Francisco de Miranda

Francisco de Miranda

A Transatlantic Life
in the Age of Revolution

KAREN RACINE

A Scholarly Resources Inc. Imprint
Wilmington, Delaware

Scholarly Resources Inc.
104 Greenhill Avenue
Wilmington, DE 19805-1897
www.scholarly.com

Library of Congress Cataloging-in-Publication Data

Racine, Karen, 1967–
Francisco de Miranda, a transatlantic life in the Age of Revolution /
    Karen Racine.
        p. cm. — (Latin American silhouettes : studies in history and
        culture)
    Includes bibliographical references and index.
    ISBN 0-8420-2909-5 — ISBN 0-8420-2910-9 (pbk. : alk. paper)
    1. Miranda, Francisco de, 1750–1816—Journeys. 2. Venezuela
—History—To 1810. 3. Venezuela—History—War of Indepen-
dence, 1810–1823. 4. Revolutionaries—Venezuela—Biography.
I. Title: Transatlantic life in the Age of Revolution. II. Title.
III. Latin American silhouettes.

F2323.M6 R33 2002
987'.04'092—dc21
[B]   2002070707

To my parents, Bob and Barb Racine,

whose love and support have

earned them an entire library

full of dedications

ABOUT THE AUTHOR

Karen Racine is assistant professor of history at Valparaiso University. She received her B.A. from the University of Saskatchewan and both her M.A. and Ph.D. from Tulane University. She has received post-doctoral research fellowships from the National Endowment for the Humanities at the John Carter Brown Library, and the Mexican Government's Secretariat of Foreign Relations. Along with Ingrid Fey, Dr. Racine is the editor of *Strange Pilgrimages: Exile, Travel, and National Identity in Latin America*, and numerous articles on the independence era in Latin America. She is completing a book on Latin Americans in London, and a textbook on modern Latin American history.

CONTENTS

ACKNOWLEDGMENTS

First I would like to thank Susan Wanat, head of the Inter-Library Loan Department at Valparaiso University's Moellering Library, who located dozens of obscure titles for me, always with a smile and more quickly than I could possibly have hoped. I also gratefully recognize the many archivists and librarians who helped me identify and consult Miranda material in their collections: Sally Holterhoff (Valparaiso University Law School), Lisa Starzyk-Weldon (Boston Athenaeum), Carrie Foley (Massachusetts Historical Society), Doctora Ermila Veracoechea (Academia Nacional de la Historia, Caracas), Rick Ring and Valeria Gauz (John Carter Brown Library), Tricia Buckingham (Bodleian Library, Oxford University), and Dr. Iain Brown (National Archives of Scotland). This biography was partially funded by grants from the National Endowment for the Humanities, the Everett Helm Research Fellowship at Indiana University's Lilly Library, and three summer stipends from Valparaiso University's Creative Work and Research Committee. Their financial support is acknowledged here and is sincerely appreciated.

I have learned much from friends and colleagues in the field who have spoken about Miranda with me over the years and provided an induction into the historical profession. In this capacity, I want to thank Rolena Adorno, Timothy Anna, Christon Archer, James Dunkerley, Judy Ewell, John Lombardi, John Lynch, and Jaime and Linda Rodríguez. I am especially thankful to have benefited from the guidance and gentle criticism of Iván Jaksić, whose careful attention to detail in his biography of Andrés Bello was a source of constant inspiration to me; he also read the manuscript in its entirety and provided useful suggestions at a critical point. As always, I thank Bill

Beezley and Rick Hopper at Scholarly Resources simply for being themselves.

During many trips afield to carry out research for this project, I was welcomed by friends who generously opened their homes to me. Ann and Lisa Newman made the wonderful city of London even more special during two separate visits. Also in London, Garry Fast shared his flat and provided some good Canadian expatriate conversation. In Madrid, Silvina Montenegro graciously allowed me to stay with her while she worked on her own important research. In Santiago, I spent a month with Patricio and Mimi Morales, whose children, Blanca and Albano, greeted me with a smile at the end of each long day at the archives. In Mexico, I stayed with my good friend Margarita Sánchez Rodríguez on two occasions and continue to appreciate both her generosity and her joyful spirit. In Caracas, Pedro Sosa generously gave me copies of Miranda's *Colombeia* and introduced me to the workings of the Academia Nacional de la Historia. Also in Caracas, Karl Krispin generously helped me to obtain permission to use the Arturo Michelene painting for the book's cover. John Fea read Chapter 2 and provided some useful comments on the nature of revolutionary society in the United States. Finally, this book would not exist without the extraordinary help of my research assistant, Jonathan Halm, who painstakingly followed up leads and scanned thousands of pages searching for the details that matter so much in biographies. His work is visible in every paragraph.

Like that of Francisco de Miranda, my circle of friends is spread throughout the globe. Our lives have taken us in different directions, but it is always a great pleasure to meet up and spend time with them, and I sincerely appreciate their efforts to maintain contact in a world of busy schedules. For their friendship, good humor, and keen insight I would like to thank: Robert Aguirre, Stewart Berringer, Louise Buckmaster, Betsy Burow-Flak, Trevor and Kim Campbell, Ellen Steinberg Coven, David Dressing, Ricardo Fagoaga, Lee and Ben Farrow, Ingrid Fey and John Lazar, Valeria Gauz, Douglas Keberlein, Hendrik Kraay, Kris Lane, Beatriz Gallotti Mamigonian, Rachel May, Salvador Méndez Reyes, Ken Mills, Blake Pattridge, Jeff Pilcher, Ian Rawlinson, Dave Reid, Matthew Restall, Michael and Heather Thiessen-Reily, Eugenia Roldán Vera, Sharon Rowley, Pedro Santoni,

Colleen Seguin and Alan Bloom, Philippe Seiler, Cami Townsend, Drew Wood, and Reuben Zahler. Dwayne Morrison created the maps within the book and has brought more than his cartographic skills to my life. My family has grown and changed during the seven years of this book's evolution. They remain my most constant source of support and have provided encouragement and praise when both were sorely needed. I would like to thank my parents, Bob and Barb Racine; my sister Janet Racine and Dale Murray; my sister Nicki and brother-in-law John Ault; my cousin Laura Migneault; and my grandmother Mona McLeod. Although I benefited from many people's suggestions while I wrote this biography during one sunny Saskatchewan summer, I am, of course, solely responsible for all errors, omissions, and shortcomings that this work may contain.

INTRODUCTION

He was one more incognito in the city of illustrious incognitos.
—GABRIEL GARCÍA MÁRQUEZ, *Bon Voyage, Mr. President*

Francisco de Miranda was a remarkable man in an age of remarkable men. Although history remembers him as "the Precursor" of Spanish American independence, Miranda was besides that many other things. He was at various times a Spanish military officer, an informant for the British in the Caribbean, a colonel in the Russian army, a commander of French Revolutionary forces in the Netherlands, a lobbyist for South American independence on the payroll of the British government, a leader of a disastrous expeditionary force to the Venezuelan coast, and, finally, a member of Congress and *generalíssimo* of the Venezuelan First Republic. He knew many of the era's important political figures personally, including George Washington, Alexander Hamilton, Thomas Jefferson, James Madison, Joseph Haydn, the Abbé Raynal, Russian empress Catherine the Great, French Girondin leader Jacques Pierre Brissot de Warville, Maximilien Robespierre, Thomas Paine, William Pitt, Lord Castlereagh, abolitionist William Wilberforce, utilitarian philosophers James Mill and Jeremy Bentham, and Simón Bolívar among many, many others. Miranda was multilingual, read voraciously, and traveled extensively throughout the United States and Europe, including Russia and Turkey. He kept a meticulous, informative, occasionally ribald diary, and infamously charmed both women and men wherever he went; rumors persist to this day that Miranda and Catherine the Great were lovers. It is true that there is no shortage of allusions to amorous conquests in either his diaries or his voluminous correspondence.

Miranda epitomized the universal man of the Enlightenment. He read all the right books, possessed all the appropriate social graces, and spoke the rhetorical language of liberty and equality that tied together intellectual, political, and social circles on both sides of the Atlantic. Strange, then, that this phenomenal man who spent his entire adult life far removed from his native land and people should become the precursor of Spanish American emancipation and the architect of the hemisphere's independent national identity. By nature Miranda was a cosmopolitan intellect, a man dedicated to the search for universal truth and progress. Yet, at the same time, the experience of living abroad amid foreign languages and cultures produced in him an intense devotion to his beloved and unique America, its people, and their political rights. Slowly, as the years passed during which the Spanish Crown's animosity kept him from his Venezuelan homeland, Miranda consciously redefined himself as an American and used his personal contacts and prestige in Europe to advance the cause to which he had devoted his life. He loved the idea of America, even as his personal circumstances slowly and inexorably drew him away from a practical understanding of its reality.

This particular process was both ironic and the source of Miranda's tragic end. He was a man of the eighteenth-century Enlightenment, raised in an era when wars were waged according to European standards of gentlemanly conduct, and he was unable to rise to the challenges of a fundamentally new kind of conflict. The struggle for Spanish American independence pointed the way forward to a new type of war, in both its form and its meaning; the Spanish American wars for independence may have more in common with the nineteenth-century process of national unification in Germany and Italy, or even with the twentieth-century decolonization movements, than they did with the dynastic warfare that had engulfed Europe (and its colonies) for the previous four centuries. Miranda's battle experience was gained during service with the grand continental armies of Spain and France; his military strategies derived from his reading of the ancient Greek and Roman histories and from reviewing professional armies such as those of Frederick the Great in Prussia. Essentially trained as an eighteenth-century European soldier, Miranda was not equipped to fight a nineteenth-century American war. He expressed little interest in the guerrilla tactics being used in Spain against Napoleon, nor did he stop to consider what the Spaniards might have learned from that experience. He failed to comprehend the emerging concept of a total war, an all-out battle of one ideological system against another, in which there was no real distinction to be made between combatants and noncombatants. The Spanish American wars for independence, epitomized by Simón Bolívar's notorious declaration of "War to the Death" in 1813, required a strong stomach and a willingness to suspend not just the rules of war but those of humanity as well. While nineteenth-century German strategist Carl von Clausewitz declared that war was simply the continuation of politics by other means, Miranda would have agreed with those of his own, earlier generation in the age of democratic revolutions who viewed honorable, negotiated political solutions as preferable in every case. Laboring under this outdated idea, Miranda was unable to comprehend that after the French Revolution, warfare, like political society itself, had changed forever.

His political ideology, such as it was, also contained a fatal flaw. Miranda was a clever man but not a deep thinker. In arguments, he was quick-thinking and opportunistic and had an excellent memory for details. By all accounts he was passionately devoted to the ideas of liberty and freedom; even his enemies grudgingly admired the consistency with which this frustrating man held to his beliefs. Yet, although he had read widely and knew many of the era's most influential politicians and philosophers personally, Miranda did not trouble himself to think realistically about the true implications of the revolutionary doctrine of liberty, fraternity, and equality for a region as deeply divided by race, ethnicity, and socioeconomic status as Spanish America was on the eve of its nationhood. Like so many other good people of his era, Miranda seemed to assume that the mere advent of liberty itself would bring happiness and harmony; in his optimism, he made the same error Marx did a generation later, when he also assumed that human behavior could be determined by its conditions and that, once this truth was understood, those sectors regarded as oppressed would be easily and willingly manipulated into painless improvement on their own behalf. Miranda did not seem to perceive that democracy is a dangerous, messy business, no more suitable for the faint of heart than fighting a modern war.

Francisco de Miranda grew up in the fundamentally aristocratic society of colonial Caracas, and throughout his adult years he constantly sought the acceptance of other cosmopolitan members of the Atlantic world's reformist circle. Although his pride never allowed him to mention it, the Canary Islander Miranda family had not been welcomed by Caracas's ethnic Basque elite, and so the young boy had grown up among them as an outsider. He left those bitter memories behind when he went to Europe to reinvent himself, but undoubtedly Miranda nurtured secret dreams of returning to Venezuela as an internationally renowned hero-liberator, a man of action able to bring independence to his homeland while his father's effete persecutors simply stood by and watched. In his secret heart, Miranda hoped that those arrogant men might even bow down and offer thanks to him, the son of an upstart immigrant merchant. In fact, Miranda spent his whole life preparing for that imaginary day. He traveled and studied. He wrote and lobbied. Eventually, his reputation spread, and he became an international celebrity, a must-have guest at any liberal host's dinner party. He hobnobbed with royalty and conspired with cabinet ministers; he dined with generals and danced with society ladies. In fact, his notorious exploits led the famous Caribbean writer V. S. Naipaul to include Miranda in two historical novels that treat postcolonial issues in a transatlantic context: *A Way in the World* and *The Loss of El Dorado*. In Naipaul's estimation, Miranda was a chronically out-of-touch character whose heart ultimately belonged to Europe.[1] Comparing Miranda to Sir Walter Raleigh, two foreign men whose dreams of military glory brought them to Naipaul's native island of Trinidad, the author deemed them both to be reckless adventurers who were more comfortable with theories than with practice.

Although his memory has been warmly eulogized by patriots, politicians, and historians since his death, Miranda was more controversial in his own day. Perhaps more often than any other Spanish American figure, Miranda has been compared to Don Quixote, the proud and bumbling hero of Miguel de Cervantes's eponymous novel. Napoleon Bonaparte, who did not care for Miranda, called him "a saner version" of Don Quixote. Two disgruntled survivors of the failed Leander Expedition to Venezuela in 1806 also resorted to the same literary metaphor. John Edsall said that "Don Quixotte's [*sic*] encounter with the wind-mill was a fool to our performances," while John Sherman recalled bitterly that their expedition "must have appeared to every calculating mind, farcical and Quixotic."[2] President John Adams of the United States never met Miranda but offered a strongly-held opinion of the man nonetheless: "He is a knight-errant, as delirious as his immortal countryman, the ancient hero of La Mancha." Adams told a colleague that he "considered Miranda as a vagrant, a vagabond, a Quixotic adventurer and cared no more about him than about Abraham Brown or Parson Austin."[3]

Two editorials in the *Barbados Mercury* in September 1806 resorted to the same imagery. The pseudonymous Rolla commented that "[w]hoever undertakes an enterprise of danger and novelty generally insures the imputation of a Quixotte [*sic*]" and was sure that for his efforts at liberating a continent Miranda risked having "his name descending to posterity on the fame parallel with the hero of La Mancha." That same week, the author of another article took a more optimistic and romantic view of Miranda's exploits, predicting that "[h]e will demonstrate to the world, that though his enterprise has been called rash by some, Quixotic by others, and by all deemed dangerous, that it is in his power to take and preserve a position on *Terra Firma*."[4] Because his dreams of emancipating an entire continent seemed so grandiose, and yet so desirable, to liberal-minded colleagues on both sides of the Atlantic, Miranda inevitably recalled in their minds that other lone hero of classic Spanish literature who also refused to recognize as insurmountable the obstacles placed before him. It would be tempting to attribute these references to the Hispanophilia that accompanied the Romantic era in the first decades of the nineteenth century, except that the memory of Cervantes's hero has also been resurrected as the title for the most recent Spanish-language biography of Miranda, written by the eminent Venezuelan historian Tomás Polanco Alcántara, *Francisco de Miranda, ¿Don Juan o Don Quijote?*[5]

As Polanco's title suggests, the other major stereotype is that of Miranda as a Latin lover, a Don Juan, a Lothario type who was bent on romantically conquering all the women he met, just as he seduced their husbands, fathers, and brothers with his dreams of emancipation. Stephen Sayre, a rogue and a speculator, gossiped with Henry Knox about Miranda's rumored affair with Catherine the Great; Thomas Paine also repeated the story to a friend in 1806 as though it were factual common knowledge. More recently, sensationalist authors have sold Miranda biographies with such lurid titles as Stewart Halpine's *The Altar of Venus*, and Jacques Cazotte's *Miranda, 1750–1816: Histoire d'un séducteur* [The Story of a Seducer].[6] Even the two major biographies of Miranda in English, William Spence Robertson's *The Life of Miranda* and Joseph Thorning's *Miranda: World Citizen*, fall into the dangerous trap of employing cultural stereotypes of Miranda as a passionate Latin male, overcome with violent tendencies and unable to control either his emotions or his libido.[7] Robertson discreetly expurgated some of the more explicit parts of Miranda's diary, but he left a tone distinctly disapproving of such behavior in his various books and articles on the man. Of course, Miranda's personal attitudes and sexual activities were no more or less extreme than those of his contemporaries. Eighteenth-century men and women were far more comfortable with the pleasures of the body than were their nineteenth-century children. Although it is true that Miranda visited prostitutes and engaged in many love affairs, a practice that continued even after he chose a mate and began a family, he was not a wanton womanizer and did not indulge in orgies or prey upon women simply to add another notch on his belt. Quite the opposite, in fact; in some ways, Miranda could be cold and formal, even prudish, in his dealings with women. He enjoyed their company, respected their minds and their opinions, and even viewed them as valuable partners in the dawning age of liberty and happiness. If the image of Miranda as Don Quixote continues to have some resonance, Miranda as Don Juan bears some reconsideration.

The challenges to Miranda's biographers are not those faced by students of lesser men. Miranda took care to preserve as much documentary evidence of his historical importance as possible. In Caracas's Academia Nacional de la Historia, carefully preserved in a glass-sided, marble display case topped by a proud eagle, sixty-three volumes of the Precursor's personal papers are kept. The contents of his personal archives have been published, albeit with several typographical errors and arranged in only a vague semblance of order, making that massive amount of information available to the researcher. Materials relating to Miranda are scattered in libraries and repositories from Chile to Russia. There are literally hundreds of existing secondary studies of Miranda's life and work, most of uneven quality. Of course, his experience must be understood in the context of the era in which he lived. A biographer could drown in the ocean of books available on the American and French Revolutions, the Napoleonic Wars, the struggle for Spanish American independence, and the wars of the Ottoman and Russian Empires. Conscious of the potential for footnotes to become unwieldy, I have endeavored to keep them to a minimum, referring to secondary sources only where there is disagreement or where a specific work is directly utilized.

The major outlines of Miranda's biography are well known but his life's meaning continues to be hotly debated. The year 2000 marked the 250th anniversary of his birth and provided a timely occasion to reevaluate just what it was that Miranda accomplished for America.[8] Ultimately, he was important not because he himself brought independence to his fellow citizens but because he convinced them that they could do it for themselves. From his vantage point in Europe, Miranda acted as a magnet for disaffected Spanish Americans from all over the continent. He was able to introduce them to each other and to important North American and European sympathizers. Through his supreme, and supremely personal, efforts, Miranda created a network that spanned the Atlantic world; he fed the Spanish American patriots' conviction that they were joining a fight for freedom that, because it was clearly the system of the future, could not fail. He gave them a sense that they were not alone and that they could not lose. What more could one single man contribute to the great cause?

1

A PATRIOT FOR ALL SEASONS
Youth (1750–1782)

These are the times that try men's souls. The summer soldier and the sunshine patriot will, in this crisis, shrink from the service of his country; but he that stands it *now*, deserves the love and thanks of man and woman.
—THOMAS PAINE, *The American Crisis* (1776)

America was a place where dreams were meant to come true. Its twin promises of personal freedom and material advance tempted thousands of Europeans each year to leave their homes and make the arduous journey across the Atlantic in order to secure part of that dream for themselves. Tenerife, a lush tropical island in the Canary Islands, had fallen on hard times since the devastating volcanic eruption of Mount Teide in 1704. Aggressive English pirates managed to steal away whatever little remained of the island's once-vibrant economy after the boiling lava flow and endless blanket of ash had incinerated the vineyards. As a direct result of this economic depression, approximately 120,000 Canary Islanders relocated to America during the middle decades of the eighteenth century, eventually making the overseas population greater than the numbers who remained at home.[1] One young Canary Islander, Sebastián de Miranda Ravelo, had grown up watching his neighbors sail westward and became determined to join them in America one day. As soon as he was old enough, he hopped aboard the first ship that passed through the dying port and never looked back. Miranda headed for Caracas, a rapidly expanding city near the northern coast of South America where there was a well-established community of fellow Canary Islanders to soften his landing. Gradually, through his ethnic contacts and by dint of his own efforts, Sebastián de Miranda succeeded in establishing several businesses of his own, including a textile factory and a bakery. The dynamic and determined young immigrant attracted the attentions of local beauty Francisca Antonia Rodríguez de Espinosa, whose family saw great promise in his future and accepted his proposal of marriage on her behalf. The two were wed on April 24, 1749, and their first child, a boy, was born less than a year later. Sebastián de Miranda had followed his dream to America, and America had not let him down.

The baby was feisty from the start. He was small and solid, with two little balled-up fists that he seemed to shake at the world. Still in the glow of their new marriage, the proud parents christened their son Sebastián Francisco. The bishop of Caracas, Monseñor Manuel Machado y Luna, officiated at the baptism in the metropolitan cathedral on April 5, 1750; the fellow Canary Islander who had solemnized the couple's marriage ceremony, Don Tomás Bautista de Melo, agreed to assume the important duties of godfather.[2] After the ceremony, the jubilant couple retired to their nearby home to celebrate and to reflect on the happy future that surely awaited them in that land of bounty and opportunity. Sebastián Francisco was eventually followed by nine siblings: Ana Antonia (1751), Rosa Agustina (1752), Micaela Antonia (1753), Miguel Francisco (1754), Javier (1755), Francisco Antonio Gabriel (1756), Ignacio José (1757), Josefa María Rafaela (1760), and Josefa Antonia (1764), most of whom did not survive into adulthood; in 1791, only Ana Antonia and Rosa were still alive.[3]

As a child, Sebastián Francisco was particularly close to his brother Francisco Antonio Gabriel, who gave him unwavering admiration and was his first follower. After the younger brother's untimely death in the mid-1770s, eldest son Sebastián Francisco gradually dropped the use of their father's forename and began to introduce himself simply as Francisco de Miranda; for this reason, his name and vital statistics have often been confused with those of his younger brother. Both the Bibliothèque Nationale in Paris and the British Library in London, for example, erroneously identify him as Francisco Antonio Gabriel de Miranda in their catalogues. Much of the obfuscation surrounding his origins is due to Miranda himself, who occasionally stretched the truth in order to present a background more consistent with his self-image. Writing in 1808, his English associate William Burke repeated the story that "Francisco de Miranda was born in 1754 in the city of Caraccas. His ancestors, originally Spanish, had passed to the New World, above two centuries ago."[4] It seems that later in life, Miranda shaved a few years off his age and tried to claim a longer, whiter lineage in America. To his European friends, Miranda also liked to point out that noted French naturalist François-Raymond Joseph Depons reported in his popular *Travels in South America* that in the sixteenth century a certain Peter Miranda had built the village of St. Francis on the spot where Caracas now stood.[5] His rejection of his father's Christian name and the concerted effort to ascribe to himself a long and illustrious American heritage suggest that Miranda's political agenda encouraged him to distort his own personal background to make it more suitable for the Precursor to Spanish American independence.

In the beginning, however, he was still just plain Sebastián Francisco, a stocky, reasonably bright young boy being educated in Caracas in the company of his younger brother Francisco Antonio Gabriel. Like most Spanish American boys of their class, they were tutored by Jesuits, Jorge Lindo and Juan Santaella, whose exercises were augmented by a prominent layperson, Narciso Yépez. The Miranda boys received a thorough grounding in Latin, mathematics, and the catechism from their tutors and then entered into the Academy of Santa Rosa. On January 10, 1762, Miranda enrolled in the lower class at the Royal and Pontifical University of Caracas, where his curriculum included two years of Latin training, the rote memorization of Father Gerónimo de Martínez de Ripalda's *Catecismo de la doctrina cristiana* [Catechism of the Christian Doctrine] (1591), and a study of the first three books of Antonio de Nebrija's *Gramática de la Lengua Castellana* [Grammar of the Castilian Language] (1492).[6] Upon successful completion of his course in September 1794, young Miranda moved into the upperclassmen's ranks and continued working through the rest of Nebrija's grammar. He also began a formal study of rhetoric using the texts of Cicero and Virgil. The Miranda boys and their classmates, all privileged young men from Caracas and its environs, spent hours each day ritually conjugating and declining verbs, translating orations, endlessly working on orthography, and practicing prosody.

Miranda always insisted that he had enjoyed his youthful hours spent reading philosophy and metaphysics, although he wished that more emphasis could have been placed on modern languages and political economy. His early education did, however, instill in him a lifelong love of the Greek and Roman classics. Although at least one historian has tried to claim that Miranda's "name is absent from the published roll" of the university's graduates, it seems clear that he did receive a baccalaureate degree in the humanities in June 1767.[7]

Eighteenth-century Caracas was an exciting place to grow up. Located on the fringes of the Spanish Empire, the city did not have the entrenched civic and religious bureaucracy of either Mexico or Peru, yet it was geographically well positioned to exploit trade opportunities in both the Caribbean and the Amazon regions. For that reason there was a certain energy and romance to the place. Diego de Losada had founded the small settlement of Santiago de León de Caracas in 1567 with a small public school and an economy based mainly on cacao and tobacco. Slowly, the city of Caracas began to assume greater regional prominence, until it declared itself to be the capital of Venezuela in the mid-1700s.[8] The Spanish system of colonial administration was byzantine and complex, with many overlapping layers and jurisdictions. In the eighteenth century, as Spain's power declined, the new Bourbon kings instituted a series of reforms intended to make the empire more efficient and profitable. Prominent among their reforms was an effort to reduce the size of administrative units; consequently, Caracas was upgraded to a full captaincy-general in 1777 and received its own *audiencia* (judicial council, or supreme court) in 1787. The number of educational establishments also expanded under the Bourbon monarchs; Caracas's small college was promoted to the status of a full university in 1722 and a seminary was established at Mérida in 1785. In order to reduce the costs of defense and to stimulate trade, in 1728 the Spanish Crown granted an exclusive trade contract to the Caracas Company (Compañía Guipuzcoana, literally Guipuzcoa Company, named after a Basque province) in exchange for its promise to curb piratical activity and protect the coast from incursions by the British, Dutch, and French. With this economic incentive, many Basque families immigrated to Venezuela and became fabulously wealthy landowners. By 1749, however, other eth-

Basques' took over — people resented it (handwritten)

nic groups resented the Basques' stranglehold on the region's trade. Juan Francisco León led a popular uprising against the Caracas Company's exclusive privileges, prompting the royal reformers to ease restrictions on trade until they finally rescinded the Caracas Company's contract in 1781. Clearly, Sebastián de Miranda and his Canary Islander family rose to prominence in Caracas at an exciting and change-filled time in the city's history.

Caracas was not a large city, even by eighteenth-century Spanish American standards. The insularity of its social and economic elite was in inverse proportion to their numbers. Although the potential for wealth and fortune was as limitless as the region's resources, the jealous Basques and others who were already in the upper strata perceived any newcomers as a threat to their own power and prestige. At first, still under the impression that America represented an escape from the rigid structures he had left behind in Europe, Sebastián de Miranda did not feel the wrath of the Creole Caracas aristocracy. He was a young man with a young family and was too busy establishing his own fortune to worry much about a public persona. Nevertheless, he made sure and steady progress and gradually rose to a place of prominence within the Canary Islander community. When the reformist governor José de Solano y Bote decided to reorganize his territory's defense and create a new local militia to be known as the Compañía de Blancos Isleños (Company of White Canary Islanders) in 1764, he naturally tapped Sebastián de Miranda to be its captain and leader. Miranda was given special responsibilities for recruitment, operation, and training and for the levy of goods and forced labor to support the militia's material needs.[9] For five years he directed a regiment of seventy or eighty men in a manner that was by all accounts fair, effective, and efficient. Along with the title he also gained the right to wear a captain's uniform, to wield an official baton, and to direct the city's annual celebration of the Day of Our Lady of Candelaria.

Sebastián bore his title proudly, perhaps a little too proudly for the tastes of his jealous *mantuano* fellow citizens. In 1767, a rival faction formed its own militia and drew its members from Caracas's most important families, including some whose names would be linked with the Mirandas for decades to come: Ponte, Tovar, Miyares, Uztáriz,

Bolívar, Landaeta, Palacios, Arias, Herrera, Blanco, and Aristeguieta.[10] This company has been derided by historians as the Compañía de Nobles Aventureros (Company of Noble Adventurers), employing a pun that allows *aventurero* to be translated alternately as "intriguer" or "undisciplined troops." When Sebastián de Miranda received an honorary appointment as an officer in the New Battalion of Creoles, town gossips began to snipe that the interloper was not all he purported to be. Indeed, in such a small and close-knit ethnic aristocracy, the Crown's elevation of a young immigrant to a place of prestige in the Creole military establishment was clear evidence that the colonial authorities were staging a slow but conscious assault on the local elite's status and on their region's autonomy.

Francisco de Miranda, the future Precursor of Spanish American independence, was almost nineteen years old when two local aristocrats, Don Juan Nicolás de Ponte and Don Martín Tovar Blanco, lodged a complaint that his father was "a mulatto, a government henchman, a mere shopkeeper, an upstart, and unworthy" of the honors heaped upon him. The pair persuaded the Caracas *cabildo* (town council), which they and their cronies dominated, to arrest the senior Miranda on spurious charges that he had falsified documents, misrepresented himself, and failed to provide true accounts of his racial heritage. The very next day, having no stomach for such unpleasantries, Miranda requested an honorable military discharge from Governor Solano, who granted it but upheld Miranda's right to retain his ceremonial dress and privileges. The contentious appointment thus renounced, Sebastián de Miranda quickly set about clearing his name. On July 1, 1769, he produced notarized genealogies attesting to the purity or, more accurately, the "cleanliness" of his blood in order to erase the suspicion that he may have had African ancestors.[11]

It was imperative for Miranda to document the cleanliness of his family's blood because its purity was a prerequisite for his children to attend university, marry in the Church, enter military service, or secure government employment. From that time onward, all of Captain Miranda's energies were channeled into a never-ending series of depositions, petitions, meetings, and appearances before tribunals. Governor Solano himself was personally sympathetic, recognizing the charges for the vindictive act that they were, but understood that he had to keep the delicate ethnic factions of his territory in balance. Solano did, however, pass the case on to his superiors in Spain with a note attached that supported Miranda's defense.[12] A Royal Patent issued on September 12, 1770, and signed by no less than Charles III himself upheld Solano's position and confirmed Sebastián de Miranda in his title and honorary position. The immigrant had prevailed. With that decree the nasty business would seem to have been resolved, but bitterness remained between the Mirandas and the *mantuano* elite.

Sebastián Francisco de Miranda was deeply wounded by the treatment that his successful father received at the hands of his adopted countrymen, and he suffered a tremendously complex emotional reaction toward all sides of the bitter dispute. Obviously he was angry at Tovar, Ponte, and the rest of the local aristocracy who could not permit talented men to advance based on their own merits. On the other hand, as a young man sensitive to his family's honor and just beginning to desire more independence for himself, young Miranda was embarrassed by the charges of a tainted lineage and was suddenly made keenly aware of his father's own personal limitations. As bitter as he may have felt toward the Caracas faction, he also resented his father's political impotence and ultimate dependence on a distant royal authority to validate his accomplishments. Both sides were diminished by the petty conflict, and Miranda decided that he needed to escape his stifling hometown for a while. He was at a perfect age to convince his parents that he ought to go abroad and eventually persuaded them that he should travel to Europe to complete his education before enlisting in Spain's military service. While the lawyers and notaries were was busy rehabilitating the family's public status, young Miranda reasoned, they might as well prepare his petition for travel permission at the same time.

In order to secure a passport and enter into official service, all applicants had to certify their legitimate birth and the purity of their blood, and provide documentation of their family's socioeconomic status. In January 1771, lawyers filed a petition on behalf of "Sebastián Francisco de Miranda, native of this city, and legitimate son of Captain of Militia Sebastián de Miranda and Doña Francisca Antonio Rodríguez Espinosa" who "wished to serve His Majesty with my person in the Kingdoms of Spain, according to the best of my predilections and talents."[13] As evidence of his fitness to serve, Miranda presented his parents' marriage certificate, proof of his baptism, a sworn statement of his current unmarried civil status, and other testimonies that not only listed his academic accomplishments but also proved that he regularly took the sacraments in faithful observance of his Christian duties. Tovar and Ponte's mean-spirited charges were acknowledged and refuted by the documents that his lawyers had prepared, which were appended in order to remove any lingering suspicion. The hopeful youth received letters of recommendation from several prominent local citizens, including educators Antonio Joseph Muñoz Aranguren and Bartolomé López Méndez, Brother Joseph de la Sierra, and the current rector of the cathedral, Dr. Jacobo Montero Bolaños; provincial treasurer Manuel de Salas and interim accountant Juan Vicente Bolívar attested to Miranda's secure finances and certified that his family's accounts with the state were in good standing. Even the governor and captain general Solano lent his support to the youth's application, perhaps as a way to extend an olive branch to the Mirandas for their recent persecution.

At high noon on January 25, 1771, at not quite twenty-one years old, Francisco de Miranda stood on the shore at La Guaira waiting impatiently for the Swedish frigate *Prince Frederick* to carry him far away from the unpleasantness of the past two years. His mind was overflowing with the limitless possibilities that stretched out before him. Just as the father had dreamed of an escape to America to find material success and more personal freedom, the son yearned to return to Europe for access to the cosmopolitan culture that he had encountered so far only in books and conversations with travelers. He imagined himself debating intensely with learned philosophers in the tradition of his ancestor Francisco de Miranda (1679–1744), who taught theology in the prestigious universities of Salamanca and Valladolid. Perhaps he would enter the Spanish military service and perform heroic deeds as Juan de Miranda had done at the naval Battle of Lepanto (1571), which halted the advance of the Ottoman Empire in the Mediterranean.[14] And of course, young Francisco always expected that he would cut a dashing figure in the salons of Madrid, where he would seduce the city's most eligible and attractive young ladies. In short, Miranda was like all adventurous young men; he simply wanted to get out into the world to see it for himself. His parents, on the other hand, had a less romantic view of the pending experience. While Francisco gazed anxiously at the waiting ship, enduring his mother's fervent last hugs and kisses and her entreaties to be safe, his father stood back stoically and watched the scene unfold. Where the Caracas-born Francisca was terrified that she would never see her son again, Sebastián de Miranda already knew that his boy would be disappointed by the even more rigid class structures he would find in Europe. That a disappointed Francisco would return to his American roots someday, however, was something the boy had to find out for himself.

So, on that day, Miranda's life changed. He was twenty years old, newly independent, and setting sail on the high seas, bound for adventure. He pulled out his diary and began to scribble the first of thousands of pages that would follow over the course of his lifetime. For most of the voyage from La Guaira to Cádiz, Miranda faithfully recorded the date, the weather, and the ship's position. Occasionally he also mentioned interesting landmarks, strange birds, or aquatic creatures that they encountered along the way, including a pod of "*unbelievably monstrous* whales." Following the death of a Swedish sailor in February, Miranda laconically commented that the unfortunate man had been buried at sea "with all the solemn rites of his [Lutheran] Sect."[15] Like his father, Miranda observed the rituals of the Catholic Church throughout his life, but his own particular worldview was secular and practical. He was curious about other faiths and always condemned religious intolerance. To pass the time, the youth peppered the ship's pilot with many questions, in the process learning much about trade winds, navigational instruments, and how to read the skies for portents of bad weather. Finally, on March 1, after a journey of nearly six weeks, the *Prince Frederick* hove in sight of Cádiz. In his longest diary entry to date, Miranda excitedly described the first nights spent in Spain at the home of his father's distant relation, Señor José D'Aniño, near the so-called Castle of the Four Towers; ironically, forty years later, Miranda would be brought full circle to end his life in chains in that same prison fortress. At that time, however, he was young and footloose in Europe at last, supported by his father's funds and teamed up with a new shipboard friend, Francisco de Arrieta, "the best chap in the world, once you get past his uncouth appearance."[16]

After cleaning themselves up and purchasing a few new outfits to dispel the impression that they were country bumpkins, Miranda and Arrieta set out for Madrid on March 14. Along the way, they stopped to inspect various country palaces, churches, and monasteries, all of which Miranda breathlessly, if somewhat repetitively, pronounced either "beautiful" or "magnificent."[17] Passing through Córdoba, Miranda witnessed the remnants of the Moorish presence in the region's art and architecture everywhere he looked. Having been raised on countless tales of Christian heroism during the Reconquest, he marveled at the perfect image of Christ crucified that one pious captive had scratched on a jail cell's wall using only a single fingernail. When their coach broke down, the pair sought assistance from one of the many German agricultural colonies they passed en route. They met up with a fellow American, Don Miguel de Florez, a "son of Quito" (Ecuador), who happened to be the military commander of the region and a "man of much erudition who showed [Miranda] his Library of Latin, French, English, and Spanish books, all very well chosen."[18] When the coach broke down a second time, the intrepid friends carried on by foot, leaving their baggage behind and walking for miles in a ferocious wind. They arrived in Madrid on March 28, ready to explore life at the center of the Spanish Empire.

As he had promised his parents, Miranda engaged tutors and set about furthering his formal education which, after all, had been the ostensible purpose of his trip. He was particularly anxious to improve his abilities in modern languages, correctly viewing them as a passport for further travels on the Continent. With his exasperated French tutor in tow, Miranda moved about incessantly, venturing afield to explore the royal palaces at San Ildefonso, Segovia, and El Escorial. Everywhere he went he displayed a keen sense of art history and knowledge of the Greek and Roman classics as well as emerging natural sciences like botany, but his most frequent and effusive praise was always reserved for book collections. Already prone to visions of grandeur, Miranda took particular note of the portraits of illustrious men that hung in the Escorial's library, including Cicero, Nebrija, Horace,

Boethius, Zenon, Pliny, Demosthenes, Socrates, Euclid, Ptolemy, and Terence. Someday, young Francisco vowed, his own image would be hung on the wall of greatness. He also made note of the lone American contribution to the royal room, the sword of "El Inca" Garcilaso de la Vega, who had fused European and American literary traditions a century earlier.[19] In Madrid, not only was the prince's study filled with "very excellent English, French, German, Latin, and Spanish books, and, above all, a General History of Plants and Animals in English with illuminated Maps," it also boasted a fine collection of mechanical devices, rubber instruments, globes, and a special tool for writing three copies of a letter at once.[20] There were samples of petrified trees (including a bit of Peruvian ebony), preserved flowers, animal specimens, a collection of crystals, and a deck of leather playing cards that Miranda mentioned, were "used by the American Indians." Admiring their craftsmanship, he took pride in the patience and abilities of the distant artisans, acknowledging the accomplishments of his countrymen at a time when their natural talents were being disparaged by European philosophers. At the Royal Palace of Retiro, he recorded seeing a species of deer sent from Mexico, adding pompously that the French word would be *élan*, in English *elk*.[21]

If young Miranda in Europe was already feeling himself drawn to things of American origin, the other marked personal tendency visible in his diary was his attraction to military sites and scenes. Just as he had consistently recorded all the American plants, animals, and persons that he encountered in Europe, so too did he mention all the statues, battlefields, and armaments he visited. At the Retiro Palace he raved about an excellent painting of the Battle of Constantinople, and he admired the heroic mounted statues of Spanish kings defending their land. At the New Palace in Madrid, images of Julius Caesar's funeral attended by legions of Roman gladiators were singled out for special mention. It is not surprising that he was attracted to scenes of martial glory. As Miranda neared the end of his academic courses, he started the process of enlistment in the Spanish service and anticipated taking his place alongside other famous generals in the annals of history someday. In January 1773, Miranda's father transferred 85,000 *reales vellón* (silver coinage) to Madrid in order to secure for his son a place as a captain in the Princess's Regiment. Miranda's days as a student had come to an end and his new career as a military officer was about to begin.

For a year and a half, the newly-minted Captain Miranda moved with his regiment between various garrisons in North Africa and the southern Spanish province of Andalusia. The Empire had two important bases in North Africa: Ceuta, located directly across the Strait of Gibraltar; and Melilla, slightly further to the east. Spain had held possession of these two ports since 1580 and 1496 respectively. Since the fall of Granada in 1492, when the Christian Spaniards drove the Muslim Moors out of the Iberian Peninsula, the Spanish Crown planned to extend the Reconquest across the Strait of Gibraltar into Africa.[22] Furthermore, constant piratical activity hampered Spanish trade and transportation in the Mediterranean, adding an economic incentive to the already strong religious zeal to try to secure European control over North Africa. Morocco's Alaouite rulers made overtures to King Charles III, hoping to arrive at a friendly truce that might benefit both dynasties; in 1767, Jorge Juan successfully negotiated a peace treaty in Marrakech. Nevertheless, the Alaouite sultan Mohammad ibn Abdullah continued to press for the return of European-controlled cities in his territory; in 1769 he recaptured Mazagan from the Portuguese and demanded that the Spaniards return Ceuta and Melilla as well. On December 9, 1774, Spain declared war on the Moroccans and blockaded British shipping to prevent them from sending aid to the sultan. Miranda got his first taste of combat in this conflict.

✢ Time spent in Africa was important in Miranda's intellectual development because it provided the crucible for his growing hubris and started his patriotic inclinations moving in a new and dangerous direction. Even from the time of his youth and early adulthood, Miranda had always believed that he was better than his peers, that he had a certain genius or destiny that others must be made to recognize. This is not a personality trait that tends to make life as a common soldier either tolerable or satisfying. At the same time, the task of guarding remote outposts of a colonial presence that was unwelcomed by the natives started Miranda thinking about the parallel implications for Spanish America. When an opportunity arose to act on both his ego and his Americanism, Miranda moved quickly. In a letter to the inspector general of the Royal Army, Count Alejandro O'Reilly, he wrote that "[h]aving learned that an order has been passed on to my regiment which proposes that all meritorious officers who wish to do so may transfer to America with a promotion in rank," he suggested that he could serve the Crown better and be deployed more usefully if he returned to his homeland.[23] In his petition, Miranda assured that the military authorities that he was worthy of this promotion in light of his "superior talents," not the least of which was his facility in modern languages. It was a brash claim for a young man who had been in the Spanish military service for less than a year. Although it was certainly possible that Miranda, age twenty-four, was homesick and anxious to live among his own people once again, it is more likely that he sought the new assignment in order to advance himself through the military hierarchy as quickly as possible. He had a healthy self-image and he sought the public status that would match it. If he could be promoted and serve in America, where his family's detractors could witness his rapid rise, so much the better.

Although Miranda had framed his arguments in a way that would suggest it was his desire to serve his country more than any consideration of personal interest that had led him to request the transfer, O'Reilly preferred to leave the impatient young American captain in Africa a while longer. Miranda therefore stayed with the Princess's regiment and entered into another tour of duty on African soil at the end of November 1774.[24] The reinforcements arrived with little time to spare. The Moroccan sultan's forces attacked Melilla on December 9, 1774, beginning a 2-month siege in which Miranda gained his first real exposure to direct military action. During that time, he learned many important lessons. He noted that the Spanish presence seemed to lack the support of the "resident Moors" in Melilla, who had either deserted the town's environs or remained behind only to sabotage their occupiers' efforts; in their actions, Miranda saw for the first time the hostility of a national people toward their foreign subjugators. Although his correspondence and diary do not specifically mention America in this context, as a bright, well-read young man, Miranda could not have failed to perceive that the new theories of government by consent were beginning to reshape the contemporary world. At the time, however, thoughts of freeing his own people lay in the distant future.

In 1774, Miranda was an ambitious 24-year-old army captain, still anxious to distinguish himself within the Spanish imperial system. Although to his credit, unlike some of his peers, he never expressed hatred of the Moors or their faith, Miranda was intent upon carrying out his duties in an effective, professional manner. He described the Moors without much apparent rancor simply as "the Enemy." Each night, Miranda wrote several pages in his diary that recounted the day's events, giving a particular attention to practical issues of supply, order and discipline, and personal leadership. The Spanish garrison was continuously supplied by ships from Málaga and the Levant that landed regularly with arms, powder, foodstuffs, and relief forces. Nevertheless, the siege was long, constant, and draining. Miranda expressed his esteem for Melilla's Spanish governor, who had promised that he "would defend the Plaza until the last drop of blood was shed."[25] Very early in his career, the young captain observed that wartime produced a particularly dramatic sort of patriotism. He remembered this lesson and learned to manipulate public emotion in support of his own cause over the next several decades.

New Year's Day 1775 brought little hope of relief as the enemy bombardment continued unabated. The unpredictable Mediterranean winter weather conspired to keep the convoys at bay, and the enemy ominously had set about constructing a trench around Melilla to cut off any hope of land-based supply. Miranda noted that despite their exhaustion and fear, his fellow troops fought back with "ardor and zeal"; one brave fellow took a rifle and manned a parapet for hours on end.[26] Yet the captain's respect for the opposing Moors was also apparent; he recognized that they fought with equal devotion and skill and had a fanatical desire to rid their territory of foreign control. Indeed, he saw his opponents as humans who had as much in common with the Spaniards as they did in dispute. For example, he commented that on January 19th the Spaniards gathered in their plaza in celebration of the king's birthday; on the twenty-first the Moorish Muslims held a similar religious celebration with bonfires that lasted the whole night.[27] In Madrid, Miranda had bought a copy of the

Koran, which he pulled out and read occasionally to understand the people and the culture he faced in North Africa. This sort of cross-cultural contact in a colonial context, coupled with his intellectual interest in the Enlightenment ideals of self-government, led Miranda gradually to start to think about American political conditions in a new light.

The North African conflict was settled with a treaty of friendship and commerce signed by Count Floridablanca and Mohammed Uthman in 1780. Although he does not appear to have played a militarily decisive role in the siege at Melilla, Miranda's ego nonetheless received a boost for having participated in the action and for having served his commanders well. In April 1775 he approached Commander Bernardo O'Connor Phelan, again asking for a transfer. Miranda pointedly reminded his superior officer that he had come to Melilla "in the capacity of volunteer (not thinking of anything else but taking my turn) in order to serve in the defense of this place."[28] Shortly afterward, he sent a similar petition directly to King Charles III, respectfully suggesting that his recent services in Africa made him a suitable candidate for military decorations, although he conspicuously left the particulars of the meritorious conduct undescribed.[29] Miranda even went so far as to suggest that awarding the prestigious Order of Santiago might not be inappropriate in his case. His letters went unanswered.

By 1776, Miranda had been away from his homeland for five years. He had met many new people and acquired many books that had been unavailable to him in America. He had learned much about the vast empire of which Venezuela was just a small part by traveling throughout Spain and by serving in its colonial garrisons. As he matured and accumulated more life experiences, Miranda's thoughts began to turn westward. He had learned the hard way that Spanish arrogance often meant that Americans, however talented they might be, were looked upon with disdain. Furthermore, he had witnessed with his own eyes the hatred the Moorish people felt for their foreign occupiers, and he had read books that declared that colonies might be more productive as independent entities. What might this mean for Spanish America? He had surmised that Americans were different from Europeans before he had even left South America, but that fact had only become clearer as he lived and worked among Spanish soldiers.

If the Spanish army had had such great difficulties quelling local rebellions in Morocco, so near to its own shores where the supply lines and travel times were much shorter, what might happen if trouble should break out in America? After the siege at Melilla, Miranda's correspondence and diary both indicate that he was starting to confront the serious implications raised by his experiences and his literary investigations.

Transferred to Cádiz once again, the city that played host to so many of the decisive moments in his life, Miranda picked up a newssheet in June 1776 and read that a revolt against British colonial authority had erupted in Boston. An energized Miranda immediately took up his plume and crafted an artful letter to the minister of the Spanish Navy, González de Castejón, in which he attempted to wheedle a furlough so that he could advance his linguistic and mathematical skills in a more academic setting.[30] One month later, the new inspector general of the militias, Don Martín Álvarez, received a similar request in which Miranda employed his characteristic rhetorical strategy of alternately flattering and berating his superiors. Although he addressed Álvarez as "My Lord of the greatest veneration, a person who was known for protecting and encouraging great talent wherever he saw it," Miranda went on to complain that he could not "deny the great disgust in which I find myself in this current situation, lacking the faculties with which I can use my ideas which, by continual study and some travels I have acquired in this profession, in spite of having solicited [a change] repeated times and sacrificing myself in the outpost of Melilla."[31] For his service, Miranda felt obliged to ask for the benevolent minister's support to protect the "honorable ambition of an individual whose only wish is to spend his life in the service and glory of his fatherland." These may have been Miranda's true sentiments, but in retrospect his perception of where his fatherland lay was slowly starting to shift. He clearly wanted to get back to America; the exact destination did not seem to matter. In desperation, he once asked to be allowed to join Pedro de Cevallos's expedition, which was heading for Buenos Aires.[32] Miranda argued brazenly that he was asking for "no more protection than I perceive that I merit." His self-important harangues did indeed attract the notice of his superiors, who chose to reward his petitions not with the desired transfer to an

American battalion, but rather with some time in jail to cool off. During the two years after his brave service at Melilla, Miranda found himself briefly incarcerated on charges of troublemaking and insubordination on at least three separate occasions.[33]

Amazingly, Spanish commanders continued to return Miranda to the bosom of his regiment despite the mounting evidence that he was too headstrong ever to submit willingly to authority. Furthermore, it appeared that Miranda was starting to question the nature of the Spanish imperial system by exhibiting an excessive interest in works of English political economy. Not only did the royal army's administrators fail to remove the troublesome captain from the rank and file, they actually seemed to provide the stimulation for his growing radicalism. For example, in December 1775, Miranda traveled to Gibraltar with some of his fellow officers in order to conduct a tour of the British base there. By providing his introduction to English military officers and the vibrant merchant community on "the Rock," as that garrison was called, Spanish officials gave Miranda free access to an alternative worldview. While the Spanish Empire had retained a strong centralized and authoritarian impulse despite the reforms of the Bourbon monarchs in the eighteenth century, the British had emerged from their Glorious Revolution of 1688 as the champions of constitutional monarchy, free trade, and social conservatism, a combination that held growing appeal for Spanish American Creoles like Miranda.

Ever the purposeful traveler, Miranda took detailed notes about his observations in Gibraltar and relished the opportunity to practice his spoken English. He had met John Turnbull, a young partner in the British firm of Turnbull and Forbes, when the latter was in Cádiz and they continued to keep up a correspondence after Turnbull returned to Gibraltar. Their friendship eventually became one of the longest-standing and most significant of Miranda's life. Turnbull consistently used his personal and business connections to introduce Miranda into high-level circles of British government and society, provided him with refuge and financial support for over forty years, and eventually acted as executor of Miranda's estate.[34] Turnbull was immediately taken with Miranda, a young soldier who seemed to embody the ideal virtues of the cosmopolitan eighteenth-century man:

erudition, wit, military skill, and a passionate devotion to liberty. When he returned to Gibraltar, Turnbull wrote a note to Miranda thanking him for being such a gracious host and sending him copies of the English books that Miranda had requested; Turnbull regretted that he could not locate a set of Lord Bolingbroke's collected works but promised to send the volumes as soon as he could manage to procure them.[35] With his new friend Turnbull supplying the incentive, Miranda began to move closer in spirit to the anglophone Atlantic world.

Miranda continued to accumulate books and to read as a way to pass the time while he was stationed in various outposts with his regiment. In 1778, the Princess's guards transferred back to Madrid, the center of imperial power and high society, and Miranda was overjoyed. As usual, he made extensive notes during the journey from Cádiz to the capital, including the distances traveled daily, sights seen along the way, the names of persons with whom he lodged, and countless other mundane details. He showed particular interest in the construction and decoration of churches in the villages they visited, and also in the stables of major landowners. While in Córdoba, Miranda waxed eloquent about its Moorish architecture and praised the horses of the both Marques de Villaseca and a gentleman named Francisco de Savallos; indeed Miranda believed that such "perfect and useful animals" were a national treasure of the country he still called "our Spain."[36] The reference was also a sly jab at the tendency of European Spaniards to use the possessive *nuestra América* (our America) when speaking of their overseas territories. Having traveled to Spain and realizing how dependent the country was on America's mineral and agricultural wealth, Miranda's perception of where the real power in the Spanish Empire lay had begun to shift.

In Carolina, Miranda marveled over the visible transformation of the region that Pablo de Olavide had accomplished under directions of the king; the forward-looking bureaucrat had cut roads out of mountains and opened up the region to unprecedented economic development. At the time, however, Miranda had no way of knowing that Olavide would fall into official disfavor and eventually become his coconspirator in Paris during the 1790s. Miranda took care to record the population of each town through which he passed: Las Cabezas (700), Utrera (4,000), Arahal (2,500), Fuentes (2,000),

Guadalcazar (100), Santa Cruz de Mudela (1,500), Baldapeña (2,000), Membrilla (80). These figures reflected the growing tendency to equate a healthy and growing population with the state's own power, a correlation that the subsequent generation of Spanish American independence leaders would be obsessed with. From his earliest days, Miranda had an interest in the experiences and a respect for the abilities and virtues of people outside his own class. In Olias, quite near to Madrid, he met with a "peasant who discussed national customs and laws that the public faith deposited in public scribes and not in the most senior Person of the State, with all the vehemence and force of a Montesquieu or a Beccaria."[37]

Despite his occasional spurts of usefulness, Miranda's haughty demeanor continued to plague his superiors. In October 1779, Colonel Don Juan Roca renewed his complaints that Miranda spent too much time reading and too little time following orders.[38] There were eleven charges in all, ranging from lesser offenses such as the unauthorized purchase of regimental supplies, to the loss of twenty-three uniforms and various other financial irregularities, to the more serious charges of violence and abuse of his authority. Roca listed complaints that he had received from many soldiers in the Princess's regiment that Miranda meted out justice unevenly; they claimed that he failed to punish Sergeant First Class Antonio Gervolés, who had brutalized three cadets, and when a new recruit failed to respond quickly to his instructions, Miranda himself had battered the poor boy badly enough that he was put in the hospital in critical condition. In response to these charges, Miranda blithely suggested that he was being framed, that he in fact had been an excellent servant of the king, and had even gone so far as to pay for some of the regiment's supplies out of his own pocket. As for the complaints of brutality, Miranda claimed, either they were trumped up or the harsh punishments had been merited. Indeed, Miranda took pride that "always, when any soldier in my company complained to me with foundation, I gave him the corresponding satisfaction, correcting the subject who had exceeded his authority." Nonetheless, throughout the next forty years Miranda's underlings consistently grumbled about the excesses of his particular brand of discipline, so there must have been some legitimacy to Roca's report.

On the other hand, Miranda's amorous side also began to reveal itself during these same years. The earliest love letters in his personal archive date from 1779, when he was living in Cádiz and seems to have been juggling two romances at once. In a series of brief but sweet entreaties, a young lady named Pepa Luque wrote to the man she variously called her "*querido amigo*" (beloved friend) or "*vida mía*" (my life) or "*Miranda de mi corazón*" (Miranda of my heart). In an all-too-familiar romantic scenario, she complained that her father refused to let her out of the house to see her young man or even to attend the theater, causing her to lament "the slavery in which I live."[39] A short while later, the deceived and heartbroken Pepa cried to Miranda about her fear of encountering him with "her competitor" in the street some evening, indicating that Miranda was indeed playing the field. Pepa's rival must have been a certain María Teresa, whose letters were sprinkled with even more impassioned expressions of devotion to the young captain. More unstable than Pepa Luque, María Teresa implored her dashing beau, "Do not forget me, or deceive me, or treat me falsely, and do not put another in my place" because, as she cried, "I am so sad that nothing can make me happy but you, in you I find my joy and my consolation, and with you my five senses are heightened and my heart and thoughts are all yours."[40] Such rabid expressions eventually drove him away; Miranda liked the attentions of pretty women, but he always distrusted these sorts of romantic emotional outbursts. Unfortunately for both women, but just in time for Miranda to beat an easily explainable retreat, his regiment moved again, cutting short what had become an awkward situation for him.

Miranda's superiors had tired of his irascible presence among them and so, in April 1780, they approved the transfer that he had been requesting for so long. Spanish troops were being sent to the Caribbean to participate in the final stages of the American Revolution. Miranda joined the Regiment of Aragón, which was preparing to leave Cádiz to retake Pensacola and the Bahamas from the British. Although he had been away from home for over a decade, the desire to see his family again does not appear to have been one of Miranda's articulated motives for returning to America. His mother had adopted the habit of a Mercedarian nun and died in a Caracas convent in June 1777, without much comment or reaction from her distant son.[41]

Furthermore, Miranda rarely mentioned his father and only sporadically corresponded with his favorite sister, Rosa. His thoughts and actions were always for himself. As his own departure gift, Miranda purchased some new books and catalogued what he proudly called "the beginnings of a famous library."[42] In 1780 his personal collection already exceeded 325 titles in several modern languages, reflecting his special interests in military history, mathematics, the classics, and contemporary political economy. If the list is indeed a true gauge of Miranda's reading habits, by 1780 he was familiar with Abbé Raynal's treatise on the benefits of free trade between Europe and America; Bartolomé de las Casas's sixteenth-century attack on the Spanish conquistadors' actions in America; Cornelius de Pauw's insulting attack on Americans' abilities; John Locke's *Essay on Human Understanding*, which asserted the rights of the governed to rise up and take back control when their leaders transgressed their civic responsibilities; and Lord Bolingbroke's essays on historical destiny and patriotism. Clearly the 30-year-old seasoned traveler and military veteran who returned to America in 1780 was not the same sheltered boy who had left La Guaira a decade before.

Spanish king Charles III wished to flex his imperial muscle in the American theater in order to curtail the British encroachment upon his royal dominions that was beginning to occur as the British attempted to compensate for their losses in the northern part of the hemisphere. With his usual lack of proportion and foresight, the Spanish king sent a massive fleet to engage the British at Pensacola and thereby take the pressure off the North Americans' floundering armies. The battle was also intended to have the important side effect of reestablishing the Spanish presence in Louisiana that had been threatened by the growing French colony there. This expensive 1780 expedition, also known as the Army of American Operations, consisted of seven entire columns of troops—12,146 veteran infantrymen, sent over in eleven warships, two frigates, one cutter, and one packet boat.[43] Although Miranda's regiment fell under the direct command of Victoriano de Navia, the entire fleet was headed by none other than José Solano y Bote, the very same man who had supported his father, Sebastián de Miranda, against the charges of the Caracas aristocracy ten years earlier. Following stops in Puerto Rico and Santo

Domingo, the convoy lumbered into Havana in early August, with many of the men ill and suffering the physical effects of a long sea journey. Once he was able to recover his health and regroup from the voyage, Navia took the first opportunity to promote the troublesome Miranda out of his command. In this way, the Venezuelan found himself stationed as aide-de-camp to the acting governor of Cuba, Juan Manuel de Cagigal.

It was a fortuitous match. Miranda and the governor got on well because Cagigal respected his aide's abilities and gave him a certain degree of latitude in his actions. During their two years together, Cagigal managed to secure Miranda's promotion to full colonel and consistently praised his work to the well-connected field marshal Bernardo de Gálvez, the governor of Spanish Louisiana. By October 1780, Gálvez had succeeded in pushing the British out of Mobile, and further advances toward Florida seemed imminent. The Havana-based troops prepared to join him on the mainland but their commanders wisely waited until the worst of the hurricane season had passed; the first group finally departed on February 28, 1781. The Spanish convoy landed at Galveston on the morning of March 3 and moved on to their final destination, the Island of Santa Rosa near Pensacola, six days later. The British were waiting for them. Vice Admiral Parker and Major General Campbell had readied 1,700 men, including Indian and African auxiliaries, to defend the British colony.[44]

In his meticulously kept diary of the battle of Pensacola, Miranda recorded each day's events just as he had done previously at Melilla.[45] His observations reveal a soldier who is professional, accurate, and well versed in both military history and tactics. He referred to the British as "the Enemy," in exactly the same way as he had identified the Moors. The pitched battle lasted for two months, March through May 1781, and, in the end, the numerically superior Spanish forces emerged victorious.[46] At 3 P.M. on Tuesday, March 8, the English finally raised a white flag and asked for a conference to discuss the terms of capitulation. Spanish troops occupied Pensacola two days later. Because he was one of the few Spaniards present who spoke English adequately, Miranda met with a British delegation to negotiate the surrender and to arrange an orderly transfer of power. Although he performed his tasks with his customary panache, he must have felt some affinity for his British counterparts. He always enjoyed talking with English people and felt himself drawing increasingly closer to their views on political economy and government by assent (albeit aristocratic assent).

Once the *Te Deums* were sung, the Spanish flag was hoisted in the plaza, and all the rum was gone, attention turned toward consolidating the Spanish victory. Following the battle of Pensacola, as everywhere, there was some looting and much opportunism. Miranda himself scooped up all the potentially valuable historical documents he could find, including a journal of the siege written by a British officer. He also used the occasion to augment his growing library; for a mere fifty-six-and-a-half pesos he bought twenty-four volumes of English-language books from the hastily departing residents who could not afford to take all their possessions with them.[47] In this way, he acquired works by Lord Chesterfield, William Robertson, John Milton, and Joseph Addison. He also purchased at least three African slaves, named Bob, Perth, and Brown; although some historians claim he bought the men as an altruistic act, as the "best way to help them gain their freedom," Miranda later gave the slaves to an English associate whose intentions surely were not as benign.[48]

The Battle of Pensacola rightly looms large in the voluminous Mirandian historiography; many biographers point to his first personal encounter with the American Revolution as the time when he "first thought of spreading revolution to Spanish America." José Luis Salcedo-Bastardo called Pensacola the "Mirandian Sword of Damocles, where the Precursor had a double revelation: one, the liberty, independence and unity of all America (in theory and in practice) and second, the method or *modus operandi* to attain such a precious goal."[49] It seems clear, however, that Miranda had probably entertained such thoughts long before 1781. Some claim that Miranda made a crucial contribution to the successful outcome of the American Revolutionary War when he helped to raise £35,000 in Havana to supply French admiral François Joseph Paul de Grasse's forces on the Chesapeake and at Yorktown. His exact involvement in that undertaking is unclear, however. Although one historian romantically recounts the way in which Miranda charmed Havana's ladies into donating their jewels to the cause, another points out that Miranda could not possibly have done that since he was no longer in Cuba at the end of August 1781, when the funds were raised.[50] In any case, whatever the actual truth of the story, it was not in Miranda's interest to deny it; in fact, in some cases he and his friends actively built up his revolutionary credentials by repeating this tale to people they needed to impress. Trinidad's governor Thomas Pownall told British prime minister William Pitt in 1790 that Miranda had offered "decisive service in the cause of the liberty of the United States" through his financial contribution to de Grasse's expedition. Whether it was true or not, the persistence of this rumor is another example of Miranda's consistent effort to burnish his reputation as a lifelong friend of American liberty.

Despite his slow advance through the ranks of the Spanish military, Miranda continued to have problems with authority. Cagigal and Solano, his partisans and sponsors, were always treated favorably in Miranda's diary and correspondence, but Bernardo de Gálvez was not. During the action at Pensacola, Miranda had been promoted to lieutenant colonel and Cagigal to lieutenant general. Eight months later, the ambitious Venezuelan applied to Governor Gálvez for a promotion to full colonel; Cagigal sent along a detailed letter of recommendation and support.[51] The request was denied. Characteristically bearing a grudge toward someone who failed to recognize his brilliance, Miranda subsequently bristled at identifying Governor Gálvez by his formal titles of Commander or General or Governor, preferring instead to refer to him simply as Mr. Gálvez. Bearing a grudge against such a high-level official did not bode well for Miranda's future in the Spanish imperial system; Gálvez's uncle was José de Gálvez, the powerful minister of the Indies, and his father was Matías de Gálvez, a prominent judge on the *audiencia* of Guatemala.

Part of the trouble was that the Miranda family curse was again rearing its head. Rumors and suspicions started to surface surrounding Miranda's relationship with various English officers in the Caribbean. One officer, John Campbell, had toured Havana's fortifications in late 1781 and somehow managed to wander beyond the permitted zones; government officials blamed Miranda for the breach in security, even though it appears he was not even on the island at the time. Cagigal, always full of faith in his friend and aide-de-camp, had sent Miranda to Jamaica in August 1781 with credentials to arrange a prisoner exchange and handle various other sensitive matters. Miranda's secret instructions contained fifteen points that charged him with securing the release of nearly 900 prisoners, attending to their immediate needs, and arranging for their safe passage to Cuba; he was also requested to make discreet inquiries about the possibility that the Spanish navy might purchase English ships and other maritime supplies in Jamaica. At the same time, Miranda was asked to conduct low-level espionage work under the noses of his British hosts. Cagigal asked his trusted assistant to bring back a classified report of Jamaica's military capabilities, detailed plans of its major towns and ports, maps of the island's fortifications and bays, and estimates of the British naval and ground force troops stationed there.[52] Miranda arrived off the island on September 4, and promptly managed to offend the British governor of Jamaica, John Dalling, by failing to accept his first dinner invitation. Whether it was merely an oversight by an inexperienced diplomat or a show of bravado intended to send a message that he was not coming with cap in hand, the tactic worked. Despite this initial unpleasantness, it seems that Miranda used his legendary charm and gracious conversation to win over the governor in fairly short order, who happily granted the envoy full permission to travel wherever he wished on the island.[53] Their negotiations proceeded quickly and smoothly. The men reached an agreement for the prisoner exchange, which was formalized in an 18-point document on November 18. Miranda set about the second, unpublicized part of his mission while he waited for the ships to be prepared.

Miranda quite clearly enjoyed spending time with his new British friends. He wanted to practice his English-language abilities and to talk with them about their nation's history and current trends in political philosophy. Anxious to gain their esteem and confidence, he probably spoke a little too freely about the Spanish side of the battle in Pensacola. In Jamaica, as in every place he traveled, he bought copies of all the books that interested him. He also entered into a fateful deal with a local merchant speculator named Philip Allwood, who dreamed of a fortune that could be made by gaining access to the restricted Spanish American market. Always anxious to augment his own income whenever he could, Miranda agreed to fill the holds of the newly purchased ships returning to Cuba with Allwood's goods, which would then be sold in the Spanish dominions at a tidy profit for both men. It seemed like a clever idea at the time.

Expecting to return to a hero's welcome with 900 released prisoners of war and two sparkling and much-needed new ships for the Spanish Caribbean fleet, Miranda instead found himself unexpectedly assailed with charges that he was a spy and a conduit for British merchants. Furthermore, his reading habits rendered him even more suspicious; he was accused of being "a traitor, an Anglophile, a smuggler, and a disloyal intriguer who was possessed of books prohibited by the Inquisition and indecent paintings."[54] A mid-level official in the Havana military administration, Juan Patiño, sent these charges all the way to Madrid, complaining to minister of the Indies José de Gálvez that Miranda was a "notorious smuggler" who had introduced Allwood's contraband into the island under the protection of his co-conspirator, Governor Cagigal. With both their reputations called into question, Cagigal leapt to his friend's defense, assuring Gálvez that throughout their long association, Miranda had consistently exhibited that "zeal, activity, penetration and knowledge which characterizes a good official who serves his profession with honor and glory."[55]

The charges were ludicrous, clearly the result of the jealousy and political intrigue that characterized the entire Spanish colonial bureaucracy. Because he was personally ambitious and because he interacted comfortably with foreigners, small-minded colleagues projected their own insecurities onto Miranda and refused to see anything but the worst in his actions. No evidence has ever been found that Miranda passed on military secrets to the British or gave them maps and plans of Havana's fortifications. He seems to have been the victim of a bureaucracy in which different branches contradicted each other's orders. According to some documents, he had royal permission to purchase the ships in the British port, while others seem to indicate that the king himself specifically forbade Miranda from carrying out that part of his mission to Jamaica.[56] To make matters worse, the old animosity between Miranda and his former commander Bernardo de Gálvez had been simmering since they had served together in Florida, and Gálvez took the first opportunity to put the troublesome lieutenant colonel in his place. His powerful uncle issued orders for Miranda's arrest, claiming that he had acted without authority in Jamaica.[57]

Officials in Madrid initiated an investigation that dragged on for over a decade until Charles III ultimately acquitted Miranda in 1799. Nevertheless, in 1782 the situation looked dire indeed. José de Gálvez ordered Miranda to be kept incommunicado while the case proceeded, but Governor Cagigal managed to have his protégé released into his custody. In August 1782, Miranda fled into the hills surrounding Havana, where he kept himself hidden from authorities while attempting to clear his name through the publication of a series of newspaper articles.

As the year 1783 approached, Francisco de Miranda found himself at a crossroads, both personally and professionally. At this crucial juncture, as he faced further persecution for his success within the Spanish system, Miranda may have received letters that intensified sentiments that had been smoldering in his breast for quite some time. Unmarried and in his early thirties, Miranda had given his youth to the service of the Spanish Empire. The Venezuelan had professed loyalty to his distant sovereign and served him on three continents. Yet, as he looked forward to his future career in the army, he began to realize that there could be no glory there for him. A natural leader by intelligence and disposition, Miranda was also a liberal, one who was increasingly anxious to put the abstract concepts of freedom and equality into practice. Then, out of the blue, he claimed to have received letters from Venezuela sent to him from the same *mantuano* families who had persecuted his father almost fifteen years earlier. In a momentous document retained in Miranda's archives, Juan Vicente Bolívar (father of the future Liberator, Simón Bolívar), Martín de Tovar, and the Marqués de Miyares described the state of affairs in his homeland for the young officer. They told him that "the lamentable state of this province today, and the general desperation [and] tyrannical measures of this Intendant (who seems to have come here for no other reason but to torment us, like a new Lucifer)" had brought Caracas to the brink of revolution. The trio rejected the dastardly actions of the *godo* (Goth, meaning Spaniard in America) and shared Miranda's opinion of "damned Minister Galvéz (who is crueler than Nero and Philip II combined)."[58] After running through a litany of complaints against the Crown, the self-appointed Caracas representatives suggested that some aggressive and defensive action needed to be taken, perhaps inspired by their American neigbors to the north who had so recently thrown off their colonial chains. Venezuelans were searching for their deliverer and Miranda, the older men pleaded, "[Y]ou are the first-born son of whom the motherland expects this important service." The letter was exactly calculated to appeal to Miranda's self-image and arrived at a time when his faith in the Spanish imperial system (and his place in it) was at an all-time low. The letter may also, however, be a forgery. Its vocabulary, its cadence, and the nature of the charges it contains all tend to mirror Miranda's own personality and style. Whatever the true origin of this document may be, it encapsulates the young man's attitude at that crucial juncture and says much about the way he chose to direct his life from that time forward. He would never be a Spaniard; after 1783, Francisco de Miranda was an American.

Hearing that he was about to be rearrested, Miranda made a radical decision. He resolved to leave the Spanish military service and take himself into exile until he could be guaranteed the public recognition and personal security he desired. Some uncertainty remains about his movements in the final weeks before he defected, as well as disagreement about just how far into his confidence he took friends such as the ever supportive Juan Manuel de Cagigal, but it seems likely that he made his life-altering decision alone. After all, even the hint of conspiracy would have potentially fatal consequences for any friends implicated in the real nature of his plan. Instead, he concocted a story that he was going to Spain to clear his name and restore his reputation. At sea, near the port of Matanzas in Cuba, Miranda wrote to Cagigal that an "unexpected accident and strange circumstances" had caused him to discover that he was about to be rearrested on the charges of treason in the Campbell incident, even though he was "more innocent and pure than Socrates."[59] He reminded Cagigal that although he had served their nation faithfully, without concern for his own fortune or physical well-being, he realized sadly that he could not expect to receive a free and fair trial. For this reason, he had determined to travel to Spain via the North American colonies to clear his good name at the Imperial Court. Another letter to Cagigal dated the same day hinted at a more convincing, deeper motive for his desertion: "The experience and knowledge that one can acquire, visiting personally and examining with studied intelligence in the great book of the universe and the wisest and most virtuous societies of which it is comprised. Their laws, governments, agriculture, police, commerce, military arts, navigation, sciences, arts etc. are those things that can only ripen the fruit and complete in some way the *obra magna* [great work] of forming a solid man of progress."[60]

Miranda intended to travel first through the United States and then onward to Europe in order to perfect his education in the ideals and practice of liberty. The springtime of his youth had turned into a season of discontent.

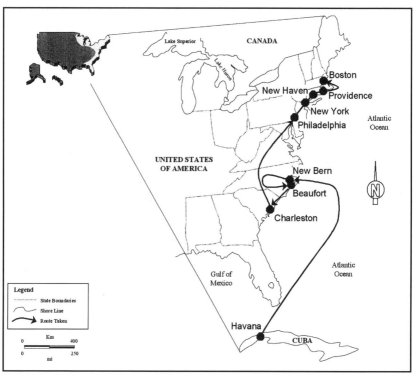

Francisco de Miranda's tour of the United States, 1783–84

2

FINDING THE FOUNDING FATHERS
Miranda's Tour of the
United States (1783–84)

Put none but Americans on guard tonight.
—GEORGE WASHINGTON, circular letter to his regimental commanders
(April 30, 1777)

When Francisco de Miranda stepped onto the American sloop *Prudent* in Havana's harbor on June 1, 1783, he never looked back. In his mind, he had escaped the clutches of a tyrannical Spanish bureaucracy and was setting sail to join a bold new experiment in American republican democracy. With that short journey, he would leave behind the antiquated monarchical past and begin to embrace the system of the future. Miranda, like the authors of the Declaration of Independence, was acutely aware of his historical moment; leaders on both continents shared the conviction that the nineteenth century would be an American century—America for Americans. Miranda had been raised in the same sort of cosmopolitan Atlantic world as his counterparts to the north; they had read the same books, studied the same languages, framed their rhetoric with the same biblical and classical allusions, and shared the same resentment toward a distant colonial authority that controlled their political destinies. Dating back to his days as a young military officer in Cádiz, Miranda had been following the progress of the American Revolution through newspaper accounts and eventually decided that he should see it for himself. There was much to be learned from books, but nothing could compare to witnessing the living example of a revolution in liberty in his own hemisphere.

Miranda left an important account of his travels through the United States at a crucial period in its early republican history.[1] In 1783, the war was all but over and the work of setting up an independent government was just beginning. The country was jubilant in its victory but was also suffering from an economic depression and widespread physical destruction brought on by the war. During the eighteen months that he traveled throughout the United States, Miranda met and forged important personal relationships with many of the era's major military, political, and financial leaders, including George Washington, Alexander Hamilton, Samuel Adams, Henry Knox, the Marquis de Lafayette, Aaron Burr, Thomas Jefferson, James Madison, and the presidents of both Harvard and Yale Colleges. Yet what makes Miranda's diary so valuable as a historical source is his keen interest in the common folk's life-style and political opinions, not just those of his elite friends. Miranda exhibited little of the snobbery that is typical in great men. He mixed well with all social and economic classes and took pains to inform himself about the conditions of rural and working Americans. If anything, he idealized the simple life, seeing in the dignity of poor people's work a complicated (even contradictory) amalgamation of his brain's republican individualism and his heart's lapsed Catholic communalism. Patriotism, as Miranda came to define it through his travels in America, meant the freedom to pursue one's goals, thoughts, and abilities unfettered by governmental interference or dictates; at the same time, freedom carried a sacred duty to contribute to the greater good of the nation. As he came to the United States consciously self-identified as a student of the American Revolution with a view to extending it to his own people, Miranda shared the inclination to trust in voluntarism and the goodness of the human spirit expressed by the Founders of the new United States.

During the same two years he spent observing the workings of the Republic, Miranda's intellectual and political development reveals a strikingly modern paradox. A fugitive from Spanish justice, Miranda was essentially stateless; as he traveled independently throughout the Atlantic world, however, he became increasingly nationalistic.[2] The Precursor of Spanish American independence left Venezuela in 1771 and did not return to his native soil for forty years, but his American rhetoric became ever more vehement with each passing year. Cut off from his fellow Spanish Americans, Miranda had to adapt to life in a new language, a new climate, new food, and new social mores. Yet his ability to interact with the North Americans, and later the Europeans, whom he met during his travels was made easier by the fact that they all shared a common outlook. The Atlantic world in the age of revolution was indeed a tightly-knit place. Families had branches on both sides of the ocean. Companies scattered their agents throughout the region. National origin was not yet a prerequisite for any government service. Miranda's life is the clearest and most elegant example of the transatlantic orientation of his social class.

The fugitive lieutenant colonel's flight to freedom was short and uneventful, except for the ship captain's unexpected decision to change course and land at New Bern, North Carolina, instead of Charleston, South Carolina, as the passengers had contracted. Annoyed, Miranda docked there on June 10, cleared customs, and made the required declarations that he was free from smallpox and other transmissible epidemic diseases. Finding himself alone in a new country, he made his way inland thirty-five miles to New Bern, which was the state capital at the time. He took lodgings at Mr. Oliver's clean and respectable tavern and, as freshly arrived tourists the world over do no matter how tired they may be, he immediately set about investigating his surroundings. Miranda had been in active military service for thirteen years, with all his movements watched and his travels prescribed for him. At last he was able to follow his own feet. Everything was new to him. He wanted to understand the United States, to share in the victory of its independence and learn how to extend its success to his own land. In America, the theories he had only read about were coming to life before his very eyes, and it was terribly invigorating.

As a healthy, red-blooded young man, the first thing Miranda noticed was the behavior of American women. There was a striking difference in the ability of women to enjoy public space compared to those of Mediterranean Europe or Spanish America, causing him to muse: "The married women maintain a monastic seclusion and a submission to their husbands such as I have never seen. . . . Once married, they separate themselves from all intimate friendships and devote

themselves completely to the care of home and family. During the
first year of marriage they play the role of lovers, the second year of
breeders, and thereafter of housekeepers. On the other hand, the unmarried women enjoy complete freedom and take walks alone wherever they want to, without their steps being observed."[3]

Clearly there was much to learn about this new country and its
people's habits. Miranda promised himself he would be a diligent student even if it meant speaking to every woman (and man) he encountered. Historian Robert Darnton, in his study of banned books in
prerevolutionary France, has rightly pointed out the undeniable connection between liberty and libertinism, "a combination of free thinking and free living, which challenged religious doctrines as well as
sexual mores."[4] In other words, a predisposition to challenge authority and to express one's love of freer action in the public sphere translated into looser attitudes in private behavior as well. Miranda certainly
displayed that quality, one so marked among educated gentlemen-
philosophers throughout the eighteenth-century Atlantic world. As
an example, following a journey of twenty-three miles from New Bern
to Beaufort, Miranda was pleasantly surprised to find that there was
no embarrassment at all when he suggested that the innkeeper's teen-
aged daughters, the deliciously-named Comfort and Constance, continue their conversations with him in his bed.[5] As a young man with
a pronounced appetite for the company of women, this sort of sexual
liberty seemed to augur well for republican democracy.

Upon unstudied first glance, the exhilarating freedom he noticed
in American gender relations seemed to extend to class relations as
well. Still in South Carolina in early September 1783 when the cessation of hostilities with England was announced, Miranda was pleasantly surprised to find that "leading officials and citizens of the region
promiscuously ate and drank [roast pig and rum] with the meanest
and the lowest kind of people, holding hands and drinking from the
same cup. It is impossible to imagine, without seeing it, a more purely
democratic gathering, and it confirms what the Greek poets and historians tell us of similar concourses among those free peoples of
Greece."[6] Miranda was trained to view liberty through the lens of the
classics; Greek and Roman references abound in his diary and in his
political concepts, just as they do in the works of every active writer

or public figure in the Atlantic world at the same time. The Greek notion of all citizens sharing equally in the exercise of public duty no matter what their station appealed to him, and he imagined that he was seeing it in action, whether the observation was accurate or not. Miranda had a lifelong aversion to the idea that wealthy people were automatically the worthiest and highest-quality citizens; what mattered to him were virtue, enlightenment, public spirit, and gentility. For example, when he visited two Quakers who had homesteads on the Newport River, Miranda found that one was rich and ignorant while the other was poor but more generous and educated.[7] Obviously, he concluded, wealth alone did not make a good citizen.

Always distrustful of unthinking authority, Miranda's lack of traditional religious piety soon got him into trouble with his various hosts in America. Often he became bored on Sundays, which were set aside as the Lord's Day with all activities except prayer and reflection were proscribed. This was quite a change from the festive Sundays he had experienced in the Spanish world, when families strolled the public parks, enjoyed musical performances, and celebrated with lively dinners together. Attempting to blend into his new environment, Miranda grudgingly took up some quiet, amusing activity to pass the time on the Lord's Day. On more than one occasion his hosts severely reprimanded him for playing cards or reading nonreligious tracts on a Sunday. Once Miranda "let loose loud laughter" when a scandalized local woman complained that he was blasphemously playing his flute on that sacred day. This behavior, Miranda noted contemptuously in his diary, indicated that "crass superstition is present in all peoples of the earth, even the most civilized."[8] Quaker Robert Williams piously tried to instill some proper reverence for the Lord's worship in his new foreign friend by sending him some Bible verses, ones that were well chosen to provide Divine support for humans' work on Earth.[9] Having grown up in a Catholic culture that stressed social status and charitable works, Miranda was curious about the relationship between Protestantism, individualism, and revolution. He did not, however, ever manage to see how adopting a somber disposition on Sunday made for more sincere Christianity or benefited society as a whole. Anglo-American attitudes such as these mystified him until the end of his days.

By August 1783, Miranda had finally made his way southward to Charleston, where he had originally expected to land two months earlier and where his prearranged contacts were anxiously awaiting him. He brought letters of introduction to the lieutenant governor of South Carolina, Thomas Bee, from both James Seagrove, an American merchant in Havana, and Havana governor Juan Manuel Cagigal. Four days later, Bee held a grand reception for Miranda that was attended by local dignitaries and interested citizens alike. There Miranda made his first acquaintance with many military figures of the Revolutionary wars, including former commander of the Army of the South Nathanael Greene, General William Moultrie, Colonel William Washington (a relative of George Washington), Colonel Jean Skey Eustace (who later became Miranda's sworn enemy in France), as well as many civil officials and those in the liberal professions. In his diary, however, Miranda spilled more ink praising the attributes of the women in attendance, including the lovely Miss Townsend, whom he coyly described as "my inamorata."[10] During subsequent weeks, as the generals ferried Miranda around from battlefield to fortification to shipyard, he took time to describe the men's countenances and characters more fully. His highest compliments were reserved for people such as General Moultrie and Judge Heyward, men of solid republican values: good judgment, austerity of habits and manners, patriotic spirit, and moral resolution. Miranda praised Mr. Hudson, a man who managed to contain rebellious factions during an antirevolutionary uprising, for his "[g]ood judgement, considerable education, and a love of the sciences, society and humanity."[11] To a large degree, this was how Miranda viewed himself as well.

After spending time investigating the South's social relations, agricultural production, military fortifications, and political landscape, Miranda was ready to continue on his journey through the Republic. With an enthusiastic set of introductions from his new Charleston friends to help him gain entry into northern society, Miranda left for Philadelphia on November 2. He was part of a cosmopolitan group that included a businessman from Port-au-Prince (Haiti), a Prussian diplomat, and a New Jersey farmer with his daughter and niece, both of whom, he reported, "were merry in the American fashion."[12] Sailing up the Delaware River near Wilmington, Miranda saw evidence of the recently-ended hostilities wherever he looked. There were charred buildings, maimed former soldiers, and abandoned armament stands. One of the most impressive sights appeared along the banks near Billings' Point when his ship passed a nasty-looking *chevaux-de-frise*, which was a type of barrier composed of spikes set up to obstruct British vessels after the enemy gained control of Philadelphia in 1777; a second *chevaux-de-frise* further upriver left barely enough room for his own ship to pass through. Miranda was quite taken with the Americans' inventiveness and marveled that it "could have been the sublime and universal genius of Doctor Franklin" that had produced such an invention. Indeed, Benjamin Franklin's reputation was clearly on Miranda's mind as he approached Philadelphia. In his diary he listed with excitement the many contributions of that "great friend of society": a new and more efficient system of chimneys, shaving soap, "and numerous other inventions and minor discoveries which, although not so brilliant as those of the laws of electricity and others of this character, are much more useful to humanity."[13]

Miranda loved Philadelphia. It seemed to him to be the most republican of cities. He stayed in lodgings at the Indian Queen Inn, where Thomas Jefferson supposedly resided while he wrote the Declaration of Independence. No wonder such a sublime document came into being here, he thought; Philadelphia seemed to be Reason incarnate. Miranda deemed his room to be the cleanest, most spacious, regular, and decent that he had yet encountered. Philadelphia's streets were straight and set out on a logical grid pattern with ample brick sidewalks for pedestrians. At regular intervals in front of houses, wooden pumps had been constructed that provided convenient access to clear water for urban residents. He admired the architecture and the small, clean, and comfortable houses that were "plain and simple, like the dress and habits of the first inhabitants."[14] Unlike those found throughout the Spanish world, Philadelphia's public market was such that even "decent women are wont to go to it in the morning and bring home pieces of beef in their hands, without soiling themselves or giving off any bad odor . . . such is the propriety and cleanliness with which everything is regulated!"[15] The streets were illuminated at night and guards were posted at each crossing to ensure the safety of all citizens. As a patriotic traveler, one already beginning to envision himself as a founder of an independent Spanish America, Miranda made special note of the city's collection of over a hundred portraits done by Charles Willson Peale to commemorate those citizens and foreigners who had contributed to the success of the American Revolution. Such a public display, Miranda commented, "not only offers entertainment and pleasure to the curious and educated traveler but also sheds light on history and forms patriotic and virtuous ideas in the youth. . . . Certainly this example should be imitated by all other nations which value virtue and good taste!"[16] He was reminded of the galleries of heroes he had viewed in Spain and was more determined than ever that his own portrait would take a central place on a similar patriotic memorial in Caracas someday.

His first order of business was to present himself at the home of the Spanish envoy, Francisco Rendón, to whom he had a letter of introduction from Cagigal. Because the news of Miranda's status as a deserter had not yet made its way through the Spanish bureaucracy to Rendón, he received the young lieutenant colonel with full honors and insisted that the visitor stay with him while in Philadelphia. Indeed, Cagigal's recommendation seemed to confirm Miranda's story that he was an innocent officer traveling to Spain to clear his name in a dispute brought about by his enemies. The letter explained to Rendón that Miranda was the victim of "certain vexations occurred lately with the Minister of the Indies [José de Gálvez], promoted by the Envy of some dirty rivals who resented him and who provoked a falling out."[17] Cagigal even authorized Rendón to release any funds to Miranda that the unfortunate man might require, charging them against his own accounts in Spain. Because his travels seemed to have been sanctioned at a high level, Miranda easily gained entry into respectable society in the United States.

This happy situation, coupled with word sent ahead by his Charleston friends that Miranda was a charming, erudite, thoroughly engaging, and liberal figure, meant that the invitations soon came pouring in. At Rendón's residence, Miranda made his first acquaintance with Gouverneur Morris, a one-legged New York representative to the Continental Congress who had made a vast fortune in land speculations. Morris subsequently became a leading Federalist and was the American minister to France at the time of Miranda's imprisonment there in 1793, yet Miranda's initial impression was that of a man "who has more ostentation, audacity and tinsel than real value."[18] Gouverneur and Mrs. Morris invited him to a ball on January 6, 1784; the merchants of Philadelphia invited him to dine with them at the City Tavern; the ministers of both France and the United Netherlands asked him to dinner.[19] Just as Miranda gained prestige and further access from his association with leading citizens in the various cities he visited, so too did those citizens feel validated by the obvious interest and admiration of a cultivated foreigner. Both sides shared the impression that they were fighting the same battles of enlightenment against ignorance, freedom against tyranny, America against Europe, the new against the old.

Although he was quite open to new people and places, Miranda revealed one of his particular national prejudices in his paranoia toward the "Gallic cabal" that he thought he detected around him.[20] Spaniards had always feared and distrusted their French neighbors. This attitude spilled over to their American colonists, whom they exhorted to be on the watch for potential French infiltrators. Caracas itself had fallen victim to a French raid in 1766, so Miranda was sensitive to that kingdom's territorial ambitions in America. Furthermore, Miranda's pride as a military man was wounded when he discovered that North American citizens tended to value French people and culture above the Spanish even though both countries had made valuable contributions to the thirteen colonies' war against the British. On a personal level, he found the French to be arrogant, narrow-minded, and prone to bureaucratic centralization in their affairs. When he met Monsieur Barrière, a learned immigrant in the service of the American military, Miranda deemed him to be "one of the very few Frenchmen I have known on this continent who is capable of recognizing, notwithstanding his native prejudices, the advantages of a free government as compared with any other despotism, and who is a good republican!" Later introduced to Marie Joseph Paul Yves Roch Gilbert du Motier, the Marquis de Lafayette, an internationally renowned war hero who had fought with Washington on the Brandywine and at Valley Forge, Miranda sniffed, "[H]e seems to me a mediocre character, invested with that activity and perpetual motion of a Frenchman. . . . This trip of the Marquis seems to me one of those

legerdemains with which France is wont to delude human nature and
which on many occasions have had the desired effect; but to the eyes
of those who see well, they are nothing but ridiculous political farces."[21]
Although he loved the work of French *philosophes*, Miranda always
had a hard time reconciling himself to the presence of living Frenchmen, especially when their talents rivaled his own. He always felt a
closer affinity with the British and those partial to British aristocratic
constitutionalism. For example, he praised traveling merchant Joaquín
de Quintana as "one of the very few of my countrymen who have
penetrated the marvelous arcanum of the British constitution."[22]

A keen observer of the status of gender relations in the places he
visited, Miranda found Philadelphia's women to exhibit a certain reserve in their manners. Because they were often segregated from men
and typically received a less rigorous education, their conversation
was tentative and their range of subjects less broad. Miranda believed
that women should be encouraged to attend public gatherings and be
welcomed at all places of social intercourse, "at which the contrast
and variety of manners and customs broaden the outlook and create
in us an open, frank, and generous manner—a quality sometimes
much more valuable in society than those which stem from wealth
and vast knowledge."[23] As examples of his pedagogical theories,
Miranda held up the persons of Mrs. Powell, Miss Sally Shippen,
Miss Moore, Miss Molly Coxe, Miss Peggy Chew, and "the Quaker
Misses," Susan and Rebecca Morris and Isabella Marshall. His "*amiga
querida*" (sweetheart) at the time, Miss Polly Vining, was an exuber-
ant lass who taught him to skate and to play the popular card game
Comet. Miranda often exchanged books with women, evidence that
he respected their intelligence and recognized their ability to enter
into serious philosophical discussions. Mrs. Montgomery, for example,
thanked him for the loan of two books, but apologized that she could
not return the third, a volume of Helvetius, because she had "absolutely fallen in love with it and cannot think of parting with it."[24] In
exchange, she hoped he would accept a history of the Revolutionary
War written by an eyewitness who had lodged in her mother's house.
Mrs. Burr thanked Miranda for loaning her his copy of *La philosophie
de la nature* (The Philosophy of Nature), which "displays strength &
elegance of mind mingled with philanthropy. From his sentiments &

Col. De Miranda's taste we are convinced there are souls that escape the prejudices imposed by sophistry."[25] Miranda loved to converse with women. He enjoyed playing the part of tutor to the ones who had the shrewd sense to flatter his genius, and he especially admired bright women who were knowledgeable and cultivated in languages and the fine arts. Music was one of his favorite feminine subjects of discussion. Mary Walton sent a thousand thanks to him for loaning her the major works of Rousseau, which she read "with much attention," particularly his ideas on music.[26]

Miranda was both amused and bemused by the austerity of the Quaker heritage in Philadelphia. Formally known as the Society of Friends, the Quakers denied that priests or public rites were necessary for salvation; their approach to religion, truth, and understanding originated in meditation and personal reflection. They also believed in the equality of all people and refused to bow down before those who claimed to be their superiors. Quakers disdained frivolity and artifice and vowed to lead honest, simple lives devoted to the betterment of themselves and their neighbors. Although he greatly admired the values of cleanliness, regularity, and humility practiced in Philadelphia, Miranda was nonetheless irritated to find that the Quakers' and other republican moralists' influence in civic life meant that there was neither a proper formal theater nor other houses of diversion in that city.[27] In fact, he was appalled that the sheriff had actually chased out of the city a troupe of bad actors who had set up a makeshift stage. At the same time, he chuckled over their American inventiveness; in their attempt to evade the local ordinance that forbade dramatic performances, the actors clutched scripts while on stage so that they could claim they were performing a simple reading and not offering a play for entertainment. Even dancing was occasionally banned as part of the moral restrictions imposed by the Continental Congress during wartime. To Miranda, such unnecessary self-denial seemed ridiculous and hopelessly outdated. After all, it was the eighteenth century, well past the time for silly religious superstitions or dour wartime observations to prohibit innocent fun. He believed patriotism was a dish best served warm and accompanied by lots of rousing music.

Nonetheless, as a freethinking liberal person formed by a Catholic upbringing, he was heartened to see that such foolery did not extend into the realm of private beliefs; even though dour Protestants predominated in Philadelphia, every religion and sect was permitted and all felt free to worship openly in the manner that suited them best. Happily, in the United States, women seemed to be valued in spiritual life as well. Attending one Quaker service, Miranda was shocked to hear a woman's voice reading aloud some passages and to find that women and men shook hands at the conclusion of the meeting, calling each other "friend" without deference to gender or status. At the same time he railed against what he perceived to be excessive piety in North Americans, their efforts to protect religious tolerance pleased him. Meeting the founding fathers and mothers of the early American Republic, Miranda wanted to believe that the positive values produced by Protestant culture (namely hard work, ingenuity, reserve, greater social and economic mobility, and personal humility) were an integral part of what he called the new "American system." Inevitably, this system should be extended to include his South America as well.

Miranda was keenly aware of the significance of the American Revolution in world history. He was even more aware of the place its leaders were guaranteed by their glorious service to the march of liberty and freedom in the New World. The idea that he might have a similar role to play for his own people had been growing steadily since the days of his service in Africa. In America, he hoped to study ways in which his dreams might be put into practice. As an avid consumer of international news while in Europe and in the Caribbean, Miranda had followed the actions of General George Washington and specifically brought letters of introduction to him. Miranda got his chance to meet the famous man in Philadelphia. On December 8, 1783, George Washington passed through the city on his way to join the Continental Congress at Annapolis. The Revolutionary hero's entrance made a deep impression on Miranda, whose reaction was made plain in his diary entry for that day:

> Children, men and women expressed such contentment as if the Redeemer had entered Jerusalem! Such are the excessive fancies and sublime estimation which this fortunate and singular man enjoys in the entire country, although philosophers are not lacking who examine him in the light of reason and conceive a fairer idea than that which the high and

low multitude imagines. . . . Just as the rays of the sun, shining upon burning glass, concentrate in the focus and produce such an admirable effect in physics, so do the achievements and deeds of many individuals in America reflect upon the independence and concentrate in Washington! A usurpation as capricious as it is unjust.[28]

Despite Miranda's barely concealed jealousy, the next day he too made the obligatory pilgrimage and went with Francisco Rendón to pay respects to the illustrious Washington. Cagigal's letter introduced Miranda as a man of "character, instruction, and other qualities that have always recommended him to me with singular distinction, as I hope they will to you as well."[29] Even Rendón was not immune to the giddy response that Washington elicited from most of those who encountered him; Rendón once asked Washington to give him leave "to permit me to love him as a Citizen as I have revered him as a Father of his Country and the insurer of domestic happiness" for his people. True to the classical rhetorical framework that their entire generation shared, Cagigal called Washington the "Fabius of our times," referring to Quintus Fabius Maximus, the great Roman commander who used delay tactics and a strategy of calculated exhaustion against Hannibal's invading Carthaginian army in the Second Punic War.[30]

Such devotion irritated Miranda, particularly if he was not its subject. Although he later reported proudly that he himself had the pleasure of dining with Washington every night that the general stayed in Philadelphia, Miranda clearly had a complex attitude toward the man. He felt Washington as a mortal human being was "circumspect, taciturn, and has little expression, but tranquility and toleration make him tolerable. I was never able to see him set aside these qualities, despite the fact that wine flowed with humor and merriment after dinner and that, when drinking certain toasts, he would stand up and give his three cheers with the rest of us. It is not easy to form a definite opinion of his character, and so we will suspend judgment for now."[31]

Meeting military figures like Washington and Lafayette, so beloved and destined for historical immortality, made Miranda both jealous and increasingly anxious to duplicate their feats. For his part, Washington really had little need to pay any attention to an odd traveling foreigner, no matter how engaging or well-informed the young man might be; he was too busy founding a nation. Unlike Miranda, whose hazy idealism often overwhelmed his better judgment, Washington was not so much a philosopher as a pragmatist. At the exact time of his brief encounter with Miranda in Philadelphia, the general's attention was focused on the nature of future relations between the United States and Spanish America; he was not as inclined to see the same cultural affinities based on ideals of liberty and democracy as were Miranda and others of that Atlantic generation. By November 1783, Washington's thoughts were already turning to the consolidation and expansion of his hard-won territory beyond the Ohio River and up to the St. Lawrence; he was most anxious that the Spaniards and the British settlers be kept out of that zone, as "it is by the cement of interest that we can be held together" and such emigrants "can have no particular predilection for us." Washington also had selfish financial reasons for wishing to fence off the opening American West from potential interlopers; he was a republican landholder with personal titles to vast tracts in the Ohio Territory himself. As an example of the dangers of "otherness" in the American hemisphere, Washington specifically pointed to the threat posed by Spanish Americans.[32] During their brief meeting, Miranda undoubtedly felt snubbed and, in turn, his wounded pride colored his own impressions of the famous American general. Years later in France, however, Miranda exaggerated his personal association with Washington in order to bolster his reputation, while retaining mixed feelings about the existence of another American general whose greatness outstripped his own: "The President of the United States, whom I knew personally, did not secure the confidence of his fellow citizens by any brilliant qualities, which, in point of fact, he did not possess; on the other hand, he did win all the hearts by his fairness of outlook as well as by the righteousness of his intentions; it has been this sense of fair play that dominated his choice of the ablest, most enlightened colleagues, who, with such conspicuous success, have helped to consolidate the liberty and happiness of their people."[33] Fairness. Right intentions. Elevation of ability. Concern for the liberty and happiness of the people. These were distinctly American virtues, praised in one great American by another who hoped to diffuse them southward among his own people as part of their shared hemispheric project.

Miranda the soldier always loved to talk tactics and battles with experienced men and, after his meeting with Washington, began to take a renewed interest in the historical process of the Revolutionary War. In Delaware, with his British friend Captain Rutherford and two American veterans, he visited the site where the Battle of the Brandywine took place in September 1777. Drawing on his companions' memories and his own extensive reading, Miranda mapped out the entire battle that had handed a serious defeat to Washington and his 12,000 men. With the greatest of care he examined the site and all the various troop movements, finally pronouncing his verdict: "I did not understand why Washington exposed himself to such an obvious danger; nor why [British] General Howe did not cross the river at Chadds Ford and attack him immediately with his entire army."[34] Miranda the traveler was also Miranda the historian, and his private investigations were animated by the same desire for accurate, first-hand history that motivated his generation of intellectuals throughout the Atlantic world.

Miranda experienced his first real taste of winter while at Philadelphia. The day he spent along the Brandywine left him in "agony" from the cold; he claimed that he lost all sensation in his nose, hands, feet, and ears and could not even dismount from his horse. Another journey, this time in Mr. Vining's phaeton, was undertaken in temperatures so severe that none of the travelers could hold the reins for more than ten minutes. Miranda found that the best remedy for this inconvenience was "[g]ood tea, good supper, good bed, and a robust and not bad-looking servant girl."[35] He did enjoy skating and took his first walk on the ice, which he deemed pleasurable and scientifically interesting.

Having studied Philadelphia's people, products, and political climate, Miranda judged that it was time to move on to New York. His continuing presence in the city had become awkward after rumors of his status as a deserter finally reached Philadelphia in mid-January; those less kindly disposed toward him began to murmur that Miranda was not at all the innocent on the way to Spain in search of legal redress that he purported to be. Clearly he had to leave town immediately or risk both compromising his kind host and friend Rendón and leaving himself vulnerable to exposure or arrest. Already feeling slightly

paranoid, Miranda began to speculate that local French agents were
intriguing against him because they thought he might disprove their
lies about the lesser role that the Spanish had played in the Caribbean
theater. Indeed, he wrote: "[T]hey began to fabricate a thousand tales
and hatch dark plots to find a way to induce me to let them cackle in
their hen-houses and continue my trip to another part. Rendón, the
poor man, was out of his wits, not knowing what to do under such
circumstances, but I penetrated the whole mystery. . . . So I abandoned to scorn these Gallo-political rivals . . . and my friend Rendón
avoided a very difficult situation for which he gave me a thousand
thanks."[36]

And so, on to New York it was. Miranda left Philadelphia at the
inhuman hour of 3:30 A.M. on January 16, 1784. The inexpensive
stagecoach he took had the additional security benefit of allowing
him to take his luggage along instead of sending it separately, so that
his belongings would not escape his watchful eye. Traveling nine or
ten miles per hour, the coach made slow progress because the unbearable temperatures forced the party to stop at public houses regularly
to warm their hands and feet. Miranda himself was so chilled that he
refused to get out of the coach in order to lighten the load and thereby
lessen the dangers of falling through the ice when crossing frozen
streams. Such churlishness must have angered his companions, who
were not as willing to bear the risk. At 10 P.M. the coach crossed the
frozen Delaware River at precisely the same place as General Washington had done on Christmas Eve 1776, when he surprised the Hessian troops at Trenton. The reverential silence of his traveling
companions as they passed over the sacred spot again reminded
Miranda of his hero-rival's omnipresence in the emerging American
national consciousness and no doubt worsened his mood.

Originally Miranda had planned to spend just a short time in
New York, travel onward to Boston, and then depart for England, but
the cold weather forced him to change his plans. Instead, he decided
to seek comfortable lodgings and to hunker down and wait for warmer
temperatures while undertaking a fuller educational tour of New England. In New York City, he secured a room at Mr. Ellsworth's excellent inn on Maiden Lane for seven *pesos fuertes* weekly, not including
firewood and liquor.[37] Much to Miranda's annoyance, his 16-year old

Scottish indentured servant, a boy named John Dean, escaped upon arrival even though their contract had obligated him to serve Miranda for two and a half years. Miranda grumbled that he had "bought [Dean] for ten guineas in Philadelphia, on board an Irish ship bearing a cargo of more than three hundred male and female slaves" and had considered the boy to be "honest and mischievous, but the event proved to the contrary."[38] Even though he had a healthy contempt for snobbish class relations, his previous acquisition of slaves at Pensacola and his subsequent purchase of John Dean's personal servitude contract reveal that Miranda possessed the same attitudes toward domestic service as other upper-class men and women of his era.

The longer he stayed in the United States, the easier Miranda found it to insert himself into the social and political life of the cities he visited. He was an assiduous collector of introductions and always arrived with a valise full of recommendations from friends and relatives in one town to those in the next. After all, Miranda knew how to be a good guest and, in a country just beginning to recover from a devastating war, a gallant, erudite, entertaining foreigner who enthusiastically admired their new system was welcomed everywhere he went. New York proved to be no different. Residing there for more than five months, he dined with the best families, romanced their daughters, and talked politics with important men. One historian has characterized Miranda as "a champion name-dropper of his time, and he buttonholed all around him who would listen."[39] He soon gathered an impressive pile of calling cards and invitations to dinner as well as to those gatherings popularly known among New York's politicians as "dancing assemblies." Happily, New Yorkers were more inclined to enjoy themselves than Philadelphians had been.

One of the more notorious liaisons of his American tour was conducted clandestinely with Susan Livingston, the daughter of the fabulously wealthy Peter Livingston. Miranda always liked women. He especially liked smart women and he chose his women smartly. Susan seems to have been the first one to affect him deeply; she was twenty-seven years old, pretty, well-connected, and fatally attracted to danger, a combination he found difficult to resist. Their courtship began typically, through an exchange of books, Miranda taking the role of tutor and loaning Susan copies of works by two of his favorite authors: David Hume and the Abbé Raynal. The coquettish Susan sent him little notes of thanks, flattering his brilliant choices and expressing her gratitude for exposure to such sublime ideas. In early January 1784, Susan's curiosity about the mysterious foreigner was piqued sufficiently to inquire on behalf of her friends, who "take a *great* interest in all that concerns you, & wish to have a particular information of your *political situation* [as] there are some things *insinuated* that are not in the least advantageous to *your* honor."[40] Over the next months, her letters became longer and more intimate and eventually had to be delivered secretly through a trusted courier. Fashionable society being what it is, however, rumors about their liaison eventually surfaced, causing some in her circle to joke that Susan was destined to become the "Queen of the Incas."[41]

Susan's sisters and girlfriends, however, merely giggled at such a prospect and poked fun at the absurd foreigner's airs. Eventually, they were concerned enough about impetuous Susan's compromised position to raid Miranda's room during one of his frequent absences from New York; the girls apparently broke open his trunks so they could rummage through his books and papers to search for any incriminating evidence regarding his affair with Susan. Upon returning and finding his things in disarray, he quarreled with the interlopers, denying that any inappropriate relationship with Miss Livingston had existed because, as he told them, "he requires three months' acquaintance with a lady before he enters into conversation with them to avoid the great error of not adapting to the idea & turn of the lady." That comment was disingenuous at best and it certainly did not fool Susan's self-appointed protectresses. Months later, Sarah Vaughan declared herself pleased that Miranda had finally departed the country and did not "venerate his character sufficiently to wish his return."[42]

Not everyone agreed with her. Thomas Paine, the republican author of *The Age of Reason* and *Common Sense*, met Miranda that spring in New York and later recalled that he had found him to be "a man of talents and enterprise."[43] John Adams never met him, but knew by reputation that Miranda had the character of "a classical scholar, a man of universal knowledge, of a great general, and master of all the military sciences, and of great sagacity, an inquisitive mind, and an insatiable curiosity."[44] Many important and powerful men listened to Miranda, whose conversation was explicitly turning toward the dream of extending the American Revolution to the Southern Hemisphere. Describing the inevitable march of liberty to his New York audiences, which not incidentally would open vast new commercial markets to them as well, it was not difficult to capture their attention. One of these listeners, William Duer, immediately sensed a good business opportunity and latched on to Miranda with friendly insistence. He had been a member of the New York State Convention and a delegate to the Continental Congress, and would become assistant secretary of the treasury as the federal government began to take shape. He was also less than honest; Duer was eventually imprisoned for embezzlement and died in prison. At the time he met Miranda, however, Duer was a well-connected entrepreneur actively seeking foreign ventures in which to make a quick fortune. Small wonder that Miranda's plans attracted him. Miranda also met Stephen Sayre, another speculator who had approached the king of Prussia in 1777 with his own plan to set up an independent empire in America based on the island of Dominica.[45]

Among his longest-standing and most important New York friendships, however, was the one with Alexander Hamilton, whose wife was a member of the extended Livingston family. For the next twenty years, Miranda and Hamilton (who had been born in the Caribbean, educated himself, and rose on his own merits) exchanged personal letters and shared plans for an emancipated Spanish America.[46] Each new friend and convert to his cause strengthened Miranda's confidence and gave him further legitimacy. Years later, writing to his friend Armand Gensonné in Paris in 1792, Miranda recalled somewhat melodramatically: "In the year 1784, in the city of New York, I formed a project for the liberty and independence of the entire Spanish-American Continent with the co-operation of England. That nation was naturally much interested in the design, for Spain had furnished a precedent by forcing her to acknowledge the independence of her colonies in America."[47]

Letters of introduction provided by his new acquaintances bear out this assessment. In two such letters Mr. S. Knox described Miranda as "a Spanish Gentleman, who visits our Country, to view more nearly

the scene where such great things have been performed by compara-
tively small means," and wrote that he wished him "to receive a proper
impression of our domestic character" so that it may "firmly impress
the Idea, that we are at least equal to our neighbors in these points."[48]
Clearly his hosts were as anxious to make a good impression on
Miranda and were as concerned about living up to his idealized view
of their society as he was to secure their friendship and approval.

Because New York had been the scene of so many battles in the
Revolutionary Wars, Miranda used his extended stay in that state to
analyze its commanders' strategies. Fending off the cold internally
with liquor and externally with fireside conversations, he made his
way to West Point. Upon arrival, he was delighted to find that no one
was particularly interested in the stranger, or made any particular inquiries as to his purpose in being there; that, Miranda raved, was a
healthy change from Germany or France, where suspicion of outsiders reigned supreme and a thousand investigations into one's credentials and permissions would have been launched. Staying with William
Hull, the fort's commander, he inspected various muskets, munitions,
sabers, bayonets, and other artillery. The most impressive sight, however, was the famous chain across the Hudson River from Fort Clinton
to Constitution Island that had prevented navigation during the war.
Miranda deemed it "an exertion of the genius, industry, and bold
spirit of the people who produced it! Its cost is said to mount to seventy thousand pounds, and had the King of Spain paid for it, doubt-
lessly it would have been more; but I do not think it cost them the
tenth part of this sum."[49] He also visited Fort Clinton, Fort Putnam,
Fort Wyllys, and Fort Webb, and dined with several war veterans who
still resided in the area; in fact, Colonel McDougall's son gave him
the best pippins he ever tasted. Hull was sufficiently impressed with
Miranda's military knowledge and abilities to mention him in a letter
to Major General Henry Knox, in which he passed along a note of
Miranda's that clarified some points about his service in European
garrisons.[50] In this way, and with the aid of willing new colleagues,
Miranda the soldier and military historian continued to outrun his
reputation as a deserter. Information was fast becoming the new currency, and Miranda's stores were full.

Miranda also continued to prosecute his investigations into the lives of common American citizens. In his diary, he recorded a story that he had heard in New York about a local farmer who had approached the French general Rochambeau for the payment of rent while the foreign troops were using his land. When he obtained no satisfaction, "this republican rustic" brought out the sheriff to arrest the powerful general right in front of his own soldiers; Rochambeau was detained until the nominal cost of damages and rent, just fifteen pesos in the end, was paid. Ah, said Miranda, therein lay America's secret. Everyone, no matter what his status, was equal before the law. He asked, "[H]ow is it possible that under similar protections the most arid and barren countries would not flourish? And that the most pusillanimous and abject men would not, within a short time, be honest, just, industrious, wise and brave?"[51] Undoubtedly he also enjoyed hearing about a Frenchman being taken down a peg.

Along with his many branches of research, Miranda also took time to indulge himself in the activities that passed for entertainment during the freezing New York winter. At the town of Footway Bridge, near the Passaic River, he visited Peter Van Weetle, cheerfully known as the "Child with the Big Head." Although a fully-grown and bearded adult, Peter's body corresponded to that of a 6-year-old boy, yet his cranium was "so monstrous that it seems to be that of a giant; doubtless it is about as large as three heads of ordinary men, and the greater enormousness is in the upper part."[52] The unfortunate youth could not lift his head and had to remain prostrate all day, being tended by a servant girl. Most remarkably to Miranda, the invalid enjoyed good health, conversed happily and rationally, and appeared completely accepting of his fate.

Miranda, on the other hand, continued to try to dodge his fate. In April 1784, he received an angry letter from his Havana merchant friend James Seagrove, warning him that the Spanish magistrates finally had pronounced their sentence upon Miranda for desertion: the loss of his commission, a stiff fine, and exile to Oran for ten years. In other words, he could no longer legally claim to be a Spanish military officer. Furthermore, Seagrove complained that "it was truly imprudent of you to mention my name as assisting at your escape. If you have mentioned it to Rendón & some others who are in Phi[ladelphi]a it will undoubtedly be known—as a Gentleman and a Man of Honour I call on you to stop."[53] With the receipt of Seagrove's letter, Miranda changed tack and no longer depicted himself as an innocent victim seeking redress; instead, he found it more convenient to present himself as a victim of Spanish tyranny, a fugitive from the political persecution of an arbitrary and tyrannical government. Miranda's New York friends easily accepted this change to his public persona. Many were anti-Catholic and already inclined to believe in the myth of Spanish barbarism, based on tales of the dreaded Inquisition and their cruel treatment of Indians that had long been current in the Anglo-American popular imagination. In a letter of introduction to his brother-in-law, British assistant secretary of the treasury George Rose, Miranda's starry-eyed merchant friend William Duer painted a portrait of the fugitive Venezuelan as a man who has "met with that Fate, which has often befallen the man of virtues, and Talents in an Arbitrary Governement [sic], the Prosecution of bigotted [sic] and intriguing men." As the cloud of suspicion was likely to follow his new colleague to England, Duer asked Rose to use his position to protect Miranda and to arrange an interview with the prime minister so that he could provide accurate details of the resources, population, and politics of both Americas, North and South.[54]

After a considerable gap in his diary, Miranda resumed taking notes on May 28, 1784, as he boarded the sloop *Schuyler* destined for upstate New York. The environs of Albany struck him as so fertile and aromatic that he imagined that he could be in Puerto Rico, Cuba, or some other part of "our American continent."[55] Just as he had shared a youthful loyalty to "our Spain" with his European brothers, by 1784, Miranda had begun to relocate his political allegiance to an American hemispheric context. His new friends and neighbors to the north seemed willing enough to overlook the charges of desertion and continued to recognize his military status; in fact, the members of the patriotic military Society of the Cincinnati invited him to dine as their guest of honor at Cape's Tavern on July 2, shortly before his departure from New York. Despite such attention, he was anxious to start moving eastward in the pleasant summer months. When Miranda arrived at New Haven, Connecticut, on Sunday, July 25, as usual, he found no activity in the streets. With little else to do in the new town, Miranda attended the afternoon service of Reverend John Murray, a firebrand preacher from Boston whose system preached universal salvation. Miranda was bored. After the sermon, the indefatigable traveler went in search of the president of Yale College (now Yale University), the Reverend Dr. Ezra Stiles, who unfortunately was out of town. Instead, Miranda set himself down by the fire and spent the next two rainy days reading Robert Watson's *History of the Reign of Philip the Second, King of Spain* (London, 1777), from which he imbibed the English predisposition to view Spaniards as evil, priest-ridden, and superstitious.

Stiles returned to town and immediately returned Miranda's call. Describing his new friend as "a Spaniard a native of Caraccas in Terra [F]irma So[uth] America, [who] was educated in a college in the City of Mexico," Stiles deemed Miranda to be "a learned Man & a flaming Son of Liberty." He proudly escorted the foreign visitor around Yale's campus and let him observe various classes in optics and algebra, where Miranda noted approvingly that "these sciences were explained to students in the most simple and natural manner." He attended the Hebrew class taught by President Stiles, which he found slightly more arcane and difficult, and then the pair spent the rest of the day together drinking wine and bandying about "college pedantries" until 10:00 P.M. In fact, Miranda and the president of Yale were inseparable over the next few days, examining books in the library, recording temperatures, visiting tourist sights, and watching a burial procession in which men and women seemed to intermingle freely.[56]

Because both Stiles and Miranda were bibliophiles and part of a shared transatlantic community of learned men, they spent much of their time together discussing books and matters of education. Miranda proclaimed the Yale College library to be "nothing special" because it possessed only two or three thousand volumes of very common titles, a few telescopes, and "a few other bagatelles of natural history."[57] On the other hand, Miranda, who was a master at presenting himself as the person his audience wished to see, left President Stiles with the breathless impression that he had a "p[er]fect Acquainta[nce] with the policy & Hist[ory] of all Spanish America. He gave me the manner of Educa[tion] in the Colleges in Mexico & so[uth] of all N[ew]

Spain."[58] After describing Spanish America's standard curriculum, the cost of tuition, and the process of academic administration in detail, Miranda estimated that there were around 500 students at the College of Mexico when he studied law there for a year. Miranda apparently told Stiles: "[T]here are no great Literary Characters in N[ew] Spain [ie. Mexico]—nor can there be—for Geniuses dare not *read* not *think* nor *speak*, for fear of the Inquisition, wh[ich] keeps out all books, lest it sh[oul]d effect sedition. There is a close League between Ecclesiastics and Civilians—they mutually support one another. No free enquiry."[59]

Miranda also painted a dark picture for the scandalized North American in which he claimed to have been obliged to pay twenty dollars for two volumes of John Locke's *Essay on Human Understanding*, with the promise that they would be burned immediately after he had finished reading them. Furthermore, Miranda claimed, the Inquisitors had taken away his own personal book collection amounting to 2,000 volumes without offering any compensation at all. Of course, no such thing had happened. Miranda had never set foot in Mexico, but he was playing upon the gullible North American's prejudices against the dreaded Inquisition in order to generate sympathy and to forge a common cause between the recently successful North Americans and their neighbors to the south.

Since his encounter with the Quakers in Philadelphia, Miranda had become fascinated with the historical and cultural bases for the legislation of public morality. While in New Haven he undertook primary research at the local archives because he wanted to understand the nature and process of the town's infamous Blue Laws, a set of strict ordinances dating from 1639 that governed the observance of the Sabbath not only in New Haven but throughout Connecticut and the rest of New England as well. For example, if a person drank to someone's health, kissed his wife in public, dallied with women, or had frequent suppers on a Sunday, he would be fined and lashed. "Such," scoffed Miranda, "was the fanaticism and way of thinking among these people a century and a half ago."[60] During his tour of New England, Miranda continued his investigation into American religious history by reading the notorious Cotton Mather's book called *Magnalia Christi Americana: Or the Ecclesiastical History of New En-*

gland (London, 1702); an incredulous Miranda branded it "one of the most curious and authentic documents one can imagine of the fanaticism and mistaken thinking which at that time (eighty-six years ago) prevailed throughout this continent and is a worthy companion of the extraordinary Blue Laws of New Haven!"[61] Miranda was deeply disturbed to see that the Revolution had failed to eradicate both the morality laws and the attitudes that had given rise to them. He once attended a "wearisome sermon" in which a preacher refused to baptize a child until the father publicly confessed that he had sinfully "covered his wife before marrying her." Never before in his life did the indignant Miranda suffer himself to be in the presence of such shameful and irrelevant declarations. "What barbarity," he scowled. In his contempt for religious attempts to legislate morality, Miranda shared much with atheistic and agnostic philosophers and public officials on both sides of the Atlantic Ocean in the age of revolution.

Because there was little else to do in New Haven, Miranda found himself sitting through church concerts and attending many tedious vocal performances. After one such evening threatened to test the limits of his endurance, Miranda returned to his room, as he said, "tired and glutted with church up to the eyes."[62] In fact, he found New Haven so dull that he spent most of his time there reading. When one of his teeth began to pain him, several ladies gathered around to watch the extraction, such was the desperation for entertainment in the tiny college town. Instead, Miranda occupied himself with his purposeful travels. For example, he visited Mr. Webb's tannery, which he described enthusiastically as being potentially "one of the richest and most flourishing manufactories in the universe." Miranda took careful notes of the man's special equipment and techniques, remarking that a similar establishment would be a treasure for Caracas or Buenos Aires.

Miranda was indeed a good traveler. He was curious, cordial, not particularly concerned with his own material comfort, and anxious to learn as much about his temporary environment as he could in such a short time. For example, near Hartford, Connecticut, he stopped at a café where he spent an hour and a half sitting in a chair in the corner of the room simply observing "the different groups, individuals, and conversation my ears and eyes could penetrate."[63] Upon spying a storekeeper in Windsor reading Charles Rollin's *Ancient History of the Egyptians, Carthaginians, Assyrians, Babylonians, Medes, Persians, Macedonians, and Grecians* (10 vols., London, 1738–40), he immediately engaged the woman in a discussion of the book and asked for her opinion as to who were the greater men, the ancients or the moderns. Of course, the patriotic woman unhesitatingly replied, without a doubt "[Benjamin] Franklin was superior to Aristides [the Just, Athenian statesman]." Miranda was impressed that in the United States, even women and shopkeepers read for their own edification and could converse intelligently in political discussions. For this reason, he had high respect for the public libraries in the towns he visited, seeing in them the repository of civic virtue and universal education. Entering the public library of Wethersfield, which contained a scant 300 volumes, Miranda nonetheless wagered those books had been read more times than all the volumes in the Escorial (the royal palace near Madrid) taken together.[64] He liked to think of America as a place where all citizens had their own contribution to make, no matter what their economic or social status. Occasionally, when journeying by road, Miranda stopped his horses at the homes of laborers in order to observe their character and customs, both of which impressed him favorably.[65] This sort of tourism was, of course, condescending to the degree that it reduced working folk to the role of exhibits in a human zoo, but he was among the travelers of his era who cared enough to seek access to experiences beyond those of his own social class.

The Venezuelan's curiosity extended to racial distinctions as well. Waiting for a ship to take him to Newport, Rhode Island, he observed a ship worked by a crew of Indians. Miranda noted approvingly that "in the performance of their work they behave with circumspection and decency, without ever getting drunk or committing any irregularity during their employment. Through this we see that these beings are as apt for everything as anyone else and that the man who acts with innate prudence has a superior character to risk."[66] Of course, by identifying the ways in which the example before his eyes contradicted the popular image of North American Indians, Miranda subconsciously reveals the degree to which he was informed by those expectations as well. He recounted the famous example of

Phillis Wheatley, an enslaved African who learned to read and write and who eventually gained a reputation in Europe for her literary productions. Although Wheatley's situation was not typical of the public respect given to persons of African descent in America, Miranda himself believed that "the rational being is the same in whatever form or aspect. The most cruel laws of forbearance and the enjoyment of the most exalted pleasures are preserved in this Negro being."[67] Through his travels in America, Miranda's growing conviction that human beings were formed by their legal, social, and economic environments started to take root. If one could improve their conditions, one could improve the people themselves.

Although Miranda was a jovial sort of man, still just thirty-four years old and devoted to all manner of entertainment, he was deadly serious when it came to politics. Throughout New England he engaged in animated parlor conversation over a wide-ranging array of topics; but when the subject turned political, his attitude instantly changed because, he believed, "in this matter, one cannot make jokes."[68] The only other area of his life that he took as seriously as his politics was his liquor. In Connecticut, Miranda and his friends carried with them at all times equipment for making rum punch "in the most republican manner," even when they were engaged in a tour of a distillery. To his way of thinking, alcohol production revealed "the spirit, energy, and industry of these people" who patriotically distilled the juice of cornstalks to make whiskey when they could not obtain molasses during the war.[69] The business was both delicious and highly profitable. Many a time Miranda hoisted his flask to toast American inventiveness and shouted, "Long live democracy!" He was often irritated by people who refused to share his alcohol-induced joviality, including General Jedediah Huntington, who he thought "resembles Washington not a little in this respect."[70] The double standard is all the more ironic, given the sobriety he had praised in the Indian shipbuilders.

Arriving at Newport after a lengthy delay, Miranda befriended a certain Dr. Newman, with whom he drank a cup of grog and discussed the man's various medical cures and scientific discoveries. No doubt as a result of Miranda's polite inquiries into the matter, the men took a purposeful evening stroll, of which Miranda euphemistically recorded in his diary: "led to the temple of one of the best nymphs, where he left me well recommended. After he had gone, we directed our steps to the altar and there consummated a solemn sacrifice to Venus. At ten o'clock I returned to my lodging and read until bedtime."[71] Two days later, he visited his nymph a second time to pay further homage to Venus. Indeed, Miranda explored all types of women on his travels. It was part of his research and part of his romantic identity. On Sunday, September 5, as he sat in silence for two hours at a Quaker gathering, he amused himself by "examining slowly the dress and countenances of the female concourse." Sounding almost surprised himself, he found that he was powerfully attracted to these women who had not a grain of powder on their faces nor a hint of perfumed oil on their bodies.[72]

At the same time, Miranda could be judgmental or even prudish when the mood struck him. For example, in New London, a Spanish immigrant merchant named Gabriel Sistaré forced his friendship on Miranda, although the Venezuelan found him to be "completely coarse and ignorant, even for a Catalan." Once Miranda learned that Sistaré had taken a mistress despite having a wife back in Spain, and that he had had seven children by her, he sniffed that the illegitimate youngsters were "as wild as their father and as dirty as their mother." Clearly the Catalan man was a savage. Miranda asked Sistaré about the presence of other ethnic Spaniards in the region and was told there was only another objectionable Galician named José Antonio Linares. To himself Miranda lamented that the only "samples of the Spanish nation for these people to form a criterion of our character, manners, customs etc., in this region [are] Sistaré and Linares, and in the other Miralles and Rendón. Long live the damned government!"[73] Miranda was always sensitive to the impression that he and his fellow nationals might make upon liberal Europeans or North Americans; he knew that if Spanish Americans were viewed as untrustworthy, impetuous, or uneducated, it would drastically reduce the support that he might win for his emancipation project. As a result, Miranda manipulated Anglo-Americans' existing prejudices against Spaniards when it suited his immediate needs, and endeavored to correct their false understandings when such misinformation might cause his enterprise harm.

By September 16, Miranda had finally made his way to Boston, the last major city on his pilgrimage through the Republic. He had brought with him many letters of introduction to the city's leading citizens, including one that perpetuated Ezra Stiles's misidentification by labeling Miranda as "a Spanish Gentleman from Mexico."[74] In Boston, he made another influential friendship that would last throughout his lifetime. General Henry Knox was a founding father of both the Society of the Cincinnati and the U.S. Military Academy, and subsequently held the position of secretary of war for nearly a decade (1785–1794). Miranda especially liked Knox because he, too, had come from a working-class background and shared similar intellectual interests; Knox had begun life as a simple bookseller, raised himself up through the militia, and became, Miranda believed, "one of the best informed on the theory and practice of the art of war of the many *caudillos* I have known on this continent, including 'The Idol' "—a sarcastic reference to Knox's close friend, George Washington."[75] Knox escorted Miranda throughout the city, showed him important Revolutionary and commercial sites, and introduced him into Boston political circles. Together, Miranda, Knox, and other like-minded men including Alexander Hamilton, Samuel Adams, and Christopher Gore formed a discussion group that they referred to as their "symposium." Without a doubt, eager Boston merchants wished to support Miranda's emerging plan to emancipate South America, in order to gain access to millions of potential consumers. A memorandum in Henry Knox's handwriting, dated Boston, November 23, 1784, contains estimates for the cost of provisioning an expeditionary force of 5,000 men; attached to it is a ranked list of North American officials who could, presumably, be drafted into service for such a project.[76]

In Boston, Miranda met with Samuel Adams, the famous leader of the Massachusetts Radicals who helped draft that state's constitution in 1780. Adams was a man as serious about politics as the traveling Venezuelan was, and the two had extensive conversations about the science of legislation. For his part, Miranda raised two substantive objections about the nature of the North Americans' constitutional visions: ⅄

The first was, how is it that in a democracy the foundation of which was virtue, no position whatever was indicated for it, and on the contrary all the dignities and the power were given to property, which is precisely the poison of the republic? The other was the contradiction I observed between admitting as one of the rights of mankind the worship of a Supreme Being in the manner and form one chooses, without giving predominance by law to any sect, and later excluding from every legislative or representative office the man who does not swear he is of the Christian religion! Weighty solecisms no doubt.[77]

Adams promised to chew on these questions but his answers have not been recorded. Miranda later put the same questions to Nathaniel Folsom, then governor of New Hampshire, who agreed with him that a constitution that required all to swear allegiance to the Protestant faith as a prerequisite for holding public office was indeed philosophically defective. By 1790, all other states' legislators seemed to have come around to Miranda's views and declared complete religious toleration; Adams' Massachusetts continued as a religious establishment until 1833. As part of their discussions of the best way to construct a new state's institutions, Adams provided Miranda with exact calculations of U.S. finances, expenses, and economic regulations, including its war debt and the interest accrued. Miranda thought that taxes were too high and he particularly objected to something called the "faculty" tax, an arbitrary amount levied by state officials on a person's abilities or personal qualities; instead, he suggested that it would be better to allow businessmen to put a voluntary contribution in a public box, the amount to be based wholly on their "honor and conscience," as was the norm in Holland.

Ever an astute student of government, and increasingly anxious to watch republican democracy in action, Miranda attended the General Assembly, where he said he "clearly saw the defects and inconveniences to which this democracy has subjected itself by placing the legislative power in the hands of ignorance." Apparently, one delegate rose in the middle of a debate he did not understand and began to recite couplets. Another, after listening to a discussion for two hours, had to ask what the subject of the vote was before he could cast his ballot. Miranda blamed this embarrassing display entirely on the power given to property, which created a situation such that the members of the legislature did not owe their position to any particular talent or virtue, but rather to their wealth and desire for public prestige. In general, Miranda thought that such crass mercantile attitudes infected all aspects of Boston society, including its residents' intellects and their conviviality. He listed seventy-four women he had met and conversed with while in Boston, including thumbnail sketches of their personalities and physical attributes. He lamented that the only school available for unmarried women to learn customs, graces, and stimulating conversation were the tea parties they threw for themselves. For this reason, the women were highly deficient in all respects and had a self-preoccupation such as he had never seen.[78] To be fair, he added, the men were not much better. Apparently all that they had been able to invent in the way of public entertainment in Boston was a card game on Monday evenings followed by a light supper of cold meats. Miranda was not impressed. Their preoccupation with trivialities and appearances Miranda put down to their mercantile occupation, noting that "[c]ommerce will always be the principal downfall of democratic virtue."[79] Once again, money did not always make for good citizens.

As a dedicated student of military history and tactics, Miranda could not visit Boston without making the obligatory trip to Bunker Hill. He took with him a veteran of that action, as he always tried to do when visiting military sites, in order to obtain accurate and firsthand information. He was surprised to find that the battle actually took place not on Bunker Hill itself, but rather on an opposite height known as Breed's Hill. Miranda, with his highly developed sense of public memory, worried what would happen when some future Polybius, intending to record the "history of this military action, encounters the contradiction between the name of the position and that of the event, unless a monument erected now for immortality on the very spot clears up this doubt?"[80]

He also traveled to Cambridge to see Harvard College, which he found to be a reasonably erudite place. The library contained an impressive 12,000 volumes, though weighted too heavily with English-language titles alone for his taste; and the institution's display of natural history was downright abysmal, limited to a monstrous tooth from some unidentified carnivorous animal. Furthermore, the college lacked a proper observatory and Miranda found its scholars to be the most slovenly he had yet encountered. He accepted a dinner invitation from the president, Dr. James Lloyd, on October 18, 1784, and presented the college with a silver medal that had been engraved in Mexico City by G. A. Gil to commemorate the founding of its Academy of National and Public Law. This gesture was intended to begin forging hemispheric solidarity in cultural as well as in political relations.

As a tourist, one bent on useful historical investigation, Miranda also wanted to visit Salem, the site of the infamous seventeenth-century witch trials. As usual, he had a letter of introduction to some-one there, in this instance a prominent local attorney named William Wetmore, who happily agreed to accompany the foreigner to the vari-ous places of interest in the town. As he had done in New Haven, Miranda specifically sought out local archives in order to research original documents from the colonial era. In his diary, he seemed to be particularly disturbed by a list of punishable offenses committed in Salem in 1667: a husband and wife had been whipped and fined for having fornicated before marriage, and others had been lashed for their failure to attend church or simply for taking the Lord's name in vain by saying "By God." That these commonplace and inoffensive private acts should call down such public wrath was shameful in his estimation; noting the similarity to New Haven's Blue Laws that he had studied earlier, Miranda pronounced his utter disgust with those "times of crass fanaticism."[81]

Yet, on occasion, Miranda showed that he recognized just how deeply Puritanical attitudes still clung to life in New England despite the great many changes of the past hundred years. He loathed "Dam-nation Murray," a controversial Presbyterian minister he had once heard in Newburyport who launched into his sermon by calling for the "extirpation of pagans, Mohammedans, the Antichrist (the Pope) and his sectaries, heretics." In a country and an era that prided itself on religious toleration, Miranda clearly saw that Murray's words im-plied that "for a moment, the entire universe, except for his flock, was excluded from the Divine Protection. Barbarous! Ignorant! . . . [Murray] continued until twelve-thirty when he finally stopped bray-ing."[82] The habit of dour Sunday observations permeated all levels of American society. In fact, some cart drivers and ferry operators re-fused to conduct passengers on the Lord's Day; even those who agreed

to do it secretly for double fare invariably felt nervous and were superstitious about their chances for safe passage. Sunday observances
throughout the Anglo-Saxon world continued to unnerve and annoy
Miranda throughout his entire life.

If the more unthinking and dogmatic Protestants continued to
plague him, Miranda always felt attracted to the Quakers' simple way
of life and professed an affinity with their social conscience. Dr.
Waterhouse, a theologian he had met at Harvard, informed him that
the Quakers had a standing committee that met weekly in London to
address grievances and to pay a proportion of the tithes and church
taxes that fell disproportionately on the poor. Whenever these wretched
folk faced debtors' prison as a result of the impossible taxes levied by
the Anglican Church (often sums that were twice those paid by the
clergy themselves), London's Quaker committee stepped in and paid
the balance so that the lawsuits would be dropped.[83] From each according to his ability, to each according to his need; Miranda's sense
of fairness and public virtue predated the nineteenth-century social-
ists by half a century.

By the end of 1784, Miranda was tired and his health was suffering from nearly two years of constant travel. He had seen many things
and his mind was reeling with the possibility of becoming the Washington of South America. Yet, the timing seemed wrong. He felt in-
tensifying pressure from the Spanish Crown's investigations into his
desertion and subsequent activities during his U.S. tour.[84] Throughout New England, Miranda's movements had been monitored closely
and he was beginning to fear that the Spanish ambassador would soon
seek a warrant for his arrest. Nevertheless, the trip had made him
somewhat of a celebrity and laid the practical foundations for his long
quixotic struggle to spark the fire of revolution in Spanish America.
His accumulated knowledge and his Atlantic connections would be
the sticks that Miranda would rub together to strike that spark. John
Adams, who despised Miranda, recalled:

> It was a general opinion and report, that he knew more of the families,
> parties and connections in the United States than any other man in them;
> that he knew more of every campaign, siege, battle, and skirmish that

had ever occurred in the whole war, than any officer of our army, or any statesman in our councils.

His constant topic was the independence of Spanish America, her immense wealth, inexhaustible resources, innumerable population, impatience under the Spanish yoke, and disposition to throw off the dominion of Spain. It is most certain that he filled the heads of many young officers with brilliant visions of wealth, free trade, republican government etc.[85]

Nevertheless, in 1784 the timing for Miranda's emancipation project was premature and he still had much to learn. On November 29, he contracted a passage from Boston to London for twenty-two guineas on the ship *Neptune*, which departed slightly behind schedule on December 15. William Duer loaned him money for the trip and Stephen Sayre toasted him with the words, "Good voyage and health to you!" He had come to the United States to find its Founding Fathers and, having won their acceptance, he turned his attention to the next stage in his career as a student of government and society. It was time for the gentleman's grand tour of Europe.

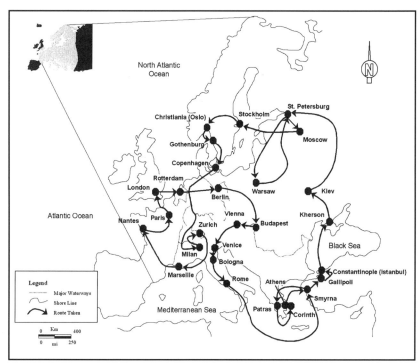

Francisco de Miranda's tour of Europe, 1785–1789

3

THE GENTLEMAN'S GRAND TOUR
Travels in Europe, Asia, and Russia (1785–1789)

One ought, every day at least, to hear a little song, read a good poem, see a fine picture, and, if it were possible, to speak a few reasonable words.
—GOETHE, *Wilhelm Meisters Lehrjahre* (1796)

January was not the best month for an Atlantic voyage. The winds were biting and incessant; both the air and the water were frigid. Fresh fruits and vegetables were scarce among the provisions, and the passengers' only amusement was gossip about illicit shipboard romances. None of that mattered to Miranda, however; he had made the 6-week trip across the ocean twice already and, at age thirty-four, was a seasoned traveler. In fact, he enjoyed time spent at sea, cooped up in a cabin with his precious books, pausing occasionally to stroll the decks for exercise and to take his meals with the others. In preparation for his entry into English society, Miranda studied the works of Scottish political economist David Hume, which he enjoyed immensely, and read William Robertson's *History of the Reign of the Emperor Charles V* (1749) and *History of the Discovery and Settlement of America* (1777), the latter of which was the first English-language work to treat Spain's colonial activities with some sympathy.[1] Like nearly everything Miranda touched, the ship on which he booked passage, the *Neptune*, departed Boston under controversial circumstances; just one year after the American Republic's cessation of hostilities with England, the ship's Captain Callahan was rumored to be carrying 60,000 guineas worth of gold coins back across the ocean, an embarrassing reminder of the still-unequal balance of trade with the former rulers. Indeed, the *Boston Sentinel* even dared to brand Callahan a Tory smuggler, which in those days were fighting words that fell just short of calling someone a traitor.[2] By then familiar with the argumentative and self-absorbed North American character, Miranda chuckled to himself over this debacle while he cracked open the pages of a new diary in which he intended to record the next phase of his preparation to be an Atlantic revolutionary. Just as he had spent seventeen months traveling throughout the United States to observe the inner workings of an emerging republican democracy, now the cosmopolitan gentleman felt he needed to make a European grand tour in order to complete his self-education, to learn about other systems of government, and to make important transatlantic contacts for his plan to emancipate Spanish America.[3]

Several weeks later, as the *Neptune* sailed up the Thames and approached London Dock, the clouds parted and Miranda was overwhelmed with emotion. Looking left and right, he was "positively certain that in this river alone there are more ships and more commerce than in all the other rivers of the world together!"[4] He also observed the bodies of dead pirates hanging in the gallows along the shores as a warning to all those who would cheat the Crown's customs agents of their due. Nevertheless, Miranda did dare to quibble with those agents who demanded more than the half-guinea he was prepared to pay to get his possessions released from the ship; as a result, many of his trifling goods were seized. Chagrined but undaunted, he piled his remaining books and clothes into a waiting hackney coach (the eighteenth-century equivalent of a taxicab) and made his way to the Royal Hotel at Pall Mall. It was February 1, 1785, and Miranda was finally in London. Nothing else really seemed to matter.

Miranda was well prepared for his new adventure. He settled in permanent lodgings on the second floor of Mr. Rayson's home at 104 Pall Mall, paying a guinea and a half per week. Immediately, Miranda was struck by "the opulence, culture, and magnificence of this Country."[5] It was easier to make friends and acquaintances than it had been upon his arrival in North Carolina, both because his spoken English was much improved and because he had brought many letters of recommendation from his important American friends. Entrepreneur

William Duer, for example, asked his overseas associate William Brummel to introduce Miranda into Lord North's circle, saying that "[t]his Gentleman is from Disposition and Reflection a Citizen of the World, which he traverses [with] a View of Increasing Stock of Knowledge, which is already far from being Inconsiderable."[6] Miranda had come purposefully to England, a country he admired as the "Nation of Philosophers," in order to study its constitutional arrangement and learn the secrets of its maritime power. His archives contain calling cards and a list of addresses that reads like London's social register: the earl of Shelburne, the earl of Effingham, scientist Joseph Priestley, General Robert Melville, Lord MacDonald, the recorder of the City of London, Francis Egerton, brothers Samuel and Jeremy Bentham, Count Andreani, and countless others.[7]

Although Miranda was known to be a deserter from the Spanish army, Ambassador Bernardo del Campo nonetheless received Miranda warmly and often invited him to dine at the official residence. In fact, the men frequently attended the theater together. The full extent of Miranda's plans to bring down the Empire were not yet known; he was still considered a minor figure and therefore the ambassador opted simply to befriend the young man and see if he could be persuaded back into the fold. For his part, Miranda was not yet willing to divorce himself completely from the Spanish orbit. He wished to secure an honorable discharge from the military service that would override the Havana tribunal's earlier guilty verdict; in that way, he might reclaim his title and restore his reputation while removing the constant threat of capture and imprisonment. Del Campo pretended to help him with his case and even offered to write to Spanish minister of state Count Floridablanca on Miranda's behalf. Perhaps, del Campo wondered, some sort of resolution that would be satisfactory to all parties could be reached.

Miranda set out his case in a letter to Charles III dated April 10, 1785, but, as usual, his tone was all wrong. In his petition, Miranda attempted to explain to the king how His Majesty's own minister of the Indies, José de Gálvez, had done malicious injury to an innocent lieutenant colonel who had been serving loyally in America. Miranda outlined his entire autobiography, drawing attention to his vast erudition as well as the many great services he had rendered to the

Spanish Crown while in Africa, Europe, and the Caribbean. He explained how all his trouble with authorities in the past had been the result of the jealousy of others, their desire to persecute him and frustrate his talents; the final provocation came when he was falsely charged with bringing contraband into Havana in 1782. Eventually, Miranda told the king, he had no choice but to flee to the United States in order to escape "such a powerful cabal" and travel in "more civilized countries of the world." Miranda claimed that he had written to the Spanish authorities several times while in the United States, but that his missives must have been intercepted somehow. Since his flight, he told the king, he had exerted serious efforts to acquire detailed knowledge about the military history of the young Republic and to make important contacts that could prove useful to the Crown. Upon arrival in London in February 1785, Miranda continued to explain sweetly, he had immediately presented himself to Minister del Campo and had been trying to set things right. He feared that his friend Juan Manuel Cagigal might have been unjustly imprisoned on his account and wanted to assure the king that the former governor "had no part in my flight from Havana"; he asked that Cagigal be released from any unfair judgments that may have resulted from that erroneous assumption. The most revealing, and ultimately fatal, claim that Miranda made, however, was his steadfast insistence that the greatest disadvantage that a man of his talents suffered was to have been born an "American." Despite his personal genius, education, accomplishments, and patriotic devotion, he had come to realize that to the people in power he would never be anything more than American, and therefore suspect and second-class. Always audacious when it came to money, Miranda not only asked the king for an honorable discharge and the reinstatement of his rank, he also requested both the repayment of the original fee that his father had paid for his commission and two years of unpaid back salary. Once this matter was resolved, he taunted the king, he intended to use his experience to guide America's youth.[8]

Clearly Miranda could not possibly have expected such an insolent letter to win its stated goals; his appeal must have been more of a dramatic gesture, asking for the sky but inviting certain failure. Considering his precarious national status and his perpetual poverty, this was a subconsciously rebellious act that allowed him to tweak Spanish officialdom one last time before he really cut himself loose from the Empire and became its open enemy.[9] Alarmed, Bernardo del Campo preferred to pretend he was Miranda's friend so that he could keep a close eye on this increasingly dangerous American for the Spanish government.[10] As the petition wound its way though the system, a potentially ugly situation was temporarily stabilized, meaning that Miranda could relax, enjoy the London sights, and learn what he could about the workings of English society and government.

Since his flight from Havana, Miranda was always short on money and had to rely on friends' generosity or occasional disbursements from his family. It was difficult to maintain his pride while seeking financial support from friends both new and old. Still trying to keep up appearances, Miranda wrote to his youthful traveling companion Francisco de Arrieta, who had by then returned to Caracas, that nothing much was new; Ambassador del Campo was paying him a thousand honors and distinctions. The summer weather was mild and suited him just fine, but he was still waiting for his salary to come from Havana; could Arrieta please send him 2,000 pesos in care of Matías de Gandásegui, the Spanish vice consul in London, as a short-term loan? Despite the money trouble, Miranda told his old friend brightly, England was all he had hoped it would be: "Philosophy, the [study of] government, scientific academies, Parliamentary assemblies, and the society of scholars and statesmen occupy all my time at the moment, with the supreme benefits that in some way mitigate the gravity of my severe [financial] adversity."[11] He told virtually same thing to Francisco Rendón, who he asked to pass along greetings to their friends in Philadelphia and New York, listing twenty specific names. Both "money hypochondria" and the compulsive desire to be remembered by everyone left behind are typical of an exile's psychology and reflected in Miranda's sense of displacement.[12] Similarly, the traveling Venezuelan became more conscious of his American identity while he was abroad, surrounded by a different language, a different climate, a different cuisine, and new cultural practices.

To combat his worries and to reassure himself that his travels did indeed have a vitally important and patriotic purpose, Miranda roamed around the British Isles with a vengeance. Any philosopher worth the title had to make the pilgrimage northward to the University of

Edinburgh to meet Adam Smith, the author of *The Wealth of Nations*
and a major figure of the Scottish Enlightenment. Miranda made
that journey but never managed to secure an interview with his hero
despite many attempts.[13] He did, however, renew his friendship with
Colonel William Steuben Smith, U.S. president John Adams's son-
in-law, who had been one of Miranda's acquaintances during his days
in New York. At the time, Smith was serving as the secretary of the
U.S. legation in London and pursued an active friendship with
Miranda, although Adams himself later claimed to have known nothing of their association.[14] On the Fourth of July 1785, planning to
celebrate Independence Day together, Smith paid his "respects to
Col[onel] de Miranda as a friend to the rights of mankind & the
Happiness of society."[15] Smith and Miranda become increasingly intimate while in London, even exchanging silk stockings if one or the
other ran short. They shared an interest in military sciences and decided to make a tour of the European continent, timed to arrive in
Prussia for the annual military review in the fall. Bernardo del Campo
watched these developments with trepidation and sent notices to the
various Spanish embassies throughout Europe, warning them that a
suspicious person may soon present himself in their midst. Monsieur
Longprès, the Paris chief of police, was put on alert and all ambassa-
dors were instructed to pump travelers for information about Smith's
and Miranda's conversations and movements.[16] From Madrid, Count
Floridablanca apparently issued orders for Miranda's arrest, but del
Campo ignored them in favor of a strategy that was designed to gather
incriminating information about his relationship to potential Spanish American malcontents.

His insincere petition to the Crown notwithstanding, it is clear
that Miranda did not hide his desire to persuade leading British citizens and government figures that they should support Spanish American emancipation. Even public newspapers took notice of his ideas.
Shortly before he left for his European tour in August 1785, London's
Political Herald and Review printed the following coy description of
an unnamed visitor:

> In London we are well assured, there is this moment a *Spanish American*
> of great Consequence, & possessed of the confidence of his Fellow-
> Citizens, who aspires to the Glory of being the Deliverer of his Country.

He is a *Man of Sublime Views & penetrating Understand[in]g, skilled in the antient [sic] & modern Languages, conversant in Books* & acquainted with the World. He devoted many years to the Study of general Politics; the Origin, Progress, & Termin[atio]n of the different species of Governments, the Circumstances that combine & retain Multitudes of Mank[in]d in political Societies; & the Causes by w[hic]h these Societies are dissolved & swallowed up by others. This Gentleman hav[in]g visited every Province in North America, came to England, which he regards as the Mother Country of Liberty, & the School for Political Knowledge. . . . We admire his Talents, esteem his Virtues, & heartily wish Prosperity to the noblest Pursuit that can occupy the Powers of a Mortal, that of bestowing the Blessings of Freedom on Millions of his fellow men.[17]

Already at that early date, Miranda was constructing a public image of himself as a legitimate representative of Spanish Americans' political aspirations, and he was using the press to legitimize that notion. Back in the United States, the *New Haven Gazette* reprinted this article in its issue of November 3, 1785; its editor speculated that "[t]his Description very exactly answers the Character of Col. Francisco de Miranda, who spent several days in this city in August 1784." London's *Morning Chronicle*, a daily newspaper that had emerged recently as a liberal counterpoint to the well-established but conservative *Times*, printed an extract of that same article, too; the British editor elaborated for his readers the well-founded reasons for Spanish Americans' growing discontent, namely "that jealousy which confined the appointments of government in Spanish America to native Spaniards, and established other distinctions between these and their descendants on the other side of the Atlantick [sic] . . . it has sown the seeds of a deep resentment."[18]

In London in 1785, Miranda was already articulating a Creole consciousness that drew upon a wide array of sources from throughout the philosophical Atlantic world: the theories of John Locke, who argued that the people had a right to overthrow illegitimate and tyrannical rulers; the nature and practice of the successful American Revolution; and Spain's abrogation of the historic compact that had brought the Americas into the Empire after the Conquest. The eighteenth-century Bourbon Reforms, an attempt on the part of the Spanish Crown to rationalize and modernize its colonial system, actually ended up alienating Americans who felt threatened by a more activist central goverment. When Europeans continued to receive preferential treatment in the appointment of senior state, military, and ecclesiastical positions, American resentment grew. When the Bourbons expelled the Jesuit order from their territories in 1767 because they were perceived as a threat to imperial security and order, many Americans who had fond memories of their Jesuit tutors were angry. By the 1780s, Creole revolts in America were becoming increasingly common, meaning that Miranda's ideas would find a ready audience.

Miranda and Smith left London on August 9, 1785, to cross the English Channel on their way to The Hague. They arrived in Holland and were immediately accosted by customs agents who "threw the dice to see whose fortune it would be to plunder and impose upon us—for this purpose there is a large box and a pair of dice standing in the Intendant's door."[19] Both men were immediately put off by the aggressiveness and defensiveness of the Dutch people they met, astonished that a journey of six hours could produce such a change in national disposition. Where the British were "daring and active," the Dutch were "cautious and heavy." The pair again quarreled with a local magistrate upon arrival in Rotterdam, but soon adjusted their expectations and settled into the first leg of their tour. Miranda and Smith never quite got used to the "incivility" of the Dutch; both were shocked one afternoon to witness a woman who "set down her basket and pissed in the middle of the street before the window which I stood at."[20]

The men were purposeful travelers. They visited hospitals, asylums, legislatures, prisons, markets, military sites, and places of historical or cultural importance; they attended theaters, balls, and concerts in order to learn as much about the conditions of other nations' people as possible. For example, in Holland, Miranda toured a workhouse, an innovative place where criminals could discharge their punishments in ways that were publicly useful and rehabilitative rather than merely retributive and harsh; sentences could be reduced to reward sobriety and diligence. Appropriately, women were responsible for passing sentence on female convicts. The Dutch took a similarly practical approach in their orphan asylums, where children were taught to "read, write and work," and idleness was unknown. As a man of the Enlightenment, Miranda was drawn to the notion that people were formed by their environment and was willing to believe that a change in offenders' conditions could rehabilitate their behavior. In fact, everywhere he went Miranda was reminded that the Netherlands had been a Spanish colony until they threw off their yoke in 1648; since that time, as an independent country, the Dutch had changed themselves into a modern, wealthy nation. If the conditions were right, Miranda extrapolated, the far larger and resource-rich Spanish American regions could certainly do the same. He and Smith continued onward to see sights in The Hague, Amsterdam, Leiden, Arnheim, and Haarlem, stopping to gaze at the wonders of the famous University of Leiden. They visited churches of various denominations and studied the complex system of dikes and fortifications, but generally looked forward to leaving the Netherlands for Prussia, which they did on August 17.

Immediately upon entering the German province of Westphalia, the pair observed that "agriculture lessens and the effects of despotism and sanguinary laws shew [sic] themselves." Smith was disgusted at the obvious Catholic religiosity of the towns through which they passed; one such community had at each entrance "the person marked by the [C]hristian-religion as the Saviour of mankind, [who] is suspended on a cross in full figure—a spectacle disagreeable, impious and absurd."[21] He mentioned that a "filthy monk" crossed their path, and that frequently they ran into "images, crusifiction [sic], wheels, racks, poverty, and filth" in Westphalian towns. Towns in Lower Saxony did not appear to be much better, although Hanover showed more promise. As cultivated eighteenth-century men, Miranda and Smith still had close personal associations with rural life, but their hearts and souls led them to prefer the city's stimulation. After a journey of three soggy and uncomfortable days, their tempers started to show; Miranda was annoyed that their servant had allowed their clothes to get wet, while Smith took refuge from the tension in his cigars. As a way to unwind, Smith recorded euphemistically that he "bought the cherries of a Brunswick girl—never did any lass dispose of them with more vivacity—she suplied [sic] me during my stay." Indeed, Miranda and Smith seem to have tasted the fruits of many women, both paid and unpaid, throughout their European tour. Smith once remarked blithely, "Miranda had a curious scene with a Virgin to whose questions of conscience he would not for a moment submit." In fact, they were pleasantly surprised to find that Berlin abounded in prostitutes, because the Prussian king's policies actually protected and promoted that profession, using the logic that a large population naturally contributed to a powerful nation.[22]

Throughout the Atlantic world, useful and up-to-date information was a sort of currency that allowed Miranda and Smith to gain entry into the drawing rooms of all sorts of prominent figures. They spent an hour with Prince Ferdinand of Saxony, who wanted to hear firsthand accounts about North America and its recent Revolutionary history. They visited "a Jew-philosopher," Moses Mendelssohn, who also had many questions for them and with whom Miranda "took up his text and preached liberty and independence with as much zeal as ever the King of the Jews established his religious system."[23] The Marquis de Lafayette, an acquaintance from their days in the United States, advised the pair to emphasize their martial backgrounds, which would make the best impression of all on the militaristic Germanic people; Smith huffed that he did not come to be seen and waited upon but rather to learn something of the military arts so that he may be more useful to his country. Perhaps because he still needed to win converts to his cause, Miranda was more anxious to ingratiate himself with his hosts; Smith recorded that his Venezuelan companion "seems very fond to give every favorable impression relative to America—he is much attached to its happiness and dignity—my god, is he a *chevalier* [gentleman]."[24] It made sense: Smith's country had already won its independence; Miranda's country still needed all the friends and good impressions that he could make.

As both Miranda and Smith were military men, their main purpose in traveling to Prussia was to study its much-vaunted military machine. Accordingly, they toured battle sites, inquired into conditions of military service, and conversed with veterans wherever they went. Near Berlin on September 5, the excited pair attended a military parade and an artillery exercise; on the eighth they rose early to watch the field maneuvers of General Moellendorf, which they enthusiastically pronounced to be "superior to panegyric." The friends explored the fortress at Spandau, visited a school that trained the children of the poor to be enlisted cadets, and went on to tour the mili-

tary academy for the sons of elite families. The martial character of
the Prussian state was obvious and onmipresent; its army's professionalism and recent expansion led the travelers to surmise that a continental war with France might be looming.

Agents of the Spanish Empire continued to shadow the pair wherever they went. Miguel Josef de Azanza, the Spanish ambassador in
Berlin, monitored their movements and sent disturbing reports back
to Madrid. First, the Marquis de Lafayette, a French hero of the American Revolution and avowed enemy of Spain, had been spotted consorting with Smith and Miranda.[25] Second, Azanza informed his
government that the outlaw Miranda had received the Prussian king's
permission to attend royal military exercises at Potsdam, "which was
the principal object of his voyage."[26] Switching to a numeric code,
Azanza passed on the small bit of good news that at least Miranda had
not formally presented himself at the Court and did not appear to be
under the protection of any other member of the foreign diplomatic
corps. Just as his counterpart Bernardo del Campo had done in London, Azanza also attempted to befriend Miranda without raising his
suspicions in order to gain insight into his activities and future plans.
In fact, in a letter to del Campo from Berlin, Miranda enthusiastically
described the Potsdam maneuvers as "the military emporium of the
century," and said that he had found Azanza to be "most agreeable
and helpful."[27]

Their tour continued at a breakneck pace through Leipzig to
Dresden and Hamburg, traveling ever eastward until they reached
Prague on September 8 and their ultimate destination, Vienna, on
September 14. These two cultured men were also interested in studying the fine arts of the cities they visited, and they frequently attended
theater performances in the evening despite having only a limited
grasp of the German language. In Budapest, at the palace of Prince
Nicholas Esterhazy, Smith and Miranda met the composer Joseph
Haydn, to whom they had brought letters of introduction. Haydn
was pleased to spend two whole days escorting the enthusiastic foreigners around the Royal Palace, showing them its library, portrait
galleries, gardens, and theater. Haydn and his new friends also spent
much time discussing music, one of Miranda's favorite subjects and
hidden passions. Miranda also pressed Haydn for information about

the number and treatment of the palace's servants so that he could make accurate notes in his diary. Miranda and Smith visited a school for "the instruction of the dumb and deaf" and were amazed to see the children's arithmetical and communicative abilities on display.[28] They toured a large hospital capable of tending 5,000 patients, the botanical gardens, and several collections of natural history. In Vienna, Miranda examined the royal library, which contained 12,000 historical manuscripts, including Hernán Cortés's first letter to Charles V from Mexico in 1519 and a bound volume of rare Mexican hieroglyphs. Wherever Miranda went, he added to the ever-expanding arsenal of American knowledge that might be useful in his battle against the Spanish Empire.

Miranda and Smith parted ways when their tour of northern Europe reached its end. Smith had to return to his duties at the American legation in London, while Miranda wanted to continue on to Italy, France, and Greece, perhaps even venture to Turkey and as far afield as Russia. Employing his usual charm, Miranda persuaded Smith to loan him £230 in cash for the journey (which, to his credit, he eventually repaid).[29] The friends shook hands, promising to meet again when they could, and Miranda set off alone for Italy. He kept a meticulous diary of the distances traveled, the nature of the terrain, the temperatures, and any sort of economic activity in the regions through which he passed.[30] Along the way, he found himself discussing George Washington's character and the military arts with an Austrian count who had been kind enough to take him to see the Military College at Neustadt in all its aspects: classrooms, dormitories, refectory, library, swimming pool, and drilling areas.

Moving from Trieste to Venice, Miranda may have felt a small connection with his homeland; Venezuela, "little Venice," received its name from the early settlers who thought its many waterways recalled the unique Italian city. Arriving on November 12, he was enchanted with the city's famous sights: the Lido, the Doge's Palace at the end of the Bridge of Sighs, and all the other magnificent buildings that seemed to emerge from the water itself. Immediately, Miranda climbed into a gondola and set about delivering his letters of introduction to Spanish chargé d'affaires Ignacio López de Ulloa, Italian senators Pietro Zaguri and Angelo Quirini, and private citizens Pietro Rombenchi,

Francisco Giorgio May, and Pietro Nutricio Grisogno. His mission completed, he stopped at a café on his way to the San Benedetto theater where he saw a "seriously awful opera that pained my soul."[31] Miranda also made arrangements to take private classes in the evenings with an Italian language tutor. The next day, Zaguri collected Miranda and the two visited the Ducal Palace and its wonderful art collection on the way to attend a senate session. There, Miranda noted, the debates proceeded with none of the formality of the British Parliament, which seemed to indicate that what passed for participatory government in Venice was really little more than "despotism dressed in a wig and black robe."

More important, Miranda had come to Italy hoping to meet some of the Jesuits whom King Charles III had exiled from his Spanish American dominions in 1767 as part of an attempt to increase state control over the Catholic Church and over education in the colonies. The move prompted outrage from Creole Americans, most of whom had a sentimental attachment to their teachers and saw this edict as further evidence of a jealous and vindictive Crown meddling in their affairs. Most of the Jesuit exiles passed through Madrid but eventually settled in Italy, either in Leghorn, Venice, Rome, or Bologna. On November 13, his second day in Italy, Miranda set up an appointment with Don Esteban Arteaga SJ, a former Spanish Jesuit also renowned for his musical scholarship. Arteaga was mercurial and arrogant, and had few close friends; in the words of one Venezuelan historian, he was "a human paradox, dwarfish of body but a giant of intelligence."[32] Although he had resigned from the order in June 1769 to enroll in humanities courses at the University of Bologna, Arteaga remained a clearinghouse for information about the Jesuit exiles in Europe. Believing as he did that "theology is a false science, or better said, an anti-science," Arteaga and Miranda shared a skeptical, even slightly hostile attitude toward organized religion.[33] Accompanied by the brother of Spanish minister of state Floridablanca, the Conde de Moñino, they sipped coffee in the Piazza di San Marco and later attended the theater. Miranda and Arteaga seem to have been inseparable during the eight days he stayed in Venice; they visited churches, attended operas, and strolled along the many waterways and bridges, including the famous Rialto. In his diary, Miranda remained circumspect about the subject of their conversations, no doubt fearing that his papers might be seized someday. He did, however, record that on November 19, Arteaga brought him a valuable list of Spanish American exiled Jesuits who were currently residing in Bologna.[34]

Having obtained this information, Miranda made preparations to leave Venice. He had seen the major sights and was anxious to make useful contacts for his emancipation project. Moreover, Miranda did not have a favorable impression of either the "idle and worthless" Venetian nobility or the "horrible and unbearable theaters"; even traipsing from "bordello to theater and theater to bordello" had become tiresome to him. He left on a rainy November 21 and found himself in a flea-ridden guesthouse in Padua that night. Typically, he spent one day hurriedly exploring that city (especially the Olympic Park, which he felt was ruined by excessive ostentation), and then quickly departed. He was tired. After months of hectic travel, the gentleman decided to stay in Verona for eight days, simply resting in bed and reading. He wanted to reflect on all he had seen and to collect his thoughts before seeking out the Spanish American Jesuits, his fellow countrymen, all exiles like himself.

Miranda arrived in Bologna on December 12, intentionally installing himself at the San Marco lodge, which was known to be a favorite haunt of the exiled Spanish American Jesuits.[35] Yet, oddly, nowhere in his Italian diary does Miranda indicate that he actually sought out the many famous American authors who could be found there. For example, Francisco Javier Clavijero, Juan Ignacio Molina, Francisco Javier Alegre, Andrés Cavo, Diego León Villafañé, Felipe Gómez Vidaurre, and Diego Abad all resided in Italy during the months that Miranda visited that country.[36] Like Miranda, these erudite, knowledgeable Americans had been shocked by the erroneous beliefs prevalent in Europe about America, and had set themselves the noble task of correcting such misinformed impressions. As a result, they were highly prolific, producing massive general histories about the various regions of America, biographies of important Americans, and institutional histories of the Jesuit Order and the Catholic Church in America. Miranda was certainly aware of at least one of the Jesuits' accounts; years later he recommended Molina's *Compendio della storia geografica e civile del reyno del Chili* (Geographical, Biographical, Natural, and Civil History of Chili) (1776) to James Mill for commentary in the *Edinburgh Review*, and also gave a copy to Thomas Jefferson for the strategic information he felt it contained.[37] Unfortunately, no records exist that indicate Miranda approached any of these men on either of his two Italian tours, leading one scholar to conclude that a conspiracy between Miranda and the Jesuits to promote Spanish American independence is "the stuff of pure novel."[38] From Bologna, Miranda traveled to Rome, a historic city he had longed to see since his days as a university student in Caracas.

Not surprisingly, Miranda spent nearly two months in Rome, by far the longest time spent in one single place during his continental grand tour so far. As a security precaution, Miranda was traveling under the name Colonel Martín de Mariland, a fiction that indicated both his sense of humor and his attachment to the United States. Fluent in both Latin and Greek, he was humbled to find himself in the same city in which his ancient heroes had lived. While there, he investigated every historical site that he could find as a necessary part of his gentlemanly education. Classical Greece and Rome were the major inspirations for intellectuals and politicians throughout the Atlantic world in the age of revolution. Daily newspapers on both sides of the ocean quoted Tacitus in Latin; public monuments portrayed leaders in classical motifs and garb; schoolchildren recited classics in Latin or Greek for their public speaking competitions. Miranda's personal library contained over 200 volumes of Greek classics and thirty volumes of Cicero alone.[39] Once in Rome, the first thing Miranda had to do, however, was to visit his banker and draw some money from his account. He headed to the area of the Spanish Steps where English travelers tended to congregate, but could not secure satisfactory lodgings there. Instead, he managed to wangle an invitation to stay at the private home of Ana Manzoli, who had close family ties to the Vatican hierarchy. Miranda was happy there. Signora Ana installed him in the very quarters in which Benedict XIV had stayed before being named pope; she fussed over him and served his favorite hot chocolate drink in his room each morning.[40]

Manzoli was an excellent political hostess, introducing Miranda to Tomás Belón, a former resident of Peru and the only other exiled Jesuit (besides Arteaga) that Miranda mentioned in his travel diary.[41]

Once again, despite their shared background and political sympathies, their acquaintance has been described as "purely casual"; meetings were always held in public places and neither party has left evidence of any conspiratorial conversations that may have occurred.[42] Quite likely Miranda feared that his diaries might be captured someday and wished to avoid committing incriminating evidence to paper. While in Rome he bought a copy of Francisco Javier Clavijero's *Historia Antigua de Mégico* (History of Ancient Mexico) with the express intention of having it translated and published in London. Perhaps not coincidentally, an English-language edition of this work did appear in 1787 as *The History of Mexico, collected from Spanish and Mexican Historians, from Manuscripts and Ancient Paintings . . . by Abbé D. Francisco Savero Clavijero*.[43] Italy was a major destination for any gentleman's grand tour, and Miranda was no exception. He spent much time thinking and reading about the Roman Empire and raiding its history for useful comparisons to the nature and structure of his own avowed enemy, the Spanish Empire. By reading classics of the past, he hoped he might discern the key to defeating his own imperial enemy.

Suffering from a persistent violent headache and bloody stools, Miranda crossed the Adriatic Sea on the difficult passage from Italy to Greece in April and May 1786. As an exotic foreigner, he found that local political chieftains in the northern provinces of Greece flattered him with excessive attention; one even sent a harem to dance around him while he was seated Turkish-style on a rug, the dancers making movements that the occasionally prudish Miranda declared to be obscene. He stopped briefly at Smyrna and Patras, where he was the guest of honor at a 4-day wedding, carefully noting down details of the preparations and ceremony in his diary. By June 5 he had made his way as far as the celebrated Mount Olympus, where he stopped to admire the view. Upon arriving in Corinth, a city whose "decadence is in proportion to all the rest of the country after the revolution of 1770," he had another of his habitual arguments with the customs agents, who eventually let him pass through without paying duty on his belongings.[44] In Corinth, he introduced himself to the local commander, who asked him about America and his family, observing that Miranda looked awfully young to have traveled so much; later that same day, a Turkish woman laughed at him and asked why he did not have a mustache if he was really an adult as he claimed to be.[45] Irritated, Miranda set out alone to explore the temple of Neptune with its Doric columns, of which he noted condescendingly that there were only eleven and not fourteen, as the French architectural historian Julien David Le Roy claimed in *Ruines des plus beaux monuments de la Grèce* (Ruins of the Most Beautiful Monuments of Greece) (1758). After a long, hot day of educational sightseeing, Miranda retired to his room, hoping that the opium his host had provided would cure the headache that continued to plague him.

As he made his way to Athens, Miranda indulged himself in the many public bathhouses that characterized Greek towns. He saw the ruins of the Temple of Ceres, the supposed Temple of Hercules near the forest of Nemea, and something he understood to be the amphitheater of the ancient Isthmian Games. Passing the island of Salamis, Miranda let his imagination wander back nearly 2,300 years to relive the famous naval battle that Themistocles had described so eloquently; from memory, Miranda sketched out the Greek and Persian troops' various positions and maneuvers and marveled at the smallness of the field on which the battle actually took place. The next morning, June 17, he visited the port of Piraeus to see the Lion's Gate and the graves of Themistocles and Simon. Miranda was overjoyed to find himself wandering in the footsteps of the ancients, and admired the "exactitude and topographic fidelity" with which their historians had managed to endow their accounts.[46] After much difficult travel, by boat, by donkey, and on foot, Miranda arrived in Athens on June 19. He still suffered from a blinding headache and immediately sought the advice of a doctor, who prescribed a cycle of purgatives for the treatment of an infected bladder. Miranda submitted to the treatment but continued to punish himself with an exhausting itinerary.

In Athens, as he had done in Rome, Miranda aimed to see all the sights that he had read about as a student. In general, Miranda tended to favor Greek design and architecture based on simple and clean lines over the more ostentatious and pompous Roman styles. This preference extended to political abstractions as well; he preferred the Greek ideal of a small state built on a virtuous citizenry over a Roman-style, vast militaristic empire. He was a knowledgeable critic of all that he saw and wrote sophisticated comments in his diary, often remarking in amazement, "what beauty!" or "what sublime proportions!" Anxious to use his Greek, Miranda read and transcribed the long dedications found on many of the ruins, one of which led him to believe he had discovered the "prisons of the Areopagi" right where they should be found, next to the statue of Philopapus (Caius Julius Philippapus, son of Caio). In the same way, he located the Demosthenes Lighthouse, the Arch of Theseus, and the Pantheon of Adriano. He toured the temple of Jupiter at Olympus, the temple of Augustus, and the Stadium, which especially impressed him because it had been built "at the expense of simple citizens."[47] Miranda undertook his grand tour not just for his personal enjoyment and education, but also to expand his understanding of human liberty and the science of government so that he might be able to serve his own people better when their turn for independence finally came.

Deciding that he would indeed continue on to Turkey, Miranda once again passed through the hot, mosquito-ridden port of Smyrna, which he detested. He spent several days there, visiting other expatriates and preparing for the next leg of his journey. At the home of Richard and Edward Lee, he met an Englishman named Mr. Hayes, "a great Fox-ite who seemed well versed in the current political intrigues of his country" and with whom he spoke of politics for "an infinity."[48] Yet he remained cagey, knowing that news of his activities constantly filtered back to London and from there to Madrid. Miranda's former traveling companion William Steuben Smith played his part in keeping the Spanish government off his friend's scent. Smith sent a note to the Spanish legation's secretary Matías Gandásegui containing the false information that "Colonel de Miranda was well at Naples in the tenth of March [1786] and proposed to be expeditious in his movements to London."[49] Bernardo del Campo assured his superiors that he was indeed keeping a file on the "various machinations of malcontents of our America" from his perch in England.[50] In the days before photography, however, it was difficult to provide distant consuls with accurate ideas of the person for whom they should watch. Using multiple pseudonyms and adopting various disguises, Miranda managed to stay one step ahead of his pursuers.

On the voyage to Turkey, Miranda encountered new sets of behaviors and prejudices that continued to challenge the assumptions with which he had been raised. He observed a group of thirty-two young African men traveling to Constantinople to sell their textiles; he viewed them as "poor people . . . yet upon reflection they are always singing and seem more content than others on this ship." From his fellow passengers he learned that the Turks detested the French for their bad behavior and their increasingly aggressive military presence in the region. Watching Arabic and Turkish passengers eat with their fingers and share the same plates, Miranda marveled at how strange it was "to note the equality with which this nation admits and treats with the blacks, yet at the same time scorns and refuses to treat with the French!" Passing the ruins along the coast of Troy toward the Dardanelles, he recognized that the view was "exactly as the ancient poets had described it." He saw the ruins of Sestos and Abydos, which recalled for him the myth of Hero and Leander (the name he later chose for his firstborn son), and pondered the sight of Gallipoli. Getting closer to home, the ship's captain boasted that "if it was not for [Turkey], half of Christendom would die of hunger"; an unusually defensive Miranda shot back, "I suppose that is the reason that you have ceded half the Crimea then?"[51]

Miranda finally arrived in Constantinople (today Istanbul) on July 30, 1786. He was immediately fascinated by its exoticism: the mosques and their minarets, the strangely-dressed multitudes, the pungent odors of its marketplaces and the tranquillity of its fragrant gardens. Most of all, Miranda noticed the seemingly endless number of stray dogs and cats. His first stop, as always, was to see his banker, here named Mr. Ahrens; then he continued on to deliver the various letters of introduction. Immediately, Miranda was welcomed into the European expatriate community that consisted of diplomats from Holland, Sweden, and France, merchants from England and Austria, their families, and various hangers-on. He spent several days touring the sights and, in the evenings, engaging in amiable conversation while listening to the women sing and play the piano. In distant Constantinople, Miranda and the other Europeans recreated their familiar parlors, thereby keeping the strange Turkish world at bay for at least part of the day. He was surprised to meet a Frenchman, Monsieur Vodreuille, who had been to Caracas recently, and plied him with questions about his friends and family back home. Indeed, the frequency with which Miranda encountered travelers with whom he had friends or places in common indicates just how closely intertwined the social life of his class was throughout the Atlantic world.

To his credit, Miranda rarely had harsh words for the people and places he visited; he preferred to learn from them and to record what he saw. In a Muslim country once again, he observed that their mosques were every bit as piously constructed as Christian churches were, and occasionally he found them to be even more aesthetically pleasing. In fact, Miranda pronounced the interior of Hagia Sophia to be more impressive than St. Peter's Basilica in Rome, St. Paul's Cathedral in London, and El Escorial in Madrid. He was annoyed to find, however, that Turkish parents did not place much value on their children's education or literacy. As he ambled around the city, he was mortified when women spit on him and children threw rocks at him under the mistaken impression that he was a Frenchman. Miranda sampled the Turkish coffee and tried smoking a pipe in the Turkish style, through a bottle of clear water so the smoke would be humid and fresh, which he deemed to be "a good refinement." Several times he found himself in the presence of Muslim holy men known as "whirling dervishes," whose devotions and motions left him mystified but impressed.[52]

Miranda spent just over two months in Turkey; he was perhaps the first Spanish American to visit that country. He spent each day walking and talking with locals and recorded vast amounts of information in his diary each night. While there, he read about the history and culture of the Ottoman Empire and took care to search out rare books and original manuscripts whenever he could gain access to them. As an indication of the cosmopolitan culture to which he belonged, Miranda found himself reading a Turkish military treatise written in French and printed in Austria.[53] As ever, he was fascinated by the "marvelous science" of tactics and was pleased to gain some insight into the Turkish mind from it. Miranda thought that more translations should be made from the Turkish language so that "we would understand them better, and have a truer opinion of them than generally reigns in Europe." After all, Miranda noted, proverbial wisdom holds that "*a wise enemy is better than an ignorant friend.*" Perhaps flattering himself, he also recorded: "*A man who speaks many languages is worth more than several others put together.*"[54] He realized that he was as much of a curiosity to the locals as they were to him; he laughed when a group of small children accosted him because they wanted to feel his strange clothes and then pretended to make war on him so that they might make him their slave. As he traveled throughout the Atlantic world and into Asia, Miranda became more aware of his unique American identity through his many encounters with other people and cultures. As he tried to learn about their ways, he also sought to answer his hosts' questions about Spanish America, a process that inevitably heightened his own national feelings.

As time passed, Miranda began to make plans to venture into Russia. He had already prepared the way by cultivating friendships with the Russian merchants, military officers, and diplomats who lived in Constantinople. From them, he solicited letters of introduction to the military commanders at Kherson and the necessary passports. Russian envoy Bulgakov advised Miranda on the impenetrable nature of Russian society and politics. When he finally arrived at Kherson in Russia on October 7, 1786, with a pain in his kidneys and "a mind unclouded by prejudice," Miranda was unlike any other foreigner who traveled to Russia in the eighteenth century.[55] He did not bring with him expectations that the vast empire was inferior to western Europe; his friend Joseph Ribas, for example, had warned Miranda that Russia was a "premature nation." Yet Miranda himself seemed to have great respect for the land and its people, and for this reason his diary is a particularly valuable historical document. While in Russia, he continued his habit of visiting prisons, schools, hospitals, cemeteries, factories, farms, and military installations and of interacting curiously with people of all classes. From his observations, one can learn much about the nature of that country at the zenith of Catherine the Great's reign.

In Kherson, Miranda quickly put his letters into circulation and awaited the invitations and callers who were sure to come. He spent most of October at his hotel, getting caught up in his diary while waiting for the quarantine placed on travelers from the Orient to pass. For reading pleasure he pulled up by the fire and lost himself in *Le Pornographe*, a book by Nicolas Restif de la Bretonne about the regulation of prostitution; he declared himself much pleased by the author's

erudition, not to mention the subject matter. Restif de la Bretonne
was a notorious libertine who advocated reforms in the areas of education, gender relations, laws, and language; he has become known as
"the Rousseau of the gutter." Once again, liberty and libertinism joined
forces in the eighteenth century. However strongly his reading matter
managed to get Miranda's blood pumping, he nevertheless found the
Crimean cold to be "diabolical and almost unsupportable; truly [he
said] this is a species of penetrating coldness far worse than that of
North America."[56] Miranda, who rarely complained about anything,
railed bitterly against the "Devil's cold" throughout his stay in Russia.
His local friends, mainly military men with whom he conversed in
French, just laughed and told him to carry on. They all amused themselves by playing whist in the evenings, a card game that was popular
on both sides of the Atlantic.

Miranda's interest in military history resurfaced in Russia. In
Kherson, he became acquainted with Korsakov, the commander of
the city's fortress; with Mordvinov, the commander of the arsenal;
and with Prince Viasemsky, the Imperial Army's second-in-command.
He and the local English agent Mr. Benson visited all the military
installations and explored each of them in depth. A Russian regiment,
Miranda learned, "is, in truth, a small town which contained all the
necessities of life in itself, so that it is ready to move the instant it
receives its orders."[57] To further his own understanding, Miranda read
Voltaire's history of Russia in the era of Peter the Great, and found its
observations each day more accurate.

His dislike of the French character continued to be fortified by
the individuals he met in Russia. He pronounced a young Russian
major with whom he had spent some time to be pretentious and su-
perficial and therefore was not surprised to learn that the man was
actually French. Similarly, one evening he was mortified to find that
his "wretched friend Monsieur Roux has been singing bordello songs
to the daughters of Mr. Rosarovich, lasses of fourteen and fifteen, an
age noted for the loss of innocence and good reputation . . . damnable
is the demonic French character and the fates which have bound me
together with this uneducated man."[58] He remained critical of "that
damned Gallic frivolity that has contaminated the human race," and
swore that never again would he enter into close friendship with any

Frenchman.[59] The two quarreled and Roux asked Miranda to take his belongings and leave his house because he was "not being used to be treated with contempt by any man."[60] Miranda happily complied with the request and went to stay with the Prince and Princess Viasemsky, probably as a good a political move as a personal one. Field marshal and Russian prime minister Prince Gregory Potemkin was coming to prepare the Crimean provinces for Empress Catherine the Great's famous tour of her new territories, in 1787. Potemkin was Catherine's former lover and an able administrator; the exaggerated story persists that he constructed dozens of false towns for her to visit during her Crimean tour in order to make the region seem more prosperous, although it cannot be denied that Potemkin truly did stimulate economic growth in the Russian Crimea. Once again present at a historical moment, Miranda's friends bought him a new uniform so that he would be respectable and presentable to Potemkin when he arrived. Yet, just as he had done previously with Lafayette and Washington, Miranda remained critical of Potemkin in his diary. He roundly condemned the minister's policy that had forcibly relocated 65,000 Greeks and Armenians in order to populate the Muslim provinces with Christians, only to leave the refugees suffering in starvation on the frontiers of Asia. Furthermore, as he watched dozens of impoverished workers prepare suitably ornate lodgings to house Potemkin, Miranda commented with disgust that "[Potemkin] did not fancy paying the artisans who worked for him and so, like all the world over, that class is getting screwed."[61]

Miranda met Potemkin on January 2, 1787, and was received with all the normal attentions paid to a distinguished traveling foreigner of his class. Together they dined and listened to performances of Luigi Boccherini's quartets. Potemkin and his coterie wanted to know all about Miranda's years in the presidios of Africa and about the Pensacola campaign. Despite Miranda's private contempt for Potemkin's character, publicly the two got on well enough for the prince to invite his new protégé to return with him to the capital, St. Petersburg. Miranda quickly agreed. Belgian consul Van Schouten gave him thirty gold ducats for his journey and the Princess Viasemsky offered him her fur-trimmed coat. Potemkin, Prince Nassau, Miranda, and a handful of others set out on January 5 for Kiev, where the group intended to join Catherine and her entourage. Patronizing their strange foreign friend, the Russians told Miranda not to be afraid when the carriage used frozen rivers as roadways; even though he surely had not experienced such a mode of travel in his country, they assured him it was quite safe. Their conversation ran the gamut from literature to history to politics. Potemkin and the others plied Miranda with particular questions about England and "our America, about which nations I saw that they had no accurate idea."[62]

Not wishing to appear to be fawning over royalty, Miranda pretended that he might leave the party before they met Catherine and continue on to St. Petersburg alone, a suggestion that shocked Minister Potemkin and that he and the others immediately refused to sanction. Miranda could not, they responded incredulously, pass so near to the empress at Kiev and fail to pay his respects to her. It would be an unforgivable slight. No, they insisted, he must accompany them to the Imperial Court and meet Her Majesty, who was a scholarly and enlightened woman; Catherine, they assured him, was always anxious to meet foreigners who might feed her curiosity about the world beyond Russia's borders. In the end, Miranda agreed to wait and meet Catherine before traveling further. Of course, that is exactly what he had intended to do all along—to make the empress's acquaintance and solicit her support for his emancipation project. In his own inimitable way, Miranda had managed to seem humble and disinterested while manipulating others into confirming his prestige and the demand for his presence. Becoming increasingly anxious about protocol as Catherine's arrival neared, his friends arranged for Miranda to obtain a dress uniform and sent out for a special sword, prompting the amused Venezuelan to exclaim, "Great Heavens! What trifles and absurdities!"[63]

Miranda caught his first glimpse of Empress Catherine the Great of Russia in a Kiev cathedral on February 13, 1787. Although she was raised as a Lutheran in Germany, when she married into the Russian royal family Catherine converted and began to take Communion in the Greek Orthodox tradition. At the ceremony, the archbishop covered her in kisses and professions of loyalty and faith. Miranda found the whole spectacle slightly ridiculous and claimed that he used the time during the long service to study the cathedral's construction and architecture. The next day, Valentine's Day, at precisely 11:30 A.M., Count Bezborodko presented Miranda to Catherine; when he stooped to kiss her hand, he was impressed that the unpretentious Catherine removed her fur muff, but took care to note in his diary that he steadfastly refused "to fall all over himself and genuflect in front of royalty." The empress took an immediate interest in the handsome stranger and invited him to join the evening's feast. After the meal, she peppered him with a thousand questions about Spanish America and his travels. Her attentions flattered Miranda, of course, but he also truly appreciated her intelligence and the "goodness and excellence of her [h]eart." Their paths crossed several times over the next few days, as Catherine toured the city of Kiev and attended dinners in her honor. He heard from one nobleman that the empress found him "sincere and learned, exactly the type of man that she liked." Catherine notoriously liked all sorts of men during her long life, but Miranda was certainly one of her favorites for a time.[64]

At each meeting, their conversations rambled over a wide range of topics: the Inquisition, North Africa's garrisons and culture, European literature, Russian history. Catherine was open and frank, not at all egotistical despite her semi-divine status as empress, and she had an attitude toward her earthly subjects that Miranda found refreshing and modern. Before long, rumors of a more intimate relationship between the two began to surface. Two years later, in 1789, Miranda's friend Stephen Sayre gossiped that he had heard that the Venezuelan "had traveled to great advantage, nothing has escaped his *penetration*, not even the Empress of all the Russias, I believe—a mortifying *declaration* for me to make, who was 21 months in her Capital, without ever making myself acquainted with the internal parts of *her extensive and well-known Dominions*."[65] Thomas Paine, too, recalled that "[Miranda] did not tell me of his affair with old Catharine [*sic*] of Russia, nor did I tell him that I knew of it."[66] Yet most historians agree that a physical relationship between the two was unlikely.[67] Although Catherine was well known for her many lovers, she tended to be serially monogamous and was involved with the dashing Count Dmitri Mamonov at the time. Furthermore, the empress was fifty-eight years old when they met, Miranda was just thirty-six, and he himself described her love for him as "the affection of a mother."[68]

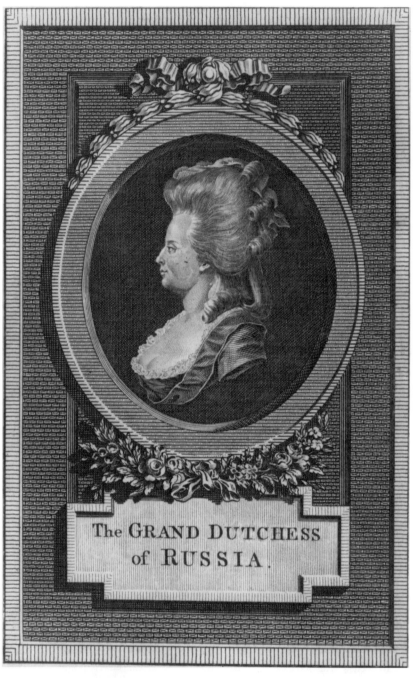

Catherine II, Empress of Russia. National Portrait Gallery

Nevertheless, their relationship was intense enough to provoke Potemkin's jealousy and Miranda's former friend and protector began to try to hurry the foreigner on his way.

Catherine's interest in Miranda was more than just a pleasant personal diversion. At the exact moment that Miranda arrived in her court, Russian explorer Grigorii Shelikov returned from Irkutsk to report that he had founded a settlement on Kodiak Island. Catherine and her advisers, it seems, were debating the possibility of expanding the Russian Empire eastward from Siberia into North America. The recent discovery of valuable sea otters in the Aleutian Islands had attracted her attention and suggested the need for a more serious and visible Russian presence in the Americas. Catherine's pointed questions about the nature of Spanish rule in America, therefore, were not disinterested. For his part, Miranda understood that he also had something to gain from the Russians' national agenda. If he wished to initiate a movement for Spanish American emancipation, he would need the backing of at least one major international power, both to provide funds and supplies and to exert diplomatic pressure. Both sides wondered if the other would be a useful ally in their respective political projects.

Miranda spent much of his time in Russia talking about America, not just with Catherine, but with others as well. Although the two had not met before, French envoy Louis-Philippe, the Count de Ségur, had toured the United States in 1783; furthermore, as a youth Ségur had spent four days in Caracas, and so the two men were able to exchange fond recollections of both places. Like Miranda, Ségur had known the Arestiguieta family in Caracas, and remembered Miss Bowen and Miss P[olly] Scott in Boston. Imagine, thought Miranda, to come all the way to Russia, "only to find here men who have been in my house!" The Prince of Nassau introduced Miranda to Lewis Littlepage, an American, who gave him the sad news that their mutual friends General Gates and General Greene had died recently. The Atlantic world's social space clearly was not as distant or great as its geographical dimensions might suggest.[69]

In Russia, Miranda's preoccupation with his emancipation project seems to have intensified. He remembered that he rambled on about nothing but "politics and more politics." He was pleased to find that

Ségur also felt disgust at the actions of José de Gálvez and the rest of the Spanish Ministry of the Indies in America. With an unnamed young Swiss diplomat he recalled many "long republican conversations." Always circumspect in his diary for fear of self-incrimination, he evidently talked with Potemkin, Mamonov, and Catherine herself about "it," an allusion to his plans to revolutionize South America. On April 12, Mamonov reported to Miranda that the Empress had sanctioned his plans, saying "[t]hat my way of thinking appeared to her to be very good . . . that as she did not know the *place* [Venezuela] she was not able to give me counsel as to the execution [of the plans] but that later she would tell me more in regard to the matter."[70] Some of his time was spent in purposeful study. Still not reconciled to the freezing Russian temperatures, Miranda used his time indoors to read Machiavelli's *The Prince*, whose doctrine he found "not good, but true . . . oh what suffering is produced when one tries to copy the malice and general character of the human race! Particularly those who command and govern the majority!"[71] He also never failed to comment on the devilish intrigues that seemed to characterize the Russian court, although his diary does not reveal much bitterness even when he himself began to fall victim to its petty rivalries. Miranda always pretended to be innocent of such activities, but it is clear that he also knew how to play their games. Both Potemkin and Ségur quickly began to resent the clear favoritism that the empress showed toward Miranda, and they orchestrated an educational trip to Poland in March 1786 to remove him from her side for a while. Ségur described Miranda as "a well-educated and spiritual man, audacious and given to intrigue."[72] The cynical Frenchman was amazed at the way Miranda had persuaded the empress that he was "a martyr to philosophy, and a victim of the Inquisition." Miranda recorded in his diary that Ségur once told him that he "was a great courtier, as in a short time I had been able to make the Sovereign take an interest in me, when she did not address a single word during a month to many foreigners of note."[73]

Miranda traveled to Poland in an official Russian state coach with an invitation from Polish king Stanislaus Augustus II, who expressed as much interest in Spanish America as did his former lover Catherine the Great. Although the diversion was entertaining and instructive,

Miranda hurried back to St. Petersburg to rejoin the empress's court so that the progress he had made with her would not be undone in his absence. Nevertheless, he had been gone long enough for someone to whisper in Catherine's ear about the imprudence of openly flouting the Spanish king's wishes and harboring a fugitive. On March 29, 1787, Catherine asked Miranda to give up any idea of returning to his homeland, where he was sure to be persecuted for his ideas; instead, she suggested, why not join her court permanently with a handsome state salary, a title, and a furnished home? Naturally the offer flattered Miranda, who replied that while there was no one who "loved the Empress more than I, . . . surely the thing is impossible."[74] He explained to her that "[o]nly a great and interesting matter such as the one that presently occupies my attention would be able to make me decline the sweet and agreeable pleasure of being able to repay you with my services for all that which I owe to Your Majesty's benevolence."[75]

Potemkin and Ségur were not the only ones anxious about Miranda's influence over Catherine. From London, envoy Bernardo del Campo had warned his counterpart in St. Petersburg, Pedro Normande, to watch out for the fugitive Miranda.[76] When Miranda appeared in St. Petersburg in July 1787, Spanish representatives there protested furiously and tried to have him arrested. The secretary of the Spanish Legation, Pedro Macanaz, charged Miranda with impersonating an officer and asked for his extradition; Macanaz also complained that Miranda was passing himself off as a noble count without any legitimate claim to that status. As he usually did when dealing with authorities who opposed his wishes or actions, Miranda shot back a nasty and sarcastic letter that essentially said he would not deign to respond to Macanaz's charges. The secretary's threats, he said, were not only ridiculous but were presented in the sort of unrefined language that the official could only use with those who had the misfortune to be his inferiors (which, presumably, Miranda was not!).[77] The brouhaha enveloped the entire diplomatic and expatriate community. Ségur claimed his status as French envoy required him to stay out of the whole mess, but British ambassador Fitzherbert supported Miranda. Catherine refused to hand over her pet to the Spaniards; instead she put an end to the controversy by bestowing on him the

title of Count Miranda, granting him 10,000 rubles, and guarantee-
ing him the protection of her embassies throughout Europe, should
he ever have need of their services. Miranda recalled that she told
him, "[I]f the Spanish Empire was in danger on my account, I could
be in no better place than in Russia as it was the most distant from
Spain than any country—and that as regards the feeling which Her
Majesty had for me it had nothing to do with the rank I had in Spain
but was due to my personal qualities."[78] In the end, there was little
more that Normande and Macanaz could do except to grumble and
pass the disturbing information on to Madrid.

Despite his successes with the empress, Miranda suffered bouts of
depression common among all exiles and travelers. He felt dreadfully
lonely when his servant, whom he described as a frightful glutton, left
him in a remote area without a translator and therefore unable to
communicate. Able to converse in at least five languages but not Russian, Miranda noted, "[W]hat a disadvantage for a traveler not to know
the language of the country! I get desperate at times and feel like
letting everything go to the Devil!" When his mood got too black, he
even feigned illness and avoided his friends. "Sadly I took the coach
back to Petersburg, wrapped in my black thoughts, feeling that my
fate was against me, in the situation in which I find myself at this
moment, due to the falseness of men . . . I went to bed and passed a
sad and melancholy night."[79] He assuaged some of his homesickness
by imagining his travels to be patriotic work undertaken on behalf of
his people. During the entire year he spent in the Russian Empire,
Miranda set himself the task of studying various public policy measures and engaging in the intellectual life of the places he visited.[80]
For example, he met the famous Dr. Samoilovich and discussed that
man's theories about inoculations. He learned happily that the death
penalty was nonexistent in Russia for any type of crime, and read
English Quaker John Howard's tracts on prison reform. Miranda
toured schools everywhere he went; he visited the universities in Moscow and Kiev, and learned that the government sponsored several
public schools that were "of tremendous utility" to the nation, although one schoolmistress he saw was "more heavily painted up than
a clown." In Moscow he toured another school where classes were
taught in French, Russian, German, Latin, Italian, and English and

where students took their morals class in Latin, "as if Russian was lacking in expression!"[81] His notebook full and his curiosity sated, Miranda left Russian soil, embarking in Kronstadt for Sweden on September 7, 1787.

When he arrived in Stockholm, his first act was to present himself and his credentials to Count Andrei Razumovski. The Russian ambassador invited Miranda to stay at his official residence but recommended that he keep a low profile while there because the Spanish had posted spies everywhere. Miranda continued his purposeful travels in Scandinavia, journeying northward to examine the mines at Uppsala and stopping to survey the Royal Library, where he accidentally bumped into Gustav III. The king subsequently arranged for Miranda to tour his much-vaunted House of Industry, a sort of workhouse where the indigent and unemployed could gain access to productive materials for a nominal charge and raise themselves out of their wretched conditions through their own efforts. It had a punitive dimension as well; beggars could be forcibly institutionalized there in order to have acceptable work habits instilled in them. Miranda deemed the House of Industry to be an "excellent way to do away with the laziness existing under a monarchical government."[82] His notion that the social and economic environment conditioned one's behavior was reaffirmed by what he saw in Sweden. King Gustav requested a private interview with Miranda, during which the two men chatted affably and shared similarly unfavorable impressions of the brutal and exploitative Spanish Empire. Each man was anxious to impress the other. Insecure Gustav, in particular, wished Miranda to take away a positive opinion of Sweden, and Miranda wanted to win a powerful friend for his cause. The vain Venezuelan later recorded with evident pride that the king had enjoyed conversing with him very much. When the Spanish ambassador, Ignacio María del Corral y Aguirre, began to protest about the outlaw's presence and initiated a request for his arrest, Miranda decided to slip quietly out of the country and continue his tour of Scandinavia.

He spent most of November 1787 in Christiania, Norway, visiting the sorts of places that habitually interested him: libraries, military establishments, mines, ports, and forests. Miranda was impressed with Scandinavia, writing "[I]t is a noteworthy thing to see the degree

of civilization, of instruction and elegance in which these people here
live . . . it is the result of commerce and communication which they
have with England and Holland."[83] He found the women to be very
good-looking and so did not reject the list of "Nymphs of Cythera"
(the ancient center for the cult of Aphrodite) that Count de Ranzau
had given him for his use. Yet, not all were furtive nights of paid
pleasure; in Gothenburg, Miranda experienced the second of his major love affairs. There he met Catherine Hall, the wife of a wealthy
British merchant, and fell deeply in love. So, it seems, did she. At the
end of December 1787, Miranda noted in his diary that he lunched
with Catherine, "who is very upsetting to me . . . after cultivating a
little tenderness, which I note is beginning to appear, I went home to
write." Miranda and Mrs. Hall went out together for many long, private carriage rides, in which they exchanged a thousand kisses and in
all likelihood something more. On one amorous expedition, their
coachman purposely made the carriage lurch, Miranda snarled, "*so
that it was most embarrassing*" for the lovers. Another time, a knock on
their door from some unexpected French visitors interrupted the lovers "in their bliss."[84] Eventually he realized that he must extract himself from an impossible situation, despite the pain to both involved,
but not before they vowed to sustain their love through frequent letters. Catherine gave Miranda her silhouette in a locket along with a
snippet of her golden hair; in exchange, she took one of his brooches
and promised to wear in on her breast forever. The monthlong affair
might have ended there, but for a footnote of possible historical significance: rumors persist that Miranda derived the color scheme for
the independent Venezuelan flag from his beloved Catherine Hall:
yellow for her hair, blue for her eyes, red for her lips.[85]

Miranda spent the first half of 1788 traveling throughout northern Europe, availing himself of the Russian diplomatic corps' protection in the places he visited. Count Bernsdorff of Denmark wrote to
a friend that he was:

> impressed with Miranda's personality: I have seen few men better in-
> formed. One would have more confidence in him if his imagination did
> not, from time to time, carry him beyond the realms of reality. . . . It is
> certain that I have never seen a person better informed as to the program
> for revolutions in South America than he is, and also in regard to every-

thing which concerns it.—He is not a partisan of the means or methods of revolution, but he is enthusiastic as to the basic principles of liberty, which in truth may appear sweet to the inhabitants of a country which is absolutely oppressed.[86]

It is clear that Miranda's twin obsessions continued to gather force throughout his European travels as he became more aware of his American identity; he wished to gather as much useful information about European nations as he could, while building support for the notion of an independent Spanish America. It was in Copenhagen at the end of January 1788 that Miranda received first news of the Túpac Amaru revolt that had shaken Peru. Led by José Gabriel Condorcanqui, a descendant of Peru's pre-Columbian Inca royal family, a series of revolts against the exploitative Spanish policies toward the indigenous population broke out across the Andes between the years of 1780 and 1783. Miranda must have felt both delight and dread upon hearing of these rebellions. On one hand, they confirmed his idea that the Spanish American colonies were ripe for revolution; on the other hand, he worried that the pace of events might quicken and he would lose his chance to be their leader. Disturbed, Miranda spent very little time in Denmark, which he found intolerably dull anyway, and hurried on to northern Germany.[87]

In Schleswig-Holstein, he dined with the Hessian prince. The two men spoke about "interesting matters" for over an hour one day and the next day had an extensive interview about North America that was conducted in English. Oddly, the prince inquired whether Miranda would like to hear his horoscope and then proceeded to describe the Venezuelan's life experiences over the past decade "without making a mistake."[88] Apparently, the cards predicted that England would indeed support his expeditionary dreams. Although Miranda professed a lifelong distaste for superstitious beliefs, like many people, he nevertheless felt happy when the occult pointed in his favor. Still, the long arm of the Spanish Empire was never far behind him. In Hamburg at the beginning of April, Miranda received a warning from the Russian ambassador that sufficiently frightened him to run back to his hotel and lock the doors while pondering an escape. He adopted another pseudonym as a precautionary measure; for the next several

Crayon portrait of Francisco de Miranda; it was his favorite likeness. Western History Collections, University of Oklahoma Libraries

months he became Monsieur de Méran, a Livonian gentleman traveling for leisure on a Russian passport.

Miranda spent most of May in the Netherlands, passed the summer in the Rhine Valley, and then returned briefly to Italy for a second time in August.[89] In Milan, he sought out Cesare Beccaria, the author of *On Crimes and Punishment* (1764), which condemned capital punishment, and the two had a lengthy conversation about America. He moved on to Zurich in September, where he made the acquaintance of Johann Kaspar Lavater, a well-known Protestant pastor and author of several books on physiognomy, which is the art of determining a person's character based on facial features. Lavater asked if Miranda would allow his portrait to be painted for his collection of notable persons. The pastel image was completed in less than an hour, and Miranda himself pronounced it to be a good likeness. Finally, Miranda thought, his face was starting to join others on the portrait walls of greatness. In Switzerland he also sought out British historian Edward Gibbon, author of *The Decline and Fall of the Roman Empire* (1776–1788), who shared his personal opinion that England had lost nothing with the independence of the Thirteen Colonies but £100,000,000 of national debt. If true, this could be an argument that Miranda might use to persuade the Spaniards to leave America; they would be strengthened, not weakened, by a similar emancipation of their colonies.

Miranda finally entered France, an essential stop on any gentleman's grand tour, in the early months of that fateful revolutionary year, 1789. Miranda's timing was always excellent. He arrived at Marseilles where he called on "my friend" the Abbé Guillaume Thomas Raynal, whose authoritative and popular book titled *Philosophical and Political History of the Settlement and Trade of the Europeans in the East and West Indies* (1770) had already run through thirty editions by 1789. Raynal's arguments seemed to sanction more autonomy for colonies and to uphold their residents' right to revolt against distant, unresponsive authority; for that reason, he was exiled from Paris and his works banned by the Catholic Church. Raynal was suffering from a bout of rheumatism but he nonetheless received Miranda with eagerness and affection. When the conversation turned to American affairs, Miranda found to his great dismay that the abbé felt less confident about Spanish America's revolutionary preparedness than he had been previously; Raynal told him that "the nation was not yet *ripe*, and that the general ignorance which dominated, on every side, was incredible."[90] Clearly Raynal's disillusionment said more about the current conditions in France than it did about faraway Spanish America (which he had never visited), but Miranda was taken aback nonetheless.

Miranda despised many of the conditions he witnessed as he traveled northward through France to Paris. At Rochefort, he cursed the town's principal economic activity, namely the African slave trade with Guinea. In Nantes, he conversed with a sea captain who described to him the way in which Africans were brought aboard in chains, and "packed in rows like sardines. Poor unfortunate souls." In contrast to Great Britain, where leading politicians and average citizens were already calling for the abolition of the barbaric trade, Miranda found their French counterparts to be vain, ridiculous, frivolous, and living in a sort of slavery to fashion themselves. For example, when Madame Candeille made a spectacular musical debut, Miranda observed contemptuously that the next morning he saw no less than eight pianofortes on the street being delivered to jealous ladies who could not bear to be out of the spotlight themselves. Miranda always detested the affectation he associated with the French; in this regard he agreed with Rousseau, who stated that "luxury destroys hospitality." From his vantage point, the French upper classes' insularity and lack of social concern meant that they were destroying themselves in "perfectly *mad* fashion, and not doing themselves or anyone else any good by it at all."[91] After one particularly painful dinner during which he could not manage to engage a single foppish person in a conversation that made any sense, Miranda left in disgust and went back to his room as soon as the meal was finished.

When Miranda finally reached Paris in May 1789, the city was in a state of turmoil. Rapid social and economic change had produced dislocation in all aspects of French life. The bold new democratic ideas of French Enlightenment authors, coupled with the successful example of the American Revolution, resulted in an increased number of revolts throughout the country. Just as they were the most politically active and discontented elements in Spanish American society, in France, too, the merchants and middle classes clamored for more representation and meaningful opportunities to participate in public life. When Miranda arrived in Paris, public pressure had forced the king to call a meeting of the Estates-General for the first time since 1614. Amid great jubilation, elections to this legislative body were held on May 5, 1789. Once again, Miranda managed to be at the center of events when a historic moment occured. Sensing that the political situation was volatile, and knowing that France was ruled by a Bourbon monarch who had close family connections to the Spanish king, he wisely preferred to remain inconspicuous. Unfortunately for the historical record, he also abandoned his usual habit and failed to record any impressions of the important events that he must have witnessed in that fateful month of May 1789.

It is clear that Miranda visited the palace at Versailles, where he was annoyed that a halberd-wielding guard made him kneel in respect to the king. He was scandalized to learn that 18,000 people resided at the palace, the vast majority of whom were employed either in the bloated French bureaucracy or in serving the needs of the royal court. He remained in Paris until June 8, having some emergency work done on his teeth by a clever, democratically-inclined dentist who talked nonstop about the rights of man. Tiring of living in hotels and fed up with the squabbling French, Miranda decided that it was time he started to make his way back to London, the closest thing he had to a real home. Of course, his movements continued to be monitored. From Paris, the Conde de Aranda was pleased to inform Bernardo del Campo that information sent by Spanish ministers in Russia, Sweden, Denmark, and Poland had allowed him to determine Miranda's route and schedule; del Campo could expect that the traitor would soon embark from Calais, headed for Dover.[92] As a precaution, Aranda had sent out an arrest order with a description of the suspect to all the ports along the Channel, asking them to watch out for Miranda.

Miranda arrived in England with a broadened mind and an address book bulging with the names of international friends and supporters he had met over the past four years. Once he was safely reinstalled in his former lodgings, Miranda wrote a grateful letter to

Catherine the Great, thanking her profusely and sincerely for her patronage and protection. He realized that without her kindness, he would have fallen victim to the agents of the Spanish Empire at least a dozen times or more. Her ambassador to London, Count Vorontsov, had inscribed Miranda's name on the list of embassy personnel, which he felt should be sufficient to ward off all potential Spanish intrigues against him. He closed the letter by offering a prayer that "the Supreme Being allow the estimable life of Your Majesty to continue forever, to bring happiness to your subjects and for the consolation of the entire human race."[93] Matthew Guthrie, an Englishman he had met in Russia, described Miranda as a "native of Mexico [who] is a rare instance in the modern times of a Spaniard becoming an enlightened and liberal Philosopher in spite of every obstacle thrown in their way by the dark confined Politic of the Country guided by the gloommy [*sic*] inquisition whos [*sic*] monkish rod strikes out of their hand every book that could dispel the Gothic darkness in which they are enveloped . . . I must own I had no idea befor [*sic*] I made his acquaintance of the true State of Spain and its Colonies." Providing Miranda a letter of introduction to Dr. Black, a chemistry professor at the University of Edinburgh, Guthrie praised him as a hero "who is actually traveling to study men and things in their ordinary habits and common appearances and not for any purpose of frivolity."[94]

Miranda's international prestige had grown considerably during his grand tour of Europe. He had learned many things that he hoped would become useful to his countrymen when their independence was finally achieved. The Venezuelan gentleman's grand tour had made both his dreams and his self-importance grow.

4

THE REVOLUTIONARY DRESS REHEARSAL
Miranda and the French Revolution
(1790–1797)

> Make the Revolution the parent of settlement, and not a nursery of future revolutions.
> —EDMUND BURKE, *Reflections on the Revolution in France* (1790)

The eighteenth century brought the dawn of the information age, a time when people began to realize that accurate knowledge brought with it both power and advantage. Francisco de Miranda understood that information had become the new currency and he consciously exploited his position as an authentic American at the courts of Europe to assert his own political agenda. He enjoyed a close, albeit frustrating, relationship with British prime minister William Pitt (the Younger), whom he bombarded with memoranda and expeditionary plans. Miranda also kept track of all Spanish Americans who ventured to Europe so that he could make contact with as many of them as possible in order to start building a revolutionary network. Miranda's hunger for useful information, a condition linked to his exile status, also awakened in him a sense of American identity. To speak of America, to remain engaged politically, and to appear authoritative were means for him to maintain his connection with his homeland, to remain relevant to its political conditions while residing on the other side of the world. Exiles tend to blend their personal identities with those of their nation as a whole, in a romantic effort not to be forgotten.[1] Miranda was certainly no exception to this egotism born of isolation; his emerging vision of the Spanish American continent and its potential was so large that it could not be viewed in its entirety except across an ocean.

Miranda had useful information to spare. As early as 1787, his emancipation project was on the lips of several high-level British officials, one of whom erroneously reported to Lord Hawkesbury that "Colonel Meranda" was the best source for South American information because he "has been in every part of those extensive Empires (except Chilie [*sic*])." British supporters tended to reflect an English pride that was still wounded from "the part that Spain took in obtaining the Independence of North America and [wanted to] return them the Complement [*sic*] in Liberating Spanish America."[2] Yet Miranda also kept up his contacts in the U.S. government, always believing that he might need their aid someday as well. To his dear friend U.S. Secretary of War Henry Knox, Miranda wrote from London that he was "very happy to see the flourishing State in which N[orth] America is grown . . . and wished that my own poor miserable Country in the South could say the same!" He liked Knox's proposal to create a militia and advised him that Lord Melville and "some other professional men" were considering a similar proposal in England at that very moment as well; all seemed to agree that "the forme [*sic*] of the Roman Legion is infitely [*sic*] superior to any other organization or military arangement [*sic*] we know yet!"[3]

Pitt and Miranda discussed the possibility of a British-sponsored expedition to South America in a secret meeting held at the prime minister's country estate in Kent, Hollwood House, on Sunday, February 14, 1790; it was Pitt's custom to retreat there with close associates "when he wanted to discuss any particular plan in quiet."[4] Naively believing that his departure for America was imminent, Miranda obligingly handed over ten Spanish-language documents with English translations outlining local conditions and political sentiment in Spanish America. This early incarnation of the Miranda Plan married British parliamentary forms with indigenous American nomenclature and included a hereditary executive (known as "the Inca") and legal power vested in a bicameral legislature. The Inca would appoint both *caciques* (lords) who would serve life terms in the upper chamber and also the members of a House of Commons who would serve for 4- or 5-year terms. The *caciques*, in turn, would choose *ediles* to be in charge of ports, canals, vessels, monuments, and feasts; the lower House would choose *questors* to control the finances, just as the Commons did in Britain. The citizens at large would choose *censors* who would guard over the politicians' and youths' morals. All told, it was a strange hybrid of ideas from Britain, ancient Rome, indigenous America, and the United States, a highly unworkable system that was clearly the product of a mind whirling in distant isolation. Beginning his eloquent proposal with the bold assertion that "Spanish America desires England's aid in shaking off the infamous oppression in which Spain has mired it," Miranda's ego pretended to speak for an entire continent.[5]

The factual documents that accompanied Miranda's imaginary Incadom were obviously of more immediate interest to Pitt. Along with Miranda's utopian design for a civic government, Pitt received detailed memoranda on the population, mines, products, consumption, revenues, and military power of all the Spanish colonies in America. Miranda submitted plans of Havana's fortifications and environs, and detailed accounts of the Túpac Amaru and Comunero revolts derived from some eyewitnesses he had met in Europe. His calculations suggested that only 12,000 to 15,000 foreign troops in total would be required for a successful emancipation expedition. In exchange for such a nominal commitment, England's freedom-loving citizens would not only be on the side of moral righteousness, they would also gain innumerable commercial opportunities, including a potential canal route to the Orient through Panama. Pitt was indeed interested. Reliable information about Spain's dominions in America was difficult to come by, since the jealous Bourbons went to great lengths to exclude foreigners from their colonies. Miranda took the prime minister's indulgent reception to mean that he should begin packing his bags for a triumphal return home; it would be sixteen more years, however, before Miranda's first expedition actually landed in Venezuela.

Undaunted, Miranda kept his end of the bargain. He sent Pitt copies of all further details as requested, with computations "made according to the best information I have received lately, and the essential part collected by myself on the spot."[6] Like exiles everywhere, serving as a lobbyist and a clearinghouse for information was the best way for Miranda to remain connected to America. He provided a useful service to both the British government and the Spanish American people and had achieved a level of respect as London's best source for accurate American data. His passion is linked to his exilic status; psychologists note that for exiles, "the enormous importance of work as an organizing and stabilizing factor in psychic life cannot be over-emphasized."[7] Of course, Miranda had been living outside Spanish America since 1780, and had personal knowledge of Venezuela and the Caribbean alone; the rest of his insight came from the same source as it did for other Europeans—from newspapers, books, and interviews with other travelers.

On May 6 and 7, 1790, Miranda sent another seven bundles of plans to Pitt and Home Secretary William Wyndham, Lord Grenville, which included a more fully fleshed out scheme for the future government of America, further details of conditions in Peru, New Granada, and Venezuela, plans for an American constitution, and a list of the Jesuit exiles in Europe. He also included a map that identified the region for the first time as "Colombia."[8] While he waited for Pitt to digest his latest communiqués, Miranda jubilantly set out on a tour of the English countryside and made the rounds of London society to promote his vision. He enjoyed socializing, but America's business always came first; when Francis Egerton, the third earl of Bridgewater (and an enthusiastic patron of inland navigation) came to call, Miranda apologized that "some important business" had demanded his prior attention.[9] As the months passed slowly with no word from Pitt, his spirits began to blacken. By the end of May 1790, he sent an irritated note to the prime minister requesting immediate and decisive action: "Sir: Conscious of the multiplicity of business that lays upon your mind at this present moment, I would not trouble your attention on maters [sic] of *great importance*, & very consequential to this nation did not require for a few minutes your atention [sic].—Therefore, I request an *appointement* [sic] either, in the Country, or here in the Town, that I may communicate to you . . . this very important subject."[10] America was first and foremost in Miranda's mind and he expected everyone to share his sense of urgency.

Significantly, in London and throughout his travels, Miranda viewed the Atlantic world as a unified political space, partly because he needed to convince British and U.S. politicians and merchants to risk involvement in Spanish America, but also because he knew those countries' leaders well and admired their spirit of liberty. He truly viewed Anglo-Saxon culture as a role model for his Spanish American compatriots. Liberty was a shared project; its advance in one region would guarantee its progress in others. For this reason, he wanted to keep abreast of the policies being introduced on both sides of the Atlantic. Miranda wrote to Henry Knox several times, always reminding him of their discussions in the Boston symposium and seeking descriptions of the inner workings of the ongoing constitutional project in the United States.[11] He also solicited inside information from his friend and Secretary of the Treasury Alexander Hamilton about his designs for equitable taxation and a national banking system founded on paper money, both of which seemed to Miranda to be guided by "principles of *honor* and *dignity*, rarely seen in modern governments!"[12]

When months passed with no word from America, Miranda was sincerely hurt, asking why "not one of my friends in that part of the world shows atention [*sic*] it seems, to this part of the old." Eventually Knox did reply, sending warm greetings and passing on the delicate news that the letter Miranda had enclosed for "his female friend," most likely Susan Livingston, was being returned to him because as a married woman she "conceived her situation rendered it improper" to correspond with other men. She still professed a sincere friendship for Miranda, if that was some small consolation for him.[13] The lonely man felt dismayed and began to realize the great personal sacrifice that his commitment to Spanish American emancipation had exacted. He was forty years old, had no permanent home, no real profession, and no steady income. Exiles typically feel isolated and suffer from persecution complexes, real or imagined. In April 1790, Miranda drafted a letter to King Charles IV of Spain in which he complained that the Crown's agents were harassing him and preventing him from leading a free and normal life. He suffered under the constant surveillance of Spanish agents and persecution from its bureaucrats, Miranda claimed: "thus compelling me to sacrifice all my property and income and, what is worse, to renounce the pleasant society of my parents and other relatives in order to seek a country that would at least treat me with justice and assure me civil tranquility."[14] In his mind, he was always the victim, the idealistic hero who had been condemned to lead a wandering, rootless life because of the threat that his greatness posed to nervous authorities. The condition of exile fortified both his distorted self-image and his sense of American identity.

While in London, Miranda continued to associate with friends from all parts of the Atlantic world in order to keep himself informed about the current state of international politics. He had met Gouverneur Morris (currently serving as the U.S. representative in France) while in New York in 1784, and occasionally paid calls to the American legation in London. Morris learned from Miranda that during the Nootka Sound dispute, Spain had agreed to allow free navigation on the Mississippi River, and that Portugal, the United States, and Spain were all deputizing legations to negotiate a settlement to the detriment of Great Britain.[15] Because Morris considered Miranda to be "deeply in the interest of Britain," his willingness to impart such bad news about his protector lent him credibility in Morris's eyes. Similarly, Miranda kept Henry Knox informed about public sentiment in Britain's capital as it might affect American interests.[16] Nevertheless, he was playing from both sides of the deck; Thomas Paine recalled the time when Miranda showed him some letters, one of which was a short note from Pitt confirming the payment of £1,200 for his services rendered in the Nootka Sound incident; once he realized just exactly what it was that Paine was reading, Miranda quickly snatched it back, saying, "O, that is not the letter I intended."[17]

Miranda nipped at Pitt's heels for almost two years before he could no longer ignore the obvious. Miranda was broke, kept on a shoe-string by a government that had no immediate intention to follow through on his plans, and felt keenly the humiliation of his position. Over time, he came to view Pitt as "an egotistical monster" whose evilness "supersedes that of Machiavelli" because he valued commercial interests above the American people's happiness.[18] Plea after plea went to the prime minister "to come to a deffinitive [sic] resolution upon the affairs in Question" because of the "uneasiness that such a long suspect [sic] ought to produce in my mind!"[19] Miranda's letters to Pitt became progressively more officious and betrayed a real tone of offense, until finally Miranda requested the return of all his papers in order to put an end to the whole "inconvenient" business.[20] Finally, all hint of Miranda's former friendship with Pitt was absent in his note of August 26, 1791, which read: "Col. de Miranda presents his most respectful Compliments to the Right] Hon[ourable] W. Pitt—requests the favour of an audience, to terminate his affairs in any Mode whatsoever; as the unfavourable terms to himself shall be more acceptable, than the personal Injury he has sustained in an involuntary Delay of moree [sic] than a year."[21] Pitt held all the power in their relationship; he was the prime minister of the most powerful nation in the Atlantic world, he held the purse strings, and he even controlled Miranda's ability to exit the country.

By early 1792, Miranda had given up hope that an English-led invasion of Venezuela would take place anytime soon. He was bitter and angry, to the point of making those around him uncomfortable. He sent a final note to Pitt on March 17, attacking the prime minister's integrity by saying that he had reneged on promises made in the name of his nation's people and that he had the temerity to claim that he had waylaid such important papers as the ones Miranda had confided to him personally.[22] Miranda was insulted to find that Pitt thought he was only after money when his sole wish had been for the liberty and happiness of his country. In his mind, their association was terminated. Miranda would leave England, with or without Pitt's permission. If the British would not let him fight for freedom in America, perhaps he could interest the French in his dream of extending liberty across the sea. But for Miranda it was a difficult decision to make. All his adult life he had felt drawn to Anglo-American forms of constitutional democracy and, despite his clear republican sympathies, he generally felt more sympathetic toward the monarchist British model rather than that of the United States; he did not believe Spanish America was ready for the responsibilities associated with a republic. Miranda had found much value in the French Enlightenment authors' ideas but, in the end, could not overcome his personal distaste for the French themselves. His diary is filled with derogatory references to the French; he once stated his agreement with novelist Pierre Choderlos de Laclos that the French nation had "passed from infancy to decrepitude without ever having reached maturity."[23] If he was ready to give up his London base and relocate to Paris, the man must have been very frustrated indeed. Miranda left Piccadilly station at 5:30 A.M. on

March 19, 1792, and slipped out of the country to join the French Revolution.[24]

Of course, the French had designs on America themselves, more specifically on Spanish possessions there. Since Miranda's previous visit to France, the pace of events had quickened and the Revolution

Miranda at the time of the French Revolution. Bibliothèque Nationale, Paris

had spread to its Haitian colony as well. The Estates-General had met in 1789, with the limited goals of fiscal reform and the presentation of grievances to the king. By June 17, in the face of King Louis XVI's intransigence and waffling, the members of the Third Estate, mainly merchants, professionals, and the emerging bourgeoisie, rose up and declared themselves to be a National Assembly. The king sponsored a ham-handed attempt to dismiss the new legislative body but relented after the mob stormed the Bastille fortress on July 14. In 1791, the Assembly approved the Declaration of the Rights of Man and Citizen, which created a constitutional monarchy and a single-chambered

Miranda as a general of the French Republic. Bibliothèque Nationale, Paris

Constituent Assembly and which required all clergy to take an oath of loyalty to the secular authorities. When certain liberal elements grouped in a society known as Les Amis des Noirs (The Friends of the Blacks) voted to extend equal rights of French citizenship to their overseas colonists, including mixed-race mulattos, the ideas of the French Revolution spread quickly to Haiti. On August 22, 1791,

50,000 enslaved Africans in Haiti, led by the voodoo priest Boukman, rose up and killed 2,000 whites and burned 180 sugar plantations in the infamous Night of Fire; the planters' vicious counterattack lasted for three weeks and left approximately 15,000 to 20,000 mulattos and Africans dead. For the next thirteen years, the French tried unsuccessfully to regain control of their most profitable colony, unleashing a bloody race war that struck fear into the elites of nearby slave societies in the southern United States, the Caribbean, and Spanish America. This was the fray into which Miranda stepped when he returned to France in the summer of 1792 to discuss his emancipation plan with interested moderates there.

The fateful meetings took place over several days in August 1792 at the home of the republican mayor of Paris, Jérôme Pétion de Villeneuve. Pétion had suggested to the minister of war, Joseph Servan, that Miranda should enter the French military service, an idea to which the minister was amenable except for the annoying detail that Miranda was a foreigner and the Revolution had already begun to turn xenophobic.[25] By August 22, Pétion had convinced Servan that the formalities could be worked out. The minister offered a position as field marshal in the Armies of France to Miranda, who found the idea "agreeable enough" but wished to be assured that his salary would continue to be paid after the war, since he would have to renounce "all my income from other parts" in order to accept the commission. Servan could offer no such guarantee but promised sweetly that "France could never forget the foreigner that was generously sacrificing himself under these circumstances." Miranda asked for some time to make his decision. For two days he wondered whether he ought to risk cutting his ties to England forever. He thought about Pitt and all his broken promises. He thought about the Spanish Crown, which monitored his every move. He thought about his friends in the distant United States, who were occupied with their own complicated affairs and not yet able to advance his cause. He thought about his Russian patron Catherine the Great, who was struggling against factions in her realm and realistically would not able to do much for him either.

There seemed to be nowhere else to turn. And so, on August 25, 1792, Miranda went to Servan and struck the fateful bargain; he agreed "to serve the cause of liberty with all that I had in my power and they, in the name of the French Nation, would defray the cost of my salary and employ me after the war, in preference to French officials, because as a foreigner my services are more meritorious under these circumstances." As a cosmopolitan citizen of the Atlantic world, Miranda could rationalize that his efforts to advance the cause of liberty in one nation were the same as fighting for liberty in another. Yet the demands that Miranda attached to his contract reveal that, even though he was temporarily shifting his energies, his ultimate focus remained on the project of Spanish American emancipation. He asked for the title of field marshal and a salary of 25,000 *livres*, which would be "enough to live honestly in France," but most significantly stated: "[I]t is necessary that the [Spanish American] cause be protected vigorously by France, and that I am permitted (the moment the occasion presents itself) to occupy myself principally in its happiness, establishing the liberty and independence of that country, to which I have attached myself voluntarily, and in which the United States and England have promised their assistance at the first possible conjuncture."[26] With that, the deed was done; he had signed away his soul to the very same French devils whose manners, affectations, and intrigues had so disgusted him during his European travels. He hoped it would not be a mistake.

In the month that followed Miranda's recruitment into the French army, conditions arose that would damage his credibility and set back his Spanish American cause for at least a decade. On September 1, the Provisional Executive Council confirmed his title of field marshal and lieutenant general based on the inaccurate understanding that he previously served as a brigadier general in the American Revolution.[27] Although it is unclear where this assumption originated, Miranda certainly did nothing to discourage it; eventually he would have to defend himself against charges of inflating his experience in order to deceive the French people about his qualifications. In the beginning, however, it seemed to be a good match. Miranda was well respected for the broad scope of his knowledge of tactics, weaponry, and military history, and he even took his precious collection of military books with him into the field. He had not, however, been in an actual combat situation for a over decade and had never fought a traditional ground war.

Francisco de Miranda, general of the Army of the North, 1792, by Arnaudet. Châteaux de Versailles et de Trianon, Versailles, France. © Réunion des Musées Nationaux/ Art Resource, New York

On September 11, 1792, Miranda joined Charles-François Dumouriez's forces, known as the Army of the North, which were battling Prussians and Austrians near the Belgian border. With Miranda in charge of its left flank, the Army of the North made consistent and daring advances and, for a time, was the soul of France. Dumouriez became a popular hero as he stormed first Valmy and then Jemappes. Yet these victories obscured his darker side. From the beginning, Dumouriez was a rogue element in the French army; he had both an inflated opinion of himself and a dangerous tendency to flout author- ity when he thought he knew better. For example, his aide-de-camp Thiébault recalled that Dumouriez's action in late 1792, "in spite of the orders from the Government and the opinion of all the other generals in the army, was the saving of France."[28] This sort of independent judgment could be tolerated, even overlooked, as long as the French forces remained victorious; when the tide started to turn against the French forces, however, Dumouriez's contempt for the central authorities' wishes was less well received.

In the early days, Commander in Chief Dumouriez was delighted with the abilities of his subordinate Miranda. Servan and Pétion were also pleased with Miranda's decision to join their Revolution and his successful efforts to help spread liberty beyond their borders. In 1792, the possibilities for the French Revolution's advance seemed limitless. In November, Jacques Pierre Brissot de Warville, a leading member of the centrist Gironde majority in the National Convention, wrote to Dumouriez: "This Revolution must be made in Spain and Spanish America. All must coincide. The fate of this last Revolution depends on one Man alone; you know him, you esteem him, you love him; it is Miranda. . . . Although the Ministers were at a loss recently to replace Desparbes at Saint Domingue [Haiti]—a sudden thought occurred to me; I say *appoint Miranda* . . . I am certain that his appointment will strike Spain with Fear and curse Pitt with his dilatory Politics."[29]

Indeed, Brissot had a scheme already worked out in which Miranda could have his Spanish American revolution, as long as he did not mind leading the "turbulent Whites" to become "the Idol of the people of Colour." After he had done France's bidding in Hispaniola, Miranda would be free to undertake his long-desired incursion to the Spanish Main. Pierre Vergniaud, a member of the Convention's Commission on Colonies, was also pleased at the propaganda coup of having Miranda join the French Revolution, telling him:

> Every man owes himself to his country, General. No one knows this sacred maxim better than you. Every good citizen should indicate the persons who he knows are able to serve the public welfare usefully, that is what decided me to write to several representatives that in the present circumstances you alone were capable of governing the colony of Santo Domingo, not only because you are both a great General and a good republican, but because you know better than anyone else the Spanish character and customs, and you will be able to inspire in them the great-

est confidence, when they would regard any other as a conquering enemy, and consequently with the greatest distrust.[30]

Miranda was aware that his acceptance of such a commission would
provoke both Spain and England. Yet he also knew that he was no
expert on the French Caribbean; the plan seemed unworkable to
him, but he agreed to come to Paris in order to talk about the matter
further.[31]

*General La Morlière receiving the surrender of the citadel of Anvers on November 28,
1792, by Félix Philippoteaux.* Châteaux de Versailles et de Trianon, Versailles,
France. © Réunion des Musées Nationaux/Art Resource, New York

In fact, Miranda was willing to talk with anyone who would listen. While Brissot was grooming him to spread the French Revolution to the Caribbean, Miranda continued to write to Knox and
Hamilton about the future of "our dear Country America from the
North to the South" and to remind them of the plans they had made
together at their symposia in Boston a decade earlier. He warned them
that William Steuben Smith would bring coded plans that would "shew
[*sic*] how things are grown ripe & into maturity for the Execution of
those grand & beneficial projects we had in contemplation at New
Yorck [*sic*] the love of our Country exalted in our minds with those

Ideas, for the sake of unfortunate Columbia." America should be ruled by Americans. Americans should aid Americans.[32]

The Brissotin plan to send Miranda to the Caribbean theater in 1792 came to naught, and the field marshal returned to the Army of the North in time for the occupation of Antwerp, the Belgian city that had capitulated on November 29. Miranda's immediate goal was to restore order and begin to implement the sort of republican liberty for which he thought he had been fighting; to him that meant establishing a participatory and representative government under the rule of law, and imposing strict integrity in officials' activities. Toward those ends, Miranda issued circular letters ordering his commanders to both protect and assist Citizen Pierre Chépy, who had been sent from Paris to investigate charges of corruption among the Northern army. Furthermore, they were to move quickly to "maintain order and tranquility and procure for the People the means by which they can name their own Representatives."[33] He was not above placing a levy on the newly liberated Belgian citizens, however. French troops desperately needed funds to continue their advance because the National Convention in Paris had none left to spare. By December 26, Miranda sent a message to Antwerp's leaders demanding "a loan of £300,000 in the name of the French People, in order to cover the costs of the garrison and the fortification of this place."[34]

As winter melted into spring, the terrain became inhospitable; rain, snow, and constant marching had made the roads impassable and the soldiers found themselves covered in "chalky slush."[35] In January, Dumouriez traveled to Paris for consultations with the government and left Miranda in charge of the Army of the North in his absence. On February 13, acting commander in chief Miranda issued a rousing circular letter to "his brave brother armies" informing them that the National Convention had declared war on England and the Netherlands for "their acts of hostility and aggression, in hatred of our holy Liberty." He appealed to the "[c]ourage, union, discipline, and watchfulness" that had allowed them to vanquish the despots and closed his patriotic letter with the first lines of "La Marseillaise": *"Allons, enfants de la Patrie, le jour de gloire est arrivé"* (Forward, children of the Fatherland, the day of glory has arrived).[36] The National Convention ordered Miranda to lay siege to Maastricht with his exhausted and undersupplied troops, and he obediently began to organize his 15,000 men into position on February 21.

By March 1, the Austrians had smashed through French lines and maneuvered 35,000 well-fed and well-equipped troops into counterposition. Miranda and the French forces were vastly outmatched. His men broke ranks and retreated in all directions in a most disorganized manner. Miranda and General Valence gathered the forces that they could and reassembled at Louvain, but it was too late. The damage was done. More than 100,000 demoralized peasant conscripts from Miranda's battalion and the others simply quit and went home in time for the planting season. Dumouriez returned and managed to wrestle Tirlemont from the Austrians on March 15 but, after hearing of the mass desertions and fearing a loss of morale back in Paris, he made the fateful calculation that what the Revolution needed to reenergize itself was a single great and decisive battle.[37] His decision to stage an attack on Neerwinden, therefore, was made for political reasons rather than being based on sound military strategy. It was a thorough disaster. French forces were trapped, broke ranks, and fled in all directions. In his *Memoirs*, Dumouriez asserted that the battle would have been won easily if only the coward Miranda had held his position at the bridges of Orsmaël and Neerhelpen; instead, Dumouriez blamed his "foreign" general for allowing an "inconceivable" retreat, and not bothering to pass on a single message to his fellow commanders about the changed circumstances, an omission that he claimed cost the French a further 2,000 men.[38]

Of course, there was more than enough blame to go around. General Custine, for example, operated with his usual rhodomontades. General Valence's experienced opinions were discounted as the ruminations of a doddering old fool. But it was his beloved General Miranda who bore the brunt of Dumouriez's criticism. On March 19, Dumouriez wrote to the new minister of war Jean-Nicolas Pache, that Miranda and General Champmorin both had performed miserably and fled the battle at Neerwinden in a disorganized and dishonorable fashion.[39] Thiébault echoed these sentiments, saying that Neerwinden had been planned beautifully but executed badly; as Dumouriez's aide-de-camp, he was of the opinion that "Miranda, who ought to have held his positions against the attacking force, committed not only the error of letting his troops get out of hand . . . but also the grave mistake" of failing to notify Dumouriez of their defection.[40] Similarly, Paul François Jean Nicolas, Vicomte de Barras, a radical leftist politician, thought that "this Peruvian general, the most intriguing of Europeans, was a most gifted man; his memory is not to be conceived; he could speak every language, discoursed cleverly about war, but knew not the way to wage it, as he had demonstrated in Belgium in 1793."[41] Not everyone agreed, however; Jean-Baptiste Louvet de Couvray, a pudgy, bespectacled moderate Gironde deputy in the National Convention, believed "Miranda was in all regards irreproachable . . . and that the plans sent from Paris were too risky and therefore appropriately modified by him."[42] Equal contempt emanated from both camps. Dumouriez was jealous of Miranda and charged him with insubordination along the lines of a contemporary Brutus; Miranda firmly believed that Dumouriez had sacrificed him and his men for no justifiable end at Neerwinden.

Back in Paris, the Revolution was taking a dangerous turn. Manipulated by Maximilien Robespierre and the more radical Jacobin faction within the National Convention, Miranda's Gironde patrons found themselves attacked on all sides. Robespierre was almost maniacally paranoid, harboring suspicions that William Pitt and the Prussian king were plotting an invasion of France. As Robespierre's Reign of Terror began to make itself felt, dissenting opinion was increasingly interpreted as counterrevolutionary and all foreigners were suspected to be enemies of the French people. Miranda, a popular, independent-minded liberal Venezuelan appointed by the Gironde, became caught up in the dense web of Parisian political intrigue. The matter was made even more complicated because Dumouriez himself actually was a counterrevolutionary who harbored monarchist sympathies. He had been angry that the Convention failed to provide adequate funds for the French army and had initiated a conspiracy to march on Paris in order to overthrow them and restore a branch of the Bourbon family to power. Before Neerwinden, Dumouriez had tried to recruit Miranda into his plot, but the Venezuelan flatly refused to have anything to do with the coup and threatened to send warnings to his friends in the Convention. After the disastrous battle, the treacherous general in chief concocted a plan with Georges-Jacques

Danton, a Jacobin deputy sent to investigate rumors of Dumouriez's sedition, to pin the blame on Miranda in order to clear his own name and remove a potentially damaging rival in the process.

Miranda appeared before the National Convention on March 29, 1793, and made a long, detailed, occasionally stirring, speech.[43] It was not enough to placate the Jacobins, who wished to use Miranda's case as a example to weaken the Girondin members' influence as the power struggle between the two factions worsened. At 8 P.M. on Monday, April 8, 1793, Miranda presented himself before a special session of the War Committee. For the next three days, his interrogators asked him a series of sixty-three technical questions, mostly dealing with provisions, tactical decisions, communications networks, and the precautionary measures he had taken to protect French troops. When asked why he had attacked Maastricht, Miranda replied that he had received a written order from Dumouriez to which he "conformed exactly"; luckily, his lifelong habit of maintaining an archive of all his papers allowed him to produce documents that supported his claim. Miranda explained that he did not have "the authority to do anything other than that which my orders prescribed for me, as the Executive Council made it clear that I should execute all that General in Chief Dumouriez orders me to do, as he has sole charge of the conduct of military affairs." Furthermore, he was not able to augment his troops "without disobeying the orders of the General in Chief." General Valence was also ranked above him in seniority, and Miranda occasionally had to defer to his judgment and wishes. When asked if he had ever thought that he would be able to defeat Maastricht through a simple bombardment, Miranda replied simply, "I never thought so personally, but the General [Dumouriez] did, and consequently he gave me those orders." Miranda entered into evidence Dumouriez's written order to "attack from the right between Orsmäel and La Chapelle de Béthanie with your troops and those of General Champmorin" so that the enemy would be outflanked. As the disastrous events proved, that did not happen.[44]

Responding to Dumouriez's charge that he had absented himself from battle like a coward, Miranda vociferously replied that he never spent a moment away from his headquarters except for the morning that the siege was lifted when he dared to go out to the heights to reconnoiter the scene. Trying to explain the situation that precipitated the disorganized retreat from Neerwinden, Miranda reported that the enemy had a far more advantageous position, that the French forces fought valiantly for three hours, but were seriously outmatched; the inexperienced and terrified peasants broke ranks and fled in confusion. Miranda, who was always supportive of his troops, told the Committee that if there was any fault to be found, it certainly was not with the simple soldiers who "when well-led, cover themselves in glory . . . I do not pretend to excuse the infamous disorder and pillaging by troops led by bad commanders . . . but the principal cause of the disorder falls on the General-in-Chief who did not apply the necessary remedies, or the means that could have been employed to prevent such an occurrence."

The Committee asked Miranda straightforward questions intended to assess the field activities and behaviors of a ragtag army comprised of under supplied and undertrained volunteers; they appear neither to have been thirsting for his blood nor anxious to have Miranda condemn others to save himself. Instead, the overall impression that emerges from Miranda's testimony before the War Committee is that of a skilled general doing the best he could under difficult circumstances. He showed himself to be respectful of his fellow commanders' efforts, albeit critical of Dumouriez's judgment, and it is clear from his responses that Miranda felt isolated and frustrated throughout the whole campaign. Not until the final five questions did the Committee ask Miranda about Dumouriez's political sympathies, foreshadowing the paranoid direction in which the Revolution soon headed. When questioned whether he had ever heard Dumouriez issue any opinions about the Assembly itself, Miranda responded simply, "Yes, often I have heard him say that half of the members are imbeciles and the other half are scoundrels."

The contentious affair continued through the rest of April and into May 1793, taking on aspects of a public relations battle as well. Dumouriez and his partisans blamed Miranda for the failures at Neerwinden and, more ominously, hinted that his untrustworthiness was due to his status as a foreigner. Miranda's camp issued their own printed counterattack, which was subsequently translated and disseminated in an English edition throughout the Atlantic world. In it,

Miranda stated that he fully expected to be cleared officially of the specious charges but, "Till then, I rely on the justice of my country and submit the following Correspondence to the unbiassed [*sic*] judgment of Public Opinion."[45] Significantly, both sides sought support beyond the French borders and throughout the Atlantic world for their interpretation of events. The *Pennsylvania Gazette* reprinted Dumouriez's letters that blamed Miranda for the defeat and retreat, calling his version "the best account yet arrived of the situation."[46] Miranda retaliated by reprinting Dumouriez's orders to attack (and then quickly retreat from) both Maastricht and Neerwinden, commenting that the commander in chief's "very inaccurate statements of the action can neither change the nature of facts nor adulterate truth." Miranda also published his letter to Deputy Pétion in which he had proven his loyalty to the Convention by exposing Dumouriez's secret plot. He warned the deputy that "I can tell you . . . those persons have made indirect proposals with great art and caution, highly offensive to my patriotism and my unshaken love for liberty . . . I even believe there is a cabal to get rid of me, as they wished to do to you before the 10th of August." Miranda would commit nothing further to paper.[47]

The Convention named a Revolutionary Criminal Tribunal, composed of five judges, a jury, and a public prosecutor, which conducted a full investigation into the charges against Miranda in May 1793. Its hearings were open to the public, and Miranda was kept in the Conciergerie, a sort of holding facility, while the proceedings took place. His defense lawyer, Claude-François Chaveau-Lagarde, has been described as "a brilliant, courageous, very remarkable advocate who had the audacity to contest with the mob for the lives of many."[48] Chaveau-Lagarde's unpopular clients eventually included Queen Marie Antoinette, Gironde leader Jacques-Pierre Brissot, and Charlotte Corday, the royalist assassin who stabbed radical Jacobin leader Jean-Paul Marat to death in his bathtub. Miranda, of course, was the star witness at his own trial; one observer said, "[Miranda] pleaded his case with such sublime energy as proved that his powers as an orator were not inferior to his talents as a general."[49] Thomas Paine, Joel Barlow, and Thomas Christie all agreed to vouch for Miranda's character at the trial. Thomas Christie, who was the local agent for the

English firm of Turnbull and Forbes, affirmed that "Miranda did not come to France as a necessitous adventurer; but [I believe] that he came from public spirited motives." Thomas Paine agreed. He told the tribunal: "It is impossible for one man to know another man's heart as he knows his own, but from all that I know of General Miranda, I cannot believe that he wanted to betray the confidence which the republic has placed in him, especially because the destiny of the French Revolution was intimately linked with the favored object of his heart, the deliverance of Spanish America—an object for which he has been pursued and persecuted by the Spanish Court during the greatest part of his life."[50]

Years later, when asked of his impressions of Miranda, Paine recalled that "his leading object was and had been the emancipation of his country, Mexico."[51] Because of his well-known republican and populist sympathies, Paine was one of only two foreigners (the other was Anacharsis Cloots) to take a seat in the National Convention; Paine did not, however, vote for the king's execution and rightly feared the increasing violence and radicalization that he witnessed around him. As one biographer noted, "the day the Convention voted to try Miranda, Paine abandoned hope for the French Revolution."[52] Before long, the famous republican author of the *Rights of Man* and *Common Sense* would also be arrested and put in a Luxembourg prison without fair representation or hope of appeal.[53]

As leading counsel for the defense when Miranda's trial for "high treason and complicity with the General in Chief Dumouriez" opened, Chaveau-Lagarde addressed his words to the "citizen jurors."[54] He noted that it was an extraordinary thing that a man known for his devotion to liberty should be persecuted by despotism "from one pole to another." As proof of his international reputation, Chaveau-Lagarde listed the virtuous men who had recommended Miranda, a veritable who's who of the eighteenth-century Atlantic world including Benjamin Franklin, George Washington, Alexander Hamilton, General Moultrie, Nathanael Greene, Thomas Paine, Samuel Adams, Lord Melville, Joseph Priestley, Charles James Fox, and many notable others. As evidence that Miranda could not have conspired with "his mortal enemy, the liberticide Dumouriez," Chaveau-Lagarde adopted a biographical approach, showing how Miranda had sacrificed his fortune, personal ambition, and private loves in the name of liberty. Yet instead of becoming bitter, Miranda was "happy because he has the opportunity to render to his fellow-citizens an honorable account of his conduct."[55]

Turning his attention to the weeks preceding the catastrophe at Neerwinden, Chaveau-Lagarde described Dumouriez's schemes for the conquest of the Low Countries as "worthy of a filibuster," a ridiculous operation undertaken for the general in chief's personal interests at the expense of the French army. He then pulled out a letter from Miranda to General Lambert dated January 1793, which warned that the Army of the North was being used for illegitimate, aggressive campaigns unrelated to the peaceful protection of liberty. When Dumouriez ordered him to take Maastricht, Miranda had no choice but to obey; even so, he took the prudent measure of writing to the War Ministry for clarification of their goals and policies.[56] In March 1793, Miranda told Dumouriez that the army belonged to the Republic, not to his personal or individual whims. When the order came from Paris to arrest Generals Lanoue, Stengel, and Valence, Dumouriez hissed that he could just as easily add Miranda's name to the list, but Chaveau-Lagarde told the jury, "that brave man [Miranda] replied *as a loyal servant of the Republic, he would obey no law that was not addressed to him.*" When Dumouriez ordered their outnumbered and outflanked troops to attack, Miranda protested that the orders were "contrary to the rules of [military] arts."[57]

Chaveau-Lagarde rested his case on May 15, leaving the jury free to follow their conscience. In his summation, he stressed Miranda's extreme self-abnegation, telling the rapt audience that the lawyer "had to force [Miranda] to give me details so that I could defend him, like Socrates after his arrest."[58] It was in no way possible that he and Dumouriez were accomplices, as the latter was "*an intriguing courtesan, an ambitious and vain swashbuckler, a false and vile man.*" There was no chance that Miranda would be complicit in a conspiracy with such a man, nor could he be blamed for a failed outcome because "the art of war is an art of conjecture."[59] The battle of Neerwinden was destined to fail because the general in chief ordered it without sufficient information and against both reason and the rules of war, forcing his troops to fight against both the terrain and superior artillery.

Not only did Miranda not issue these flawed orders, he actively opposed them, just as the patriotic Roman general Manlius Torquatus had done when he patriotically slew his own son for disobeying an order by staging an unauthorized attack that dragged Rome into an unwanted war.

The jury came back with a unanimous verdict. Miranda was declared innocent of all charges against him. The chamber erupted into enthusiastic applause; even the nasty state prosecutor Antoine Quentin Focquier-Tinville joined in the celebration. Praise for Miranda's patriotism poured forth from all quarters. British expatriate author Helena Maria Williams lauded his actions because "his personal friendship for Dumouriez did not lead him to forget that his first duty was towards that country which had entrusted him with its defense."[60] The Bishop of Antwerp believed that "wherever the General Miranda will go, he will be followed by the respect and all the admiration due to notable talents; for he is the man of letters, the philosopher full of courtesy as well as of vast knowledge, the brilliant leader."[61] Miranda retired to a house on the outskirts of Paris where he intended to recover from the trial amid his books and growing art collection. Unfortunately, events soon overtook his plans. At the end of May, the radical Jacobins successfully wrested control of the National Convention from the moderate Gironde. On July 10 the most famous Jacobins, among them Louis de Saint-Just, Georges Couthon, Lazare Carnot, and Maximilien Robespierre, formed the so-called Great Committee, which quickly moved to consolidate its own brutal hold on power. Along with the Committee of Public Safety, the Great Committee instituted the Reign of Terror and ruled France as a virtual military dictatorship for over a year; during that time several thousand suspected enemies of the state were guillotined.

On July 5 the Committee of Public Safety ordered Miranda's rearrest along with many of his Gironde friends and protectors in the National Convention. Robespierre personally hauled Miranda before the Committee and charged him with being "the chief defender and abettor of the Gironde and Girondism." One sympathetic friend believed that Robespierre's animosity toward Miranda was caused by "that general hatred which he bore towards all men of talents . . . [thinking] that the existence of such a man was dangerous to his own."⁶² Yet Miranda's actions seemed calculated to invite the radicals' wrath. He commented pointedly, and in print, that "I have always carried the cult of liberty in my heart. For this cause I have lived. Consequently it is enough for me to be a friend of freedom, without any theatrical displays of my sentiments. Those who love the people, both by nature and by principle, are *not always the ones who shout endlessly* about their devotion to the common man."⁶³ Those who shouted endlessly were, of course, the radical Jacobins, who claimed to act in the name of the people while sending them to their grue-some deaths. The second time he was arrested, Miranda was spared the trouble of a trial and was packed off to La Force prison without even being sure of the nature of the charges against him.

While entombed in La Force prison, daily expecting to be taken to the guillotine, Miranda passed the time reading, saying that he "endeavoured to forget his present situation in the study of history and science."⁶⁴ One fellow prisoner, patriot editor Luc-Antoine Champagneux, recalled: "Interesting conversation, varied and pro-found knowledge, and the principles of an austere virtue made me prefer Miranda's company to that of almost all other prisoners . . . his studies concentrated principally on the science of war . . . and I can say that I never have heard a discussion with any other person on that subject with so much depth and substance."⁶⁵ Other jailhouse com-panions included Girondins Pierre Vergniaud, Charles-Éléonore Dufriche-Valazé, and the former Marquis Achille Duchâtelet; the men took tea together each evening in order to discuss the books they had read during the day, "avoiding as much as possible the subject of poli-tics, which affected them too deeply."⁶⁶ Both Miranda and Duchâtelet had procured poison tablets that they swore they would take rather than let themselves be dragged to the guillotine. One by one, Miranda's French friends met unpleasant and unnatural deaths as the Terror grew in fury. Jean-Marie Roland died a suicide; his wife Madame Roland, Pierre Vergniaud, and Jacques-Pierre Brissot all were guillo-tined; and poor Jérôme Pétion's corpse was found in the countryside, half eaten by wolves.⁶⁷

Miranda directed several petitions to the Convention, protesting his innocence and sending documentary proof. He never received a response. Even when Robespierre "the Incorruptible" fell from power at the end of July 1794 during the so-called Thermidorean Reaction that ended the Reign of Terror, Miranda remained in prison. Hoping to take advantage of the changing political climate, he approached the reconstituted Convention with another open letter sent on August 7, in which he claimed to be a victim of "the perfidious influence of the infamous Robespierre."[68] Still, no reply. In mid-September, prison conditions began to take their toll on his health and Miranda was placed in the infirmary. By autumn, several notable persons felt secure enough to take up the ailing man's cause. Urged by the newly-appointed U.S. ambassador to France, James Monroe, and by Thomas Paine and his other prominent international friends, the Convention agreed to debate Miranda's case. His allies argued eloquently that Miranda was indeed a guiltless friend of liberty who had been wrongly imprisoned by a jealous Robespierre; his detractors claimed he was a Spanish spy and a closet monarchist who wished for a Bourbon restoration in France. On January 4, 1795, Miranda sent another angry open letter to the "Representatives of the French People," denouncing his illegal confinement. He hated the "execrable maxim of Couthon and Robespierre which holds that *individual rights must be sacrificed to the public interest*, this is the base on which they build their tyranny." The Committee had charged him with every contradictory ideological crime imaginable: joining the Dumouriez conspiracy but also acting disloyally toward Dumouriez; first espousing federalism, then Capetism (monarchism, derived from King Louis's surname, Capet), then being a republican but not a sufficiently revolutionary one. It was all nonsense, Miranda said. In the end, he was nothing less than a French citizen who ardently loved liberty, who had been promised a decent salary for his efforts and yet had been repaid only with persecution and imprisonment, "in the name of *Public Safety and without just cause* . . . What a country!"[69]

After much debate, the Committee of Public Safety ordered Miranda's release on January 15, 1795. He left La Force prison with his head still attached (he was luckier than most in that regard), and brashly took up residence near the Rue St. Honoré at the center of political Paris. His first tasks were to request the return of his personal effects, including all books and manuscripts, and to arrange for the public circulation of his open letters. Because of his long opposition to the Terror's extremism, Miranda was a popular public figure, attractive to liberal men and women alike. He engaged in a relationship with the pretty but troubled Delphine de Custine, who was the wife of a fellow general and a former lover of the Comte de Ségur. As usual, the romance was more serious on her part than his.[70] His magnetic personal qualities aside, it is not difficult to imagine why Miranda appealed to women with liberal inclinations. In 1792 he had criticized an all-male National Convention that was willing to extend civic membership to people of color but not to women. He wrote to Pétion, "To my way of thinking, I recommend just *one thing*, wise legislator: the *women* . . . Why is it that in a democratic government, fully half of the individuals, the women, are neither directly nor indirectly represented although they are subjected to the same severity of the law? Why can they not be consulted at least in the laws that concern them most (marriage, divorce, girls' education etc)? I must confess that all these things seem to me to be strange oversights and worthy of consideration on the part of our wise legislators."[71] For all the historical snickering about Miranda's reputation as a slippery Lothario type, it is to his credit that he was one of the very few eighteenth-century men who were able to perceive that liberal ideals logically extended into the realm of something approaching more equal gender relations in the public sphere as well.

Linking his personal liberty with that of humanity as a whole, Miranda continued to fight for the true nature of the French Revolution. He lashed out at the excesses of the Terror in a daring political pamphlet called *Opinion du général Miranda sur la situation actuelle de la France et sur les remèdes convenables à ses maux* (Opinion of General Miranda on the Current Condition of France, and the Remedies for Her Troubles) which he released symbolically on the anniversary of the American Revolution, July 4, 1795.[72] This work was a curious mixture of political ideology and personal justification, a highly revealing essay in which Miranda linked his own persecution with that of all the French people; this sort of hubris is typical of exiles who demand that "the world shall take notice" of their plight and their greatness.[73] In his *Opinion*, Miranda wrote:

The first duty of all good citizens is to come to the aid of the fatherland when it is in danger. After the terrible shocks brought on by atrocious tyranny and anarchy which is undermining France, the only hope for the majority of the nation and the great friends of liberty, is to be found in the union of clear-minded and virtuous men who, by their insight and energy can save [the Revolution]. Place hope in the magnanimity of those such as myself who are victims of the Terror [who can] set aside their outrage and sacrifice their individual resentments in the name of the general interest, so that they may sustain liberty when it becomes dangerously threatened.[74]

Clearly Miranda saw himself as the embodiment not just of the French people, but of all those who would fight for liberty wherever tyrants existed. His 23-page manifesto explicitly condemned the arbitrariness of the current government, which seemed to have forgotten that it was the servant of the people that it claimed to represent. Instead he called them "assassins," "brigands," and "evil tyrants" who used calculated violence to inspire terror and obedience when they should have brought peace, order, and happiness. Miranda openly opposed the expansionist goals of Paul François Jean Nicolas Barras and his favorite general, Napoleon Bonaparte, suggesting instead that the best way to spread liberty was to set a desirable example that others would wish to emulate; he knew that war and conquest would only create resentments and make enemies. Similarly, he opposed any branch of authority that was left unchecked. He recommended that the various branches of government be kept separate, each charged with oversight of the others. Furthermore, he wrote, each individual citizen had a sacred duty to monitor the government and to act "vigorously on his own behalf." In this way, no single person or cabal could dominate the social body, but such an approach also placed a high burden of responsibility on individuals' virtues.

Miranda's public words carried a great deal of authority in Paris because of his close personal association with U.S. and British governmental leaders, his extensive travels, and his academic studies. He was also one of the few voices willing to criticize the excesses of the Terror openly. In March 1795 he sent copies of his publications to be circulated in America, reminding Henry Knox of "my sentiments for our dear *Colombia*, as well as for all my friends in that part of the world, which has not changed the least bit" despite the evil turn of events that had caused the downfall of liberty in France.[75] Nevertheless, judged by the ideas expressed in his *Opinion*, Miranda stands closer to the aristocratic traditions of England than to the more egalitarian conception of democracy espoused in the United States. In a sense, he argued for a meritocracy, or at least a civic virtuocracy. He favored "*One* or *two* men of quality at the head of the executive power who ardently desire the happiness of the nation," who would appoint six ministers of talent and genius to help administer the land. One potential model was the Athenian Senate, a body that proposed laws to the People's Assembly, which could then adopt or reject them.[76] He did, however, suggest that in contemporary times it might be useful and fair to allow the popular chambers also to table legislation for debate.

Miranda's short but sharp-edged pamphlet hit its target. The new executive governing body of France, the five-member Directory, could not fail to realize that his words were a direct assault on themselves and their predecessors; disturbingly, Miranda's personal popularity and the brisk sales of his *Opinion* seemed to indicate that his sentiments were shared by many. He continued to receive invitations to the best Parisian soirées, including one at Julie Talmy's home where the rising young Napoleon Bonaparte pronounced Miranda to be a saner incarnation of Don Quixote. Napoleon apparently rebuffed Miranda's dinner invitations, and there was no great affinity between the two military men. The ambitious Corsican believed that Miranda was a spy for either the Spanish or the British, albeit one with "a sacred fire burning in his soul."[77] At one point in late summer, Miranda's former patron Joseph Servan resurrected the idea that the Venezuelan might be sent to govern the island of Saint Domingue, but the proposal never gained much momentum and then was made moot by the ever-changing Parisian political climate.

In early October 1795, officials uncovered a royalist conspiracy centered around the French National Theater. Apparently, constitutional monarchists had expected that the fall of Robespierre in 1794 and the promulgation of a new constitution in 1795 would allow them to regain some representation in the Convention; on August 22, however, sitting members passed a decree that required at least two-thirds of the next Convention's delegates to be drawn from the current membership, thus circumventing the loss of their legislative control through free elections. The moderates and monarchists were outraged and plotted revenge. On October 5, the "Day of Sections," street violence erupted and over 300 people were killed when the National Guard joined the protesters. Although Miranda cooperated with the government to put down the rebels, his enemies nonetheless used this as an opportunity to resurrect old rumors and smear him once again. The Convention ordered Miranda's rearrest on October 21, 1795, as a coconspirator in what has come to be known as the Vendémiaire Plot. He went into hiding on the outskirts of Paris.

Because he was left in an untenable position, a wanted man without any consistent means of financial support, Miranda found himself consorting with some unsavory characters. While he was proscribed from Paris, he took up with a low-level official in the Ministry of Foreign Affairs named Louis Dupérou. Miranda was finally captured at the end of November, interrogated, and released. Although he himself requested that the Council of Five Hundred permit him a proper and public trial to answer their charges, the Directory apparently wished to avoid further publicity and instead dusted off an old law that could be invoked to expel troublesome foreigners. They demanded that Miranda leave the country and "gave him twenty-four hours wherein to leave Paris and the territory of the Republic."[78] He stalled for time, pretending to put his affairs in order and to gather up his belongings under constant police surveillance, all the while protesting that the order of expulsion was not only unconstitutional but illegal; Servan had granted Miranda the protection of full French citizenship when he entered the service in 1792. Officials disagreed; Barras thought that he and the Directory had treated Miranda gently, considering that he was "deeply implicated" in the Vendémiaire Plot. Helena Maria Williams remarked scornfully that "Miranda was ambitious, but he was scarcely a royalist."[79] When the gendarmes knocked at her door one evening after dinner with an arrest order from the Directory, Miranda tiptoed out the back door and left his embarrassed hostess to stammer some sort of an explanation. He returned to the countryside and lived clandestinely until the Directory lifted the decree of expulsion on April 25, 1796.

The Arc de Triomphe, Paris. Photo by Karen Racine

Miranda's name inscribed on the Arc de Triomphe, along with other officers of the Army of the North. Photo by Karen Racine

Miranda kept up an active correspondence throughout his political persecutions and viewed his own fate as being inextricably bound up with that of oppressed peoples everywhere. He watched with nervousness as Napoleon Bonaparte rose rapidly through the military's ranks and took the Revolution's forces in an openly imperialistic direction. He condemned this sort of cultural arrogance for the detrimental moral effects it had on the conquered people, the loss of their public artifacts, and the destruction of their liberty and independence. In a voluminous exchange with Antoine C. Quatremère de Quincy, a well-known art historian and rigid academic from the ancien régime, Miranda discussed the sad fate of historical monuments in Italy under the invading French forces, and the demise of Continental art in general under the Terror. Quatremère de Quincy had also been imprisoned in the wake of the Vendémiaire Plot. He published a 74-page booklet that came to be known as the *Lettres à Miranda* (Letters to Miranda) in July 1796 in which he outlined "the prejudice that has caused the displacement of artistic monuments in Italy, the dismemberment of its schools, and the destruction of its galleries, museums, and collections."[80] Since his tour of the United States more than a decade earlier, Miranda understood the value of public art and memory (the accurate preservation of the Bunker Hill battlefield site, for example), and recognized that these important places and pieces were part of humanity's international cultural heritage. One nation did not have the right to destroy or restrict access to the great accomplishments of another. France did not have the right to do it in Italy, and Spain did not have a right to cordon off and deny access to its American colonies either.

By 1797, Miranda had clearly become disillusioned with the French Revolution and turned his thoughts back to his old friends in Britain and the United States. When yet another coup occurred in September 1797 and Miranda found himself listed among those undesirable persons about to be deported to French Guiana, he decided to leave France voluntarily. By that time he had concluded that he needed solid evidence of a legitimate political constituency if he hoped for better luck with Prime Minister Pitt the second time around. Accordingly, Miranda and a small group of like-minded Spanish Americans met in Paris in December 1797, declared themselves rep-

resentatives of their various regions, and signed an official petition to
be presented to Pitt as proof of Spanish America's desire for self-
determination; in actual fact, the signatories represented only themselves in this so-called Paris Convention. Venezuelan Miranda,
Peruvian José Godoy del Pozo y Sucre, and Chilean Manuel José de
Salas signed the treaty, with French fellow-traveler Louis Dupérou
witnessing the act as secretary.[81] Others in Miranda's expatriate Paris
circle, including Peruvian Pablo de Olavide, Cuban Pedro José Caro,
and Venezuelans Francisco Iznardi and Ignacio Bejarano, may have
contributed to the scheme but did not sign the final document.[82] The
Act of Paris contained several specific instructions, all debated and
unanimously sanctioned by America's three self-appointed representatives, including:

1. Full independence to be secured by a treaty of friendship and alliance
with Great Britain;
    2. A guarantee of maritime protection and military assistance to be
repaid with thirty million pounds sterling immediately after independence and the rest with precious metals over an agreed span;
    3. Ideological alliances between the United States, Great Britain, and
Spanish America against "the detestable maxims professed by the French
Republic";
    4. A commercial treaty on terms most favorable to the British na-
tion, including exclusive rights to a canal route through Central America
for a specified period; and
    5. The request that Miranda head any military forces based in America
by virtue of his extensive experience and patriotism.[83]

The Act of Paris was a stunning document, not only because of
its obvious professionalism and its very early date, but because of its
clear goals, its informed assessment of European power relations,
and its intended British audience. Fifteen years later, when legiti-
mately appointed Spanish American envoys came to London to petition the British government for the same sorts of things, they did so
using strikingly similar language.[84] Pitt already felt threatened by
French expansionism and so the signatories ordered Miranda and
Olavide, as "delegates to the Junta of Deputies of the people and Provinces of *América Meridional*," to proceed to London first but if no
positive reception was to be found there, to proceed immediately to

Philadelphia to shop their plans around there. In this way, they played upon Pitt's apprehensions of the North Americans' designs as well.[85] The balance of power had shifted and, after years of experience in the thicket of Parisian politics, Miranda had learned how to exploit it to his advantage.

Miranda had always hoped that he could interest the British in his scheme. Several of his friends recalled his partiality to that country, its culture, and its governmental forms. His French cellmate Luc-Antoine Champagneux was a little hurt to find that Miranda "always seemed to me to esteem us little, and that he preferred the English. . . . He also spoke with admiration for the heroes who had fought for liberty in North America. . . . In general, I observed that Miranda had a predilection for just and virtuous men."[86] The Paris document quickly circulated among the hallways of power throughout the Atlantic world. President John Adams of the United States received a copy on August 25, 1798, in a bundle of letters from Timothy Pickering, his secretary of state.[87] Miranda and Caro sent similar packages to Alexander Hamilton and General Henry Knox. With some overstatement, Miranda told Hamilton he would wait impatiently for a reply because "[t]his is the greatest and most glorious object that has ever been presented to the world." Miranda clearly linked this matter of "great importance to the future of my Fatherland and very interesting as well for the prosperity of your own."[88]

The Paris Convention of 1797 was important because it reveals two key things about Miranda's evolving American identity. First, he realized that an American constituency was an essential prerequisite for action in modern politics, mainly to placate Pitt at that point, but also to govern successfully in the long term. Second, while in Europe Miranda began to work with other South Americans from across the continent, thereby broadening both his movement and his perception of the challenges that faced them all. In Paris he met many likeminded Spanish Americans, including Colombians Antonio Nariño and Pedro Fermín de Vargas, each of whom had been declared persona non grata by the Audiencia of New Granada for their seditious activities. Nariño had translated and printed the French Declaration of the Rights of Man in 1794 and reportedly conspired with his friend Vargas to overthrow the colonial government; Vargas had abandoned his position as *corregidor* of Zipaquirá, ransacked the region's treasury, and fled South America with his married mistress, Bárbara Forero.[89] Like Miranda before him, Nariño had approached William Pitt with a request for financial and military support for Spanish American emancipation but met with little immediate success. When the Spanish authorities later interrogated Nariño about the goings-on in London, he preferred to make only vague statements and never once mentioned Miranda's name, although the two clearly had known each other and worked together in Europe.[90]

So, with the signing of the Act of Paris, the Spanish American emancipation movement began a new, more collaborative and mature phase. Spanish Americans from throughout the hemisphere met in a European capital and began to formulate plans for their collective future. These early romantic years, conspiring in the shadow of the French Revolution, set the tone for the next decade of the Spanish American drive for independence. The Paris Convention had been signed; their mission was defined. All that remained was to build support and put the plan into motion. The Spanish ambassador in Paris warned his agents to be on the lookout for Caro, who was wearing "a black wig that imitates perfectly the hair of Negroes; and who has darkened his face and skin to the same color with a substance so effective that neither sweat nor water can remove it."[91] Dressed in this absurd manner, Caro managed to slip out of Europe, headed for the Caribbean to foment rebellion. Miranda returned to England posing as a merchant, complete with a wig and green spectacles and using a doctored passport that identified him as the American Count Mirandov.[92]

The first thing Miranda did upon arriving at Dover on January 12, 1798, was to write to his "very dear friend" John Turnbull, recounting his narrow escape from the "claws of the Directory" and expressing his desire to learn all that had passed in England during his long absence.[93] Miranda intended to remind Pitt of his agreement at Hollwood all those many years ago, namely to support Spanish America in case of a war with Spain. In 1790, Miranda had been a single voice, albeit a charismatic and persistent one, pursuing British political figures in the hallways and drawing rooms of power to support an expedition to South America. They were interested, but not fully convinced.

Miranda's prodigal return to England in 1798, however, met with a very different political climate, and he himself had gotten better at the game. He had become "Francisco de Miranda, Principal Agent of the Spanish American Colonies," with an act of accreditation and instructions signed by American representatives to lend him legitimacy. Never mind that these agents were self-appointed and the proclamation self-serving; Miranda had wrapped himself in the flag of legitimacy and popularity, and that was something the British government finally was able to embrace.

5

DON QUIXOTE IN THE CARIBBEAN
England and the Leander Expedition
(1798–1807)

He's a muddle-headed fool, with frequent lucid intervals.
—MIGUEL DE CERVANTES, *Don Quixote*

B ack in London, reunited with old friends and living in an environment he knew well, Miranda flourished. He returned to
England from France focused and more determined than ever to advance the cause of Spanish American emancipation. He had participated in both the American and French Revolutions and therefore
had a practical understanding of the nature of the changes taking
place on both sides of the Atlantic. His personal experiences in France
made him wary of excessive centralization and the dangers of unchecked power left in the hands of either the unthinking masses or a
fanatical directing elite. Great Britain, with its tradition of aristocratic
liberty and gradual, managed change from above, attracted his attention as a possible model for his own people. For this reason, he was
excited to be on English soil once again. When Miranda announced
his return to Prime Minister William Pitt, he did so in language befit-
ting his new, self-appointed station as the Voice of a Continent: "The
undersigned, Principal Agent of the Spanish American Colonies, commissioned to treat with the Ministers of His Britannic Majesty, to
renew the negotiations begun in 1790, in favour of absolute Independence of said Colonies, in the shortest time possible . . . culminating
in a treaty of friendship or alliance similar . . . to that proposed by

France and signed in 1778 between that country and the English colonies of North America."[1]

By 1798, Miranda had become politically savvy enough to stress the benefits of Spanish American emancipation to the British nation itself. At a low point in Continental relations, Britain faced hostile attacks from both France and Spain, so the possibility of securing Spanish American allies and access to important resources and markets in the New World was sorely tempting. Pitt wanted to hear what his old associate had to say, and he invited Miranda to Hollwood House for a meeting on January 16, 1798.

Miranda arrived just before 11 A.M. and Pitt greeted him without delay. Pitt was jovial and effusively lamented that eight years had passed since their last visit.[2] Since England was at war with Spain, their old discussions could be renewed less awkwardly. Pitt asked to see Miranda's credentials and the Principal Agent of the Spanish American Colonies was only too pleased to comply; he pulled the Act of Paris out of his valise before the prime minister could even finish his sentence. Of course, Spanish American emancipation remained a higher priority for Miranda than it was for Pitt, who was always more concerned with European affairs; their relationship quickly slipped into the old pattern that had been established in 1790. Miranda sent letter after letter, plan after plan, memoranda, maps, and timetables, which Pitt received in grateful silence. For the first few months that he was back in England, Miranda felt a renewed optimism, and the enthusiastic reception that his British friends accorded him more than made up for Pitt's reticence. Merchant John Pownall gushed, "Providence has extracted you from all these Evils; & preserved you for *some great purpose* . . . [you are] a Character equal to some grand Rôle in the Drama of the World, I mean the New World."[3] With this image of himself as an agent of both Divine Providence and the General Will of Spain's American colonies, Miranda's ego could not entertain the possibility of failure.

Nevertheless, when Pitt still had not responded by May, Miranda sent a gently worded reminder that the moment to emancipate the colonies had arrived and if Pitt did not act immediately, no doubt France or the United States would. Miranda knew this because he had already sent the president of the United States the same "propositions and overtures" in the name of the Spanish American colonies of which he was now calling himself the Principal Agent.[4] In his note Miranda clearly indicated his preference for British sponsorship of the expedition, but demanded action with a new confidence born of his age and position. As the dawn of the nineteenth century approached, the idea of Spanish American independence no longer seemed outlandish or heretical to many in the Atlantic world, including two types not usually found together: romantic poets and merchants. Alexander Hamilton said that he wished it would be "undertaken, but I should be glad that the principal agency was in the United States."[5] Furthermore, Hamilton told Miranda he would be "happy in my official station to be an instrument of so good a work." Miranda approached Rufus King, the American ambassador to England, who agreed, "The destiny of the New World, and I have a full and firm Persuasion that it will be both happy and glorious, is in our Hands; we have a Right, and it is our Duty to deliberate, and to act nor as secondaries, but as Principals. The object and the occasion are such as we ought not in respect to ourselves or others to suffer to pass unimproved."[6] In other words, the nineteenth century would be both an American century and a century of untrammeled material progress. Considered in such a light, Spanish American independence was not only logical but inevitable. From King, Miranda also learned that there was a Jesuit residing in London "in the service and pay of the government" who shared his views and might be a useful collaborator.[7]

Unlike older Jesuits who were content to live out their Italian exile engaged in research, writing, and contemplation, young Peruvian Juan Pablo Viscardo y Guzmán actively sought revenge against the Spanish Crown for his expulsion. In 1781, he approached the British representative at Leghorn, Italy, and offered a native's assessment of Peruvian conditions.[8] He received an invitation to relocate to England and share his knowledge with interested parties there. Barely surviving in London in the early 1790s on a meager British government pension of £300, Viscardo composed the single most important document of the entire Spanish American emancipation project, his *Carta a los españoles americanos* (Open Letter to the American Spaniards).[9] Historians have called this document "Spanish America's Act of Independence" and have compared it to Thomas Jefferson's

Summary View of the Rights of British Americans.[10] From its opening
lines, Viscardo's letter revealed its author's affinity with intellectual
trends current throughout the Atlantic world: an emphasis on sober
reflection and scientific observations as the proper basis for action,
the people's right to choose their own government, and the necessity
for that government in turn to respond to the people's desires.[11] Also
present was the emerging modern concept of nationalism, the idea
that one intrinsically belonged to the land of one's birth.

The *Carta* first set out the historical case for Spanish American
independence. By examining three centuries of "causes and effects" in
"our history," Viscardo revealed a truth so plain "that one might abridge
it into these four words—*ingratitude, injustice, slavery*, and *desolation*."
He built the historical case for independence on precedent, logic,
natural rights and origins, and the conquerors' accomplishments.
Throughout his extended argument, Viscardo stressed that their separate national identities had always opposed American and Spanish
interests. For Viscardo, de facto independence had existed in America
since the sixteenth century. American conquerors and settlers had
earned independence through their brave actions and by their permanent residence in the New World. Viscardo wrote:

> Our ancestors, in removing themselves to an immense distance from their
> native country and in renouncing the support that belonged to them, as
> well as the protection which could no longer succour them in regions as
> distant as unknown; our ancestors in this state of natural independence,
> ventured to procure themselves a new subsistence, by the most excessive
> fatigues, with the greatest dangers and at their own expense. The great
> success which crowned the efforts of the conquerors of America, gave
> them a right . . . to appropriate to themselves the fruit of their valour and
> their labours.[12]

In his view, nothing more than simple affection and tradition still
held Americans to the Spanish Crown, a lamentable sentimentality
that had caused Americans to ignore their own interests for too long:
"Led by a blind enthusiasm, we have not considered that so much
eagerness for a country to which we are strangers, to which we owe
nothing, on which we do not depend, and of whom we expect nothing, becomes the worst treason to that which we were born, and which
furnished nourishment to us and to our children."[13]

As final evidence of Spanish hypocrisy, Viscardo claimed that the Crown itself had both recognized and guaranteed de facto American independence in its own stated policies: "What would Spain and her Government say, if we should seriously insist upon the execution of this fine system, and why insult us so cruelly in speaking of union and equality? . . . This resolution, the Government of Spain has itself pointed out to us, in constantly considering you as a people distinct from European Spaniards, and this distinction imposes on you the most ignominious slavery. Let us agree on our part to be a different people; let us renounce the ridiculous idea *of union and equality* with our masters and tyrants." In other words, "Spain has been first in transgressing all her duties towards us; she has been the first to break the feeble bonds which would have been able to attach and retain us." Americans should not hesitate to declare independence when Spain treated them as different already.[14]

The second major section of Viscardo's *Carta* constructed the legal and political case for Spanish American independence. He had already proven that Spain had abrogated its treaties with Columbus and the conquerors, thereby forfeiting its rights to the New World; he then argued that Spain's Christianizing mission had long since ended, thereby nullifying that claim to continued domination as well.[15] Similarly, Viscardo thought the Spanish court had overstepped its traditional role and usurped the power of the Cortes "which represented the different classes of the nation, and were to be the depositories and guardians of the rights of the people."[16] Taking John Locke's *Second Treatise on Government* as his inspiration, Viscardo reached back into the juridical history of Aragon to find an article in the ancient constitution that decreed that "if the King violated the rights and privileges of the people, the people had a right to disown him for their sovereign, and to elect another in his place, even of the *Pagan* religion."[17] There he found the direct progenitor of the constitutionalist argument the Spanish American *cabildos* (municipal councils) would use to assert their control when Napoleon took King Ferdinand hostage in 1808. Viscardo's historical arguments went a long way toward establishing a pantheon of Spanish American heroes and anti-heroes, an essential component of modern national identity and something upon which Miranda and the next generation elaborated significantly.

For their heroes, Viscardo invited Spanish Americans "[t]o consult our annals for three centuries," where they would find "the great Columbus" whom Spain had betrayed by reneging on his contracts. Other heroes included the brilliant and authentic Inca Garcilaso de la Vega, "the young and innocent Inca Túpac Amaru," and the entire proud *mestizo* (mixed) race "who were born in this country of Indian mothers and Spanish fathers." Equally important for the invented Spanish American pantheon were Viscardo's anti-heroes: "Viceroy Don Francis [Francisco] de Toledo, that ferocious hypocrite, [who] put to death the sole heir of the empire of Peru," and all "the bloodsuckers employed by the Government."[18] Viscardo appealed to incipient Creole nationalism by drawing upon Americans' shared history and identifying their common enemies. His writings, and Miranda's subsequent enthusiastic distribution of his text, inspired a generation.

Viscardo's *Carta a los españoles americanos* was a brilliant, well-argued, and impassioned case for Spanish American independence. It incorporated Enlightenment political philosophy, legal precedent, and an appeal to history and historical memory. Above all, it confirmed the people's right to determine their own fate. He addressed his audience as "Brothers and Countrymen," spoke to them as an insider, and used that privileged position to validate his authority. Viscardo told Americans that they had a divine mission. A brilliant future awaited them, if only they had the courage to seize the rights that were theirs already: ". . . [W]hat an agreeable spectacle will the fertile shores of America present, covered with men from all nations exchanging the productions of their country against ours! How many from among them, flying oppression and misery, will come to enrich us by their industry and their knowledge, and to repair our exhausted population! Thus would America reconcile the extremities of the earth; and her inhabitants, united by a common interest, would form one GREAT FAMILY OF BROTHERS."[19]

Strangely enough, there is no evidence that Viscardo and Miranda ever met, although both were involved in similar discussions with Pitt at the same time. Miranda did not return to London until January 11, 1798; Viscardo died in that same city, bitter, cold, and alone, at the end of February.[20] United States ambassador Rufus King inherited the Jesuit's personal papers, which he subsequently loaned to

Miranda.[21] Miranda realized the significance of this cache and lost no time joining Viscardo's efforts to his own. As early as July 1799, Miranda sent a copy of the *Carta* to Pedro Josef Caro, his former Paris associate and now agent for his scheme in Trinidad, telling him to use it to rally support especially among British merchants there; by September he had sent Caro at least four other copies.[22] On November 14, 1799, Miranda passed on the same text to Alexander Hamilton, describing it as a document of "great importance for the future of my country."[23] Viscardo's open letter to Spanish Americans had become Miranda's mission statement.

Like Viscardo, Miranda was frustrated with the noncommittal semisupport of Pitt's government and was determined to seek other channels to advance his plans. In France, Miranda had used the power of public opinion as part of his defense strategy; in London, he set out to launch a propaganda war to build the moral case for Spanish American emancipation and to put political pressure on the British government. He needed to get his message out and to spread it as far and as fast as possible. The most obvious way to do this was to publish an inexpensive edition of the *Carta*. Rufus King paid the printer and Viscardo's *Lettre aux espagnols américains* appeared in London in 1799 bearing a false Philadelphia imprint to avoid antagonizing Pitt. By 1801, Miranda had translated the pamphlet into Spanish for distribution throughout America.[24] He was successful. In 1804, Spain's minister of state for despatch, Pedro de Cevallos, warned his overseas colleagues to intercept the dangerous tract.[25] Despite their best intentions, handwritten copies continued to reach disaffected Creoles throughout the continent, forcing the Mexican Inquisition to prohibit its circulation once again during the aftermath of the Hidalgo Revolt in 1810.

After so many years of dreaming and laboring in distant isolation, Miranda desperately needed to be needed, to have the value of his work confirmed for him by a South American. His prayers were answered in the person of 19-year-old Bernardo Riquelme, better known as Bernardo O'Higgins, the future Liberator of Chile. The illegitimate son of Peruvian viceroy Ambrosio O'Higgins, young Bernardo had been sent to London in 1797 to complete his education. He was enrolled at the Richmond Academy but fell in love with Charlotte

Eels, the daughter of his headmaster, and was promptly transferred to the Margate School for propriety's sake.[26] The idealistic youth was lonely and tried to persuade his guardian to let him return home, complaining that there were no other Chileans in London and that no one in that city knew anything at all about Chile.

It was at that crucial time in both their lives that O'Higgins met Miranda, a seasoned soldier and veteran traveler who was thirty years his senior and looking for a disciple. Beginning in 1798, the impressionable young Chilean spent hours at the Venezuelan general's home, sitting at his feet and absorbing both his dreams and his rhetoric. Together they pored over books on military history and tactics; in fact, legend says that Miranda himself tutored the young man in mathematics.[27] Miranda even took O'Higgins to meet Prime Minister William Pitt. Undoubtedly, having an audience with the leader of the most powerful country in the world made quite an impression on Bernardo, barely twenty years old and nursing his first broken heart. Around the same time, Miranda's old friend John Turnbull invited Miranda and O'Higgins to dinner in order to discuss potential commercial ventures between the two countries. It was the dawn of the Romantic Age, and what could be more romantic than the liberation of one's people from tyranny and oppression? By the time he left London, O'Higgins was so thoroughly stricken with emancipation fever that he unwisely wrote to his father (Viceroy O'Higgins, Spain's highest-ranking official in Peru) that he was going to hurry home "to a fruitful career serving the fatherland, or to a glorious death."[28] His father could not have been amused.

To underscore the deadly seriousness of their mission, Miranda scribbled down some private instructions for his young protégé to read and then destroy during the long sea journey home. O'Higgins could not bring himself to burn the paper and kept it in the brim of his hat for years afterward. The original text of the note has survived in two slightly different versions and is usually given the title "Advice from an Old South American to a Young Compatriot on Leaving England for His Country." With his words, the rhetorically skilled Miranda spoke not just to his young disciple but to posterity as well. As the self-appointed Precursor of the Spanish American emancipation movement, he symbolically passed the torch on to a generation not yet born when he took himself into exile to fight for their precious liberty. The "Advice" opened with praise for the young Chilean's honor and discretion and solemnly warned him of the dangerous mission ahead. Miranda rightly feared Spanish reprisals, telling O'Higgins, "[a]s you leave England, do not forget for a single minute that there is in all the world but one other nation in which you may speak of politics openly . . . and this nation is the United States." Furthermore, Miranda warned him to be careful and prudent when taking others into his confidence. O'Higgins should distrust all men over forty years of age, he said, because youth was the most natural constituency for revolution. Yet Miranda had learned that "it is a mistake to think that all men, simply because they have a crown on their head or sit in the easy chair of the churchman, are intolerant fanatics or enemies of the rights of man. I know from experience that this class contains some of the most enlightened and liberal men in South America." Miranda must have been thinking of the patriotic exiled Jesuits such as Viscardo and the important nation-building intellectual work they had undertaken thousands of miles from home. Extended residence in a foreign environment had heightened the Jesuits' sense of American identity, just as it had done to Miranda's and then to O'Higgins's. The Venezuelan reminded his student of the overwhelming power of patriotism: "I have always tried to imbue you with these principles in our conversations, and it is one of the objects that I want you to remember, not just all the days, but in each one of your hours. Love your country! Embrace this sentiment constantly, fortify it by all possible means, because only through its longevity and energy will you be able to prevail."[29]

Miranda always felt comfortable in the company of martially-inclined young men to whom he could serve as both a teacher and a father figure. More than once he fondly referred to O'Higgins as "my son." Years later a soldier in Miranda's ill-fated excursion to the Venezuelan coast recalled that the general "assumed the manners of a father and instructor to the young men," his stories carrying them to distant places and times: Troy, Babylon, Jerusalem, Rome, Athens, Syracuse, Africa, Pensacola, and France.[30]

Miranda and O'Higgins were fascinated by the idea of The Fight. After all, theirs was the Age of the Atlantic Revolutions, a generation suckled on the teats of freedom and liberty. Great nations struggled into being and the great leaders who personified them, military men like Washington and Napoleon, commanded respect on both sides of the ocean. Simón Bolívar, Bernardo O'Higgins, and José de San Martín, the three preeminent figures of the South American independence armies, all lived in Europe at various times during the Napoleonic Wars and read voraciously in Miranda's vast library of books on tactics and military history. Despite its great distance from continental Spain, everyone understood that Spanish American emancipation would imply military action; in 1801, nobody was thinking in much detail about setting up government structures. For Miranda and his generation, it was as though independence from Spain and local governance would solve all their problems, and in a large measure, they were right. The ability to control one's own commercial policy, collect taxes and utilize them for local improvements, administer justice quickly based on local norms—these were the reasonable early goals of the emancipation movement. It was logical that their attention should turn first to the immediate task at hand—ridding the continent of Spanish colonial authority. The rest could be sorted out later. Bernardo Riquelme O'Higgins returned to Chile infected with a revolutionary fever and started to spread Miranda's word.

For lack of anything else, Miranda dusted off his 1790 plan for the Inca Republic of South America and resubmitted it to Pitt. His third go-around with British sponsorship was much more concerted and no longer confined to lobbying the prime minister's office alone. He had learned that merely petitioning the government would not be enough; he had to approach several constituencies and be willing to offer them something concrete in return for their support. He had to know how to dance the quadrille and make witty small talk among potential supporters. Socializing, therefore, became Miranda's patriotic duty. The endless round of social calls, dinners, toasts, theater performances, balls, and the obligatory Sunday stroll through St. James's Park would have exhausted lesser mortals, but Miranda thrived in that type of environment. He captivated the women with his attentiveness and impressed the men with tales of heroic exploits and his famous friends. With all of them, he spoke of his dreams for an independent Spanish America and, though some dismissed his conversation as mere parlor talk, many others were caught up in the romance of it all.

By 1803, Miranda was no longer a lone voice. British military leaders and entrepreneurs urged the British government to take action, and significant elements in the aristocracy and the learned general public were not far behind. Miranda had influential friends who liked him personally and found his plans to be a worthy cause for the heroic and free British nation; if emancipation made them some money along the way, so much the better. Since August 1796, Pitt, Nicholas Vansittart, and Secretary of War Henry Dundas (Lord Melville) had agreed on the general outlines of a plan to topple the Spanish Empire from a staging ground in the recently captured island of Trinidad.[31] Miranda started to meet regularly with Vansittart, Pitt, Melville, and Sir Evan Nepean to formulate actual expeditionary plans. It was only a matter of time before the thorny question of leadership arose; Miranda quite naturally viewed himself as the obvious candidate but the politicians were less eager to put British troops under foreign command. Governor Thomas Picton of Trinidad was accepted as a compromise although he was, in the view of Arthur Wellesley (the future duke of Wellington), "a rough, foul-mouthed devil as ever lived."[32] Picton had extensive experience in Caribbean military affairs; he had led the British capture of Trinidad from Spain in 1797 and was a consistently valuable friend to Miranda's cause.

Sir Home Riggs Popham of the Royal Navy was another of Miranda's most influential advocates. Their friendship dated from August 1, 1803, when Miranda sent him a letter expressing a desire to work together on Spanish American affairs.[33] Popham had cruised off the coast of Buenos Aires in 1801 and therefore could claim to be familiar with both the geography and the local people's sentiments.[34] Popham assured Foreign Secretary Lord Hardwicke that Miranda's plans were well founded and well suited to the needs of the continent, and wrote that he was proud that Miranda "materially vests his prospect of success on my accompanying him in the command, or as a joint commissioner for the ultimate pursuits."[35] Popham and Evan Nepean both supported Miranda's 1804 plan, which called for him to go to Trinidad immediately, disguised as a settler, to reach a secret understanding with the governor and to expand his covert network on the South American continent. The pair claimed to have it on good authority that, upon landing in Venezuela, the populace "will unanimously flock to his standard." Nepean, Miranda, and Popham estimated the requirements for their expedition to be minimal: arms, clothing, one artillery company, one cavalry troop (with the possibility of one more to follow), two ships, two sloops, two gun brigs, and three cutters. Popham sent a follow-up memo to Melville advising him that several ships, including the *Argo*, the *Antelope*, and the *Leopard*, were immediately available and perfectly suited to Miranda's needs. For the nominal expense of outfitting this small force, Britain would obtain "the most liberal export channel for all our manufacture that I am acquainted with."[36] The secretary of war seems to have assented, because a jubilant Popham invited Miranda over for a cup of tea to celebrate his imminent departure for Trinidad.[37] Popham was "aggressive, dynamic, arrogant, ambitious, and intelligent with a well-developed acquisitive instinct"; we cannot be sure whether it was due to his ego or Miranda's that they petitioned Melville for more supplies and better ships within days of receiving the good news.[38]

In 1804, Miranda had been away from Venezuela for over thirty years. He had seen much and had enjoyed a great many adventures and now believed that South America cried out for him in its hour of need. An outsized sense of importance is a psychological trait common to exiles, particularly politicized exiles whose lonely struggles distort their perspective and sense of time.[39] For example, Miranda wrote to Pitt once again requesting permission to leave England for the Antilles so that he "shan't be detained any longer, from applying the personal assistance at least, that my distressed country expects of me."[40] Not only do exiles tend to overestimate their own indispensability, they also lose sense of the real mood in their native lands in direct proportion to the time and distance they have been away; surely this was the case with Miranda, a man who was so sensitive to racial politics that he papered over any African blood his Canary Islander grandparents may have had, yet in 1804, with memories of a race war in nearby Haiti still fresh in everyone's mind, he desperately suggested amalgamating the English troops in Trinidad with "the men of colour we find on [that] island; and that we get rid of those that seem weak or useless."[41] Terrified Venezuelan slaveholding landlords would have been appalled to learn that an invading force of armed, dark-skinned men was being considered. Miranda's suggestion was another classic example of his liberal impulses coupled with obsessive patriotism momentarily overtaking prudent political considerations.

This time, it was no longer simply Pitt's hesitation that prevented Miranda from sailing; British politics itself had become more sophisticated and public opinion carried more weight. Miranda had been using the press to advance his cause, forgetting that his opponents could also initiate a media campaign against him. Certainly not everyone approved of Miranda's plans or even of the man himself. His stint in France's Army of the North did not sit well with many British officials or publicists. No less a person than Attorney General Law commented cynically that Miranda would serve France, Britain, or even Russia against his own country, depending on who paid him the most. Enemies resurrected the 20-year-old claim that Miranda had been a smuggler in the Caribbean. Miranda tried in vain to remind the public that he had been cleared of those charges long ago and to persuade them that he was indeed the person best prepared to lead Spanish America into the future, because "[w]hen one has spent 25 years of one's life on a single and same object, and that this object is the study of wise principles that can plead Men to Happiness so that they can be well-applied in one's Homeland, one must not doubt my devotion to these same principles."[42] Miranda appealed to "my [English] compatriots, my friends, and to the same Government which gave me asylum and honorable support" over the past twenty years. At the same time, some of his former friends, chief among them Pedro Josef Caro, turned double-agent and began to provide information about his plans to the Spanish government.[43]

By 1805, Miranda had resided outside South America for a longer time than he had actually lived there. The great project of Spanish American emancipation had been his surrogate family for over two decades. Young, impressionable men like Bernardo O'Higgins took the place of the sons he never had.[44] Yet Miranda was beginning to tire of his transient life-style; it might have been exciting for a youthful adventurer, but was decidedly less appealing for an aging adult. Weary of staying in rented lodgings and finally realizing that he would likely remain in London indefinitely, Miranda bought a house at

27 Grafton Street, a fashionable West End street right around the corner from the newly established British Museum.[45] It was to this 3-story Georgian-style home that he brought his young wife, Sarah Andrews, whom he likely met on a tour of Northern England.[46] Very little is known about Sarah, except that she was the niece of the London portrait painter Stephen Hewson and that she came from a rural family. She does not appear to have been Jewish, as some writers have claimed. Extensive investigations by Venezuela's former cultural attaché in London, Miriam Blanco Fombona de Hood, seem to prove that Miranda and Sarah did not simply cohabitate but were actually legally married. The first of their two sons, Leandro, was born on October 9, 1803, shortly after the happy couple moved into Grafton Street and Miranda settled into a satisfying domestic life at long last. He was fifty-five years old, newly married to a Yorkshire lass, and a proud London homeowner. Slowly, over time, Miranda absorbed English cultural norms and values. Linguists who have studied Miranda's diary have even found a "slow but persistent dehispanization" as his vocabulary became progressively more cosmopolitan, full of words in other languages and therefore less Venezuelan or even Spanish in character.[47]

After 1805, Miranda gave up trying to persuade Britain's ministers that Spanish American emancipation was a lofty and humanitarian enterprise, and began arguing that it was in their own best interest.[48] Political scientist Yosse Shain has described the phenomenon of "exiles *qua* sellers" to explain the common pattern of their attempts to convince host governments that their respective interests coincide. Miranda knew that Pitt was preoccupied with Napoleon's march across Continental Europe and hoped to persuade him to extend that battle to the Caribbean, using the prime minister's own precious balance-of-power concept to argue that Spanish America had a concrete role to play as Britain's ally across the Atlantic.[49] Miranda also began to court West Indian merchants by offering the vision of a huge Spanish American market to their powerful Liverpool- and London-based lobbying groups. Although his reading interests tended more toward military history and the classics of Spanish, Greek and Roman literature, Miranda had read his copy of Adam Smith's *Wealth of Nations* and understood the power of enlightened self-interest. Perhaps merchants would prevail where politicians failed to act. Such an appeal could not hurt and it just might help.

Miranda's house at Grafton Street became the nexus of Spanish American conspiratorial activities throughout the Atlantic world. The tireless Sarah Andrews kept the candles at their home permanently lit, symbolizing not only her husband's devotion to the Great Cause but the openness of her home to all Spanish Americans who came to London. Like moths to a flame, disaffected travelers came to meet the man behind the words they had been receiving. One of them, the Colombian fugitive Pedro Fermín de Vargas, stayed shut up in the Grafton Street attic; Miranda only permitted him "to go out after dark, under the idea that his being here might be known to the Spanish Minister and his family be made to suffer for it."[50] Miranda regularly held meetings with London's most active reformists, a stellar group that included the utilitarian philosophers Jeremy Bentham and James Mill, parliamentarian and abolitionist William Wilberforce, and education reformer Joseph Lancaster.

In the wake of Admiral Nelson's victory over the French forces at Trafalgar on October 21, 1805, the threat of Napoleon's advance receded and British politicians were able to breathe more easily. This easing of international tensions meant yet another delay for Miranda's Trinidad project. It was as though it was 1792 all over again. Miranda felt betrayed and decided that he ought to send feelers to his North American friends to test their willingness to support a mission when it became clear that Pitt would not. Faced with pressure from both Miranda and U.S. ambassador Rufus King, Nepean told Pitt that he could no longer dissuade the general from going to America. Although Miranda claimed that as a patriot his goal was simply to prevent the "entry of the *modern Gauls*" into Spanish America, no one could have been fooled by this transparent nod to anti-French sentiment.[51] Using the pseudonym Mr. George Martin, Miranda embarked at Gravesend on Monday, September 2, 1805, headed toward the Western Hemisphere for the first time in twenty years. Several people on the ship died of smallpox during the long journey, adding further stress to the usual hazards presented by storms, privateers, and boredom.

When the *Polly* finally hove in sight of Governor's Island on November 9, at least one passenger gave thanks for the end of "the most boisterous and disagreeable passage I ever experienced."[52]

In New York, Miranda and his secretary, Tómas Molini, lodged at Mrs. Avery's boardinghouse near the Battery for a little more than two weeks and then took a stagecoach to Philadelphia, where Miranda conferred with some merchants from Santo Domingo. He also renewed acquaintances that he had made twenty years earlier during his tour of the emerging Republic. Young Richard Rush, son of the famed doctor Benjamin Rush and a future ambassador to England, spent two days in Miranda's company and came away from the experience starry-eyed and breathless. Miranda regaled the lad with tales of George Washington, Napoleon Bonaparte, Frederick the Great, Prince Potemkin, and the Empress Catherine, all of whom he knew personally. The amazing man appeared to possess perfectly detailed knowledge in the fields of art, botany, ancient history, literature, anatomy, and modern languages. Whether it was his disillusionment with Pitt or a desire to flatter a potentially useful ally, Miranda told young Rush that England ought not to send troops for the Spanish American emancipation project because it was better suited to be a wholly American endeavor. He complained that the British army sold its officers' ranks to the highest bidder, which meant that "a Jew with his money could get above men of talent." Furthermore, years spent in London had led Miranda to conclude bitterly that a great deal of what Montesquieu said about the British Constitution in the *Spirit of the Laws* exists "only [in] theory." These two brief but nasty comments were not characteristic of Miranda's true attitudes; he was neither anti-Semitic nor anti-British. Instead, they reveal both the soaring heights of his own ego and the depths of his frustration with a system that failed to provide him with all he felt his genius deserved.[53]

On the way to Washington, Miranda met former vice president Aaron Burr in Philadelphia. Burr was struggling at the time to recover his reputation from the fatal duel he had fought the previous year with Alexander Hamilton, and had embarked upon his own scheme to revolutionize Louisiana and the West. Apparently, Burr was not interested in joining forces with the South American and viewed Miranda as a competitor. Burr wrote:

I was greatly pleased with his social talents and colloquial eloquence. It is true, however, that I did, from private considerations, studiously avoid anything which might afford him an occasion to disclose his views. The bare suspicion of any connexion between him and me would have been injurious to my project and fatal to his; a circumstance of which he must have been ignorant. He afterward complained to his friend of my coldness and reserve, and he had reason; but I did not dare to explain, not having sufficient assurance of his discretion. As, however, there never has been, nor in any probability, ever can be the smallest collision political or other, between us, I did not suppose that any sentiment approaching to enmity existed on his part; certainly none on mine.[54]

Nevertheless, Miranda felt slighted and took an instant dislike to Burr, calling him "detestable" and "Mephistophelian," a dastardly intriguer who had killed his dear friend Hamilton. Ironically, on this point the Spanish ambassador Casa Irujo agreed.[55]

On December 7, Miranda arrived in Washington, where he and Molini took rooms at Stelle's Hotel on Capitol Hill. A week later he sent a cryptic note to William Steuben Smith, confirming that he had seen "the two gentlemen and after having spoken extensively about the matter, I believe that it is all set."[56] The men to whom he alluded were, of course, President Thomas Jefferson and Secretary of State James Madison; Miranda later claimed that both men had given their "tacit approval and good wishes" for his expedition. Keeping in mind that the United States was at peace with Spain, there could be no promise of official support, but the two hinted that they might "wink" at individual Americans' enlistment or financial contribution.[57] Madison later rejected the insinuation that their administration had done anything of the sort, saying that Smith and the others simply "fell into the snare."[58] Jefferson, too, swore "on my personal truth and honor . . . that this was entirely without foundation, and that there was neither cooperation nor connivance on our part."[59] As Madison seems to have reported both the occurrence and the substance of the secret meetings to Spanish ambassador Casa Irujo, it does seem likely that Miranda stretched the truth to suit his needs on this occasion.[60] Nevertheless, both Jefferson and Madison were consummate politicians and it is impossible that they could have misunderstood his purpose or failed to stop it had they chosen to do so. Two full weeks before his outfit sailed, Miranda sent Jefferson a copy of Juan Ignacio

Molina's *Geographical, Biographical, Natural, and Civil History of Chili*, which they had discussed in Washington, and thanked him for "the happy predictions that you pronounced on the luck that our beloved Colombia will surely have in our times."[61]

With this business successfully concluded, at least in his opinion, Miranda returned to New York and began to make preparations for the voyage. Casa Yrujo's spy network, however, had infiltrated Miranda's hotel and kept the ambassador well informed about his every move. Thomas Stoughton, Spain's consul in New York, passed on the alarming news that Miranda was loading supplies of rifles, guns, powder, uniforms, and other such munitions on a ship called the *Leander*.[62] His pikes were made at U.S. government manufactories in Westpoint and Springfield, and the mortars and cannonballs came from federal stores in New York. As financial security, Miranda pledged his valuable library in London, which was estimated to be worth over £2,000. Miranda's aide-de-camp was none other than Jonathan Smith, the son of his old traveling partner William Steuben Smith (now serving as the inspector of the Port of New York) and grandson of former president John Adams. Casa Irujo felt that this youth's presence gave Miranda's enterprise an alarmingly official character. Years later, Adams professed complete and utter ignorance that his grandson had left college and joined the expedition until the ship had already been at sea for weeks; Adams condemned the expedition and remarked unsentimentally, "I can truly say, that information that the ship had gone to the bottom would have been an alleviation of my grief. I gave up my grandson as lost forever."[63]

After so many years on the run, Miranda was obsessed with personal security and deathly afraid that his expedition might be shut down before it had even begun. For this reason, he adopted a secretive strategy for the recruitment of his American mercenaries. Most of the *Leander* Expedition's survivors later claimed that they had been tricked into joining the force under false pretenses. An unsavory character named John Fink, a butcher by trade, recruited strong, naive, down-on-their-luck young tradesmen by telling them that he had been commissioned to put together a force to go to New Orleans to guard the mail. John Edsall apparently signed up with this expectation. Others thought they were going to Washington to guard the president. Henry

Ingersoll tried to claim that he was a simple passenger on the ship, although he clearly had been engaged to work for Miranda as a printer.[64] In general, it is probably true that some of the recruits were deceived, but the majority must have had some vague understanding that they had signed on for a military tour of duty in a foreign land. The young men's overriding motivation was greed, which prevented them from asking too many questions. Moses Smith, later one of Miranda's most bitter detractors, essentially admitted as much when he wrote that he had been merely "a country lad, but the picture my friend had set before me of good pay and a fine uniform, lands and a horse, were temptations that never before assailed me." When Smith agreed to sign the contract Fink offered to him, his shaky penmanship was deemed good enough to make him a corporal, "the first prize I had ever obtained for my scholarship, and was so much the more seducing."[65] James Biggs, who has left the most insightful and erudite account of the *Leander* Expedition, recalled that Miranda's agents promised the volunteers the irresistible wages of $10 per day for colonels, $8 per day for majors, $6 per day for captains, and $4 per day for lieutenants, all made retroactively effective from January 1, 1806. In other words, someone like Edsall would immediately have been guaranteed well over $100, a fantastic sum in those days. John Sherman wrote, "[A]ll were told, and firmly impressed with the idea that nothing less than a fortune would be the reward of their labours. That money was plenty where they were going; that after they should arrive at their place of destination, they would have little else to do but hoard up treasure."[66]

The *Leander* Expedition sailed out of New York's harbor on February 2, 1806, with approximately 180 men on board. Its ultimate destination was registered as Santo Domingo and the captain's manifest contained no reference to the military stores kept belowdecks. Biggs claimed that he did not know to where they were sailing to but, to be fair, he pointed out, he had not made it his business to ask either. Nevertheless, Biggs quickly and correctly surmised that they were going to South America "with a view to assist the inhabitants in throwing off the oppressive yoke of the parent country."[67] After several days at sea, General Miranda finally made his first dramatic appearance above deck, clad in a scarlet dressing gown and slippers and with his thick white hair flowing behind him. Making its way down the eastern seaboard, the *Leander* Expedition was anything but secret. On February 25, 1806, the *Richmond Enquirer* quoted Stephen Sayre, who said that at last Miranda was putting his long-discussed plan into effect, which would "most likely change the face of affairs throughout the universe." Two months later, Sayre planted another article that claimed Miranda had rendezvoused with delegates from Mexico, Caracas, and Santa Fé de Bogotá at Trinidad under the auspices of the British governor there.[68]

On their way to Haiti, a British vessel called the *Cleopatra* came into sight and threatened to claim the *Leander* as a pirate ship. Instead, Miranda showed its Captain Armstrong his letters of introduction and their vessel was mysteriously allowed to proceed, giving the men a firmer impression that their mission had been officially sanctioned, most certainly by the British and possibly by their own government as well. A short time later, in the Mona Passage, the *Leander* fired on a Spanish ship that was suspected of tailing them; as the threatening galleon drew closer, Miranda and Captain Lewis hatched an ingenious plan to disguise their true nationality; they ordered all those who could not speak French to keep silent and thus convinced the Spaniards that they were citizens of an allied empire. Surprisingly, the scheme worked. The *Leander* arrived in Haiti's Jacmel harbor on Tuesday, February 18, 1806, where it remained for over a month. Mechanics cleaned and repaired weapons, tailors stitched elaborate and colorful velvet uniforms, and enlisted men conducted training exercises on board the ship because local officials had refused permission to land the crew on shore. On January 1, 1804, Haiti had become the first independent black republic in the world and, not unreasonably, its leaders, Emperor Jean-Jacques Dessalines and Alexandre Pétion, were suspicious of light-skinned troops arriving off their shores.[69]

The first thing Miranda did was hoist the new tricolor Colombian flag. His printers set up their presses and produced a proof sheet of Miranda's *Proclamation to the Inhabitants of South America*, which one reader tearfully exclaimed, "in point of beauty and execution far exceeded our most sanguine expectations."[70] While in Haiti, the printers cranked out over 2,000 copies of five different texts destined for

the inhabitants of the Venezuelan coast and "all parts of the world."
One such proclamation began with a typical Mirandian phrase that
managed to be humble and boastful at the same time: "Brave Countrymen and Friends: Obedient to your wishes, and to the repeated
calls of the country, to whose service we have cheerfully consecrated
the greater part of our lives, we have disembarked in this province of
Caraccas [*sic*]."[71] Promising to recover "our glory as Colombian Americans," Miranda asserted optimistically that independence depended
solely on the people's will. His years in France during the Revolution
should have taught him to be suspicious of highly centralized attempts
to control the masses and harness them to the revolutionary cause.
Miranda's proclamation, however, carried several Jacobin-style reso-
lutions, including the conscription of all (male) citizens between the
ages of sixteen and sixty-five into the patriot army; the requirement
that all patriotic citizens affix a tricolor cockade to their hats to make
their loyalties visible; that churches must fly the civic flag from their
highest and most conspicuous part; that all those who had received
authority from a foreign Spanish source be immediately discharged
and be exiled if they failed to exhibit sufficiently sincere enthusiasm
for the new regime; and finally, that all Miranda's statements and Juan
Pablo Viscardo's *Carta a los españoles americanos* be posted in all public buildings and read aloud in churches and civic courts at least once
a day. The edict ended with words worthy of Miranda's archenemy
Maximilien Robespierre: "The public good is the supreme law."

Miranda conducted a special ceremony on March 24 at Jacmel in
which all volunteers were required to take an oath of loyalty to "the
army of Colombia" that would operate according to the U.S. articles
of war. One by one, the recruits swore, "to be true and faithful to the
free people of South America, independent of Spain, and to serve
them honestly and faithfully against all their enemies or opposers
whatsoever, and to observe and obey the orders of the supreme government of that country legally appointed; and the orders of the general and officers set over me by them."[72] They further agreed to serve
until discharged by Miranda or until they had served in at least two
campaigns. At the same time, many were quick-witted enough to realize that this oath was tantamount to a renunciation of their U.S.
citizenship, so Miranda was forced to add a clause that affirmed their

ultimate American allegiance. Still, morale remained low. Moses Smith cynically noted that by that time, Miranda's men "were much more desirous of freeing themselves than of freeing anybody else."[73] A desperate mutiny occured on March 18 but was quickly put down and then officially blamed on an overzealous and drunken St. Patrick's Day celebration; after that close call, Miranda's already strict discipline became even more onerous. To instill the message that dissent would not be tolerated, Miranda ordered several young men, including Daniel Newberry of Connecticut, to be kept in irons until the *Leander* reached Aruba. Others who might have thought of escaping were induced to remain by promises of additional riches. A growing feud between Miranda and Captain Lewis over issues of authority and command added to the already unbearable shipboard tension.

The *Leander* was joined by two American schooners, the *Bee* and the *Bacchus*, which helped reduce overcrowding. The ragtag fleet landed at Aruba in early April 1806 to resupply and provide some much-needed exercise for the men. Unfortunately, the Spanish were aware of their presence in the general vicinity; a Catalan spy named José Doy had returned from Trinidad to Caracas and warned that a rebel fleet was preparing an invasion.[74] As a countermeasure, Venezuelan authorities placed an embargo on all U.S. ships. For this reason, when Miranda's tiny fleet attempted a landing near Ocumare on the morning of April 27, two Spanish Coast Guard vessels were ready to intercept them. The crew members and volunteers on board the *Bee* watched helplessly as Miranda and the *Leander* turned and sailed out of sight, abandoning them to their fate. Biggs claimed that the *Bee*'s hapless captain failed to follow prearranged signals, but he also felt disgusted and incensed that Miranda had led all of them "headlong into danger and destruction"; in contrast, an anonymous diarist reported that the *Bee* actually surrendered of its own accord.[75] The Spaniards took fifty-seven men captive, including printer Henry Ingersoll, but they may have been the lucky ones; when one young officer grumbled about the nonexistent pay and harsh conditions, Miranda grabbed him by the throat and shouted, "Hold your tongue, sir, you have no rights here but obedience."[76]

In June, rumors floated around the Caribbean that the *Leander* was resupplying in either Barbados or Bonaire. In actual fact, they were at Aruba once again. Paranoid Spanish estimates of the force's size eventually went as high as seven boats with 4,000 men, and they felt certain that the hated British must be involved. That was not an unreasonable assumption. Governor Frederick Maitland sent supplies from Grenada and the new governor of Trinidad, Thomas Hislop, promised them haven. Admiral Alexander Cochrane of the *Northumberland* was known to be sympathetic and invited Miranda to dine with him on June 7, 1806. What was good news for the multinational force was bad news for the Spanish colonial authorities. Garrisons all along the Venezuelan coast were put on high alert, requiring "all the zeal and vigilance that could be mustered to guard the King's territories from the insidious attempts of Miranda to shatter them."[77] In an ironic twist of fate, Miranda's old commander from Havana, Juan Manuel Cagigal, was at the command of a Venezuelan garrison, and any shred of affection he may have felt previously for his aide-de-camp was absent; to Cagigal, Miranda had become "that fanatic," "the enemy insurgent," or even "the perverse Miranda."

On Sunday, August 3, 1806, Miranda raised the Colombian flag for the first time on South American soil at La Vela de Coro. He and his raggedy, scared troops marched inland for twelve silent miles until they reached the town of Coro itself, which they found abandoned but for a few women and old men. Catholic priests apparently had told the frightened citizens to flee before lawless heretics arrived to rob and kill them. They need not have worried on that score; Miranda had issued strict orders that all persons and property must be respected. At one low point, Miranda's men, understandably jittery and confused by the multiplicity of languages spoken among them, accidentally fired on each another from opposite ends of the town, causing several casualties from friendly fire. At Coro, the general distributed various linen handkerchiefs decorated with portraits of Home Popham, General Beresford, George Washington, and Miranda himself surrounded by the promise, "The Dawn of Day in South America."[78] Others contained the phrases, "Not commerce but union," "Let arts, industry and commerce flourish," and even "Religion and its Holy Ministers be protected." Some flags had images of Christopher Columbus placed in the center with British colors providing the background. England was depicted as a maritime goddess with the Spanish lion lying prostrate at her feet. These carefully constructed images give clear visual insight into the sort of patriotic civic culture Miranda intended to create in Venezuela and his attempts to harness their future both politically and economically to Britain.

Although James Biggs believed that opposing Spanish soldiers never came within three or four miles of Coro, Miranda decided that they were surrounded and had to abandon the town after just a few days. The general was not prepared to let himself fall into Spanish hands. Beating a hasty retreat from Coro to the coast, able-bodied men carried their injured compatriots on litters; their exertions obviously meant that they had to stop frequently in order to relieve each other. One eyewitness claimed, "Miranda flew into a violent rage, pretending that it was an unnecessary delay," and said that "if the wounded slowed down the march they should be left behind on the side of the road."[79] If anyone wanted to complain, Miranda was prepared to shoot them there on the spot. On Wednesday, August 13, after just eleven days in Venezuela, Miranda gave orders for the *Leander* to sail away to Aruba, leaving behind a pile of well-worded proclamations, some tattered uniforms, and a lot of questions. While his disillusioned men recovered from their injuries and from yellow fever, Miranda never once visited them in the hospitals but rather sat in his comfortable quarters, "picking his teeth in silence" and saving the best rations for himself, his friends, and his dog.[80]

Miranda's landing at Coro had been a disaster in all imaginable ways. Thanks to an extensive spy network operating on three continents, Spanish colonial authorities were well-informed about Miranda's activities; they had ample warning that he was coming and simply waited for the expedition to land. Furthermore, after thirty years' absence, very few people remembered him or responded to his call. Most important, however, may have been Miranda's own conflicted leadership. Although he had been preparing for his triumphal return for most of his adult life, once the fateful day arrived, his heart simply was not in it. He had always enjoyed the sociability of preparation— meeting with governors, contractors, and investors, signing up bright-eyed recruits anxious to serve under his command—but when it came down to the actual fighting, Miranda had passed his prime. He was an old man and liberation was a game for the young. Furthermore,

Miranda had a lot to live for and all of it was back in England: his young wife and two beloved sons, an interesting and powerful group of friends, access to publishers and a vigorous public forum, a comfortable home and an established reputation. If home is where the heart is, there can be no surprise that 56-year-old Miranda wanted out of his creaking ship and back into the arms of his young family.

Ironically, while on his long-awaited expedition to Venezuela, Miranda was actually homesick for England; this is perhaps the best evidence of his conflicted national identity. As an example, Miranda did not name his vessel after an American person or place, or with a typical reference to a classical hero or lofty concept; rather, he christened it the *Leander*, in English, after his 3-year-old British son. A million details required his immediate attention, yet he still found the time to write frequent and long letters to Vansittart, John Turnbull, and his wife Sarah, instructing them in the conduct of his affairs back home. Miranda explicitly told Turnbull that he wanted Leandro to be baptized by a Roman Catholic priest but that it should be done without much fanfare and with the consent of the boy's mother.[81] There remains a particularly touching correspondence between Miranda and his young wife, who gave birth to their second son, Francisco *hijo* (junior), while the father-general was away in America. Calling him "My ever dearest G," Sarah kept Miranda informed of every detail of her daily life with the children, from bricklayers' fees to Leandro's charming antics. One of her favorite pastimes was watching when "[Leandro] getts the newspaper and setts down for some time as if he were reading, and then asks for a pen and ink to coppy it out, for thay is very good news of papa, papa is at C[or]o, and I am going, he will send a ship for me, and I shall be a G[enera]l with papa."[82] Precocious little Leandro undoubtedly learned this game by watching his equally devoted mother compile a scrapbook of articles relating to Miranda's expedition clipped from London's popular press.

Life was not easy for Sarah during Miranda's absence. She worried constantly about money, staved off an attempt by the Dulau booksellers to repossess her husband's prized library, and thwarted the occasional swindler anxious to take advantage of an unprotected woman. Most of all, Sarah was intensely lonely; she even considered taking her boys to America because, as she wrote to her husband, "without you life is become insuportable, your dear letter and my Leandr are the only consolation I can find in the midst of my trubbles my lovly children God pray them I often pray for them to be in Heven then to live in this dispiseable world—I hope one grave will contain us all and not live to feel the pangs of misery that I am forst to feel."[83] She begged him to "wright soon my ever dear sir, that is the only consolation I have, reading over and over your dear letter and the hopes of soon meething again."[84] Sarah Andrews, like other women of her class and era, did not receive a sophisticated education; her handwriting was shaky and her command of spelling and grammar weak, but the intensity of her feelings for Miranda and her children is unmistakable. Despite her literary shortcomings, Sarah Andrews exerted great effort to write long, informative, frequent letters to her faraway love. For his part, Miranda kept his young family's welfare close to his heart. He implored Vansittart and Turnbull to guard over them in his absence and used these friends as trusted conduits for his letters back home.[85]

For their part, British naval commanders were uncertain what policy they ought to pursue toward Spanish America. William Pitt had died of overwork recently and the British had been humiliated when Sir Home Popham, General Whitelocke, and General Beresford were defeated in their 1806 attempt to seize Buenos Aires.[86] Following the simultaneous failures at both Coro and the Río de la Plata, confusion reigned. Admiral Alexander Cochrane stated that he "felt himself much at a loss how to act" and had sent home for further instructions. He and Miranda decided to send the shifty-eyed Count de Rouvray to London to determine the new government's true intent. Miranda remained in Port of Spain until mid-November 1806, when Cochrane prevailed upon the general to return to England on the HMS *Alexandria* "for his personal safety."[87] London's venerable daily newspaper, the *Times*, reflected its government's ambiguous response to Miranda's proposals, alternately calling him a buccaneer or a pirate while suggesting that access to South American commerce was essential for the maintenance and support of the British Empire.[88] One contemporary observer even went so far as to suggest that Miranda had actually succeeded in his real goals for the *Leander* Expedition, namely to prove to the British government that the Spanish American coast was indeed penetrable, even to a small and underequipped force.[89]

Miranda's credibility throughout the Atlantic world was badly damaged by the *Leander* Expedition. Fifty-seven angry and resentful American youths had the misfortune to find themselves captured and locked up in a fetid Spanish American dungeon. Oddly, the Venezuelan governor appointed Juan Germán Roscio, a rising young lawyer with growing republican sympathies, to travel to the prison at Puerto Cabello in order to investigate the extent of the prisoners' knowledge of Miranda's plans and backers.[90] Whereas Napoleon had previously deemed him to be a saner version of Don Quixote, others started to wonder if Miranda was hopelessly out of touch with reality. Just as Miranda's command in Belgium had gotten tangled up in French Revolutionary politics, so the controversy surrounding the *Leander* Expedition reflected partisan struggles going on in the United States. In March 1806, New York's Republican governor charged William Steuben Smith and Samuel Ogden, both of whom were devoted Federalists, with treason for breaking the young country's neutrality laws when they outfitted Miranda's expedition; their trial turned into a full-blown assault on the reputation of the Federalist Party in the state (and by implication those in the nation's capital as well). A typical broadside screamed, "Mechanics of New York, read the heart-rending truth! *Sixty American Citizens enslaved - - - Ten beheaded and hung* by the nefarious scheme of Miranda, the would-be *King* of America [Rufus King], the Duke of Braintree [John Adams], a Burr-ite Col[onel William Smith] and a Nova Scotia Tory, F[in]k, together with a tory-federal merchant S. O[gde]n." After quoting pitiful words from an imprisoned man to his wife, the broadside asked readers how, in the face of such evidence, they could support the Tory ticket, "most of whom are the implacable enemies of the labouring mechanic and the poor man."[91]

When Moses Smith made his way back home in December 1807, instead of the hero's welcome that he expected, he found that no one at all was inclined to treat him kindly and that instead he was offered neither lodgings nor succor; at that particularly contentious time in New York politics, he suddenly realized that "the occurrences of Burr and Miranda had fatigued the public mind." Ironically, when Smith lodged a suit against John Fink for damages caused by his deception, he ultimately decided that he preferred the Spanish justice system, which was quicker and more humane than that of his own country. John Edsall, too, reported that the local Venezuelan magistrate did not believe the account of his unwitting recruitment in New York, because he could not imagine that any men could have behaved so basely in a civilized country as to enlist unwitting soldiers.[92]

The execution of ten of Miranda's officers. From The History of the Adventures and Suffering of Moses Smith during Five Years of His Life *(Brooklyn, 1812), opposite page 48.* Courtesy of the John Carter Brown Library

The question of the prisoners and the treatment they received remained a live issue in the U.S. public debate for many months. Thirty-seven captives managed to sign a petition and have it smuggled out of their jail cell with a visitor in order to have it presented to the U.S. Congress; in 1809, outraged members of the House resolved that the president "be requested to adopt the most immediate and efficacious means in his power to obtain the liberation of the peti-tioner . . . and that [an unspecified amount of] dollars be appropri-ated to that purpose."[93] From Cartagena's prison, Henry Ingersoll wrote to his parents that Jefferson, Madison, John Adams, and Rufus King all had been aware of the expedition.[94] The whole nasty business made many powerful people nervous. If the concept of plausible deniability had existed in the nineteenth century, it surely would have been invoked on this occasion. Rufus King whispered to his colleague Christopher Gore that he was certain that "our Chief [Jefferson] has kept me within the limits of extreme Caution. I cannot with honour be a volunteer on this occasion against Government, but if I am called as a Witness on the Prosecution they institute, all Reserve will be at an end; the whole must be told, and being told cannot leave any doubt of the unworthy Conduct of the Government in this Affair."[95]

Still, those in positions of prominence stuck to their stories and insisted that they had not sanctioned Miranda's expedition. The unfortunate recruits had been duped. Even William Steuben Smith dared to declare that he had not acquainted his own son with Miranda's true plans beforehand, but rather sent "him as a young companion, to share his fortunes and his fate; he was accompanied by some of his friends, capable of deeds of hardihood and valour—Worthy their leader; worthy his cause!"[96]

Smith's statements were self-serving since he was facing a lengthy jail sentence for his participation in the venture. Prosecutors lodged their complaints against Smith and his financier, Samuel Ogden, before a New York state grand jury on April 7, 1806.[97] The whole affair was politically charged right from the start; the courtroom was packed and the country's newspapers covered each day's revelations extensively. Assistant District Attorney Nathan Sanford and Republican lawyer Pierpont Edwards "for the United States" (i.e., representing the interests of Jefferson and Madison) made the prosecuting arguments; Federalist lawyers Cadwallader D. Colden, Josiah Ogden Hoffman, and Thomas Addis Emmet replied for the defense. Essentially, Republican prosecutors charged Smith with a violation of section 5 of the June 5, 1794, neutrality law that prohibited U.S. citizens from engaging in hostile acts toward foreign powers. According to the Law of Nations, the right to declare war belongs to a nation's sovereign power alone, a necessary condition to prevent international anarchy; in the United States, the right to declare war devolved upon its Congress, not the executive power or any private citizen. In reply, the Federalist defense team argued that the legal provision mentioned was intended to be time-specific and that it applied only in the particular instance for which it was written, namely to maintain U.S. neutrality in the European wars occasioned by the French Revolution. At stake were not just the personal freedom and reputations of Smith and his partner Ogden, but the issue of individual versus the federal government's rights. Republican partisans were in the process of wresting power away from the Federalists and viewed this case as a heaven-sent opportunity to tarnish their opponents as blackguards and warmongers. There was clearly enough material to proceed, and Judge Matthias B. Tallmadge moved to take the case to trial in a special July session.[98]

When Ogden and Smith's trial opened on July 15, the defense unsuccessfully requested an extension until September when some of their witnesses, notably *Leander* crew members Captain Thomas Lewis and Jonathan S. Smith and Secretary of State James Madison (who had disobeyed his subpoena and refused to attend), could not be procured. Circuit Court Judge Paterson and District Judge Tallmadge listened to the tedious and repetitive arguments about the necessity of the absent witnesses' appearance for over four days, leaving the real issues of Smith and Ogden's guilt until the end. The defense attorneys gamely tried to persuade the judges that Smith and Ogden presumed that there was a de facto state of war in existence since members of the executive branch, that is to say Jefferson and Madison, countenanced the discussion of Miranda's expedition; prosecutors and the impatient justices themselves responded that only the Congress had the right to declare war and that this constitutional fact could not be superseded by private actions, no matter what the public station of the individual. If Smith and Ogden had dared to presume otherwise, so much to their detriment. Trying a second tack, defense counsel argued that Miranda's vessel, the *Leander*, had been nothing more than a merchant ship and that the "articles composing her cargo were those of ordinary commerce."[99] When the time came for the jury to retire to deliberate and render a verdict, Judge Tallmadge informed them that the testimony was "in his mind, clear and decisive" against both Smith and Ogden.[100] In both men's cases, the separate juries took only a short time to reach their decisions and found in favor of the defendants. Popular support for the anti-Spanish, pro-American Miranda expedition seemed to have trumped the letter of the law.

The new Spanish consul in Philadelphia, Josef Bruno Magdalena, followed Smith and Ogden's trial closely in the daily gazettes and reported to Madrid that it appeared the U.S. government "did not intervene in Miranda's piratical expedition," but that the real power and influence behind him was the British.[101] Nevertheless, relations between Spain and the United States had been worsening for some time already as their empires began to bump up against each other in the American South and the West. There was a growing anti-Spanish sentiment both among the U.S. public in general and in Congress, where members were debating the propriety of a new bill that would allow the government to request the recall of an unpopular foreign ambassador; this measure was clearly an attack on Casa Irujo's dogged activity on behalf of the Spanish Crown.

Throughout the fall of 1807, reports continued to flood into Venezuela that Miranda was variously preparing new expeditions in Aruba, Trinidad, Jamaica, and Haiti, all of which were based more on fear than on fact. These rumors did, however, turn out to be politically useful as the colonial authorities in Venezuela used the threat to extort more funds from Spain to build up their coastal defense. The Venezuelan governor put a bounty of 300 pesos on Miranda's head and approved transferring an additional 600 men from both the white militias and the *pardo* (brown, or colored) militias of Aragua and Valencia to the garrison at Barlovento de Puerto Cabello as a precaution against another attack.[102] Authorities praised local citizens for "their fidelity and love for Religion, the King and the Fatherland" for having rejected the schemes of a deluded madman, and requested their further aid in burning all seditious papers and turning in suspicious foreigners. Even the distant king himself was relieved to hear that the threat had been repelled, and he ordered a Mass of thanksgiving to be said in the Caracas Cathedral on his behalf.[103] Not all Venezuelans got off as lightly; in August several Coro residents faced trials for their suspected complicity with the foreign invaders. Juana Josefa de Silva and her son Narciso de Castro, and Josefa de Moreno, Jaime Botay, and José Nicolás Alvarado were found to be "innocent, good and loyal vassals of His Catholic Majesty" and fully absolved. Pedro de Castro, María Tomasa Morales, and José Balladares were released, but the courts reserved the right to punish them in the future if their behavior continued to arouse suspicion. The harshest sentences went to Francisco Borges and Bartolomé Rivera, who were condemned to prison for three years "to set a good example for the public."[104] Ironically, both the Venezuelan authorities and Miranda overestimated the amount of popular sympathy that his ideas enjoyed.

At any rate, Miranda was ready to return to England once more by the end of 1807. For obvious reasons, he wished to avoid stopping in the United States and instead booked a passage directly from Trinidad. Governor Thomas Hislop forewarned the British politicians of Miranda's impending return, telling Castlereagh, "[H]e has taken his passage in a Ship bound for Bristol and is anxious that he may not be detained there under Alie[n] Regulations, conceiving that his earliest presence in London may be of consequence." Hislop stressed Miranda's zeal and anxiety for "the Honor & success of His Majesty's Arms, as well as for the welfare prosperity and Glory of the British Empire, towards which both his heart and Mind are as strongly bent as those of the most loyal and faithful of His Majesty's Subjects."[105] Miranda docked at Portsmouth on December 21, 1807, where he waited just over a week for a permit to proceed to London. Unlike poor Moses Smith and John Edsall, Miranda enjoyed a warm reception, complete with a Foreign Office passport that described his occupation as "General in the Army" and with parish bells ringing in his honor at the port.[106] He had come home from Venezuela.

6

GREATNESS BEGINS AT GRAFTON STREET
Following the Leader in London
(1808–1810)

My house in this city is, and shall always be, the fixed point for the independence and liberties of the Columbian continent.
—FRANCISCO DE MIRANDA (London, March 24, 1810)

Francisco de Miranda arrived home at Grafton Street on New Year's Day, 1808. There he found his happy family waiting for him: his overjoyed wife, Sarah Andrews; their 5-year-old son Leandro, who was trying very hard to appear grown-up; and the as-yet-unseen infant son Francisco, cradled in his mother's arms. Also present to celebrate Miranda's return were John Turnbull and his family, Sir Home Popham and his wife, Miranda's faithful secretary Tómas Molini, and an assortment of hangers-on. The group spent a boisterous night filled with toasts, anecdotes, and songs. After two years in his native American hemisphere, Miranda was home at last, back in London with friends where he had a clearly defined role to play. The best thing about leaving home is always the return. Miranda reappeared on the London scene in 1808 with his legendary propitious timing. Napoleon's advance across the European continent had become more threatening at the same time that interest in Iberian affairs reached a crescendo in Britain. William Pitt had died and the new Portland administration tended to view the war against Napoleon in broader terms, as a global struggle not confined to the European theater alone. For Miranda and his emancipation project that was good news, although the man himself genuinely lamented the death of a friend of nearly twenty years.

Miranda lost no time in announcing his presence to the new government. Calling on Secretary of War Robert Stewart, Viscount Castlereagh, on Monday morning, January 3, 1808, Miranda delivered the dispatches he had brought from Trinidad's governor Thomas Hislop and Cochrane Johnstone, M.P., and requested a personal audience with the secretary for himself.[1] These letters confirmed that Miranda brought with him a sort of modern currency, namely accurate information about the "precise situation of matters on the neighboring continent," which, Hislop wrote to Castlereagh, should be very useful for the British government. Cochrane Johnstone similarly felt "confident that the adoption of his plan for giving freedom to South America, would be the means of producing such a commercial intercourse with our country as would enable us to view with indifference any attempt on the part of France against England. No peace should be made with that country until this great National Object was accomplished."[2] Just two days later Miranda spent the afternoon in Castlereagh's office, sharing his recent South American experiences with the minister and discussing the possibility of a second emancipation attempt in the near future; he appears to have met with easy success. Miranda's Scottish friend Alexander Davison would be the outfitter and Nicholas Vansittart would oversee the general preparations. Miranda's project was on everyone's lips in those heady, early January days. Viscount Melville and Undersecretary of War William Huskisson asked for his papers and even the crusty foreign secretary, George Canning, commented, "[h]is representations are certainly very interesting."[3]

Miranda and his associate James Mill worked hard on the final proposal, which was ready to be turned over to Castlereagh on January 10 so that he might use it to persuade the rest of the Cabinet. The document was part biography, part posture. As a ploy designed to prey on British politicians' worst fears, Miranda stressed the very real danger that Napoleon had designs on the Spanish Empire in America; at the same time, Miranda endeavored to distance himself from the embarrassing fact that he himself had served in the French army ten years earlier. He warned that the "Gallic interest" in Spanish America was evidenced by the fact that there were already 180 French troops in Caracas, with more sure to follow. He therefore appealed to the British sense of humanity not to allow his countrymen to become "the victims of French rapine and conquest." He also prepared a specific outline of the military preparedness in the provinces of Caracas, Santa Fé, and the Pacific Ocean, complete with estimates of the troops and munitions that would be needed to intervene.[4]

Miranda returned to his previous plans and produced another version of his standard, vague outline for an independent Spanish America. There should be four large states based mainly on the existing viceroyalties: Mexico-Guatemala, New Granada-Venezuela-Quito, Peru-Chile, and Buenos Aires-La Plata.[5] He stressed that the emancipation project would be greatly aided by the existing uniformity of the colonies' civic administration, language, religion, and culture. Persuasion (rather than compulsion) would be all that most citizens needed to join the banner of liberty, since Spanish Americans were innocent, mild, and uncorrupted. Part of this excessively rosy picture was intentional, designed to minimize any lingering doubts about the project's feasibility, but his failure to acknowledge the complexity of the region's racial and cultural diversity also indicates that Miranda had a flawed understanding of the real nature of Spanish American society. It is worth noting that, in the end, the various countries emancipated themselves in almost the exact opposite order to the way in which Miranda had predicted they would; he expected his own Venezuela would rise up first, followed by Mexico and Central America, moving southward through the Andes and culminating with Buenos Aires. Interestingly, Miranda's close friend Nicholas Vansittart seems to have had more insight into these matters than Miranda did. Asked to proofread a draft of the memorandum, Vansittart recalled from his reading of Alexander von Humboldt's travel account, *Personal Narrative of a Journey to the Equinoctial Regions of the New Continent*, that there were strong regional and racial differences among Spanish Americans that might require local adjustments to the plan. Peruvians, he understood, were more intensely attached to monarchical forms. Similarly, he advised Miranda to take into account the different

Miranda's Grafton Street residence, now called 58 Grafton Way, near the British Museum. Photo by Colleen Sequin and Alan Bloom

English Heritage plaque marking Miranda's residence on Grafton Street. Photo by Colleen Sequin and Alan Bloom

historical and cultural backgrounds of American Indians and African slaves, and not lump them together as a single homogeneous group.[6]

Carefully tended by his devoted Sarah Andrews, Miranda's house on Grafton Street attracted travelers who shared his disaffection with the Spanish colonial presence in America and who wished to work with him toward its demise. For example, Monsieur Pelletier, the self-appointed agent for independent Haiti, asked for a meeting with Miranda in January 1808 to discuss their shared hemispheric interests and to outline possible commercial treaties that might arise from Spanish American independence.[7] A more significant collaborator appeared in the person of Manuel Aniceto Padilla, a 40-year-old fellow traveler from Cochabamba who had come to London with a similar agenda. While there, Padilla worked in concert with Miranda's circle and extracted from British government officials similar promises of military aid and transport for an expedition to Buenos Aires. Miranda did not completely trust Padilla, who was paranoid enough to avoid appearing on the streets in daylight, and the two men often communicated through notes exchanged by their servants. Padilla could always be tempted to join a party, however, once drinking himself into a stupor that lasted for two days after an especially boisterous feast in March 1808. The next month, Miranda wrote to his Argentina correspondent Saturnino Rodríguez Peña, informing him that he and his London-based colleagues had received approval from the British government for an expedition to Buenos Aires, which they would send as soon as the situation with Napoleon in Spain permitted.[8] Indeed, he said, "[n]ever before on Earth has a cause more sacrosanct, just, or necessary for the human race been discussed than that which we are obligated to defend by right and by duty." Admiral Sidney Smith was in the South Atlantic at the time, and took such a liking to the South American that he assigned a pension of £300 per year to Rodríguez Peña in exchange for information and reports.[9]

The British government was becoming more concerned about South American affairs because of Napoleon's territorial advances in Europe. In 1807 the British government evacuated the Portuguese royal family, its court, and the bureaucracy to Rio de Janeiro as French forces invaded Portugal. Soon afterward, Napoleon looked poised to close in on Spain as well. For this understandable reason, in the early

months of 1808, the British government did an about-face and decided that the small military force it had intended for South America
should instead be diverted to fight Napoleon in the Iberian Peninsula. Arthur Wellesley, the future duke of Wellington, said he "never
had a more difficult business than when the Government bade me
tell Miranda that we would have nothing to do with his plan." Wellesley
took Miranda out for a walk in the street, hoping that the very public
setting for this awkward conversation might reduce the volatility of
their exchange. He was wrong. Years later, Wellesley recalled, "even
there he was so angry, that I told him I would walk on first a little that
we might not attract the notice of everybody passing. When I joined
him he was cooler. He said, 'You are going over into Spain (this was
before Vimiera [*sic*])—you will be lost—nothing can save you; that,
however is your affair; but what grieves me is that there never was
such an opportunity thrown away!' "[10] Although he himself had participated in the planning of the South American expedition, right
down to minute details like the number of flints that would be required, Wellesley was a political conservative at heart. He remarked
to Lord Mahon that he "had a horror of revolutionizing
any country for a political object. I always said, if they rise of themselves, well and good, but do not stir them up; it is a fearful responsibility."[11] In order to placate Miranda, the British government agreed
to keep him on salary at £700 per year for his services as a political
consultant.[12]

In the summer months of 1808, Napoleon finally invaded Spain
and forced King Charles IV to abdicate; Charles's son and heir
Ferdinand VII also abdicated and spent the next six years "in comfortable indolence on Talleyrand's estates at Valençay," not bothering
himself too much about his lost country.[13] Napoleon then installed
his brother Joseph on the Spanish throne in what had become known
as the Bayona Capitulation. With the legitimate Spanish sovereign
thus removed, an interim junta based at Cádiz asserted its leadership
and started a 5-year guerrilla struggle known as the Peninsular War
against the French occupation. Although Miranda continued to press
the British for the renewal of his emancipation project, pleading in
May 1808 that "if we do not avail ourselves of this Grand and Providential Opportunity, we may have hereafter to lament it forever," in

reality the moment was lost.[14] There was nothing left for him to do but to remain in London, undertake a public relations campaign, and wait for the tide of events on the Continent to turn. As one of Miranda's collaborators put it, something "may be gained by interesting the nation at large in a project which has hitherto been almost exclusively the nurseling of ministers; and thus binding the government to more prompt and effectual exertions in behalf of a cause which may have become popular as well as important."[15]

Furthermore, Miranda had much repair work to do on his own reputation and personal credibility, both of which had been damaged by his earlier service in France and the unmitigated failure of the *Leander* Expedition. Even though British officers had advised Spanish Americans in London that the armed forces held no real power in that country, Miranda remained sensitive to slights of his own military record. In January, city barristers Kibblethwaite and Marryat advised Miranda not to pursue a libel case against the author of a pamphlet that had used the word "banished" to describe his departure from the Spanish service in 1783 because the word could be construed to mean a voluntary withdrawal and did not necessarily imply a dishonorable or forced exit.[16] His patron and protector Nicholas Vansittart asked Miranda for evidence that he could use to correct erroneous misrepresentations that someone had made to his Cabinet colleagues Castlereagh and Canning, charging that the 1806 Leander Expedition was nothing more than a pillaging enterprise. Creditors chased him around town; William McCulloch pressed his brother's claim of $1,314 for flour and claret wine that had been loaded onto the *Leander* two years earlier but had never been paid.[17] With Napoleon's carnivorous example fresh in everyone's mind, some cynical types complained that Miranda was also a megalomaniac with personal ambitions for his own empire in South America. In his defense, Miranda chose to present himself as a patriotic republican citizen of the world; and he responded:

> My personal views and interest will be highly gratified, and my labours
> perfectly rewarded, when I shall see the People of those Provinces, enjoy-
> ing a sufficient Portion of rational civil Liberty under a solid, permanent
> form of Government that will preserve it, and promise them Happiness:
> The situation of a private Citizen then, will be to me not only a conge-

nial and eligible one, but of a good example, I hope, to others; by shewing
[*sic*] that the true Character of a Patriot consists in being submissive to
the Laws of the Country and a useful member of the society to which he
belongs.[18]

Miranda had been moving closer to the philosophers James Mill
and Jeremy Bentham, who were expounding a doctrine based on utility, or usefulness, to the people. Their famous slogan, "the greatest
good for the greatest number," indicates the direction in which
Miranda's rhetoric and beliefs were starting to turn.

Support for Spanish American emancipation had slowly been gaining popularity among the merchant community and the general reading public, even if their elected officials and statesmen were slow to
respond. Many of Miranda's and Mill's ideas filtered out into the general public discourse on the issue; in a position paper titled "A Concise Account of the Present State of the Spanish American Colonies,"
the anonymous author argued that Spain was nothing less than a province of France, which meant that all the precious metals from South
America were flowing into the coffers of Britain's Napoleonic enemy.
Leaving aside the considerable moral and humanitarian righteousness of the Spanish American cause, Britons must consider that
continent's immediate emancipation to be nothing less than a matter
of self-preservation. By attacking Spain where it was most vulnerable,
that is to say in America, England would cut off a vital infusion of
resources to the French war machine and therefore strike a death blow
to its forces in Europe. The unnamed author of this manuscript seems
to have been a Spanish American, as he expressed gratitude to the
English nation for sheltering him in its bosom; its arguments and
rhetoric exactly follow the standard Miranda–Mill line by promising
to examine "the political system which Spain maintained with her
American colonies, the disposition of these inhabitants toward their
colonial masters, the military force with which they are defended, the
facility with which the English nation can change the present government, and the extraordinary advantages which would result to the
world in general and England in particular from this change."[19]

For the next two years, Mill and his fellow utilitarian philosopher
Jeremy Bentham would take great interest in South American affairs
and in Miranda's success in particular. Mill used his influence with

the Whig editors of the powerful *Edinburgh Review* to plant articles favorable to the Spanish American cause. The *Edinburgh Review's* editorial board reflected the liberal position of the Whig reformers and included such important public opinion makers as the Reverend Sydney Smith, Holland House librarian John Allen, lawyer Henry Brougham, and Sir Francis Jeffrey. From 1808 to 1810, the editors consistently argued that Spain had brought its recent misfortunes upon itself and thus should be left to suffer the consequences; after that date, as the revolts in Spanish America became more serious, the Edinburgh reviewers moderated their stance. Miranda, Mill, William Walton, and other savvy lobbyists actively courted the popular press in their battle for Spanish American independence; the value of positive press and favorable public opinion was one of the major lessons Miranda had learned during his years in foreign residence.

As part of the campaign, James Mill wrote a lengthy review of Juan Pablo Viscardo y Guzmán's *Lettre aux espagnols américains, par un de leurs compatriotes* for the *Edinburgh Review* in January 1809. In truth, the 34-page article summarized Viscardo's work in just over a single page and then went on to focus instead on making a detailed argument for Spanish American emancipation from both commercial and humanitarian points of view. In some cases, the language used was identical to the memorandum that Mill and Miranda had presented to Castlereagh a year earlier. In this expanded and more philosophically developed version, however, Mill built up the utilitarian aspects of the case for emancipation, stressing the "grand experiment of North America before us, which the inhabitants of the South are so ambitious to imitate."[20] He argued that the independence of the North American colonies was "far more profitable to us than their subjection" and, by extending that logic, that the independence of the infinitely more resource-filled Spanish American colonies would bring untold riches to the country with enough foresight to aid them in their efforts. Quite obviously, at the dawn of the nineteenth century, European mouths still watered at the same promise of easily obtained New World wealth and glory that their ancestors had sought three hundred years earlier. Mill, however, was less insistent on dictating political forms to the Spanish Americans. Although Miranda might have bristled at Mill's characterization of his compatriots as "indolent and superstitious," he undoubtedly agreed with his scientific formula that predicted that if one could "remove the cause [i.e., Spanish control], and the effects will cease to follow." Both Mill and Jeremy Bentham were entering a radical phase in their philosophy and were quite willing to entertain the possibility that the Spanish Americans might tend toward a republican constitution resembling that of the United States although, Mill quickly added, an American-based monarchy would afford him more personal satisfaction. As Miranda had suggested since 1790, this hereditary ruler might be called a "King, Consul, Inca or by whatever name shall be most to the public taste."[21] Six months later, in the July 1809 issue of the *Edinburgh Review*, Mill also reviewed one of Miranda's favorite books about America, exiled Jesuit Juan Ignacio Molina's *Geographical, Biographical, Natural, and Civil History of Chili*, using it as another pretext to promote his group's cherished goal.

Since his military actions appeared to be shelved, at least for the immediate future, Miranda launched on a "paper assault" against Spanish colonial authority in America.[22] It was a renewed attempt to prove the righteousness of the American cause by amassing all available data, facts, testimonials, proclamations, and similar information in order to create an overwhelming impression of Spanish American independence as both just and historically inevitable. Collaborating with the journalist known as William Burke, Miranda's group published two forcefully argued volumes on the subject: *South American Independence; or the Emancipation of South America, the Glory and Interest of England* (1807), and *Additional Reasons for Our Immediately Emancipating Spanish America* (1808), both of which reveal the general's heavy reliance on British material and moral support for his scheme.[23] His associate José María Antepara also collated several documents that glorified Miranda and validated his arguments, and published them in London under the title *South American Emancipation* (1810).[24]

In *Additional Reasons*, Burke agreed with General Whitelocke's statement while on trial for his involvement in the disastrous 1806 British invasion at Buenos Aires that "our ultimate objects—[are] those of friendly intercourse and trade with the country."[25] As the South American people found themselves "inadequate to the task of self-government, their dependence on Britain and her influence must be increased."[26] Burke urged the British government and public to act immediately and decisively to preempt the French from extending their influence in Spanish America and to save "the unemployed, starving manufacturers of Britain."[27] In his view, the fates of Britain and Spanish America were inextricably linked in the struggle against Napoleon. And, crucial in this dawning age of nationalism, the allies had God on their side, the author noting that "General Miranda appears a fit instrument, in the hands of Providence, for breaking the chains of one of the finest and most interesting parts of the globe."[28]

The book clearly championed Miranda as the movement's natural leader and bestowed on him a measure of popular legitimacy by accepting and referring to him by his self-declared title of commander in chief of the Colombian army. Of course, Miranda held no such position; just as the signatories of the Paris Convention in 1797 had represented only themselves, the Colombian army did not exist except in the minds of its London-based generals. Burke and Miranda carefully created the impression of an oppressed continent, artfully renamed in homage to its world-renowned genius-father Christopher Columbus; it was a continent impatiently awaiting British arms and institutions to deliver it from the yoke of Spanish tyranny, intellectual slavery, and economic stagnation. In crafting this image, the ideologues resurrected the age-old archetype of America as the New World, a place free from the vices and decay of the Old World and toward which Europeans could look for a safe haven and regeneration.[29] Previously America had served as a source of great mineral and agricultural wealth for Europeans, a destination for religious dissenters, a testing ground for planned societies, and a vast opportunity for economic advancement; in 1808, Burke and Miranda reclaimed these images and went on to present America as a secure rear flank from which to defend Europe, meaning Britain, against Napoleon's grand designs.[30] As the author put it, Britain, "by adopting the all-powerful measure of conferring independence on the people . . . shall in no great distance of time, more than counterbalance the loss of those now destroyed or withheld by our enemy, in the Old." Miranda was well pleased with the results of his friend's efforts; he arranged for a copy of *Additional Reasons* to be sent to the Buenos Aires *cabildo* in

July 1808 with instructions that it should be copied and distributed throughout the rest of the continent.

As a passionately political exile, Miranda always needed to feel needed. He reveled in his position as a purveyor of knowledge and an intermediary between America and Europe. As he self-importantly told Castlereagh in August 1808, his eager correspondents in Caracas and Trinidad "would be extremely anxious for further advice from me." It seems that Miranda had proposed to the Marqués del Toro in Caracas that the *cabildo* there should assume control in the absence of a legitimate sovereign on the Spanish throne, and should request that the provinces send representatives to Caracas for further deliberations. He was, however, explicit in his advice that they not accept as delegates men who were self-interested, hostile, or linked to any foreign party that might work against the true interests of the fatherland. This recommendation should be passed on to the *cabildos* at Santa Fé de Bogotá and Quito as well, so that all can "march united toward the same end." The next week Miranda sent similar advice to Saturnino Rodríguez Peña and the Buenos Aires *cabildo* and asked that they transmit copies onward to Peru, Chile, and Quito. In September, he trained his sights on Havana and Mexico, telling the captain general and viceroy respectively that recent events in Spain had proven that "the Columbian Continent cannot be governed by Europe, whose *Political, moral and civil System* is entirely different, and nearly incompatible with our tranquility and well-being in America." He suggested that they were receiving intentionally distorted information about the real state of affairs in Europe from the junta at Cádiz, and that they ought to consider deputizing a loyal and trustworthy agent to travel abroad in order to make independent inquiries. He must have felt assured of British protection while in London; in all his communications, both with private citizens and with high-level colonial authorities, Miranda made no attempt to disguise his local address or downplay his real intentions.[31]

On October 6, 1808, Miranda issued another of his signature circular letters to the *cabildos* of the "Columbian Continent," in which he tried to create a sense of hemispheric solidarity and to resurrect heroes from their recent past to serve the present struggle; for example, he described Gual and España, leaders of a 1797 patriotic revolt in Caracas, as "illustrious Americans" and not the criminals that the Spaniards had tried to depict them as.[32] He sent nine documents as appendices that he counseled Spanish American patriots to study carefully; he believed that his own personal experiences in the two great Revolutions that had preceded their own, the American and the French, could provide the rebels with some practical guidance as their own turn for liberty approached. In the early nineteenth century, lines of communication between the American colonies were almost nonexistent, so information often passed from one region to another via London. This logistical oddity allowed Miranda's Grafton Street home to be the nexus at which all patriotic dissenters could gather.

José María Antepara, an Ecuadorean liberal, followed Miranda's beacon to London in 1809 and attached himself to the Grafton Street group. Antepara was a 38-year-old gadabout with some experience in journalism and uneven training in political theory. Like Miranda, he was perpetually short of money and often got himself mixed up with shady financial schemes in order to keep his political agenda afloat. Manuel Cortés Campomanes, a Spanish defector to the Venezuelan cause, also gravitated toward Grafton Street and presented himself to the general on January 26, 1809. Cortés Campomanes had long been active in liberal conspiratorial circles, having been jailed for his collaboration with Mariano Picornell in Spain's San Blas revolt (1796) against Manuel Godoy and later in Venezuela for complicity in the Gual and España Revolt (1797). According to a contemporary observer, Cortés Campomanes was thin and light-skinned with large, black eyes, a long nose, not much in the way of a beard, a slightly hunched back, no hair on his chest, a large forehead, and black hair.[33] Miranda was thrilled to meet him and assigned Cortés Campomanes the task of infiltrating London's Spanish community because his accent would allow him to blend in unnoticed.

The Spanish Crown did not fail to take notice of Miranda's exploits. An extensive Spanish spy network was centered around The Orange, a coffeehouse near Haymarket that had its own propaganda organ in the newspaper *The Anti-Gallican Monitor*.[34] Britain had allied itself with the Spanish patriots against Joseph Napoleon, meaning that the two nations were working together in a joint enterprise;

Miranda's public campaigns therefore threatened to undermine relations between the two wartime partners. Foreign Secretary George Canning wrote to the Spanish envoy to Great Britain, Juan Ruíz de Apodaca, pretending to be shocked to learn of Miranda's alleged conspiratorial activities in London; Canning thanked the envoy for his kind note and promised to take measures to impede the general's progress. A few days later, Canning assured Apodaca that any letters Miranda might have sent to the governor of Caracas, the viceroy of Mexico, or any other Spanish American official had been written without the British government's knowledge or complicity, and that British agents in the Caribbean would intercept them wherever possible.[35] Canning was never one to be too concerned with truth or accuracy in these sorts of matters. For him, expediency was more important.

Nevertheless, by 1809, Miranda's public relations campaign on behalf of Spanish America began to pay dividends. Attracted by a carefully cultivated image of Venezuela, several prominent Londoners, including Lady Hester Stanhope, Jeremy Bentham, and even the aging abolitionist William Wilberforce, began to entertain thoughts of relocating to the tropics. Miranda and his group had portrayed Caracas as a land of unparalleled natural beauty, unlimited commercial opportunities, and a healthful climate. As part of their print strategy, the London lobbyists published translations of Francisco Javier Clavijero's *The History of Mexico* (1807) and Juan Ignacio Molina's *Geographical, Biographical, Natural, and Civil History of Chili* (1809) in order to stress Spanish America's tremendous economic potential for British merchants and politicians. Most important, however, was the region's need for useful professionals. Hester Stanhope offered to superintend a school for girls in Caracas; Jeremy Bentham thought he might be able to do "a little in the way of my trade," that is, to provide a custom-built constitutional code for the new nation, or help codify its laws at the very least.[36]

In one of the more implausible footnotes to British intellectual history, the reclusive Bentham fell under Miranda's spell and came very close to relocating to Spanish America; in 1808 he wrote to Lord Holland, describing himself as "an Englishman by birth, [but] a citizen of the world by naturalization," and requested Holland's intercession on his behalf with his personal friend, Spanish prime minister

Gaspar Melchor de Jovellanos, for a visa.[37] Bentham, it seems, had felt so "pinched by the cold of our English winters" that he desired to repair to the vicinity of Mexico City where the "[t]emperature is just what anybody pleases." He had considered as alternatives Madeira or

Jeremy Bentham, by J. Thompson. National Portrait Gallery

Tenerife in the Canary Islands, but in the end decided that "on account of its wealth, extent and novelty, Mexico is more inviting."[38] At the dawn of the Romantic era, with anti-Spanish theatrical productions like *Pizarro* and *The Inquisition* popular on the London stage, political reformers dreamed of starting over in a New World paradise. If his genius was not needed at home in England, Bentham reasoned, his expertise might be valued and recognized across the Atlantic, where he could help his friend Miranda usher in a new stage of liberty and happiness among the Americans.

In order to be allowed to travel, Bentham beseeched Lord Holland to sign "a certificate of harmlessness" (later called "a certificate of nothingness") in exchange for which Bentham would send back for Lady Holland "[a] feather or two from the crown of Montezuma, if there should happen to be such a thing left." Furthermore, he wrote: "Everything that, in the shape of *poetry* has ever issued from any press in either Mexico, old or new, from the death of Guatamozin [Cuauhté-moc] to the present day, shall be faithfully collected and transmitted to Holland House, there to be transmuted from Mexican Spanish to elegant English."

There was a lot of accurate, as well as the inevitably inaccurate, information about Spanish America circulating in London, all of which attracted serious attention in liberal and reformist circles.[39] The region's exoticism and mythical history provided enough stimulation for the romantic imagination, while its rich resources held out the promise of vast fortunes for those bold enough to seek them. Holland replied from Spain several months later that Jovellanos was indeed familiar with Bentham and his work and was sympathetic to his request, but he "conceived that the character of *Jurisconsultus*, and writer on criminal law might possibly be considered as a bad recommendation; and has therefore, mentioned those circumstances as accidental, and ventured to ground your petition on your love of botany, and of antiquities and of the precarious state of your health."[40]

Undaunted, Bentham continued to meet with South American expatriates in London and sketched the outlines of a constitution for use in the various future nations. He dined with Argentine lobbyist Don Mariano Castilla and lived next door to the very same Cochrane Johnstone who had worked with Miranda in Trinidad in 1806. He also actively pursued research into the natural history of Spanish America and requested that visitors bring him seeds and specimens of American flora and fauna, which he kept preserved in bottles of spirits in his bizarre Westminster home.[41]

In 1809, a married father of two, Miranda met the woman who was the last major love affair of his life, Lady Hester Lucy Stanhope, the brilliant but erratic 27-year-old niece of his deceased patron,

Lady Hester Stanhope, by R. J. Hammerton. National Portrait Gallery

William Pitt. Lady Hester had come from a stifling country estate to London in 1803 to serve as her unmarried uncle's social hostess and quickly shocked polite society with her unconventional ways of dress and behavior.[42] For his part, the indulgent Pitt enjoyed Lady Hester's outrageousness and took pleasure in introducing her to the most pompous and self-important people he could find, sure that some great anecdote would result; his obliging niece rarely disappointed him in that regard. Before meeting Miranda, she suffered several intense attractions to prominent society gentlemen, most notably Sir Granville Leveson-Gower and Sir John Moore. She was ripe for another romantic adventure when friends introduced her to the notorious Venezuelan general. After they met in April 1809, Miranda and Lady Hester dined together frequently. Always captivated by bright women, Miranda recorded in his diary that Lady Hester offered the most lovely, erudite, and liberal conversation ranging over several subjects. She professed to be devoted to the cause of Venezuelan independence under a system of rational liberty and was most anxious to visit that interesting country herself. Miranda was immediately besotted. He declared her to be one of the most interesting women he had ever met and despaired to learn that she was setting out for Wales the next day to take the country air for her health. Ever the coquette, before she left, Stanhope found the time to send a copy of Sydney Smith's recent edition of *Letters of Peter Plymley* to the handsome foreigner, accompanied by an invitation to visit her when she returned to the city in ten days.[43]

It should not be surprising that the couple found each other attractive. By all accounts Lady Hester was a woman who was "always happiest in the company of men, preferably those that were handsome, intelligent, and half in love with her," and Miranda was all three.[44] Calling her "the most delicious woman I have yet encountered," Miranda, for a time, was Caesar to Lady Stanhope's Cleopatra.[45] Although rumors persist among Miranda's South American biographers that Lady Hester was the true mother of one or both of his sons, the late date of their acquaintance seems to preclude the possibility.[46] This rumor draws its strength from not only the relationship between Lady Hester and Miranda, which surely existed as an intense intellectual friendship, but also from her continued interest in the education and welfare of the young Miranda boys well into the 1820s. Although she left Britain permanently in February 1810, Lady Hester kept in touch with the Miranda family and later brought Leandro, and possibly Francisco as well, to visit her in Lebanon.

In July and August of 1809, Miranda traveled throughout the English countryside, partly to visit friends like James Mill who had invited him to Oxted at Jeremy Bentham's request, partly to join in the traditional English summer activities, and partly to continue building his useful connections.[47] Vansittart had hinted that it might be a good idea to get out of the city for awhile since Apodaca had recently been complaining that Miranda continued to engage in subterfuge by corresponding with Rodríguez Peña and others. No doubt his decision to take some country air was nudged along by the removal of Lady Hester to her summer house at Bath. On his way to visit Mill, Miranda stopped by to spend some time with her, discreetly taking lodgings in an inn next to her home. The two rode horses, dined together, and met furtively in the evenings.

With a smile on his face and already many pleasant memories made during his summer tour, Miranda continued onward to visit Oxford University, where he met Dr. F. S. Constancio and Francis Gould Leckie, two men who became enthusiastic collaborators in his emancipation project. In the countryside, Miranda reverted to his tourist persona and attempted to see every sight listed in his copy of the *Oxford Guide*. He visited the university's library, which had an astounding 200,000 volumes and 30,000 manuscripts, enjoyed its botanic garden and observatory, studied the architecture of its many cathedrals and college buildings, and admired the busts and portraits of eminent British figures such as Locke, Pope, Swift, Mary Queen of Scots, and Addison. Miranda also partook in that most English of recreations, looking at rural views, and spent his evenings attending Shakespearean plays. In Wales, Miranda crossed the Monmouth Canal and saw the ironworks of Frere and Cook; there, he noted in his diary, he saw for the first time "what are called Railways, by which means Waggons [*sic*] go up and down the Mountains with considerable less Labour, as one Horse does the work of 4 or 5. Some of the Waggons come down the Mountains without any Horses, and are managed by means of a lever which is guided by a Man behind who stops or impedes the velocity of the Waggon at pleasure." Two days later, he visited another ironworks where he "examined with much attention the stupendous machine, the Steam Engine, which is the primum mobile of the whole, and saves the labour of 80 horses."[48] Miranda returned to London on Thursday, August 17, tired but refreshed from the change of scenery and excited about the new inventions he had seen.

Even spies need a holiday. Once Miranda was back in London, the Spanish diplomats and agents who had been tailing Miranda since the 1780s resumed following his activities with nervousness and reported on them with increasingly hysterical language. Colonial officials in La Plata and Caracas received warnings dated November 8, 1809, of "the renewed machinations of the traitor Miranda," whose expedition against Caracas "was as shameful for him and his backers as it was glorious for the Spanish armed forces."[49] Apodaca was watching "this revolting man" closely, but the Spanish government thought it prudent that Spanish Americans themselves be on the lookout for partisans of his growing transatlantic network, possibly operating from a base in Brazil. Apparently Apodaca had a meeting with Canning in late 1809 during which the foreign secretary professed no great estimation for Miranda's person or abilities.[50] In February 1810, Spanish spies reported that a suspicious person by the name of "N. Pavia," apparently a native of Ceuta who had been married in Havana, had appeared in London with some secretive plans for the British government about Spanish colonies throughout the Atlantic world.[51]

Miranda, in his capacity as an idealistic, eighteenth-century devotee of reason and progress, was also a Freemason. The Masonic movement was an extraordinarily powerful part of patriotic movements throughout the Atlantic world in the age of democratic revolution. As an organized entity, Freemasonry began with the foundation of the Great Lodge in London in 1717 among sculptors, artists, and others in the building trades who wished to create a voluntary moral code to regulate their members' lives and to provide aid in times of financial distress. The movement was secretive, highly organized into thirty-three grades, each with its own induction ceremony, rites, and special titles. Freemasonry has been described as a "religious fraternity without a religion," making it a perfect vehicle to spread politicized ideology.[52] Its ideals included equality, fraternity, justice, tolerance, liberty, the avoidance of moral self-destruction, patriotism, and class cooperation. In practice, this meant an adherence to political principles that advocated separation of powers, constitutions, popular sovereignty, and natural rights. A Masonic lodge could bind together persons of different classes, religions, and social status, and therefore membership became a symbol of one's modernity and forward thinking. Its origins among the working classes, as well as its conscious use of symbols associated with construction and human achievement (compasses, hammers, pyramids) indicated a growing value placed on science, productivity, and social mobility.[53] Because of the emphasis on organization and fraternalism, Masonic lodges caught on among genteel society types and military men alike. Miranda seems to have been inducted into a Masonic order while in France in the 1790s, although it is likely that he had encountered Masons among his friends long before that. A list of important U.S. and European Masons includes Marquis de Lafayette, Talleyrand, Georges-Jacques Danton, Camille Desmoulins, the Abbé Sieyès, U.S. presidents Thomas Jefferson, George Washington, James Monroe, and Andrew Jackson, Benjamin Franklin, Sir Home Popham, the duke of Sussex, William Pitt, the duke of Wellington, William Wilberforce, Henry Brougham, Lord Holland, and even literary figures such as Sir Walter Scott, Johann Wolfgang von Goethe, and Alexander Pushkin. As a Freemason, Miranda was in good company.

In London, he founded an exclusively Spanish American Masonic lodge, variously known as the Gran Reunión Americana (Great American Assembly) or the Sociedad de los Caballeros Racionales (Society of Rational Gentlemen); an affiliate was established among Spanish American expatriates in Cádiz, and the group eventually spread throughout Spanish America when patriotic travelers returned home and set up their own cells. Nineteenth-century Argentine historian and statesman Bartolomé Mitre, however, called the rumor "unfounded" that Miranda traveled to Cádiz in either 1808 or 1809 in order to plot with disaffected Spanish American Creole Masons there.[54] Miranda's Spanish American lodge in exile had four goals: to create an instrument for the formation and consolidation of the struggle for

emancipation, to give the movement a continental character, to provide a vehicle for the dissemination of patriotic propaganda, and to
provide patriots with shared political symbols of inclusion (signs, rituals, formalities, organizational structure).[55] He took as its motto
"Union, Firmness and Valor." Most leaders of Spanish American independence were Masons in affiliated societies, including Simón
Bolívar, José de San Martín, Bernardo O'Higgins, Tomás Guido,
Manuel Moreno, Fray Servando Teresa de Mier Noriega y Guerra,
Vicente Rocafuerte, Carlos Alvera, Francisco de Fagoaga, Antonio José
de Sucre, Camilo Henríquez, José Cecilio del Valle, and Antonio
Nariño. Many of these men joined the movement while visiting
Miranda's Grafton Street home. Not surprisingly, the Spanish Crown
and the Catholic Church viewed the growth of the Masonic movement with fear and alarm. A series of papal bulls condemned Ma-
sonry as a sort of irreligious contagion and added its practice to the
list of offenses punishable under the Inquisition. Similarly, civil authorities viewed Masons as seditious intriguers bent on seducing loyal
and vulnerable populations away from the government.

With the establishment of Masonic secret societies to aid in the
diffusion of their ideology and organization throughout America,
Miranda's circle began to step up their London-based activities and to
attract increasing numbers of like-minded individuals to their door-
step. Cortés Campomanes arranged for arms to be smuggled to an
allied cell in Buenos Aires to create an armed force there; as he reported, "America is beginning defensive preparations."[56] He also conferred with Antepara, who informed him that the Mexicans seemed
to look toward the North Americans as a possible military ally. On a
personal level, Cortés Campomanes disliked Antepara, who was continually engaging in questionable business deals and whose character
was, in his estimation, less than honorable; nevertheless, Antepara
was clearly decided in favor of independence and for the moment,
that quality superseded all others.[57] Cortés Campomanes took sick
and was bedridden for a month and a half, but by the end of December he felt well enough to write to Miranda and inquire about the
arrival of the wealthy Mexican Marqués del Apartado (Francisco de
Fagoaga) with his brother and his cousin, Wenceslao Villaurrutia.[58]

Vansittart, too, sent a note saying that he was impatient to learn the news of the Mexican travelers, but urged extreme circumspection in the face of Miranda's many enemies.

As 1810 opened, Miranda was a happy man. He was nearly sixty years old and had a growing young family and a respected place in London society. For all intents and purposes, he was the voice of America in Europe. His home on Grafton Street was the first stop for any Spanish American who came to the British capital, whether for business or pleasure. He provided introductions for these starry-eyed patriots to his vast circle of friends and sympathizers throughout the country and offered them access to the highest levels of government. Everyone knew who Miranda was and his appearance at any dinner party was enough to ensure its success. Living comfortably across the Atlantic, Miranda could play the role of Great American Patriot-General and still go home to sleep in his own bed at night. No wonder he was so pleased with all the idealistic young men who traveled across an ocean to meet him and take up his cause. Miranda needed London more than it needed him. He was more American, more pa-triotic, and more relevant in London society than he could hope to be in Venezuela. Although he spoke constantly of returning to *América Meridional,* for Miranda, South America was an imaginary place, dimly related to the idealized Venezuela of his youth but more clearly shaped by his thirty years of life abroad. Miranda may have been the precursor of Spanish American independence, but its true heroes were found in the next generation, those brave young men who shared Miranda's goals and began coming to London in 1810. Having received his stamp of approval, having met with other like-minded Spanish Americans from throughout the continent and ransacked British culture for the secrets to its success, they were the ones who ultimately made his dream a reality.

The year 1810 was momentous both for the Spanish world and for Miranda personally. Lady Hester Stanhope had become so disillu-sioned with English politics that she vowed to leave her homeland forever. Miranda wrote to her, his "dear and beloved Lady Hester," expressing a fervent wish that the superiority of her spirit would carry her far beyond the petty troubles in which she had become embroiled. He considered her "irreplaceable," as a lover and as an insightful adviser. In one of their last exchanges, Miranda recounted for Hester his recent interviews with Wilberforce and the duke of Gloucester, wishing that she could be near in order to discuss these events with him and offer her sage counsel.[59] She departed on the frigate *Jason* at the end of January 1810, requesting that her dear general direct future letters to her under cover to General Torrens of the Horse Guards, who would make sure that they reached her safely. Miranda probably never saw her again.

Throwing himself into his work as a way to stave off sadness was Miranda's typical response to any personal or professional setback. He had a phenomenal will to succeed and rarely allowed himself the luxury of wallowing in self-pity. Taking advantage of the growing number of like-minded Spanish Americans gathering around him in London, he hit upon the idea of producing his own serial publication to promote their common cause. His friend, exiled Spanish liberal cleric Joseph Blanco White, was publishing a monthly journal called *El Español*; another friend, outspoken Brazilian journalist, Freemason, and anti-Inquisition crusader Hipólyto José da Costa, was producing a sophisticated newssheet called the *Correio Brasiliense*. Miranda decided that Spanish Americans also needed their own advocacy organ, which he titled *El Colombiano*. Ecuadorean Antepara would be its editor; adopted Venezuelan Manuel Cortés Campomanes would be a contributing writer; Mexicans Apartado and Villaurrutia would provide funding and occasional articles, while expatriate Frenchman Juigné agreed to be its printer. Miranda, of course, was the mastermind behind the whole operation and in charge of its editorial direction. Intended to appear fortnightly beginning in mid-March 1810, *El Colombiano* represented a bold ideological leap; addressed to the "great Colombian continent," as though all American people were one, the publication ushered in a new era of hemispheric solidarity. Nicholas Vansittart, always a cautious voice whispering in Miranda's ear, received the first two issues of *El Colombiano* and warned his friend that he should exercise extraordinary care to avoid exciting the jealousy of his enemies or giving strength to their charges against him.[60]

The direction and purpose of *El Colombiano* was apparent from its opening lines. The London-based editorial group assigned themselves the task of raising the Spanish American consciousness about "the disgraceful events that have recently occured in the Peninsula, events which will most likely be followed by the entire subjugation of European Spain" and the implications that this fact held for their future happiness.[61] Antepara and Miranda explicitly stated that they wished to empower Americans with accurate information to enable them to make their own decisions, rather than having to rely on the heavily mediated reports that Madrid permitted to dribble across the Atlantic for their consumption. Issues of *El Colombiano* were dotted with translations of foreign newspaper articles and official dispatches about the ravages of the Continental war and the Regency's unpopularity in Spain itself. For example, the fourth issue opened with an article titled "Thoughts of an Englishman on the State and Present Crisis of the Affairs of South America," the point of which was anything but subtle: "All Europe knows that for many years the inhabitants of America have desired to see themselves emancipated and free of the harsh subjection in which a foreign country holds them; that is the reason that civilized Europe has loudly passed judgement that the immense population of the New World cannot be well-governed except by a government established in their own land."[62]

Taking the anonymous Englishman's words at face value as an established authority, Miranda and Antepara instructed their faraway compatriots that good government implies:

> . . . the coordination of the people's business, by which all classes join together and abandon their separate interests, in the name of peace and common happiness, all that which can be prejudicial to the others. The rich man deprives himself of all that which is contrary to the well-being of the poor; the poor of all that which opposes the happiness of the poor. Men of one [national or racial] origin abandon all that which can injure the prosperity of men of different origins, so that in this way all of society enjoys the greatest possible happiness. And this is the true meaning of the word *Patriot*.

The Spanish colonial system had kept them divided and oppressed for its own benefit and, therefore, in the eyes of the modern world and political science, the system itself was illegitimate, its demands null and void. In other words, *El Colombiano* championed the standard Creole argument about the devolution of power to the *cabildos* upon Napoleon's seizure of the royal family and Charles IV's abdication.

The appearance of *El Colombiano* unleashed a flurry of terror throughout the Spanish colonial administration, especially once its officials had determined that the hated General Francisco de Miranda, "well known for the part that he took in the horrors of the French Revolution," was behind it. A nervous functionary in London's Spanish embassy reported that *El Colombiano* was published "not in order to be sold here but in order to be sent to our Americas, exhorting them to independence." In his view the newspaper was "incendiary and subversive to all good order and tranquility and union that surely must reign in those dominions."[63] Juan Ruiz de Apodaca requested a meeting with the new foreign secretary Richard Colley Wellesley in order to discuss the objectionable publication, but was told that the country's freedom of the press laws made it impossible to shut it down; Apodaca could do little but to urge colonial officials to monitor the ports and confiscate any stray copy of either *El Colombiano* or *El Español* that might make its way into their dominions. In November 1810, both president of Guatemala Antonio González and viceroy of New Spain Francisco Xavier Venegas reported that the two serials had not yet been found to be in circulation; by January 1811, the viceroy of Peru José Abascal also confirmed that he had successfully impeded their distribution.[64] Of course, nothing was farther from the truth. In Mexico alone there were several subscribers to *El Colombiano* to be found among the liberal urban and mercantile types; Jacobo Villaurrutia, José María Fagoaga, the Mexico City *cabildo*, the Cathedral of Guadalupe's Canon José Mariano Beristain y Souza, the Marqués de Guardiola, the Conde de Medina, and several others of the autonomist movement all possessed copies of the publication despite an official government ban.[65] Furthermore, articles from *El Colombiano* were reprinted in both the *Gazeta de Caracas* and the *Gazeta de Buenos Aires*. The Spanish Americans' first great collaborative effort on behalf of their independence survived for just five issues before financial trouble forced it to shut down.

Suddenly, the pace of events in Spanish America picked up. On April 19, 1810, disaffected Creoles in Caracas ousted Captain General

Vicente Emparán; one of the leaders of this movement was José Cortés Madariaga, a Chilean canon who had spent some time with Miranda in London in 1803. On May 25, 1810, a group of young patriotic liberals in Buenos Aires also rose up and overthrew the viceroy; the leaders of Buenos Aires' May Revolution claimed that in the king's absence, governing power constitutionally reverted to the local *cabildo*, which would act as its custodians until his return. Both movements relied on similar arguments that followed the Viscardo-Miranda-*El Colombiano* line and dramatically changed the course of events on both sides of the Atlantic. Later that summer, Father Miguel Hidalgo encouraged a somewhat more radical social revolution among indigenous and rural people in central Mexico, indicating that there was indeed widespread discontent throughout Spanish America that operated on many different levels.

Revolution seemed to be on everyone's minds. Holland House librarian John Allen asked Joseph Blanco White to pass along any particulars that he might have heard about the "insurrection of Caracas," adding that he hoped it would not be directed against Spain but rather that it was intended simply to introduce freer trade and permit Creoles to rise higher in their own government.[66] Similarly concerned, the Spanish ambassador, the duke of Albuquerque, arranged a meeting with Wellesley on July 4 in which the two men discussed the turn of events in Caracas. Apparently the British foreign secretary assured Albuquerque that His Majesty's government continued its previous policy, which was to support Spain in the war against France and to protect the integrity of the Spanish American under the dominion of Ferdinand VII.[67]

The Spanish American revolution quickly crossed the Atlantic to London and made its presence felt on the streets and in the city's drawing rooms. On July 19, 1810, three Venezuelans stepped off a ship, ironically named the *General Wellington*, and passed through British customs at Portsmouth. Luis López Méndez was a 52-year-old university administrator who spoke tolerable French and whose second wife was Miranda's niece, María Rodríguez de Miranda. Simón Bolívar was a brash, 27-year-old aristocrat who had offered to fund the mission in exchange for a place as one of its members. Andrés Bello was a shy, 29-year-old government official who spoke English and had come in the capacity of secretary. Wellesley agreed to send the trio passports for travel to London but, not wishing to anger the Spanish embassy by appearing to embrace potential rebels, he informed Albuquerque immediately that the men had arrived and offered to pass along copies of any documents they might have brought for him.[68] Wellesley agreed to meet with them but insisted that the encounter take place at his residence, Apsley House, in order to make it clear to them that their talks carried no official recognition.

Their first meeting was held on the evening of Monday, July 16. Speaking in French, Bolívar and López Méndez presented their credentials and their government's requests while Wellesley listened patiently for over an hour, trying to ascertain how truthful the men were being with him. The Venezuelans used the standard argument that in the event of a threat to the Crown, power reverted to local authority constituted as the *cabildo* and that therefore their junta's actions were both constitutional and necessary. Although Bolívar and López Méndez stressed that their government was only a placeholder, guarding power until Ferdinand VII could resume the throne, and that was the constitutional reason why they had refused to recognize the Regency in Cádiz, Wellesley remained unconvinced. He retorted that Venezuela had been the only territory to make such a refusal and therefore their actions had to be viewed as nothing less than a de facto declaration of independence.[69] The discussion bounced back and forth along these lines until it became clear that neither side was going to budge from its position. Wellesley thanked the men for their kind visit and then, unexpectedly, hinted that perhaps an understanding could be reached after all. They should meet again, soon.

The Venezuelan delegates benefited from Miranda's twenty-five years of experience with the intricacies of European diplomacy. Clearly the British foreign secretary would not be willing to sacrifice Spain, his nation's Continental ally against Napoleon, for an ill-understood group of possible rebels from a half a world away. Nevertheless, Wellesley was also mindful of the potential trade opportunities that could be opened with a vast new American market, and was also anxious to create goodwill with the American colonists in order to have some leverage with Spain when negotiating peace after the war was eventually won. For this reason, Wellesley permitted himself the luxury

William Wilberforce by George Richmond, 1833. National Portrait Gallery

of several more meetings with Miranda's protégés over the course of the next six weeks. The Spanish embassy, for its part, was desperate for accurate information about what had passed between Wellesley and the Venezuelans; on July 17 its corresponding secretary reported back to Madrid, "The only thing that I know about said Deputies is that although they profess against Miranda with vehemence, he has already been to visit them in their lodgings."[70]

Employing the same sort of stalling tactics that Pitt and Castlereagh had used before him, Wellesley asked the envoys to prepare a memorandum stating their goals and to present it to him for further consideration. They did so immediately and then had to settle into a waiting game. In the meantime, Miranda took his foreign visitors on the rounds of society, presenting them to Vansittart, Lord Buckinghamshire, the duke of Cumberland, and even to the king's nephew, the duke of Gloucester, who was "a great admirer or panegyrist" of Miranda's talents and integrity.[71] The kindly parliamentarian and abolitionist William Wilberforce gave Miranda and his friends from Caracas an hourlong interview, and they were invited back for another early dinner in the middle of August.[72]

The arrival of the Venezuelan delegation in London prompted a sort of publicity war among the liberal and conservative daily newspapers. Miranda's colleagues helped him plant articles favorable to their cause in the *Morning Chronicle* and identified the trio with the legitimate-sounding title of "South American Commissioners" who represented "the Provisional Government of Caraccas [*sic*]." In contrast, conservative editors at the *Times* beefed up their coverage of those Spanish American colonies that had declared continuing allegiance to the Regency that was ruling Spain in Ferdinand's name; for example, the *Times* claimed that the Mexican people were attached to Spain and preferred to remain loyal rather than hamper the war effort with their own ill-considered actions and selfish motives. The next day, another *Times* article added that Peru also had declared itself to be loyal to the central authority; far from being viewed as brutal masters, they wished it to be known, Peruvians considered Spaniards to be their brothers across the ocean. The editors of the *Times* scoffed at those who pretended to the British public that their aid in emancipation would be welcomed, pointing out that just four years earlier

Whitelocke, Popham, and Beresford had failed miserably in their attempt to conquer Buenos Aires, and Miranda himself had been rejected at Coro.[73] Their barbs were a clear and pointed attack on the veracity of the optimistic message that the Miranda camp had been trying to set before the British public.

While they were in London, Miranda introduced the Venezuelans to other Spanish Americans who had gathered around him: Antepara the Ecuadorean; Cortés Campomanes, the Spanish defector; the Mexicans Apartado, Fagoaga, and Villaurrutia. Matías Yrigoyen arrived from Buenos Aires in mid-August 1810 with an official commission that was strikingly similar to that of the Venezuelans.[74] Together, the Spanish American men toured London, talking about the attitudes they shared and the similar conditions that faced their respective homelands. Miranda exhibited pride of place as he took them to visit the dockyards and naval hospital at Greenwich, to meet with Jeremy Bentham and talk about constitutional law, and to visit the scientifically rigorous Royal Botanical Gardens at Kew. At least one of the Venezuelans, Simón Bolívar, made a pilgrimage to Joseph Lancaster's well-publicized school for mutual education located on Borough Road. Lancaster's monitorial system used older students as tutors for the younger ones, thereby promising to educate thousands of children to full literacy in just weeks. Clearly this model appealed to fledgling governments who lacked funds and human capital for a mass education project; Bolívar promised Lancaster he would remember to send back "two young men from Caracas to learn the system under the tuition of its founder."[75]

Although the summer was enjoyable and educational for the group of progressive and liberal Spanish Americans, there was still much work to be done on behalf of their people. Both Yrigoyen and the Venezuelans continued to press Wellesley for a response to their requests for British trade, military assistance, and public proclamations of friendship for their respective juntas. Wellesley agreed to another meeting with Bolívar and López Méndez on August 10, and eventually offered them something that fell short of their full requests but represented a significant accomplishment nonetheless; he offered maritime protection from any French incursion into their territory, British mediation between "the brothers of both hemispheres" to see if any reconciliation could be effected, and a recommendation to Spain that the colonies be permitted to trade more freely with other nations.[76] Wellesley surreptitiously sent copies of all notes taken and documents presented to the Spanish ambassador, including his final proposal to the deputies.

With that, the business of the so-called Grafton Street Symposium had reached its conclusion and the various envoys started to make their plans to return home. They had been excited and energized by London's sights, smells, and sounds, but soon began to miss their own kind. Manuel Cortés Campomanes, for example, wrote to Miranda from Islington, complaining that he had not been able to leave his house for fifteen days because he was laid up with a debilitating pain that turned out to be, thankfully, rheumatism and not a case of venereal disease, as he had thought. He was most anxious to return to a tropical climate and to get away from England, where he had been "more miserable than in any other part of the world, or better said, only here have I felt bad."[77] Miranda naturally had thoughts of going back to America as well. He had written to the Venezuelan junta on August 3 to praise their wise selection of Bolívar and López Méndez as envoys; both men, he dutifully reported, had acquitted themselves with "tremendous personal honor and brought much credit to the country that sent them." With a tone that managed both to be ingratiating and to convey a sense of entitlement, Miranda mentioned his desire to be relieved of the debts that he had accumulated in the service of the Great Cause over the past twenty years while at the same time soliciting "the permission that is due to me to return to my beloved fatherland in the capacity of one of its citizens."[78] Vansittart entirely approved of his request and hoped that he would be allowed to depart for his homeland; the ever politic Vansittart recommended, however, that Miranda not book passage on the same ship as the deputies simply for the sake of appearance. It would be wise not to arouse Spanish fears any more than the news of his travels was already likely to do. Furthermore, Vansittart counseled, Miranda ought to emphasize that he was entirely enthusiastic about the possibility of British mediation between Spain and her American colonies "on terms calculated to secure the liberties and happiness of both."[79] The Venezuelan junta had its own ideas, however; its members had explicitly instructed Bolívar and López Méndez not to bring Miranda back with them. They believed that he was too old and would represent too much of a liability in the delicate international diplomatic balance they had to strike. Furthermore, Juan Germán Roscio and others believed that Miranda's personal ambition could not be trusted.

The *Times* took polite notice of Bolívar's departure from London on the *Sapphire* in early September, merely remarking that he had been content with his reception and that its editors hoped good commercial relations between the two nations would result.[80] Antepara, Cortés Campomanes, and Frenchman Pedro Antonio Leleux went with Bolívar, but Miranda wisely stayed behind to put his personal affairs in order before he slipped away without much fanfare later in October. Meanwhile, Spaniards' suspicions of the real goals of the Caracas junta continued to color their interpretation of events. Apodaca presented a note to Wellesley informing him that the Venezuelans had released sixteen enemy Frenchmen from their jails and sent them off to the United States on the understanding that "no further reason exists for detaining them any longer as that Country [Venezuela] is not at war with France." In other words, the Venezuelans were making their own foreign policy and thus renouncing their loyalty to the Spanish Empire in contradiction to their statements of allegiance to Ferdinand. A few days later, Wellesley assured Spanish Secretary of State for Despatch Eusebio Bardaxi y Azara that his government's accusation that the British had somehow betrayed their alliance by receiving the Caracas deputies in an official capacity were "extremely unjust and unfortunate," and that he wished to take this opportunity to disabuse them of that notion.[81]

Before he left England for the last time, Miranda added a codicil to the 1805 will that had been prepared before the Leander Expedition. Nicholas Vansittart and John Turnbull were designated as his executors and the bulk of his property was left to his wife, Sarah Andrews, and their two sons. His most valuable and prized possession, namely his vast personal library, was intended to be brought to Venezuela at some happier point in the future. Miranda kissed his family, trying hard to ignore Sarah's tears and promising her that they would be reunited again very soon. She did not relish the thought of another long separation, this time as a single parent to two small children who had to try to make ends meet on a very small income. Nevertheless, once again, Miranda's patriotic dreams overrode his personal attachments and he sailed away in October 1810. Wellesley informed Albuquerque of Miranda's departure but stressed that he had gone on his own accord, in a private capacity, and without British government sanction; that was his right according to the laws of the land and no impediments could have been thrown in his way.[82] In America, the Venezuelan junta gave orders to impede Miranda's disembarkation, since he was clearly an outlaw and known to be a wanted man throughout the Spanish Empire to which they were still technically loyal.[83] Because of his reputation and the many problems his presence threatened to rain down on the struggling junta, Miranda was not entirely welcome in his homeland. He owed much to the enthusiasm of his young admirer and protégé Simón Bolívar, who had ignored the junta's explicit instructions to the contrary and invited Miranda to take his rightful place at the head of the fledgling movement. Miranda may have viewed Bolívar as another admiring son, much like Bernardo O'Higgins and the others before him, but in this final important instance, he was wrong. The complicated relationship between these two powerful characters eventually soured and put a final end to Miranda's aspirations, but in 1810, at least, they were still politically close allies.

As the decade wound to a close, particularly in the wake of British-backed incursions at Coro and Rio de la Plata, Spanish Americans came to London in increasing numbers and with more concrete goals. Bonaparte's capture of Portugal and the Spanish monarchy irrevocably altered the political landscape of the Atlantic. Spanish American *cabildos* claimed that the devolution of power to local authorities in the face of extraordinary circumstances was a constitutional measure that represented order and moderation rather than revolution and innovation. The Bayona Capitulation had been a grand stroke of luck for Miranda and the Spanish Americans; they could invoke the cries of Order and Legitimacy along with their cry for Self-rule and Liberty, making de facto independence a return to tradition rather than a disruptive break from the past. This was in line with British political culture, which revered tradition, authority, and moderation and opposed sudden change as inevitably representing transient, selfish interests.[84] Through Miranda's purposeful travels, his study of political change and social conditions throughout the Atlantic world, and his conscious diffusion of patriotic rhetoric from his base in London, Spanish Americans gained a sense of the possibilities that lay before them. In 1810, Miranda made his long-awaited prodigal's return to spend one glorious year as a leading figure among his own people, the Americans.

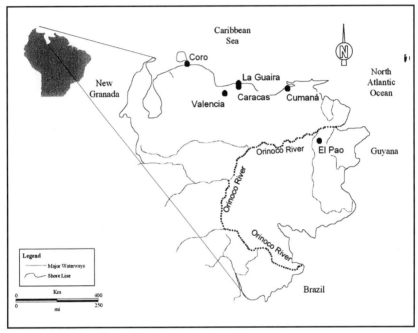

Miranda's Venezuela

7

A YEAR AMONG THE AMERICANS
Miranda and the
First Venezuelan Republic (1811–12)

You must build your House of Parliament upon the river: so . . . that the
populace cannot exact their demands by sitting down around you.
—ARTHUR WELLESLEY, DUKE OF WELLINGTON

Beginning reform is beginning revolution.
—ARTHUR WELLESLEY, DUKE OF WELLINGTON

C rossing the Atlantic for the fifth time, an old man traveling under the name of Mr. George Martin drummed his fingers anxiously on his table whenever he was seated and continually paced the
floor when he was not. Friends and acquaintances had always commented that throughout his active and adventurous life, this extraordinary man never stopped moving. Indeed, this particular ship could
not sail fast enough for him. It was as though he expected that this
voyage would be his last one. Francisco de Miranda was sixty years
old and had spent more than half his lifetime dedicated to the emancipation of his beloved homeland from Spain. Leaving his young family,
his precious library, and a history of broken promises behind him in
England, he was certain that his time in the sun had finally arrived.[1]
Following a brief stop in Curaçao for Miranda to confer with the
British governor and to hand deliver letters from his well-connected
friends, his ship finally docked at La Guaira, the same port from which
he had taken leave of his parents forty years earlier.[2] Although he had
never seen either of them again, he smiled at the sight of the shoreline

211

and remembered their parting words. Venezuela, however, was not the same place he had known in his boyhood. The capital city was larger, boasting a population of over 40,000 souls, and its better houses even enjoyed water piped indoors from the three streams that passed nearby.[3] Businesses thrived and the ports bustled with traffic from countries and islands throughout the Atlantic world. French agents mingled with American traders; British travelers dined with Spanish colonial agents. While Miranda had been away fighting for freedom and liberty in other countries, his own had become far more complex.

Unbeknown to him, Miranda was stepping into a quagmire. The patriotic movement that had deposed Captain General Vicente Emparán on April 19, 1810, had received its main support from the capital city of Caracas where bureaucrats, liberal professionals, merchants, and university students all hoped to benefit from increased personal freedoms. Led by the liberal young lawyer Juan Germán Roscio, the new ruling junta was characterized by "ability and soundness" but quickly faced serious opposition from the provinces, which had always resented the capital's power over their affairs. For this reason, provincial authorities in Coro, Maracaibo, and Guyana remained loyal to the Spanish Crown and put up military resistance to the Caracas junta, seriously weakening that fragile coalition's ability to survive.[4] In fact, one contemporary observer characterized the rivalry between Coro and Caracas as a "deadly animosity."[5] Furthermore, even in the capital city itself at least four different factions each had its own competing vision for the movement's future direction: elites in the provisional junta enjoyed their new public status but wished to move cautiously; middle-class officials and government clerks owed their livelihoods to the previous system and therefore were more sincerely loyal to the Crown; university students were enthusiastically prorevolution and given to radical rhetoric without offering substantive ideas for reform; and a sober fourth group (to which Roscio, Miranda, and Simón Bolívar all eventually belonged) had a longer-range, more practical view that included full independence and statehood.[6] It was the latter view that came to be the most widely held. Before long the Caracas junta dared to state publicly that "the political order of the other hemisphere has reduced Spain to being the victim of perfidy and oppression. . . . The connections that until today have made us *compañeros* in its fortunes have ceased to exist, because the power that moves and animates the universe has accelerated the fatal catastrophe that must separate both our worlds forever."[7] It should not be surprising then, that to the eyes of one British traveler, Venezuelan politicians' professions of loyalty to the captive King Ferdinand VII were "cold and theatrical."[8]

Miranda arrived home in Caracas on December 10, 1811. London papers reported that he received a "most cordial welcome," which was true, but it was a far cry from the hero's entrance he had hoped to make.[9] A good number of Caracas's politically active citizens remembered Miranda's ill-considered landing at Coro four years earlier and thought he was hopelessly out of touch with their current reality. Others feared that he intended to take them out of the Spanish Empire and straight into the British orbit. Still others were put off by the expectation that Miranda's years abroad had denationalized him, had made him too cosmopolitan and therefore inclined to treat native-born Americans with European-style condescension. Juan Germán Roscio, ever the gentleman, politely told the prodigal General Miranda that his "knowledge, experience and familiarity with foreign deliberative bodies" would prove most advantageous to the junta and that his native land was pleased to welcome him back.[10] In private, he remained skeptical.

Almost as soon as he disembarked, Miranda made his presence felt. He had brought with him two pieces of legislation that Jeremy Bentham had drafted specifically for Venezuela's use: "Constitutional Legislation. On the Evils of Change," and "Proposed Law for Securing the Liberty of the Press Against Persons Having the Exclusive Command of the Printing Presses of a New Country When Small in Number."[11] During the time that the two men were collaborators in London, Bentham was beginning to enter into an increasingly radical phase of his thought, and some of his energy transferred to Miranda. Bentham urged his friend to encourage the freest possible press laws for Venezuela. The utilitarian philosopher believed that the strict British libel laws had hampered free expression and he did not wish to see the same mistakes made in the new utopian social experiment that Venezuela represented for him. He further anticipated the danger that having printing presses concentrated in just a few hands might further erode the people's access to competing ideas. For this reason, Bentham urged, Miranda should labor to make Venezuela a land where one's thoughts could be expressed freely to the public without fear of censorship or reprisals. As the British owners of the *Gaceta de Caracas* suggested in their editorials, freedom of the press would be the font of "our civil regeneration."[12] In Bentham's idealized dream, the New World continued to be a place of hope, a place where the errors and restrictions of Europe could be overcome and a more perfect society could be created. Miranda would be the instrument of that glorious human achievement. Indeed, after his return, the *Gaceta de Caracas* published many extracts from the works of Miranda's utilitarian friends Bentham and James Mill.[13]

Under the general's influence, at the end of the year 1810 a group of engaged politicians and intellectuals founded the Patriotic Club, a sort of Jacobin-styled discussion group intended to build solidarity and to raise political consciousness.[14] From its inception, the Patriotic Club appeared dangerously radical to those who feared a full-blown revolution in Caracas. For one thing, its meetings were held in the poorer parts of town and its membership was open to anyone who shared the group's sympathies: both the old and the young, women, mulattos, blacks, and Indians. Under Miranda's leadership, the club agitated vigorously for full independence and started to produce its own serial publication, *El Patriota de Venezuela* (The Venezuelan Patriot). Opponents tried to tar the club with the Jacobin brush, claiming that it had many French members and that it aimed to subvert the moderate government with its wild agenda.[15] These fears were overblown and, for the most part, unfounded. It cannot be denied, however, that Miranda the statesman knew that in order to haul his country into the nineteenth century he would have to reconcile Venezuela's mutually suspicious social and ethnic groups, which had previously been kept separate not only by the strict Spanish colonial race laws but also by their ethnically-based monopolistic economic practices. Although his intellectual position on this matter was well grounded in liberal theories and practices elsewhere in the Atlantic world, no doubt the emotional side of Miranda also wished to avenge his Canary Islander father's treatment at the hands of the *mantuano* elite decades earlier. His timi..g was premature; the Caracas elite resented his ham-handed unilateral proclamations, and the rural landowners feared that any attempt to alter the conditions of the slaves in their country might lead to a massive revolt similar to the one that had recently occurred in Haiti. Nevertheless, Miranda continued to advocate his idealistic program. In January 1811 he informed British abolitionist William Wilberforce that "[t]he Slave Trade has been abolished by Law in the Province of Venezuela, previous to my arrival; and I find the benevolent feelings of the Government and People of this Country, very congenial with your Philanthropic sentiments."[16]

Miranda also started to make overtures to neighboring regions, trying to build the grand Spanish American movement he had envisioned while living in exile across the ocean. On January 22, 1811, Miranda sent his old London associate, the Chilean canon José Cortés Madariaga, as his personal emissary on a mission to the Junta Suprema del Nuevo Reino de Granada (Supreme Junta of the Kingdom of New Granada). Cortés Madariaga was charged with persuading them to "reunite in a single voice all of [Colombia's] inhabitants, so that we can more easily repel the insidious efforts of our enemies like [Puerto Rico's military commander Antonio Ignacio] Cortabarría and the Bishop of Cuenca, who never fail to use all their powers to beguile and deceive the simple and honest inhabitants of these expanding Provinces."[17] The canon did not meet with much success, but Miranda's insistence on the necessity of hemispheric solidarity for the immediate victory over Spain (and the subsequent national era) proved to be prescient. He had been advocating a continental military alliance ever since he began negotiations with the British, and had diffused Viscardo's *Carta a los españoles americanos* from his Grafton Street home in an effort to create a sense of pan-American identity among all those in the Spanish colonial dominions. His disciple Simón Bolívar, as well as other major military figures who absorbed Miranda's line during their time in London (Bernardo O'Higgins, José de San Martín), all shared a vision of Spanish American nations' independent futures as being inextricably bound together by culture, tradition, and interest.

Miranda's British friends were anxious to help him secure his position and also to ensure that events in Venezuela followed an orderly and constitutional course. Nicholas Vansittart wrote long tutelary letters to Miranda advising him to send regular and detailed reports to Venezuelan agent Luis López Méndez in London so that he could counteract the numerous false and contradictory reports that had been swirling around European capitals. He had heard disturbing reports of violence and anarchy in Mexico and Peru and counseled Miranda that "nothing will become more important than the establishment of a regular and effective police for the protection of persons and property . . . without this no government can be either loved or respected—no security can exist for domestic happiness, no improvements can be expected in industry or science."[18] Less than two weeks later, Vansittart wrote again to inquire if it was indeed true that all native Spaniards had been arrested, a report that, if accurate, would surely influence the British government and public against the Venezuelans; instead, Vansittart recommended "measures of mildness and conciliation to all classes of inhabitants in your country." He was further troubled by the junta's apparent refusal to pay back funds that had been advanced to them by various private individuals and firms in England. "You must be sensible," the prudent Vansittart wrote, "how important it is for a new government not yet officially recognized by any power to put its pecuniary credit on the most solid footing. . . . You will find this not only the means of establishing a solid credit in the future, but it will be a very considerable saving in point of economy."[19] This attitude was typical of British foreign policy, which tended to prefer managed change from above that neither disrupted overseas investments or incited violence among classes.

A short time later, Vansittart reported to Miranda that he had had a meeting recently with young Richard Wellesley (the enamored son of the British foreign secretary), who remained enthusiastic about his idol's experiment but had not yet been able to persuade his leery father to open official relations with the new junta. Young Wellesley promised to keep nagging his father about continuing the payment of Miranda's government pension to his abandoned family, as the secretary had promised he would. On the thornier public issues, Vansittart knew that Miranda was well acquainted with the difficulties of prodding British politicians out of their established course and would not be surprised to learn that they were not willing to welcome Venezuela into the international family of nations just yet. He was nonetheless pleased to learn that a Venezuelan Congress had met and that it seemed to be a "dignified, temperate and discrete" body; although he phrased it nicely, Vansittart stressed again how crucial it was that Miranda continue to furnish López Méndez with accurate information, especially now that there were other, more pernicious rumors floating around claiming that the Venezuelans were outfitting and training an offensive military force. Vansittart could not resist warning his former protégé Miranda that he feared "the indiscriminate arming among a people composed of such distinct races of men who have hitherto felt little cordiality towards each other may be productive of great internal danger and by no means be the best system of defense." As an alternative means to unite "the different races of your population," Vansittart proposed to Miranda that "a system of public education should be seriously attended to. Liberty and good order will become compatible with each other in proportion as the influence of religion and morality prevails and your people become enlightened."[20] He must also remind his colleagues that they needed to keep their finances on a respectable footing. Once again, Miranda's British friends encouraged them to follow their recipe of aristocratic reformism coupled with the benefits of capitalist expansion; they did not question that social reforms and progress would be the eventual and inevitable result of allowing the better classes to control the pace of change under their more sober, well-considered judgment.

Taking over from the junta that resigned in its favor, the rump of the First Venezuelan Congress met on March 2, 1811, in Caracas at the home of the Conde de San Javier. In their oath of office, an important shift in attitudes became discernible in this meeting. The patriotic men pledged allegiance to the sovereignty of the Venezuelan people as it would be represented in their own duly constituted Congress at home in America; they no longer felt obliged to pretend that the king or his institutions had any claim on their political loyalty. Because everyone present was inexperienced in creating governmental forms and was unsure of what to do next, the living room Congress elected an executive council that consisted of a few members who rotated duties on a regular weekly basis while plans for the larger national congress were laid. Dr. Felipe Fermín Paúl became its first president and Dr. Mariano de la Cova was named its vice president. Miguel José Sanz and Antonio Nicolás Briceño served as the secretaries. Delegates for six provinces (Caracas, Barcelona, Mérida, Cumaná, Barinas, and Trujillo) were present, while the three dissenting provinces (Guayana, Coro, and Maracaibo) were left unrepresented.

Shortly thereafter, on the first anniversary of the movement that had deposed Viceroy Emparán, April 19, 1811, a massive public celebration erupted in the streets. One historian believes that this event should be considered to be the real date for independence because "[o]n that day, the People, a new factor in the political life of the country, created Venezuelan national identity."[21] Indians paraded about town wearing sashes in the new national colors of red, yellow, and blue. Enthusiastic students sang patriotic songs while amateur theater troupes performed along the sides of the streets. Members of Miranda's Patriotic Club made their official public debut that day, proudly marching alongside the previously excluded groups with their own banners and flags. The crowds burned portraits of Ferdinand VII and other symbols of Spanish power and, for the first time, yelled, "Down with the tyrant!" and "Down with the Spaniards!" All classes and sectors of society were represented, even the Catholic clergy who blessed the event with a *Te Deum*. The festivities carried on well into the night, with public buildings and elite homes putting on an illuminated display of candles and lights in their windows and on their balconies just as Europeans and North Americans did to mark their special occasions.

At the end of the month, the capital city's politicians turned their attention once again to the business of government and preparations for the meeting of the full National Congress, which would be called shortly. Miranda may have felt that his age and history entitled him to one of the organizational committee's three seats, but he was not among the chosen; Cristóbal de Mendoza, Juan Escalona, and Baltasar Padrón received the honor instead. Because the elections for the Congress had begun while Miranda was still on the seas coming to Venezuela from England, he was chosen to serve as the member for the small and distant province of Pao, that being one of the few remaining districts left without an elected representative. British observers reported that Miranda was a member of Congress for a town that no one had ever heard of before, making it appear that "it can by no means be said that he possesses the confidence of his fellow citizens."[22] Expecting to serve on the executive, or at the very least to represent an important district in the capital, there can be no doubt that Miranda felt slighted by the younger generation in Venezuela. The members of the junta could have given him a more active and central role had they been inclined, but they were wary and preferred to keep Miranda at arm's length until his true nature and abilities could be ascertained. He was widely distrusted. One participant in the proceedings wrote, "[r]egarding Miranda . . . here [the Supreme Congress] does not look upon him favorably because of their deep reservations (which I do not understand) and which have made them suspicious of him."[23] An exasperated Juan Germán Roscio also wrote to his friend Andrés Bello in London that Miranda was proving troublesome; he was power-mad, dangerously radical, and was responsible for polarizing the country with his Jacobin-style Patriotic Club.[24] Roscio complained that Miranda had thrown open the doors of polite society to colored people, and was certain that he had the ambition of another Napoleon. The concern with racial origins is interesting, especially since Roscio's own bloodline contained some Indian ancestry mixed in with his father's Italian origins.[25] Roscio was not alone in this estimation; another friend described Miranda as "a most ingenious, cunning and ambitious Chap in his soul."[26]

On July 1, 1811, the Venezuelan National Congress convened and passed two important documents: the "Declaration of the Rights of the People" and the "Declaration of the Rights of Man in Society," both of which indicate the extreme seriousness with which constituent members took their discussions of public liberty. Unlike the French Declaration of the Rights of Man and Citizen, a publication that was widely read in the 1790s and landed some Spanish Americans like Antonio Nariño in jail simply for possessing a copy, the 1811 Venezuelan versions reveal an awareness of the dangers posed by extreme individual liberty left unchecked. Even Miranda's notion of what liberty actually meant in practice had changed over time. The Patriotic Club organ, *El Patriota de Venezuela*, reprinted a translated version of Miranda's 1795 pamphlet, *Sobre la situación actual de la Francia y sobre los remedios convenientes a sus males*, in which he had condemned the Jacobins' use of terror to advance their cause. The resurrection of this pamphlet was mean to assuage fears that Miranda and his cohorts were dangerous radicals themselves. Having spent the past ten years in England, where upper-class reformists hoped to save their own privileged positions by using piecemeal reforms to stave off something much worse from below, Miranda thought that Venezuela could benefit from his observations about the dangers that the uneducated and uncontrolled mob had presented in France during the Terror.[27] In other words, as liberalism started to mutate into its nineteenth-century forms in the wake of the Haitian and French Revolutions, people like Miranda still believed that the fatherland had a responsibility to provide for the happiness and well-being of its citizens, but they also increasingly began to argue that the people were bound by a similar duty to obey their governors and contribute to the greater good of the nation.

The congressional debate over the declaration of full independence took place on July 3, 1811, with Miranda lending the full weight of his considerable experience to the proceedings. Never a rigorous political theorist, Miranda tended to learn through practical experience. Since his time in France, he had moved away from the ideal of a federal republic such as the United States (or the type advocated by his Girondin friends) toward a more centralized, unitary system that allowed for greater executive control. Obviously, Miranda voted in favor of full independence when the ballots were cast. As he was leaving the chamber at the end of the historic session, a disgruntled delegate named Ramón Ignacio Méndez assaulted him, claiming that Miranda had not been authorized by those in Pao to support full independence.[28] Such was the personal risk that founders faced every day in the age of revolution. Miranda came away from the encounter bruised but undaunted. He had waited too long for this moment to arrive to let a little scuffle on the steps dim his day of glory.

Always attuned to symbolic dates in the history of the Atlantic world, members of the Venezuelan Congress had hoped to sign their own declaration of independence on July 4 in order to link their destiny with that of their northern neighbors. They missed the mark by one day. Nevertheless, July 4 was celebrated with sincere joy and enthusiasm in Caracas. The city's streets were once again illuminated, musical bands strolled about playing patriotic songs, and enthusiastic speech makers pronounced inspiring words before their fellow citizens in the central plaza. One member of the Patriotic Club, whose name has gone unrecorded, thundered, "[N]o foreign domination can make us happy. Their interest will always be in themselves and their fortunes, and not the prosperity of the Venezuelan people." It was hard to argue with logic like that. Invoking the North American example, the optimistic orator declared that all that was needed for 800,000 Venezuelans to throw off their chains was "constancy, energy, patriotism, love of liberty, and unselfishness."[29] In the streets, the Spanish colors were torn to pieces and replaced with the red, blue, and yellow of the Venezuelan flag. The crowd tore down portraits of Charles IV and Ferdinand VII and vowed that they would never defile their walls again. Henceforth, republicanism and liberty would rule throughout America, North and South; the days of distant monarchs were over.

Despite such symbolic violence, when the First Venezuela Republic was officially declared on July 5, it was, in the words of one North American historian, "neither irrational nor particularly chaotic."[30] Congressional debates were remarkably civil and well considered, with much deference being shown to those of dissenting opinions. Nevertheless, some disturbing trends started to emerge from the earliest days. Besides the latent regionalism that had already started to spring to life, all persons holding public employment were required to pass a loyalty test, prompting many experienced bureaucrats either to resign or to emigrate. Ethnic Spaniards were insulted daily and suspected of counterrevolutionary plots; many lost their property or even their lives as a result. Even a sympathetic observer like British merchant and traveler Robert Semple recoiled in horror at what he called "the cruelty and injustice of the new government of Venezuela." Of course, Semple viewed events through the eyes of one who had grown up in the shadow of the French Revolution; seeing waves of wealthy and cultured emigrants leaving Venezuela only reminded him of the way French Jacobins had chased out all their opposition. Both governments' policies, he felt, created a situation in which little constructive opposition was left to balance their own extreme views.[31]

The constitution was written by Roscio and Francisco Iznardi and was made public for the first time on July 14 (another symbolic date, Bastille Day in France). It was printed in the *Gaceta de Caracas* two days later, on July 16. Only six of the forty-four delegates present had refused to sign the final document. The new republic was to be called the American Confederation of Venezuela and contained seven "free sovereign and independent states": Barcelona, Barinas, Caracas, Cumaná, Margarita, Mérida, and Trujillo. Martín Tovar y Ponte became its first president, and Isidoro López Méndez, whose brother Luis was barely surviving in London on the charity of Miranda's wife, Sarah Andrews, was named the vice president. Tovar y Ponte hailed from one of Caracas' most powerful families, who had put their wealth at the disposal of the revolution; he was not, unfortunately, possessed of any lofty vision or ambition beyond doing what was immediately necessary for his position.[32] The republican experiment was faced with many challenges, both internal and external, from the very moment of its inception.

By no means a radical document, the Venezuelan constitution was an uneasy hybrid of the U.S. Constitution and, to a lesser extent, the French Declaration of the Rights of Man. Ideals that had animated the British aristocratic reformers' political culture also made their way across the Atlantic and exerted influence; the Venezuelan elites were careful to preserve their own privileges and wished to make certain that the executive would remain weak and under their control. At the same time, however, they expressed a real interest in making some important social changes, as long as the disruption created could be minimized and controlled by from above. The republic's founders abolished several antiliberal remnants of Spanish colonial system: the slave trade, the detested racial categories, and outdated race laws; but as a sop to conservative landowners, they elected to permit the actual institution of slavery to continue uninterrupted.[33] By the end of July, the Congress proudly issued a public manifesto addressed to the rest of the world, announcing its official appearance into the family of nations.

London's *Morning Chronicle* praised the Venezuelan constitution as a document "likely to give a character to all the political establishments in South America; and to determine the destiny of a large portion of mankind."[34] Yet Miranda himself was disappointed with their efforts. He had hoped that the Congress would be more ambitious and look beyond its borders to a sort of pan-American confederation along the lines that he had envisioned since the 1790s; on this point, at least, his erstwhile enemy Roscio agreed with him.[35] Servando Teresa de Mier Noriega y Guerra, in his monumental *Historia de la Revolución de Nueva España, antiguamente Anáhuac* (London, 1813), praised Miranda, who sagely criticized the Venezuelan constitution "as contrary to the preoccupations, uses, and customs of the country."[36]

From the start, the Venezuelan republican patriots faced opposition from many quarters. Antonio Ignacio Cortabarria was a special military commissioner sent to Puerto Rico to oversee Spain's attempt to reclaim the rebel Venezuelan territories. In that capacity he had vociferously opposed the Caracas junta's actions since 1810 and now, following their full declaration of independence, he attempted to refute the congressional arguments line by line. Cortabarria's strategy alternated between trying to provoke guilt in the moderate Venezuelans by appealing to their sentimental loyalty to the king, and attempting to create a real fear of the implications of their leaders' supposedly radical actions. Of Article 1, in which the representatives identified themselves as agents of the people looking to recover lost rights, Cortabarria suggested that it might be proper to ask who "*they*" actually were; if one extended the patriots' argument back even further, he said, logically these original rights belonged to "the Caribes, Motilones, Guagiros, Quiripiripas, Guaranos and other indigenous Indian nations who occupied a considerable part of this Venezuelan land" even before the Spaniards arrived.[37] Clearly no one wanted to place themselves under Indian rule. Cortabarria therefore warned the patriots that they owed their position to their Spanish ancestors and that they ought to be careful of alerting the Indians to the natural rights that had been stolen from them. Cortabarria made much of the cultural affinity between the Spanish Americans and European Spaniards, using family metaphors to describe their deep bond and painting the patriots' actions as an ungrateful and bitter divorce. He also tried to counter the Venezuelans' ideological use of juridical history by reconstructing an alternate reading of Spain's organic laws. In Cortabarria's opinion, their 1811 constitution's Article 8 deliberately misled citizens when it claimed that sovereignty devolved upon *cabildos* in the absence of a king; instead, Cortabarria argued, authority passed to the next male heir and not to Americans or their deputies. He brushed aside the republicans' claims that they had received inadequate representation and respect within the Spanish system, and he condescendingly asserted that all actions taken, or policies followed, had been done for the Americans' own benefit. It was the "crazy ambition" and "anarchy" of a few deluded radicals that threatened Americans' happiness, not the sage policies of a kindly father-king.[38]

Cortabarria urged legitimate nations not to create relations with "the usurpers"; his plea was clearly directed toward England, whose leaders had repeatedly offered to mediate between Spain and the colonies, hoping not only to secure some sort of amicable arrangement between the two opposing parties, but also to gain some commercial advantages for their own merchants in American trade as well. Cortabarria asked the rhetorical question, "What would England say if it heard that it had employed its valiant armies in the defense of a Monarchy that had already ceased to exist?"[39] As a response, his Venezuelan opponents invoked John Locke's hallowed arguments about the natural right of a people to govern themselves and pointed out that Cortabarria's own ships had attacked British shipping in the Caribbean as part of their blockade.[40] Clearly, Miranda was not the only person to realize that the struggle for liberty had to be fought in a theater that spanned the entire Atlantic world.

Two volumes published in London attempted to repair the damage that the Spanish public relations machine was attempting to inflict on the Venezuelans' credibility. The earlier one, *Discurso que puede servir de preliminar a las noticias de la última conspiración de Caracas* (Reflections That Can Assist in Prefacing the News of the Latest Conspiracy in Caracas), was intended to combat the notion that Venezuelans were somehow inherently anarchic or that violence was a certain outcome of political change in Spanish America. Essentially, the edited series of documents argued that the Venezuelans' actions had been justified because the Spanish Cortes refused to allow its duly elected representative, Joaquín Mosquera, to take his seat in that august body on the technicality that he had been born in Popayán (now part of Colombia) and not Caracas itself. The editors pointed out the utter hypocrisy of this denial since many of the European Spaniards did not hail from the town that they represented. These documents offered unmediated, pure, factual proof to counter the Spanish disinformation campaign being prosecuted throughout the Atlantic world against their errant colony. Although the title appeared anonymously, Miranda's relative Luis López Méndez most likely oversaw its production; as Venezuela's envoy to England, he continued Miranda's association with the French printer Juigné, who had brought out the five issues of *El Colombiano* in 1810.[41]

A second, more sophisticated documentary collection appeared a year later in a handsome bilingual version that was obviously directed to both Spanish- and English-speaking audiences. Again, Venezuelan representatives in London tried to make their government's case; Andrés Bello wrote the preface, which pointed out that the 1811 constitution guaranteed protection to the person and property of all foreigners, expanded rights of citizenship to include Indians, guaranteed the freedom of religion, and ended the scourge of the evil slave trade. These documents neatly turned Cortabarria's historical arguments back against him by pointing out sarcastically that if past ownership of the land was to be the standard used in determining modern governance, then "Spain belongs to the Phoenicians, their descendants, or the Carthaginians wherever they may be found."[42] Instead, Spanish America's revolution promised to be "the most useful to the human race" by providing a sanctuary for those who were persecuted elsewhere and by throwing open the continent's vast resources to the entrepreneurs of the world. In the nineteenth century, foreigners would cross the Atlantic not as conquerors or slaves, but as friends, desiring "not to destroy but to build; not as tygers [*sic*] but as men."[43] Hearing these palatable (and profitable) terms, liberal elements throughout the Atlantic world could hardly find fault with Miranda's associates in the Venezuelan First Republic. They spoke the same language.

In Caracas, however, the general himself was kept under close surveillance and given important, though restricted, responsibilities intended to keep his personal charisma out of politics entirely. The Congress gave Miranda oversight of several important domestic financial arrangements such as the reordering of the state financial system through the creation of paper money and the regulation of metals.

Quite clearly, this was not within his area of expertise; the assignment indicates an attempt to marginalize the aging revolutionary, to keep him away from the army's command for fear of his real intentions. On July 14, 1811, the anniversary of Bastille Day, Miranda unveiled the new Venezuelan flag, modeled on his previous yellow, blue, and red version. Although legend says that the colors derived from the physical attributes of his lover Catherine Hall, it has also been suggested that the yellow band signified Venezuela and the red one was imperial Spain, both of which would be separated forever by the blue band that represented the Atlantic Ocean. Several other typical Mirandian motifs appeared in the new Venezuelan coat of arms that was also presented to the public for the first time that day: a noble Indian, the French Revolution's cap of liberty, examples of American wildlife, the dawning sun of a new era, and the proud slogan, "Free Venezuela."

Shortly after the euphoria of the congressional declaration of independence subsided, the new government was faced with a serious internal revolt. The town of Valencia had refused to submit to the Caracas authorities and their demands and was raising a military resistance. The Congress's executive committee gave the responsibility for dealing with the thorny situation to Fernando del Toro and the Marqués Francisco Rodríguez del Toro, brothers from an elite family whose personal talents were not adequate to the job. When British traveler Robert Semple passed through Valencia in mid-1811, he remarked, "all was silence, mistrust, suspicion and alarm when I was there."[44] The situation could not be allowed to continue. There were suspicions of royalists in other provinces, an unseen enemy that might threaten the young republic's existence. Of the two dangers, it appeared that Miranda's ego was the lesser one, and so he was relieved of his job at the Mint and dusted off for military command once again. By July 19, 1811, Miranda had taken over the strategic planning for an operation to subdue the intransigent town.

Toward the end of the month, Miranda moved his troops toward an assault on Valencia. The rebellious townsfolk had concealed small gunboats in the bushes and tall reeds along the lake, which Miranda's scouts failed to notice. When the skirmish took place, the patriot forces of the central government were unexpectedly caught in the

crossfire and suffered serious losses. One contemporary observer recalled that during the heat of the battle, "General Miranda exposed
himself considerably and gave his orders with coolness."[45] Although
many scions of elite families, not to mention common foot soldiers,
were maimed or killed, Miranda himself escaped without a scratch. A
mere 700 ill-equipped but impassioned Valencians defended their town
from what they perceived to be an enemy occupation and drove
Miranda and his 2,600 men back to a safe distance. It was a devastating loss for him, one that reopened the painful wounds of Neerwinden
and Coro. Miranda was highly sensitive to his military reputation,
aware of the comparisons that future historians would likely make.
During the 1811 campaign, for example, the hotheaded general "got
into a hair-splitting argument over George Washington's military and
political commands during the American Revolution."[46] He was determined to make the Valencians submit with a second assault, this
one staged with more caution and less reserve.

On August 9, Miranda wrote to Secretary of War Carlos Soublette
that the "enemy" was now confined to just one part of the city and
that the "enemy" had lost twenty-five men with a further seventy-five
being taken prisoner by Miranda's forces. His choice of language reveals that Miranda had reverted to the same concise, single-word iden-
tification for his opponents that he had used with the Moroccans at
Melilla, the British at Pensacola, and the Austrians and Prussians in
Belgium. This time, however, the enemy was his own kind. In all his
years of daydreaming about the glories that awaited him as the Washington of South America, Miranda never admitted to the possibility
of having to face domestic opposition to his glorious plan. Like all the
cosmopolitan men of the eighteenth-century Atlantic world, Miranda
believed in the power of human reason to cut through all obstacles; it
was a unilinear, single-minded sort of view that assumed happiness
was better than suffering, enlightenment was better than darkness,
modernity was better than tradition, and independence was better
than dependence; presumably all thinking persons would define these
categories the same way and would inevitably reach the same conclu-
sions. If they did not, they must logically become the Enemy. According to this view, then, Miranda could see the "assassins of Coro . . .
afflicting the country under a false sense of patriotism," and Cumaná's

rebels could be branded "revolting Catalans"; in other words, all were false Venezuelans.[47]

By the next day, Miranda again reported to Soublette that his forces had occupied Valencia's suburbs and that the enemy's men were deserting to his side. He blockaded the center of the city and commenced an attack from eight different directions. The battle lasted through the night and into the next day, with the Valencians putting up serious resistance to the superior *caraqueño* troops. When Miranda cut off their water supply, the Valencians realized that all hope was lost and sent up a white flag. They capitulated on August 13, 1811. His objective achieved, Miranda again thought of his historical reputation and returned to his principles; he informed Soublette of "the terms of humanity and generosity with which I propose to treat them."[48] The general did not wish to alienate the Valencian rebels further by assuming direct control over their town as an arrogant victor bent on vengeance, but rather he hoped to reconcile them to Caracas's authority through reasonable and moderate treatment. This was the same strategy he had used in Belgium. Miranda commanded his troops to "observe the greatest order and regularity" in their occupation of the city and to "refrain from insulting any citizen, no matter what his class or station, respect all their property and houses, and pay the respect due to the ministers of religion. Do not enter any churches except as those who come to pay tribute as true Christians." He did demand that the Valencians turn over their weapons, but permitted their town *cabildo* to continue to function unmolested. Several of the uprising's ringleaders were tried and sentenced for their treason, in order to make it clear who was in charge, but the Congress either commuted their death sentences or reduced the charges. Miranda did, however, insist that all those citizens over the age of nineteen swear loyalty to the Republic, as the Constitution required.[49]

Reports reached London that Miranda had instructed his army to put down the rebellion without quarter and that thousands were believed to have perished as a result.[50] This was not quite true. Yet, after the frightfully close call at Valencia, the central government did indeed become more jealous of its authority and began to suspect that its enemies were laying traps everywhere. Accordingly, they became more paranoid and restrictive in their policies. The Congress instituted "a tribunal of vigilance" that paid visits to private homes to assess the residents' loyalties. They shut the theater in order to prevent large assemblies of people from gathering together and then banned concerts, balls, and parties as well. All males in the population were ordered to train for the militia until eventually, "it became fashionable for those of the greatest distinction to sleep at the barracks."[51] Miranda's Patriotic Club attempted to make heroes of the fallen Caracas soldiers; in September 1811, Captain Lorenzo Buroz was buried with full state honors and special cantos pronounced in his name. The government sponsored schools for "patriotic education" in order to instil civic virtues in those unwilling to accept the new order. The destruction of Valencia became a metaphor for the central government's attitude toward dissent. Its orators decried "the terrifying effects of the unfortunate divisiveness" that wracked the country; the good people of the interior should, the patriots pointedly suggested, look around them and see that "not a single European can be found among the unhappy victims" of the violence at Valencia.[52] In other words, those self-interested foreigners were using Venezuelan blood to advance their own fortunes.

As often happens when idealists find that their political utopias are harder to create than they had expected, the Venezuelan republicans turned to more heavy-handed methods to convince their opponents of their righteousness. Although they remained democrats, they also believed that "You are all equal, we would repeat to you, but this equality has limits and the maintenance of political society demands a hierarchical order among its citizens. Just as the general is not equal to the soldier, neither is the Magistrate equal to a simple citizen in the exercise of his functions."[53]

With words such as these, there can be little wonder that contemporary observers started to talk of a Jacobin coup within the First Republic, accompanied by a growing cult of personality that true democrats ought to shun. When Miranda returned to Caracas on October 29, he was treated to the hero's welcome he had long awaited. With some exaggeration, his friends at the Patriotic Club reported, "[n]ever before in the annals of the history of South America has such a fiesta been seen."[54] Shouts of "Long live the Savior of the Fatherland!" and "Long live liberty and independence!" could be heard in the streets. Devoted young virgins dressed in flowing white gowns tossed laurel leaves in his path as the victorious general entered the city. Yet, even in his partisans' own account, there is a sense that these celebrations were somewhat forced, even staged. The First Republic was in trouble and no parade could disguise that fact.

Rumors of Miranda's failing health and declining vigor started to spread throughout the Caribbean after the capture of Valencia. Furthermore, the patriots seemed to be fatally divided, their squabbles descended to the level of duels among themselves and "instances of human butchery too shocking to repeat," although the authorities did endeavor to punish the perpetrators.[55] In London, Miranda's former friend Joseph Blanco White published an article in *El Español* that warned, "Peoples of America! Liberty is not won by savagery. Those who need to employ proscriptions and terror exhibit all the signs of the most dreadful tyranny."[56] Miranda's friends James Mill and Jeremy Bentham tried to persuade him to set aside his personal enmities and look for allies in places he had previously scorned. One such person, for example, might be Aaron Burr, who was currently in London and on close terms with the utilitarian radical circle. To Bentham, Burr had expressed pleasure at learning of Miranda's return to his native country and claimed that his own "heart and feelings are, as you know, wholly and warmly with the patriots of Venezuela. [Miranda's] advent is, unquestionably, a very great boon to them. His experience in political and military life, and his literary accomplishments, justly entitle him to pre-eminence among his countrymen. But that part of Miranda's character which constitutes his greatest eulogy is the purity of his political creed, and the constancy and consistency with which he has persevered in it. On this head, he has shown no caprice, no backsliding that I have ever heard."[57]

Burr expressed a desire to mingle personally in the affairs of South America if a mutual agreement could be reached. With this news, Mill wrote to Miranda, urging him (in good utilitarian terms) to put aside his personal feelings and consider the greater good of the cause. Burr was, in his and Bentham's estimation, a man of enterprise who would be a valuable ally for the patriots.[58] Again, one's devotion to the cause mattered more than one's national origins; the struggle for liberty knew no borders in the Atlantic world in the age of revolution.

Pressure started to mount from royalists across the ocean in Spain and from King Ferdinand's sympathizers elsewhere in Europe and North America. Venezuelan republicans became the favorite target of all those poison pens who wished to focus the world's energies on the struggle against Napoleon and hoped to stave off the rapid pace of political change that the nineteenth century seemed to herald. Ignacio Rodríguez de Ribas made a case to the *caraqueño* people that "[the republicans] have deluded the unwary among you, made the majority of you victims of their slurs, and only convinced a few with their passions. Union has been destroyed for everyone, disorder arose from order, bringing with it death and disgrace, resulting in the excitement and irritation of the spirit. Decide for yourselves, inhabitants of the towns of Venezuela. . . . Remember what has happened, reflect on the present, and you will be able to predict what will happen in the future to a country where towns are pitted against the rest of the nation."[59]

The Duque del Infantado told overseas residents of the Spanish Empire that "[y]ou will find that you can only enjoy true independence when you reunite your forces with our glorious arms: peace, liberty and happiness will come to those who obey and swear allegiance to the wise Constitution [of Cádiz]."[60] Even a sympathetic constitutional monarchist in the United States urged the "Caraccassians" to return "to your love and duty; your provincial governments, under the [Spanish] Cortes, are adequate to all your civil concerns, to all the exigencies of colonial defense." Furthermore, the same author threatened, Venezuelans will surely feel God's displeasure if they do not set their affairs right: "That government is necessary to political happiness is a self-evident proposition. As it embraces order and regularity it is an emanation from deity. As the deity it is the fountain of all power; so, also, he is the God of order and wisdom (unless with Atheists who denominate matter and its organization and motions as the offspring of chance). I am not writing to you, Caraccassians, as a province of Atheists, but as professors and believers in the holy religion, whose author is God. Little argument will convince the rational of the existence of an All Supreme."[61]

Royalists allied with the Catholic Church painted the reformers as atheists and Freemasons, bent on erasing the Holy Religion from Venezuelan life. These types of arguments struck true fear into the common people in an era when even highly-educated travelers still reported seeing a species of unicorn in the Venezuelan mountains and when fishing expeditions regularly hunted mermaids in the British Channel.[62]

Then, on Holy Thursday, March 26, 1812, Caracas was rocked by a devastating earthquake. Over 10,000 people were killed and much of the capital lay in smoking ruins. In one of those fateful accidents of history, that date coincided with the second anniversary of the day that the patriots ousted Emparán and set the whole independence process in motion. Having become disillusioned with the new republican regime, Catholic priests began to spread the story that Divine wrath had sent the earthquake to avenge the Spanish king and bring down those who had dared to question secular and religious authorities. In the streets, people fell to their knees and begged for mercy from God and King Ferdinand. The aristocratic young military officer and Miranda's protégé, Simón Bolívar, scoffed at this sort of superstition and issued one of his immortal statements in response: "If nature opposes us, we shall fight against her and force her to obey."[63] Obviously his words were not calculated to assuage any of the clergy's fears. Rational patriots such as Interim Secretary of State Antonio Muñoz Tebar consoled themselves by reading foreign gazettes and learning that an increased number of earthquakes had been reported throughout the Atlantic world that year (Mississippi, Saint Lucia, St. Vincent, Germany, France, Italy, the Canary Islands), possibly as the result of some powerful comets. A scientific explanation for the earthquake might calm the fears of the members of Congress, but other citizens were not so sure.

When he heard the news of the "dreadful earthquake at Caraccas [sic]," Nicholas Vansittart's thoughts immediately flew across the ocean to his friend Miranda.[64] This turn of events would be a daunting challenge indeed. In the confusing aftermath of the disaster, on April 3, 1812, Miranda was named generalíssimo (supreme general) and head of state with full dictatorial powers. The Patriotic Club lauded this decree, reminding the public that Rome often resorted to benevolent dictators in times of crisis. Miranda was proud of the comparison and proud of his new title; he wished to have his position publicized throughout the Atlantic world so that his friends, and his enemies, would be aware of the authority his fellow citizens had entrusted to him. Miranda wrote to Jeremy Bentham, "I hope the day is not far distant when I shall see the liberty and happiness of this country established upon a solid and permanent footing. The appointment I have just received, of *generalíssimo* of the Confederation of Venezuela, with full powers to treat with foreign nations will, perhaps, facilitate the means of promoting the object I have for so many years had in view."[65] He sent virtually the same letter to British prime minister Spencer Perceval and Lord Castlereagh, telling them that "being animated with the same views toward Great Britain, whose interests I conceive, are intimately connected with the safety and prosperity of this country, I am very desirous of cimenting [*sic*] by all means in my power the existing friendship, and forming if possible, a closer union between the two countries."[66] Shortly after these letters were composed, Miranda sent his trusted secretary Tómas Molini on a mission to England to try to secure more assistance beyond the mere promises of neutrality. He also wished to reassure British politicians that the Venezuelan government that he was now leading did not intend to recall López Méndez and Bello or to end the preference given in their ports to ships flying the British flag.[67] In fact, he wished to enter into close and intimate relations with his admired British friends. Molini's secret mission, however, only fortified Miranda's enemies' fears that he was selling his country to a new foreign master.[68]

As time progressed and the republic began to cast about for new supporters to replace those who were starting to fall away, its decrees became more radical. For example, in colonial times, only white women were allowed to kneel on the carpets while praying in church, but the new leaders wished to do away with these sorts of racial distinctions in order to be consistent with their other policies and democratic values. Such a measure was enacted with some success in smaller towns first, but excited no small amount of antipathy when it was to extended to Caracas.[69] Also, Miranda offered freedom to any slave who would enlist in his armed forces for a period of ten years. This proposal enraged the landowners (most of whom were slave owners), who not only resented the implied assault on their status and property but also feared that their crops would be left unharvested if their slaves heeded the generalíssimo's call and abandoned the countryside for military life.[70] On many levels, the move made sense. Rhetorically at least, the patriots sympathized with the slaves' condition and often used terms such as "the slaves of moribund Spain" or "degrading servitude" to refer to the Spanish American Creoles' analogous plight. One orator even said that "those who would return and suffer the degrading name of servants" to the Spanish Crown did not deserve to be called Venezuelans.[71] On a personal level, throughout his long life and many travels, Miranda counted among his closest friends and associates many active participants in the international abolitionist movement: Jacques-Pierre Brissot de Warville, Alexander Hamilton, Aaron Burr, John Jay, William Wilberforce, James Mill, Jeremy Bentham, and others all shared his antipathy to the traffic in human beings.

At the same time, some of the more radical advisers who surrounded Miranda viewed the Caracas elite as insufficiently revolutionary as well. Undoubtedly he, too, still harbored some childhood scars inflicted when that arrogant *mantuano* elite had rejected his father so brutally and so publicly. José Cortés Madariaga, the priest who had started the independence movement in 1810, warned him, "[O]ur domestic enemies rush headlong toward your ruin . . . to oppose all efforts to establish a true democratic liberty on the ruins of a stupid aristocracy." In Cortés Madariaga's opinion, the capital city of Caracas was the focal point for "intrigues, cabals and perfidies" of "the aristocrats and *godos* (Goths, meaning Spaniards)."[72] A pseudonymous writer to *El Patriota de Venezuela* complained that there were "aristocrats" who considered themselves to be superior to other citizens and who falsely claimed they could be Venezuelan patriots while maintaining their loyalty to the Church and the Spanish state.[73]

Miranda determined that his "great and only objective is to form an army" because "according to the principles and systems of administration," a good government should take its form and character from the circumstances in which it finds itself. Therefore, the generalíssimo used his new position to declare martial law.[74] Interim Secretary of State Muñoz Tebar wrote to the archbishop of Caracas Narciso Coll y Prat that, in light of the clergy's scandalous actions following the recent earthquake, the Executive Power had determined that "the pernicious influence of superstition has flowed into streets and taken

over the spirit of an ill-educated people." Miranda's government, therefore, ordered him to tell his priests "not to delude the people with the
absurd insinuation that the political revolution caused the earthquake
on March 26."[75] The secularizing spirit of the Venezuelan revolution
had finally run up against institutional religion.

One of Miranda's other early goals as generalíssimo was to shore
up the patriots' military defenses, which had come under fire from
many quarters. He sent Simón Bolívar, his trusted young friend and
an able commander in his own right, to defend and hold the important garrison at San Mateo de Puerto Cabello. At the time, cynical
Venezuelans thought that Miranda was suspicious of Bolívar's ambition and wanted to send him to a remote outpost in order to remove
him from the center of the action; aware of the purported machinations against him, Bolívar apparently accepted the post but "not without repugnance." When the Executive Power asked Miranda why he
had sent the able young commander to the hinterland at a time when
there was a pressing need for him closer to Caracas, Miranda told
them "[b]ecause he is a dangerous young man."[76] It was further reported in London that the Venezuelan Congress had passed two acts
on May 13, 1812, both of which were designed to increase their stores
of arms: first, foreigners could introduce specie without paying import duty; second, foreigners were permitted to import 12,000 muskets at a duty of $30 for the first 4,000, $25 for the second 4,000, and
$20 for the final 4,000, although these fees would be waived for the
rest of the year.[77] By exiling his talented young rival to the hinterland
and allowing foreigners to increase their commercial and military presence in Venezuela, Miranda engendered further suspicion that he was
not a disinterested patriot at all, but rather an ambitious anglophile
who would lead his country out of servitude to Spain and right into
the British empire instead.

For a brief time at least, Miranda's government appeared to enjoy
some popularity outside Caracas. José de Anzoátegui reported that in
May, local chapters of the Patriotic Club in both Barcelona and
Cumaná had carried out grand processions in the public plazas, planting Trees of Liberty and shouting patriotic slogans. José Cortés
Madariaga flattered Miranda's self-image by telling him of "the universal contentment with which our fellow citizens have learned of

Simón Bolívar, Liberator of Colombia and Peru. Mezzotint by Charles Turner. National Portrait Gallery Archive Engravings Collection (D753)

that energy and Constance that you have applied toward their salvation."[78] At the same time, no one could deny that the royalists and the counterrevolutionaries were gaining force. The *Gaceta de Caracas* reprinted a royalist manifesto from the commander of the Spanish forces, Domingo Monteverde, which its arrogant editors mocked as being directed to "the incautious and the ignorant." Of course, by disseminating his words, the editors helped to spread Monteverde's message that Spaniards were the ones who wanted to "conserve the Catholic Religion, defend it, and avenge the insults heaped upon it, to guarantee the lives of the men of the cloth and encourage the predication of the Holy Bible," all of which faced extinction at the hands of the atheistic republican philosophers.[79] As Venezuelans continued to dig themselves out from under the rubble left by the earthquake that their parish priests told them had been sent as a punishment from God, Monteverde's message struck a chord in the weary and confused populace.

On July 5, 1812, the first anniversary of the declaration of Venezuelan independence, the tide turned. Miranda was celebrating his eventful year among the Americans when a breathless courier arrived with the incomprehensible news that Bolívar's San Felipe fortress near Puerto Cabello had been lost; it appeared as though the young commander and his forces had defected to the other side. Despite Bolívar's repeated warnings that his garrison was outnumbered by a factor of ten to one, Miranda refused to send him any auxiliaries, saying, "That is the way of the world. A little while ago we thought all was secure. Yesterday Monteverde had neither weapons not ammunition. Today he has both in abundance. I am told to attack the enemy. But he already has everything in his hands. Tomorrow we shall see what happens."[80] With no aid forthcoming from Caracas, Bolívar indeed lost Puerto Cabello, in the process complicating his historical reputation as a hero and a patriot. He wrote a pitiful letter to Miranda, apologizing for his failure and stating that his "soul is crushed to such an extent that I do not feel able to command a single artilleryman; my presumption led me to think that my desire for achievement and my ardent love of country would supply the talents which I obviously lack to fulfill a command." After he composed himself, Bolívar promised to send Miranda a complete account of the action, in order to "safeguard in the eyes of the public, your appointment of me and my personal honor. I did my duty, General, and if a single soldier had remained at my side, I would have given battle to the enemy; if my troops had abandoned me, it was not my fault."[81]

Miranda had no choice but to send two representatives to discuss terms of a possible surrender with Monteverde. Although José de Sata y Bussy and Manuel Aldao were perhaps the best of Miranda's advisors, they were also men of "weak character and lacking in energy."[82] After initial meetings between the two sides were completed, the Marqués de Casa León had Miranda's full authority to complete the final terms of the capitulation, and he proved to be far less trustworthy. The actual details of the agreement were known to only one or two of Miranda's particular friends, but it was reported that the patriot forces in general were dissatisfied with his decision to give in to the Spaniards.[83] The Venezuelan commission concluded its peace with Monteverde on July 26, 1812, who gleefully told his friend Fernando Miyares the next day that the rebels would "submit without bloodshed or other ravages of war, to our legitimate Sovereign" and that he, Monteverde, would be awarded the glory of occupying the territory still under the patriots' control.[84] The royalist forces entered Caracas on August 3, 1812, issuing a dramatic proclamation that opened: "Inhabitants of Caracas! One of the characteristic qualities of the kindness, Justice and legitimacy of Governments is its good faith and exactitude in complying with its promises. . . . My promises are sacred and my word is inviolable."[85] Yet within a few weeks, Monteverde and the royalists went on a counterattack, saying of the patriots that "[n]ot one who falls into my hands shall escape."

With the unpleasant reversal in his fortunes, Miranda resigned himself to exile once again and began to make plans to rejoin his family in England. It was not the worst fate one could imagine. As he sadly packed up his things and began to move his baggage to La Guaira for embarkation, the unimaginable happened. The royalists arrested Miranda and turned him over to the Spanish authorities, even though he had understood that his safe passage out of the country had been part of the capitulation's terms. Miranda, José Cortés Madariaga, Juan Germán Roscio, Juan Pablo Ayala, and several others were taken into custody and eventually sent to prison Cádiz and then to Ceuta in North Africa. They were the lucky ones; Monteverde the Avenger believed that "four walls are three too many for a prison—you only need one for an execution."[86] Eyewitness Juan Vicente Gómez recorded the extraordinary viciousness of the royalist fury in Caracas: "Morning and afternoon, shootings went on in the main square and in the slaughterhouse . . . to save ammunition, sometimes the victims were murdered with machetes and knives. . . . Over such scenes deadly nymphs could be seen running with delight, dressed in white and adorned with yellow and blue ribbons, who on the bloody and muddy remains danced the obscene dance known as the *palito*."[87] A horrified British traveler made plans to leave Caracas in the waning days of the First Republic because its streets were stained with blood and human heads were hung in cages at the entrances to the city. He blamed both sides equally for the cruelty.[88]

It was a disastrous setback for the patriots. The First Republic was dead. Most of its partisans were dead as well or had gone into exile. Luis Delpech said that the "monstruous government of the ferocious Monteverde" had determined to hunt down and kill all the Creole patriots who remained in the land "and to persuade the ignorant and fanatical mob that the earth will quake as long as a single one is left alive."[89] Mariano Montilla wrote to Luis López Méndez in London to advise him regretfully that his nephew and two brothers had been killed and the family fortune stolen; Montilla also passed on a list of the persons he knew to have been jailed and a general account of conditions in Venezuela. No doubt feeling sad but vindicated, the stateless envoy dutifully passed on this information to the British government, proving once and for all which had been the side of brutality and oppression in America. It was Spain, not the patriots. López Méndez also had these documents translated for immediate dissemination in the public press. He presented a strongly worded letter to the government that described Monteverde's violation of the capitulation's terms which, in the outraged envoy's view, was nothing less than "the consummation of acts of perfidy and cruelty that have no example before them in the history of civilized nations." In his translated version, however, López Méndez delicately omitted

Montilla's condemnation of Miranda's pact with Monteverde as an "infamous treason."[90]

Not everyone was sorry to hear that Miranda had been taken prisoner. Valencians rejoiced when they heard that he was captured and Caracas had been retaken in the name of Ferdinand.[91] One of Bolívar's staff members (later to become his ambivalent biographer), General H. L. V. Ducoudray-Holstein, blamed Miranda for his own downfall, saying that the generalíssimo's unwise conduct had increased his enemies and that his curt manner had alienated even those who might have wanted to work with him. Bolívar, too, attempted to control the historical interpretation of his role in the act by declaring more than once that he "had Miranda arrested to punish him for betraying his country, not to serve the king."[92] Furthermore, Miranda had offended many natives because he "preferred English and French officers to his own countrymen, saying that they were ignorant brutes, unfit to command, and that they ought to learn the use of the musket before they put on epaulettes."[93] To his British friends, however, the sad news of Miranda's capture was just plain demoralizing. His social experiments in Spanish America were supposed to have been the proving ground for their reformist theories. Instead, their hopes died along with his. William Allen, a Quaker chemist and administrative assistant to the duke of Kent, told Jeremy Bentham, with characteristic understatement, that he was "chagrined with hearing bad accounts of Miranda."[94]

Luis Delpech retraced Miranda's path and fled to England, hoping to find some friends and allies there. He tried to counter the "calumnies, the sophisms, and the injuries" that Miranda's enemies had been spreading, but found them to be a "multi-headed hydra of impostures, fanaticism and silliness." To anyone thinking clearly, it was impossible to believe that Miranda had sold his country to Monteverde. The old man simply was not capable of such a cowardly or self-interested act. Furthermore, Delpech believed, "it is impossible that a man who worked all his life for the independence of America could have forgotten that glorious enterprise at the end of his career, risk tarnishing his reputation in old age and dishonor his memory forever—and for such ignominy and heedlessness receive no other recompense save chains and death."[95] No, in Delpech's opinion, it was not Miranda who deserved the blame for the fate that had overtaken poor Venezuela; it was the immoral and ungrateful Venezuelan people themselves. Miranda had spent his year among the Americans, and that had proved to be more than enough time for everyone.

CONCLUSION
The Measure of the Man (1812–1816)

Eternal spirit of the chainless mind. Brightest in dungeons, Liberty! Thou art.
—LORD BYRON

Condemned to spend the last years of his life chained to a wall in a dark Spanish prison, Francisco de Miranda could have served as the inspiration for Byron's bittersweet ode to the strength of the human spirit. Although he suffered in solitude, pining for his faraway family and friends and hearing his reputation besmirched by foes throughout the Atlantic world, Miranda never stopped believing that he would escape the confines of his dank cell and live to see the triumph of liberty throughout his beloved America. The general had that sort of optimism born of a great man's ego. Because he felt certain that he could make anything happen through undying patience and the force of his own efforts, Miranda simply refused to yield. Even as he sat moldering away in Spanish custody, the old man plotted his escape and expected to return to his rightful place as the leader of Spanish American emancipation. Both he and America would be free. Liberty would triumph over despotism. There was no question in his mind, no other possibility to be entertained. That was simply how it had to be.

Of course, throughout his long life, with all his words and actions, Miranda spoke not just to his contemporaries but also to the annals of history. As a man of the Enlightenment, he understood that the events in which he was participating were of lasting importance and that generations to come would debate their processes and their meaning. Since the time when he first traveled to Spain and gazed upon a wall of heroic portraits, Miranda directed all his considerable energies toward earning a place there for himself. To preserve the memory of his friendships with important people and to provide future biographers with adequate documentation with which to immortalize his life, Miranda saved every calling card, every newspaper clipping, every letter or official pronouncement that crossed his desk. In the end, he accumulated some sixty-three volumes of personal papers that he took care never to allow to fall into his enemies' hands. Through the existence of his historical archive, Miranda planned for his chainless spirit to survive his corporeal existence. This most recent trial, he thought, would prove to be the same as all the others, another chapter in his biography, another drama for the myth. Fate, as it always does, had a different and more fitting end planned for Miranda. He would not breathe the air of freedom again, but he was permitted to conclude his life as a martyr at the hands of the cruel Spanish Empire.

After confining him to a holding cell in La Guaira for a few months, the royalist commander in Venezuela, Domingo Monteverde, transferred Miranda to more secure facilities in the fortress of San Felipe at Puerto Cabello. By then, the prisoner was sixty-three years old and suffering from an increasing series of ailments ranging from rheumatism to chronic stomach pain (likely caused by ulcers) to bronchial infections and persistent insomnia. He was malnourished and plagued by the large and vicious rats that scurried across the floor. Yet Miranda was always at his best when adversity struck. It was as though his genius grew in proportion to the difficulty of his circumstances. As he sat and waited for his fate to be decided, ironically in the same garrison in which young Simón Bolívar had surrendered to the royalists the previous year, Miranda was permitted to produce a series of documents that would be read before a panel of two Spanish judges who had been assigned to hear his case. Although the letter was ostensibly addressed to the king via these men, Caracas *audiencia* members José Heredia and Costa Gali, Miranda in fact was directing his words to the entire Atlantic world and to history.

At times sparkling with poetic language, other times boiling over with rage, Miranda's open letter equated his own fate with that of the

Spanish American people. Entering into the capitulation in good faith, he had been betrayed by the evil Monteverde, who personified the refusal of the Spanish Empire to treat its overseas citizens with equality and respect. The Spaniards had no honor and their word meant nothing. With all due respect, Miranda explained, he had been "kept in the most profound silence, buried in a dark and narrow prison restrained by bars," but avowed that such conditions could not keep him from telling the truth about the horrors that had enveloped not just himself but all the unfortunate people of Venezuela.[1] He explained the calculated and noble reasons why he had sought a truce with the Spaniards once it became apparent that the patriots had lost their military advantage; simply put, Miranda said that he preferred to arrange an "honorable reconciliation" between two members of the same family rather than risk a destructive civil war. Almost as soon as the ink was dry on the hated parchment, however, the Spaniards began to violate the letter and spirit of their agreement. Appealing to accepted rules for the gentlemanly conduct of warfare that prevailed throughout the Atlantic world at the time, Miranda outlined Monteverde's numerous violations of the capitulation's terms. The barbarous royalists arrested and executed not just the patriot combatants but also their entire families; they confiscated patriot estates and sought revenge wherever they could. No one, from the elderly to the youngest children, was spared the Spaniards' wrath. Hoping to strike fear into the hearts of his British allies, Miranda sent them a coded warning in his letter:

> I saw then with amazement a repetition of the same scenes of which I had been an Eyewitness in France! I saw multitudes of Men of the most illustrious and distinguished Ranks, Classes and Conditions, treated like the most atrocious Felons! I saw them buried with myself in the horrid Dungeons! I saw venerable age, I saw tender Youth, the Rich, the Poor, in short the Priesthood itself reduced to shackles and chains and condemned to breathe a mephitic air, which extinguished artificial light, infected the blood and led to inevitable death. I saw in fine sacrificed to this cruelty citizens distinguished by their Probity and Talents.[2]

Furthermore, Miranda charged, hypocritical Spanish officials in America had consistently refused to enact the articles of their own liberal Constitution of Cádiz, proving once again that Spain treated the colonial subjects as different and inferior. In fact, he stated from experience, "it appears to be considered as a crime against the State to have been born on this Continent."

Throughout his life, as he grew more sympathetic to Anglo-American political culture with its emphasis on constitutions and the rule of law, Miranda always tried to situate his own activities within a wider Atlantic context. After all, his vision for a happy citizenry in the future reflected a project shared by all the world's enlightened citizens. Liberty's advance in one part of the world inevitably would help its progress in another; by the same token, the existence of oppression anywhere threatened liberty everywhere. Imbued with these sentiments, Miranda drew strength from the belief that his petition, indeed all his life's work, also spoke for his friends on both sides of the ocean. For this reason, he could confidently and defiantly tell the king that "in the conception and opinion of every People, in the unshaken and uninterrupted Practice of all civilized Nations and in the Doctrine generally received of all Classical Writers on Public Law, as well as foreign and national professors," Spain's actions in America were illegitimate. According to the most basic principles of humanity, Miranda concluded dramatically, "I reclaim the empire of the law, I invoke the impartial judgement of the entire world." He asked Ferdinand to restore liberty to himself and to the people of Venezuela because, in his mind at least, the two were indistinguishable. Miranda cannily not only offered to provide security for his own release but also expressed his willingness to post bail for all those humble Venezuelans who could not scrape up sufficient funds to free themselves. He was truly a generous father to the nation.

In Spain, Miranda's appeal met with a stony silence, as he undoubtedly knew it would. He was not released, of course, but rather found himself transferred from Puerto Cabello across the Atlantic to the notorious prison of La Carraca at Cádiz, just a few blocks from the house he had occupied as a youth on his first visit to Europe. Employing the psychological defense that had served him well during his many years in exile, Miranda struggled to keep his darker emotions at bay by continuing to imagine himself to be engaged in a struggle of liberty against tyranny. In La Carraca he had few social contacts, although he did manage to befriend a Peruvian inmate named Manuel Sauri who, like himself, was charged with treason. His other close confidant was a Spaniard named Pedro José Morán, a simple man who fell under the spell of Miranda's charm and served him loyally as an unofficial secretary and servant until his final illness. There is some speculation that the mysterious woman who visited Miranda occasionally and provided financial aid while he was in La Carraca was none other than Lady Hester Lucy Stanhope, Miranda's London love who had taken herself into exile to express her disgust for the state of parliamentary affairs in England; letters addressed to this benefactress were sent to a certain Señorita Leonor de Flores who resided at Calle de San Cristobal in the Isla de León and subsequently at the Calle de San Francisco de Asís. Perhaps not coincidentally, it is true that Hester Stanhope was known to be traveling throughout Europe at that time, and she did not settle in the Middle East until the winter of 1816, after Miranda's death occurred.[3] There is no question that Lady Hester retained a lifelong sentimental interest in his young family. Leander, and possibly Francisco *hijo*, later visited her in Lebanon, and when she died in 1839, Stanhope left one of her most treasured possessions, Lord Chatham's seal, to General Miranda's heirs.[4]

The move to La Carraca initiated a final and bitter epoch in Miranda's eventful life. With Napoleon temporarily removed to the island of Elba in 1814, King Ferdinand VII returned to the Spanish throne and immediately began to reclaim his dominions. Decrying the "torrent of evil that afflicts many of my Provinces," Ferdinand, "Spain's worst king," reinstated all previous institutions of overseas domination that had been modified by the liberal caretaking Junta Suprema and the Cortés of Cádiz; he then sent troops across the Atlantic to enforce his decrees. In America, the newly energized royalist counteroffensive ran up against Bolívar's declaration of War to the Death against European Spaniards and reduced northern South America to a graveyard.[5] In January 1814, Miranda's close friend Nicholas Vansittart (who had been promoted to the post of British foreign secretary) submitted to domestic political pressure and attempted to distance himself from Miranda; because the two countries were allies against Napoleon, Vansittart's colleagues feared that public scandal might erupt if the jailed South American general's close links to the British government could be proven through the publication of the men's correspondence. Vansittart attempted to retrieve copies of any potentially damaging letters that might be found in private hands. He did not, however, ever step back from his admiration for the man himself. In a letter to Major Hodgson, Vansittart affirmed that Miranda was "a man of extensive information and considerable talents which he always directed to his favorite object of becoming the Washington of South America. He had traveled over every part of Europe and is better acquainted with the policy of military systems of the different countries than almost any man I know." Sadly, Vansittart lamented, events suggested either that the Venezuelans had "proved too violent to be controlled," or that Miranda showed less ability to manage them than his British friends had anticipated.[6]

For his part, Miranda did not lose his ability to craft a powerful political plea. Imprisonment had always aroused Miranda's finest rhetorical skills, and his last major statement, produced in La Carraca in 1814, was no exception. Hoping to use the return of the king to the Spanish throne as a pretext to assign blame for the violation of the capitulation's terms to the placeholding Junta Suprema and thereby take advantage of a change in administration, Miranda addressed a new petition to Ferdinand VII on June 30.[7] Employing his characteristic style of alternately flattering and haranguing his audience, Miranda reminded the king of the paternal expressions of hope and goodwill that His Royal Highness had circulated in America the previous year; perhaps the king did not know that his lofty sentiments had never been acted upon by his royal officials in the colonies. There was no response. A few months later, Miranda once again reminded the king, telling him that although he, Miranda, had been the first and perhaps the only American commander to be invested with absolute authority by his fellow citizens, he had nevertheless undertaken to propose "an honorable peace and sincere reunion with the Mother Country," yet for his efforts he had been repaid only with ingratitude and had been relegated to an ignominious jail cell.[8] Declaring himself friendless and without financial resources in Spain, Miranda humbly asked the sovereign for permission to gather up his personal belongings scattered throughout England and France and then transport them to Russia, where he wished to live out his days under the protection of its imperial august and benign rulers. This letter also went unanswered. After forty years spent hunting the rebel Miranda, the Spaniards were in no mood to release him.

Miranda's mood continued to spiral downward and he became increasingly more despondent and desperate. Never one to feel sorry for himself or to fret over small sums, Miranda began to barrage Vansittart with complaints that he did not have enough money to secure the food, books, and writing implements that he required in prison. His paranoia grew; Miranda told Vansittart that his Gibraltar-based bankers were shortchanging him financially and, what was worse, were preventing him from receiving outside information about the affairs of the world. Miranda pathetically wrote to his stalwart old friend that "[i]t seems that adversity pursues me wherever I go in all ways possible."[9] During the years that he was confined in La Carraca, Miranda's handwriting aged visibly, degenerating from an elegant, measured script to a wobbly, spider-like scrawl. He concluded one letter on a strangely poignant note, pleading with Vansittart to take care of his little family at Grafton Street and hoping that he would be able to join them all in London soon. Frustrated at receiving no response, Miranda wrote again on May 15 and August 15 in order to assure Vansittart that if he had imagined "for a minute that your old friend had departed from the honorable and just principles [by entering into a treaty with Monteverde] which therefore lowered me in your esteem," he felt certain that "you would have undoubtedly done the same in my place." Through a series of complicated deceptions, Miranda had managed to get some books delivered to his cell; he therefore passed the many long, solitary hours in the company of Horace, Virgil, Cicero, and Don Quixote. He took pleasure in Ariosto's lyric poems and also turned to the New Testament for solace and guidance on those occasions when his faith wavered. All these favors had cost him dearly though, and jail was not a place where one could exist without access to funds. "Be a friend," Miranda pleaded, "and send some money quickly."[10]

Miranda continued to harass his friends for information and letters of credit throughout the rest of the year and well into 1816.[11] Using the pseudonym José de Amindra (an anagram of Miranda), the general exchanged more personal, even tender, letters with Peter

Turnbull, the son of his other faithful old friend of nearly forty years, merchant and banker John Turnbull. Young Peter had gone to Gibraltar to serve in his father's company and had assigned himself the task of monitoring Miranda's treatment in jail from a distance. From that vantage point, he wrote to his father that, sadly, it appeared that the old man was likely to remain in jail for the duration of his life unless his British friends could find some means of effecting his escape. John Turnbull discreetly passed on his son's assessment to Vansittart and added a note of his own saying that Peter believed that if Miranda's friends could raise the princely sum of £1,000, they might be able to secure his release.[12] Miranda himself was aware of these machinations. In April 1816, Turnbull had advanced £266 to some shady characters who had promised to spirit the general out of his cell and deliver him safely to the arms of his British protectors in Gibraltar.[13] Using the good offices of the mysterious señorita at the Isla de León, the rest of the money found its way into the right hands and the final details for Miranda's escape were hammered out. Alas, just as they appeared to be arriving at the point of success, the conspirators' scheme was cut short by the unforeseen circumstance of Miranda's rapidly deteriorating health.

Miranda's final illness was painful and drawn out. On March 25, 1816, he experienced a violent stroke that caused his devoted attendant Pedro José Morán quite a fright; convulsing with occasional fits and drooling from the side of his mouth, the proud Miranda would have been mortified at the indignity of his appearance if he had been at all conscious. Shortly afterward, just as he was beginning to recover his strength and the use of his faculties following the stroke, Miranda suffered through one of the typhus epidemics that occasionally swept through La Carraca because of its unsanitary conditions. Although an agent reported to Vansittart on April 7, 1816, that Miranda's health was "not bad," in actual fact his days were running out.[14] Morán provided a more realistic assessment for his "beloved love's" patrons; he told them that Miranda had been wracked by "an apoplectic fit, upon the heels of which he remained with a nasty, putrid fever—for forty-eight hours his head was swollen and he frothed at the mouth."[15] Morán felt certain that the general was nearing the end of his life; therefore, according to his instructions, he took the precaution of sending Miranda's personal papers on to Gibraltar in order to prevent them from falling into Spanish hands. Peter Turnbull was glad to hear of it, but worried that the agents at Gibraltar would refuse to accept the precious cargo when it arrived, for fear of arousing Spanish distrust that would affect their mercantile affairs.

The horrible news of Miranda's dire condition prompted a flurry of letters among interested parties throughout the region. Through the judicious use of petty bribes, Admiral C. S. Fleeming had been able to persuade Spanish jailers to remove Miranda's leg irons and to move him from "a noisome and miserable Dungeon into an airy and healthy apartment where he was indulged with many comforts." Now that the general's demise seemed imminent, the admiral callously hoped to stake his claim for payment before other creditors surfaced to lay claim to part of his estate; Fleeming asked John Turnbull (as Miranda's executor) to repay all the money that he had advanced to Miranda to ameliorate his prison conditions since September 1814.[16] Peter Turnbull was disgusted to report that he had learned that several unscrupulous characters were trying to take advantage of the dying man by promising him false hope and an escape in exchange for vast sums of money. Even the conspirators that he himself had engaged fell under this new suspicion. Yet young Turnbull refused to believe that his old family friend was nearing the end. As long as there was a spark of hope left, Turnbull continued to press his contacts in Spain and Gibraltar for assistance in effecting the weak old man's escape. Although an ever-optimistic Miranda reported that he was "feeling better after the fevers that have plagued me of late and am ready to leave this Wednesday on the little voyage that you know about," he felt compelled at the same time to reaffirm his previous 1805 and 1810 wills with only slight modifications before it was too late.[17]

He had always been a fighter and this last battle for his failing health was no exception. Miranda lingered for nearly two months, fittingly drawing his final breath in the early hours of the morning of July 14, 1816, the anniversary of Bastille Day in France. Dominican friar Alvaro Sánchez heard his confession and said last rites; he later reported that the impatient patriot's final words were simply to "let me die in peace."[18] For all the grief that he had caused the Spanish empire, the fateful day's entry in the prison's record book succinctly (if inaccurately) listed the death of "Francisco de Miranda, son of Sebastián de Miranda, native of Venezuela, single, aged seventy years."[19] His body was quickly buried and all his personal effects, clothing, and bedsheets were consigned to the flames in order to prevent the spread of disease. No doubt the empire also wished to remove the last traces of a troublesome man. In 1875, when La Carraca was torn down, Miranda's bones were dug up and placed in a mass grave along with those of hundreds of other unfortunate men, rendering any attempt to repatriate them to Venezuela impossible. Today, in the National Pantheon in Caracas, the door to the Precursor's sumptuous marble tomb is held open by an eagle, symbolically awaiting the return of his mortal remains.

Miranda's devastated servant Pedro José Morán sadly wrote to Peter Turnbull to report that, "at 1:05 A.M., my beloved Señor Don Francisco de Miranda surrendered his spirit to the Creator."[20] News of the general's death, once confirmed, caused his many associates throughout the Atlantic world to eulogize him immediately and profusely. John Turnbull was deeply saddened and died shortly after receiving the news, causing his son's grief to double. Lamenting the world's loss privately in his diary entry for August 12, 1816, Lord Glenbervie recalled two occasions on which he had dined with Miranda and wrote that he had found the amazing man not only to be perfectly fluent in Spanish, English, French, Italian, and German but also to be a "good classical scholar in both Latin and Greek."[21]

London's *Morning Chronicle* mourned the death of General Miranda, who, as its editors said, "has at length fallen victim to Spanish barbarity, after an imprisonment of nearly four years in a horrible dungeon, in violation of a most solemn capitulation. Revenge pursued him even beyond the grave, monks would not allow his faithful attendant to give him any last rites: but carried off the miserable body on the mattress and truckle bed on which he expired, and committed all his raiment and everything that belonged to him to the flames. The friends of freedom and humanity will deplore the fate of a man whose aim it was to ameliorate the condition of his fellow creatures."[22] Its editors promised to launch an investigation into the true conditions of Miranda's final days, eventually assuring their readers, "[i]t is now fully ascertained that General MIRANDA died a natural death, and behaved in the most courageous manner during the whole of his captivity."[23] Jeremy Bentham was devastated, noting that he had pinned his hopes on Miranda as "one of the mainstays of South American liberty."[24] Even Richard Wellesley expressed his condolences to Miranda's secretary, Tómas Molini, with the gentlemanly sentiment that "all men, whatever their party or their principles, will lament the premature death of an individual who, through his capabilities, his knowledge, and his experiences, was capable of loaning eminent services to his country."[25]

News of Miranda's death spread quickly. Across the ocean in the United States, friends and enemies alike shared their memories of the cosmopolitan man who had spent time in their midst. For example, James Madison asked Richard Rush to send a copy of the notes that he had made after that unforgettable day spent with Miranda so long ago in 1805. Rush added in hindsight, "[t]hough Miranda has proved himself so wholly unequal to anything great in practical life, the first bursts of his literature and knowledge were calculated to make an impression upon a mind that had never knowed or viewed him through any other medium. . . . In the department of conversation he was an uncommon man. Whether his narratives were already to be trusted, I knew not enough of the inside of his character to say."[26]

Madison returned the documents three days later, agreeing that the brief conversations that he had had with Miranda convinced him that the Venezuelan "possessed a mind of more than ordinary stature, and improved by diversified acquirements." Madison nevertheless believed that his career of depredation indicated that Miranda's character was, in the final analysis, less than respectable. At least, Madison owned, it was to Miranda's credit that during the whole unpleasant business of the Smith and Ogden trials, Miranda never claimed that he had received the American government's countenance for the *Leander* Expedition.[27] Only Charles-François Dumouriez, Miranda's archnemesis from the Belgian campaigns in the 1790s, was willing to criticize Miranda openly; still harboring resentments after two decades, Dumouriez told John Quincy Adams that the Venezuelan was nothing less than a madman.[28]

Miranda had choreographed his entire life with one eye toward his historical reputation. When he died, his friends and family took care to ensure that his memory would be preserved favorably in the annals of history. In the 1820s, his son Leander joined with Colombian envoy Francisco Antonio Zea to produce a handsome English-language history of the young country; the volume contained a description of Miranda's illustrious father as "[t]he man in whose breast the scheme of South American emancipation, if not first conceived, appears to have first matured."[29] Mexican patriot Fray Servando Teresa de Mier Noriega y Guerra praised the Precursor's genuine American-ism, saying that he had wisely "*protested against the Venezuelan [1811] Constitution as being contrary to the biases, habits and customs of the country.*"[30] Perhaps out of revenge, Bolívar's disaffected secretary, General Ducoudray-Holstein, wanted it known that "[Miranda] was in every respect, a much worthier man than General Bolívar. Miranda was a profound tactician; an intrepid soldier; a man of great ability in civil administration; disinterested in his views; and who never, in the least particular, abused the dictatorial power entrusted to him by Congress during several months. He attracted to him men of talent and merit, listened to their opinions, and many times followed their suggestions. Bolívar is the exact reverse of all this."[31]

Yet even Bolívar's trusted aide-de-camp and close confidant Daniel Florencio O'Leary agreed that Miranda had "consecrated his entire life in the attainment of independence for his *patria* [fatherland]."[32] The balanced and astute O'Leary observed that Miranda "died a martyr to the cause that he embraced from his youth. Whatever his faults may have been, posterity should do justice to the sincerity of his patriotism, and nobody can deny him his notable talents and vast knowledge. While he governed in Venezuela, his greatest fault consisted in not understanding the nature of his compatriots and in not adjusting himself to the circumstances."[33]

O'Leary was right: Miranda was a man of the eighteenth century whose genius lay in raising the consciousness and confidence of his fellow Americans. Although he prided himself on being a soldier, his greatest battles were fought with his pen. When the nineteenth century arrived and demanded action, Miranda had been away from home for too long to be effective as an American commander. He fought as a European would, according to European rules of battle and for European brands of universal truth.

Miranda remained a man caught between two worlds. Although he was most comfortable in London and had created an English family for himself, America was never far from his thoughts. In his last will and testament, Miranda bequeathed part of his precious book collection to the University of Caracas. He wished that "there should be sent in my name, the Greek classics in my library as a token of my gratitude and respect for the wise principles of literature and Christian morality with which it nourished my youth. These sound teachings have enabled me to overcome happily the grave risks and perils with which fate has encompassed me."[34] Miranda had always hoped that his book collection would constitute the nucleus for a world-class library in Venezuela. The English Lord Colchester remembered Miranda's "great ardor for literature; [he had] always been collecting books for his intended library at the University of Santa Fé."[35] In fact, the books contained in his personal collection had a historical significance for the entire Columbian continent. They had been well thumbed by the leaders of the three major South American military campaigns; Bernardo O'Higgins, Simón Bolívar, and José de San Martín all read in his library at Grafton Street. Andrés Bello, the great Venezuelan poet, linguist, and jurist, also studied in the Precursor's vast library. In 1820, Chilean envoy to London Antonio José de Irisarri wrote to O'Higgins that Miranda's executors, Vansittart and Sir John Jackson, had inquired whether the Chileans would be interested in purchasing the books to become the core of Chile's recently founded national library; Irisarri excitedly reported that the collection was "generally held in great esteem in London because of its exquisite assortment of rare and classic works, and special editions."[36] Irisarri was flattered that the men had approached him first, believing that Chile was the most enlightened Spanish American nation and therefore would offer the best home for Miranda's library. O'Higgins did indeed desperately want to buy his old mentor's collection, which he called a "valuable treasure-trove of enlightenment," but the fiscally responsible Chilean Senate ultimately decided that they would have to postpone the construction of "libraries and other such aggrandizements until calmer times."[37] It was a regrettable lost opportunity; as Miranda's family became increasingly desperate for funds, his library was eventually sold piece by piece at a London public auction.[38]

Sarah Andrews was inconsolable following the news of her husband's death. As his "beloved Sally," she devoted the rest of her life to raising their sons and to preserving his memory. She remained in the Grafton Street house until her death at age 74 on December 28, 1847. Leander was a passionate and intellectual youth who inherited his father's devotion to the American cause. In 1823, he approached his father's old patron Jeremy Bentham to solicit a letter of introduction and recommendation to Simón Bolívar. Bentham described Leander's character as "altogether spotless."[39] The young man followed his father across the ocean and moved to Bogotá where he founded the bilingual newspaper *El Constitutional* (The Constitutional) and married Teresa Dalla Costa Soublette. He served in Colombia's Ministry of Foreign Relations and was secretary of its legation to London in 1830. Leander left the diplomatic service in 1839 for a stint in the world of finance; he served as the director of the Banco Colonial Británico de Caracas (British Colonial Bank of Caracas) until 1849. In the 1850s, Leander Miranda returned to foreign service as Venezuela's consul in Lima. He died in Paris in 1886.

Francisco de Miranda *hijo* had a shorter, more tragic life. Possessed of none of his older brother's social skills and all of his father's hot temper, he followed Leander to Colombia and entered military service, where he promptly got into scrape after scrape. Francisco fought with the Gran Colombian forces in Peru in 1826, but was arrested in Lima the next year for refusing to participate in Bustamante's uprising. In October 1827, because of his nearsightedness, young Francisco accidentally slighted the Dutch consul general Johnkeer van Stuers at a presidential ball when he knocked over the perfume flask of the young lady with whom the consul had been dancing.[40] Even though such contests were illegal in the new republic, the irate man challenged Miranda to a duel the next day; Francisco killed the witty and popular Dutchman at fifteen paces with a shot right between the eyes, and then had to be hustled to a safe house. He was always seen as an outsider. The newspapers described Francisco as "an English official in the Colombian service."[41] Under the patronage of his father's friend General Rafael Urdaneta, he was spirited out of Colombia and posted to a more innocuous post doing guard duty at La Guaira. In 1829, Francisco was first appointed as aide-de-camp to General Tomás

Cipriano Mosquera and then later reassigned to General José Laurencio Silva. On May 2, 1831, 25-year-old Francisco de Miranda was killed in battle; some witnesses claim he was actually taken prisoner and shot. He never married, but apparently left an illegitimate daughter named Avelina for whom his older brother searched unsuccessfully for many years.

Despite General Francisco de Miranda's extensive travels and numerous high-level political associations, throughout his long and active life, his closest relationship remained with the British. He lived in London for a longer time than anywhere else, beginning in the mid-1780s and continuing on and off until his final departure for Venezuela in October 1810. Although he had many love affairs during his long life, in the end he married an Englishwoman and his two beloved children were raised there. London was the cultural environment he knew best and the one that provided him the greatest comfort in his old age. He embraced its leaders' brand of aristocratic reformism, believing that those men who were well educated and independently wealthy would be the least susceptible to corruption and therefore the best prepared to deliberate impartially on behalf of their fellow citizens. He had studied political cultures both in North America and throughout Europe, always with an eye toward creating happiness for his own people (whether they wanted him to or not). After his traumatic experiences in the service of the French Revolution, Miranda understood all too well the danger of allowing the unrestrained anger of the masses to spiral out of control; from his North American friends, he observed that the self-interested deliberations of citizen representatives could not only slow down the pace of reform, but could also pervert the nature of liberty itself. Miranda, like the Spanish Americans whose worldview he influenced, came to prefer a constitutional monarchy that was an ill-defined hybrid of British forms, traditions drawn from the Greek classics, and elements of the American indigenous heritage.

Miranda's sense of American identity was the direct product of a life spent in exile. Virtually all of his adult life was led outside Spanish America; he retained a sort of sentimental attachment that grew in strength as each year passed, but the nature of this devotion also doomed his efforts to failure. He was an American patriot who did

not understand America. He was a great nationalist who was denationalized by his life experiences. He felt at home everywhere he went,
partly because his curiosity and extensive journeys had made him a
seasoned traveler, but also because his outlook was profoundly international. Francisco de Miranda was truly a man of the Enlightenment, passionately devoted to the idea of liberty and convinced that
the future belonged to men like himself. He had lived and fought on
four continents, schemed with the Atlantic world's most powerful
leaders, and romanced women of all social ranks. He was indeed a
remarkable man in an age of remarkable men. He had fought glori-
ously for liberty wherever he went and had been jailed on more than
one occasion for his convictions, but when death finally came knock-
ing, Miranda found himself to be just the same as everyone else—
alone.

NOTES

Introduction, Pages xiii–xix

1. V. S. Naipaul, *A Way in the World* (New York: Knopf, 1994), and *The Loss of El Dorado: A History* (New York: Penguin, 1973).

2. John Edsall, *Incidents in the Life of John Edsall* (Catskill, NY: [printed for the author], 1831), p. 15; [John Sherman], *A General Account of Miranda's Expedition, Including the Trial and Execution of Ten of His Officers* (New York: McFarlane and Long, 1808), p. 40.

3. Adams to James Lloyd (Quincy, March 26, 1815) and (Quincy, April 5, 1815), *Works of John Adams, Second President of the United States, with a Life of the Author*, Charles Francis Adams, ed. (Boston: Little, Brown and Co., 1856), 10:142, 151.

4. Rolla [pseud.], (September 6, 1806) and [anonymous] (September 2, 1806), both in *Barbados Mercury*.

5. Tomás Polanco Alcántara, *Francisco de Miranda, ¿Don Juan o Don Quijote?* (Caracas: Ediciones Ge, 1997).

6. Stewart Halpine, *The Altar of Venus: A Biography of Francisco de Miranda* (Bloomington, IN: First Books, 1999); Jacques Cazotte, *Miranda, 1750–1816: Histoire d'un séducteur* (Paris: Perrin, 2000).

7. William Spence Robertson, *The Life of Miranda*, 2 vols. (Chapel Hill: University of North Carolina Press, 1929); Joseph Thorning, *Miranda: World Citizen* (Gainesville: University of Florida Press, 1950).

8. Rafael Pineda, *Iconografía de Francisco de Miranda (retratos, estatuas y medallas, hechos y cosas relacionados con su memoria)* (Caracas: Comisión Presidencial para la Conmemoración del 250 Aniversario del Natalicio del Generalíssimo Francisco de Miranda, Ministerio del Interior y Justicia, Banco Nacional de Venezuela, 2001).

Chapter 1, Pages 1–29

1. Polanco, *Miranda*, p. 19.

2. *Archivo de la Catedral Metropolitana [Caracas], Libros parroquiales, Sección Bautismos, Libro 13, f. 196.*

3. Polanco, *Miranda*, p. 23. Thorning, *World Citizen*, p. 5, lists eight other siblings, omitting reference to Josefa Antonia, who was born in 1764 and lived less than a year.

4. William Burke, *Additional Reasons for Our Immediately Emancipating Spanish America*, 2d ed. (London: J. Ridgway, 1808), p. 66.

5. François-Raymond Joseph Depons, *Travels in South America during the Years 1801, 1802, 1803, 1804, Containing a Description of the Captain-Generalship of Caraccas and an Account of the Discovery, Conquest, Topography, Legislature, Commerce, Finance, and Natural Productions of the Country with a View to the Manners and Customs of the Spaniards and the Native Indians* (London: Longman, Hurst, Rees & Orme, 1807), 1:43. Depons (1751–1812) served as the local representative of the French government, and his account is one of the few existing records of Caracas's social life during those years.

6. "Lista de los cursantes de la clase de menores, regentado por don Antonio Monserrate desde el 10 de enero de 1762," [*Universidad Central de Venezuela*], *Archivo Universitario, Matrículas, Libro 2, Años 1673–1762*, cited in Polanco, *Miranda*, p. 29n.

7. Robertson, *The Life of Miranda*, 1:6. Miranda's diploma is signed by the University's secretary, Marcos de Madrid, and included in Miranda's personal papers, "Certificación de Estudios," (30 de junio de 1767), *Archivo del General Miranda* (Caracas: Editorial Sur-América, 1929), 1:1 (hereafter cited as *AGM*).

8. John Lombardi, *Venezuela: The Search for Order, the Dream of Progress* (New York: Oxford University Press, 1982), contains an excellent description of Caracas's rise to regional prominence.

9. David Fernández, *La familia de Miranda* (Caracas: Instituto de Estudios Históricos Mirandinos, 1972), p. 13. Sebastián de Miranda held this position from December 17, 1764, until April 21, 1769.

10. Polanco, *Miranda*, pp. 32–33.

11. Captain Sebastián de Miranda Ravelo, collection of documents, in *Archivo General de la Nación—Venezuela, Limpieza de Sangre, vol. 9, f.123*.

12. The documents from the entire case have been transcribed and printed in Angel Grisanti, *El proceso contra Don Sebastián de Miranda, padre del precursor de la independencia continental* (Caracas: Editorial Ávila Gráfica, 1950). The same author has an account of the charges in *El precursor Miranda y su familia: primera biografía general de la familia Miranda* (Madrid: Talleres Artegráfica Betancourt, 1950), pp. 19–24.

13. "Informe de Hidalguía" (Caracas, 3–4 de enero de 1771), in *AGM*, 1:4–12.

14. Thorning, *World Citizen*, p. 11. Fernández, *La familia de Miranda*, pp. 5–7, lists the military background of Miranda's European family, including their titles and places served.

15. "Diario de Navegación de la Guayra al de Cádiz, 1771" in *AGM*, 1:29.

16. "Diario de Navegación," *AGM*, 1:33.

17. "Ruta del Puerto de Santa María a Madrid," *AGM*, 1:34–38.

18. "Ruta del Puerto de Santa María a Madrid," *AGM*, 1:38.

19. "Retratos de hombres ilustres que están en la Biblioteca del Escorial," *AGM*, 1:42.

20. "Descripción del Palacio nuevo de Madrid," *AGM*, 1:43–44.

21. "Descripción del Palacio viejo del Retiro," *AGM*, 1:49.

22. W. N. Hargreaves-Maudsley, *Eighteenth-Century Spain, 1700–1788: A Political, Diplomatic and Institutional History* (Totowa, NJ: Rowman and Littlefield, 1979); Neville Barbour, *A Survey of North West Africa* (Oxford, UK: Oxford University Press, 1962).

23. "Mas por amor hacia la patria que por interés mío" (Melilla, 15 de junio de 1774), in Francisco de Miranda, *América espera*, ed. J. L. Salcedo-Bastardo (Caracas: Biblioteca Ayacucho, 1982), pp. 6–7.

24. There are four different fragmentary diaries that cover Miranda's time in Melilla, not all of which are in accordance in small details. One of the more significant discrepancies is the date of arrival; two of the diaries indicate that he arrived on December 29, although the battle clearly had begun three weeks earlier. As the diaries appear to be transcribed at least in part from each other, and amended at a later time, it is likely that he misdated these portions. The originals are found in *Academia Nacional de la Historia [Caracas], Archivo Miranda, Colombeia Africa-España-Viajes, Tomo 1, ff.177, 183, 187, and Tomo 2, ff.42.*

25. "Diario del sitio y defensa de la Plaza de Melilla contra el exército del Emperador de Marruecos quien le atacó en persona el dia 9 de diziembre de 1774," *AGM*, 1:54.

26. "Salida de Málaga para la Plaza de Melilla [segundo fragmento]," *AGM*, 1:67.

27. "Salida de Málaga," *AGM*, 1:73. A calendrical conversion indicates that this date would have been 19 Thw al-Qi'dah 1188 A.H. in the Muslim calendar. Although this reckoning means that the dates would not seem to coincide, January is frequently the month in which the end of Ramadan is celebrated by *Eid al-Fitr*, "The Feast of Breaking the Fast," and it is celebrated in the manner described by Miranda in his diary.

28. Miranda to O'Connor, "En calidad de voluntario" (Melilla, 18 de abril de 1775), in *América espera*, p. 7.

29. Miranda to El Rey Carlos III, "El mérito contraido en la defensa" (Melilla, 20 de junio de 1775), in *América espera*, p. 8.

30. Miranda to González de Castejón, "Lograr el cumplimiento de mis ideas," (Cádiz, 7 de junio de 1776), in *América espera*, pp. 8–9.

31. Miranda to Álvarez, "Un individuo que solo desea emplear la vida en servicio y gloria de su patria" (Cádiz, 7 de julio de 1776), in *América espera*, p. 9.

32. Miranda to Cevallos, "No tengo más protección que el concepto que merezco" (Cádiz, 18 de agosto de 1776), in *América espera*, p. 10.

33. José Nucete-Sardi, *Aventura y tragedia de Francisco de Miranda* (Barcelona: Plaza y Janes, 1971), p. 21.

34. For a cursory treatment of a relationship that deserves fuller exploration, see Pascual Plá y Beltrán, "Un fiel amigo de Miranda: John Turnbull," *Boletín de la Academia Nacional de la Historia* (Caracas) #179 (julio-setiembre 1962): 425–29.

35. Turnbull to Miranda (Gibraltar, 7 de julio de 1777), in *América espera*, pp. 10–11. Henry St. John, Lord Bolingbroke (1678–1751) was an influential British politician, orator, and historian who favored a form of Tory democracy that sought to strengthen opposition to the government through parliamentary inquiries and the freedom of the press.

36. "Ruta de Cádiz a Madrid con el Reg[imen]to de la Princesa año de 1778," in *AGM*, 1:121–29.

37. "Ruta de Cádiz a Madrid," in *AGM*, 1:128n.

38. Miranda, "El hecho de la verdad: respuestas a los cargos del Coronel Juan Roca," (Madrid, 22 de diciembre de 1779), in *America espera*, pp. 18–24.

39. [P. Luque] to Miranda, [1779], *AGM*, 13:183.

40. María Teresa to Miranda, *AGM*, 13:186–87.

41. Fernández, *familia de Miranda*, pp. 13–14.

42. "Principios de una famosa biblioteca," *América espera*, pp. 24–34.

43. Rafael Valery S, *Miranda en Pensacola* (Los Teques, Venezuela: Biblioteca de Autores y Temas Mirandinos, 1991), p. 57.

44. Manuel Pérez Cabrera, *Miranda en Cuba, 1780–1783* (La Habana: Academia de la Historia de Cuba, 1950), p.13. In "A Journal of the seige [*sic*] of Pensacola West Florida 1781," an anonymous British officer reported that the total number of combatants on their side was 1,200, and estimated the number of their opponents at 23,000; *AGM*, 1:191.

45. "Diario de Panzacola [*sic*]" in *AGM*, 1:142–91.

46. For details of the battle and its larger implications, see Héctor Bencomo Barrios, "Miranda y la toma de Pensacola," *Boletín de la Academia Nacional de la Historia* #255 (1981); Robert Rea and William Coker, eds. *Anglo-Spanish Confrontation on the Gulf Coast during the American Revolution* (Pensacola: Gulf Coast History and Humanities Conference, 1982); and Virginia Parks, ed., *Siege! Spain and Britain and the Battle of Pensacola* (Pensacola: Pensacola Historical Society, 1981).

47. Pérez, *Miranda en Cuba*, p. 16.

48. Valery, *Miranda en Pensacola*, p. 24; Pérez, *Miranda en Cuba*, pp. 15–16.

49. Valery, *Miranda en Pensacola*, p. 15.

50. Thorning, *World Citizen*, p. 21, and Pérez, *Miranda en Cuba*, pp. 18–19, and Nucete-Sardi, *Aventura y tragedia*, pp. 30–31 all believe Miranda played a vital role in supplying the Chesapeake Bay expedition. Valery, *Miranda en Pensacola*, p. 141, argues that his participation was unlikely.

51. Miranda, "Hace presente los méritos que tiene en el servicio," in *América espera*, pp. 46–47.

52. Copy of instructions included in Cagigal to [el Comandante General del Ejército de Operaciones Don Bernardo de Gálvez] (Habana, 6 de enero 1782), in *América espera*, pp. 47–49.

53. Thorning, *World Citizen*, pp. 21–22.

54. Valery, *Miranda en Pensacola*, p. 24

55. Cagigal to [el Comandante General del Ejército de Operaciones Don Bernardo de Gálvez] (Habana, 6 de enero de 1782), in *América espera*, pp. 47–49.

56. Copies of the documents from this investigation are located in Cuban Archives and have been reprinted in Pérez, *Miranda en Cuba*. See, for example, the royal order authorizing Miranda to purchase the ships, J[ose]ph de Gálvez, S[eñ]or Intendente de la Havana (Havana, 17 de noviembre de 1781), pp. 39–40, which is deposited in *Cuba, Archivo Nacional, Asuntos Políticos, leg. 3, sig. 31.*

57. Gálvez to S[eñ]or Gobernador de la Havana, (El Pardo, 11 de marzo de 1782), in *AGM*, 5:75–77.

58. Bolívar, Tovar, and Miyares to Miranda, (Caracas, 24 de febrero de 1782), in *AGM* (Caracas: Tipografía Americana, 1938), 15:68–69.

59. Miranda to Cagigal, (En la mar, sobre el Puerto de Matanzas, Isla de Cuba, 16 de abril de 1783), in *América espera*, pp. 57–60.

60. Miranda to Cagigal, confidential, (16 de abril de 1783), in *América espera*, pp. 60–61.

Chapter 2, Pages 31–64

1. Available in an English edition as *The New Democracy in America: Travels of Francisco de Miranda in the United States, 1783–84*, Judson P. Wood transl., John Ezell, ed., (Norman: University of Oklahoma Press, 1963). An accessible Spanish language facsimile edition appeared under an English title as *Diary of Francisco de Miranda: His Tour of the United States, 1783–1784*, William S. Robertson, ed. (New York: Hispanic Society of New York, 1928).

2. For a fuller discussion of this paradox, see the articles in *Strange Pilgrimages: Travel, Exile and National Identity in Latin America, 1800–1990s*, Ingrid E. Fey and Karen Racine, eds. (Wilmington, DE: Scholarly Resources, 2000).

3. *New Democracy*, p. 6.

4. Robert Darnton, *The Forbidden Bestsellers of Prerevolutionary France* (New York: Harper Collins, 1996), p. 90.

5. *New Democracy*, pp. 10–11. Comfort was fifteen; Constance was eighteen.

6. Ibid., pp. 7–8. Many books elaborate on this connection. See Carl J. Richard, *The Founders and the Classics* (Cambridge: Harvard University Press, 1995).

7. *New Democracy*, p.12.

8. Ibid., p. 17.

9. Williams to "Much Esteemed Friend Francisco de Miranda" (July 19, 1783) in *AGM*, 5:246–48. The verses sent were: Psalm 139:14, Psalm 8, Acts 21:14, and Romans 1:19.

10. *New Democracy*, p. 24.

11. Ibid., p. 32.

12. Ibid., p. 35.

13. Ibid., pp. 40–41.

14. Ibid., p. 42.

15. Ibid., p. 42.

16. Ibid., p. 43.

17. Cagigal to Rendón (Havana, 18 de mayo de 1783), in *AGM*, 5:243.

18. *New Democracy*, p. 46.

19. Invitations dated January 1784 and reprinted in *AGM*, 5:255–56.

20. The phrase is Miranda's in a letter to Francisco Rendón (Londres, 20 de junio de 1785) in *AGM*, 1:19.

21. *New Democracy*, p. 167.

22. Ibid., p. 45. Miranda, however, did not condone Quintana's failure to rescue a young Quaker girl who had drowned in her cabin on their voyage over from England. For a general history of cultural relations between these two countries in the revolutionary era, see Light Townsend Cummins, *Spanish Observers and the American Revolution, 1775–1783* (Baton Rouge: Louisiana State University Press, 1991).

23. *New Democracy*, p. 56.

24. Mrs. Montgomery to Miranda (n.p., n.d.), in *AGM*, 5:258.

25. Mrs. Burr to Miranda (Tuesday Mor[nin]g), in *AGM*, 5:259. This likely refers to the 1777 work by Jean Baptiste Claude Delisle de Sale Izouard that was popular at the time and available in both English and French editions. Similar titles included Baron Paul Henri Thierry d'Holbach's *Système de la nature*, and G. W. Leibniz's *Principe de la nature et de la grâce fondés en raison. Principes de la philosophie ou Monadologie*. Natural philosophy can be traced back to Saint Thomas Aquinas.

26. Mary Walton to Monsieur Le Colonel Da Miranda (Mardi le matin, 6 Avril 1784), in *AGM*, 5:265.

27. For a discussion of republican morality and public life, see Ann Withington, *Toward a More Perfect Union: Virtue and the Formation of the American Republics* (New York: Oxford University Press, 1991).

28. *New Democracy*, p. 58.

29. Cagigal to Ex[celentísimo] Señor Don Jorge Washington (Havana, 26 de mayo de 1783) in *AGM*, 5:243–44.

30. Rendón to Washington, ([Philadelphia], December 1793), *Library of Congress, George Washington Papers, 1741–1799, Series 4, General Correspondence 1697–1799*. Quintus Fabius Maximus, known as "Cunctator" or "the Delayer," died in

203 B.C.E. In contemporary times, Fabianism has come to describe a gradual or cautious approach to political change and public policy.

31. *New Democracy*, p. 59.

32. Washington to Jacob Read, (Mount Vernon, November 3, 1784), *Library of Congress, Washington Papers, Series 2: Letterbooks*.

33. Miranda's observation on Washington (1795) quoted in Thorning, *World Citizen*, p. 128. Original in *AGM*, 3:341.

34. *New Democracy*, p. 62.

35. Ibid., p. 63.

36. Ibid., pp. 65–66.

37. Ibid., p. 75.

38. Ibid., p. 75.

39. Marshall Smelser, "George Washington Declines the Part of 'El Libertador,' " *William and Mary Quarterly* 11 (#1, January 1954): 45.

40. Susan Livingston to Miranda ([New York], January 10, 1784), in *AGM*, 13:200–201.

41. The actual reference is found in Susan Livingston to Miranda (Hanover Square [New York], 1785), *AGM*, 13:214–15, in which she writes, "perhaps you will understand their allusion, I do not." Both Nucete-Sardi, *Aventura y tragedia*, p. 31 and Robertson, *The Life of Miranda* (New York: Cooper Square Publishers, 1969), 1:44, attribute the letter to Eliza Livingston, her sister, but the copy in Miranda's archive seems to be written by Susan herself.

42. Sarah Vaughan to H. W. Livingston (Thursday [November 25, 1784]), in *Massachusetts Historical Society, Matthew Ridley Papers*.

43. Thomas Paine (New Rochelle, March 20, 1806), in *The Complete Writings of Thomas Paine*, Philip Foner, ed. (New York: Citadel Press, 1945), pp. 1480–82.

44. John Adams to James Lloyd (Quincy, March 6, 1815), *Works of John Adams*, 10:134.

45. John R. Alden, *Stephen Sayre: American Revolutionary Adventurer* (Baton Rouge: Louisiana State University Press, 1983), pp. 65, 185.

46. Alexander Hamilton to Miranda (Wednesday, [New York, January–July 1784]), in *The Papers of Alexander Hamilton*, Harold Syrett, ed. (New York: Columbia University Press, 1961–1987), 3:504. The original is in Miranda's papers at the Academia Nacional de la Historia in Caracas.

47. Miranda, quoted in Robertson, *The Life of Miranda*, 1:43–44. Original dated (Paris, October 10, 1792).

48. S. Knox to James Swan, and S. Knox to His Excellency Governor Hancock, both dated (New York, April 28, 1784), in *AGM*, 5:266–67.

49. *New Democracy*, p. 85.

50. Lieutenant Colonel William Hull to Henry Knox (West Point, February 29, 1784), in *Massachusetts Historical Society, Knox Papers, reel 17, #29*.

51. *New Democracy*, p. 90.

52. Ibid., p. 94. Van Weetle likely suffered from hydrocephaly, a disease caused by excessive brain fluid that distorts the skull.

53. J[ames] Seagrove to Miranda (Havana, March 16, 1784), in *AGM*, 5:263–64.

54. Duer to Rose (New York, July 10, 1784), in *AGM*, 5:269–70.

55. *New Democracy*, p. 99.

56. Ezra Stiles, *The Literary Diary of Ezra Stiles*, Franklin Bowditch Dexter, ed. (New York: Scribner's, 1901), p. 130. See also Miguel A. Villaroel, *Miranda y la Universidad de Yale* (Caracas: Instituto de Estudios Históricos Mirandinos, 1977).

57. *New Democracy*, p. 107.

58. Stiles, *Literary Diary*, p. 131.

59. Ibid., p. 131. Oddly, in Miranda's diary, where no one else would see the reference, he compared a machine for draining mines that he had seen in Rhode Island to inferior ones found in Mexico and "all our other dominions of America," speaking as though he had seen them personally; *New Democracy*, p. 150.

60. *New Democracy*, p. 107.

61. Ibid., p. 128.

62. Ibid., p. 111.

63. Ibid., pp. 114–15.

64. Ibid., p. 116.

65. Ibid., p. 138. The Jeffersonian ideal of the small farmer was at the center of republican theory at the time and was viewed as an essential part of the emerging American identity. Another famous contemporary observer of the phenomenon was J. Hector St. John Crèvecoeur, *Letters from an American Farmer: Describing Certain Provincial Situations, Manners, and Customs Not Generally Known; and Conveying some Idea of the Late and Present Interior Circumstances of the British Colonies of North America* (1782).

66. *New Democracy*, p. 130.

67. Ibid., p. 165.

68. Ibid., p. 116.

69. Ibid., pp. 117–18. He encountered the same substitution at a distillery near Providence, Rhode Island, in September, p. 145. For a discussion of tavern culture, see Peter Thompson, *Rum, Punch, and Revolution* (Philadelphia: University of Pennsylvania Press, 1998).

70. *New Democracy*, p. 125.

71. Ibid., p. 134.

72. Ibid., p. 140.

73. Ibid., p. 126.

74. Dan Parker to the Hon[orable] Major General Knox (New York, January 25, 1874), *Massachusetts Historical Society, Henry Knox Papers, roll 16, #177*.

75. *New Democracy*, p. 164.

76. Reprinted in *América espera*, pp. 65–68. The list of North American officials is undated and is suspected to be the work of Alexander Hamilton. See *The Papers of Alexander Hamilton*, 3:586–87.

77. *New Democracy*, p. 163.

78. Ibid., p. 162.

79. Ibid., p. 163.

80. Ibid., p. 169.

81. Ibid., p. 176.

82. Ibid., pp. 186–87.

83. Waterhouse to Miranda (December 12, 1784), in *AGM*, 5:278.

84. See [Minister of the Indies] José de Gálvez's royal order to the Intendente del Exército de la Havana, (San Ildefonso, 14 de septiembre de 1784) ordering an inventory of all papers relevant to the Miranda affair. Quoted in Pérez, *Miranda en Cuba*, pp. 41–42. Original at *Cuba, Archivo Nacional, Reales Decretos y Ordenes, leg. 20, #63.*

85. Adams to James Lloyd (Quincy, March 6, 1815), in *Works of John Adams*, 10:135.

Chapter 3, Pages 67–104

1. *AGM*, 1:346–47.

2. *Boston Sentinel*, #25 (December 1784).

3. *Fragments from an XVIIIth Century Diary: The Travels and Adventures of Don Francisco de Miranda, 1771–1789*, Jordan Herbert Stabler, comp. and transl. (Caracas: Tipografía "La Nación," 1931).

4. Ibid., p. 71.

5. William S. Smith [with additions and annotations by Miranda], "Jornal de Prusia, Saxonia, y Austria en el año de 1785," in *AGM*, 1:352.

6. William Duer to William Brummel (New York, February 12, 1784), in *AGM*, 5:260–61.

7. "Direcciones," in *AGM*, 5:281, 286–87.

8. Miranda to Carlos III por vía de Floridablanca, "Vindicado su inocencia y denunciado la persecución" (Londres, 10 de abril de 1785), in *América espera*, pp. 68–75.

9. Robertson believes that Miranda wrote this letter to stall for time and to deceive the Spanish Crown as to his real intentions because he was desperate for money. *The Life of Miranda*, 1:60–61.

10. See Mario Hernández y Sánchez-Barba, "La Paz de 1783 y la misión de Bernardo del Campo en Londres," *Estudios de Historia Moderna* 2 (1952): 179–229, and Angel Grisanti, *Miranda juzgado por los funcionarios españoles de su tiempo* (Caracas: SPI, 1954).

11. "Pancho" to Francisco Arrieta (Londres, 12 de mayo de 1785), in *AGM*, 5:95–96; "Pancho" to Arrieta (Londres, 20 de junio de 1785), in *América espera*, p. 75.

12. León Grinberg and Rebeca Grinberg, *Psychoanalytic Perspectives on Migration and Exile*, Nancy Festinger, transl. (New Haven: Yale University Press, 1989), pp. 79–80, 94.

13. Arturo Uslar Pietri, *Los libros de Miranda* (Caracas: Fundación de Caracas, 1966), p. 21.

14. John Adams to James Lloyd (Quincy, March 6, 1815), in *Works of John Adams*, 10:135.

15. Smith to Miranda (London, July 4, 1785), in *AGM*, 5:280.

16. Ignacio de Heredia to Bernardo del Campo (París, 26 de julio de 1785), in *Archivo General de Simancas, Estado 8.175*.

17. *The Political Herald and Review; or a Survey of Domestic and Foreign Politics* [London] vol. 1, (August 22, 1785), quoted in *The Literary Diary of Ezra Stiles*, pp. 199–200.

18. *Morning Chronicle* (Saturday, August 20, 1785).

19. Smith, "Jornal," *AGM*, 1:354.

20. Ibid., p. 361.

21. Ibid., p. 363.

22. Ibid., pp. 393, 414.

23. Ibid., p. 384.

24. Ibid., p. 413.

25. Ignacio de Heredia to [unidentified], (París, 4 de noviembre de 1785), *Simancas, Estado 8.175*.

26. Azanza to Bernardo del Campo (Berlin, 13 de setiembre de 1875), *Simancas, Estado 8.175*.

27. Miranda to del Campo (Berlín, 1785), in *AGM*, 7:22–23.

28. Smith, "Jornal," *AGM*, 1:431.

29. Adams to Lloyd (Quincy, March 6, 1815), in *Works of John Adams*, 10:135–36. Receipt dated (Vienna, October 26, 1785), in *AGM*, 7:99.

30. Miranda, "Diario de Viena a Trieste, 1785," in *AGM*, 2:1–9.

31. Miranda, "Viajes por Italia," *AGM*, 2:10–11. See also Rafael Pineda, *Francisco de Miranda en Italia* (Los Teques [Venezuela]: Gobierno del Estado de Miranda, 1966).

32. Angel Grisanti, "Los jesuítas a quienes conoció el General Miranda (Esteban de Arteaga y Tomás Belón)," in *Cultura Universitaria* 50 (1955): 137–38.

33. Arteaga to Mateo Bosa (15 de mayo de 1790), quoted in Grisanti, "Arteaga y Belón," p. 139.

34. Miranda, "Viajes por Italia," *AGM*, 2:22.

35. César García Rosell, *Miranda y los ex-jesuítas desterrados* ([Caracas]: Instituto de Estudios Históricos Mirandinos, 1970), p. 20.

36. "Memoria de los padres y hermanos de la Compañía de Jesús de la Provincia de Nueva España," *British Museum, Additional MSS 36743*; Alfred J. Lemmon, "The Mexican Jesuit Exiles of 1767: A Profile of their Writings" (Ph.D. diss., New Orleans: Tulane University, 1981), pp. 94, 125; Ernest J. Burrus SJ, "Jesuit Exiles: Precursors of Mexican Independence?" *Mid-America* 36 (#3, July 1954): 171–72.

37. The original edition was published anonymously but the Chilean abbot Molina is usually credited as its author; Miguel Batllori claims that distinction for Diego León Villafañé in *El Abate Viscardo* (Caracas: Instituto Panamericano de Geografía e Historia, 1953), p. 104. Mill's commentary on the text's English version appeared in the *Edinburgh Review* (July 1809).

38. Grisanti, "Arteaga y Belón," p. 135. María Teresa Berruezo León claims that Miranda met Juan Ignacio Molina in 1785, in *La lucha de Hispanoamérica por su independencia en Inglaterra, 1800–1830* (Madrid: Ediciones de Cultura Hispánica, 1989), pp. 59–60.

39. *Catalogue of the Valuable and Extensive Library of the Late General Miranda* (London: William Nichol, 1828). See Antonio Cussen, *Bello and Bolívar* (Cambridge: Cambridge University Press, 1992); Frank Miller Turner, *The Greek Heritage in Victorian Britain* (New Haven: Yale University Press, 1981); Richard Jenkyns, *The Victorians and Ancient Greece* (Cambridge: Harvard University Press, 1980).

40. Miranda, "Viajes por Italia," p. 59; Thorning, *World Citizen*, pp. 43–44.

41. Miranda, "Viajes por Italia," *AGM*, 2:60.

42. Miguel Batllori, "El mito de la intervención de los jesuítas en la independencia hispanoamericana," *Razón y Fé* 145 (1952): 512; Grisanti, "Arteaga y Belón," p. 142.

43. Miranda, "Viajes por Grecia, Turquía y Rusia," *AGM*, 2:293. Clavijero, *The History of Mexico*, Charles Cullen, transl. (London: G. and G. Robinson, 1787). A later Spanish edition was translated from the Italian by José Joaquín de Mora, *Historia antigua de Mégico* (London: Ackermann, 1826).

44. Miranda, "Viajes por Grecia, Turquía y Rusia," *AGM*, 2:113.

45. Ibid., p. 118.

46. Ibid., p. 122.

47. Ibid., p. 126.

48. Ibid., p. 135.

49. Smith to Gandásegui (Leicester Square, Saturday morning [March–April 1786]), *Simancas, Estado 8.175*.

50. Del Campo to Conde de Aranda (Londres, 23 de julio de 1786), *Simancas, Estado 8.175*.

51. Miranda, "Viajes por Grecia, Turquía y Rusia," *AGM*, 2:138–41. Hero and Leander were lovers who resided on opposite sides of the Dardanelles. Each night, Hero would place a lamp that would guide Leander as he swam across the strait to visit her. During a storm, the lamp blew out and Leander drowned;

upon hearing the news, Hero killed herself. Lord Byron swam across the Dardanelles to prove it could be done, and wrote a famous poem called "The Bride of Abydos."

52. Ibid., 2:145.

53. Ibid., 2:179. The book was Ibrahim Efendi's *Traité de la Tactique, ou Méthode artificielle pour l'ordonnance des Troupes* [*Treatise on Tactics, or Artificial Method for the Organization and Deployment of Troops*] (Paris: 1749). Ibrahim Efendi (also known as Ibrahim Müteferriqa) was a printer who introduced the first movable type in Turkish and Arabic script into Turkey in 1728.

54. Miranda, "Viajes por Grecia, Turquía y Rusia," *AGM*, 2:180. Miranda's italics.

55. Isabel de Madariaga, *The Travels of Francisco de Miranda in Russia* (London: n.p., 1950), p. 23.

56. Miranda, "Viajes por Grecia, Turquía y Rusia," *AGM*, 2:197. See also M. S. Alperovich, *Fransisko de Miranda v Rossii* (Moscow: Nauka, 1986).

57. Miranda, "Viajes por Grecia, Turquía y Rusia," *AGM*, 2:208.

58. Ibid., pp. 203, 210.

59. Ibid., p. 280.

60. Roux to Miranda (Monday, December 3, [1786]), in *AGM*, 5:311.

61. Miranda, "Viajes por Grecia, Turquía y Rusia," *AGM*, 2:205, 216.

62. Ibid., 2:228.

63. *XVIIIth Century Diary*, p. 88.

64. Miranda, "Viajes por Grecia, Turquía y Rusia," *AGM*, 2:258.

65. Stephen Sayre to Samuel Ogden (London, June 29, 1789), in *Massachusetts Historical Society, Henry Knox Papers, reel 24, #70*. Sayre's emphasis.

66. Thomas Paine (New Rochelle, March 20, 1806), in *The Complete Writings of Thomas Paine*, pp. 1480–82.

67. Madariaga, *Travels*, p. 12; Thorning, *World Citizen*, p. 61; Angel Grisanti, *Miranda y la Emperatriz Catalina la Grande* (Caracas: Empresa Gutenberg, 1928), p. 6.

68. *XVIIIth Century Diary*, p. 98.

69. *Mémoires ou Souvenirs et Anecdotes par M. Le Comte de Ségur* (Paris: Henri Colburn, 1825), p. 425; Carlos Duarte, ed., *Misión secreta en Puerto Cabello y viaje á Caracas en 1783* (Caracas: Fundación Pampero, 1991), p. 301; Miranda, "Viajes por Grecia, Turquía y Rusia," *AGM*, 2:268.

70. *XVIIIth Century Diary*, p. 100.

71. Miranda, "Viajes por Grecia, Turquía y Rusia," *AGM*, 2:270.

72. Ségur, *Souvenirs et Anecdotes*, pp. 63–65.

73. *XVIIIth Century Diary*, p. 94.

74. Miranda, "Viajes por Grecia, Turquía y Rusia," *AGM*, 2:298.

75. Miranda to Emperatriz Catalina II (San Petersburgo, 15 de agosto de 1787), in *América espera*, p. 91.

76. Del Campo to Normande (Londres, 28 de marzo de 1786), in Joseph O. Baylen and Dorothy Woodward, "Francisco de Miranda and Russian Diplomacy, 1787–1788," *The Historian* 13 (1950): 52n. The document is at *Simancas, Estado 8.156.* See also Francesca Miller, "Tsarist Initiatives in the New World: Problems of Interpretation," *The New Scholar* 8 (1982): 488–501.

77. Miranda to Macañaz (Petersbourg, 14 de julio de 1787) in *AGM*, 7:24.

78. *XVIIIth Century Diary*, p. 110.

79. Ibid., p. 115 (July 29, 30, 31, August 2).

80. Miranda, "Viajes por Grecia, Turquía y Rusia," *AGM*, 2:232, 249.

81. *XVIIIth Century Diary*, p. 103.

82. Ibid., p. 125. See also Gunnar Sahlin, *Miranda i Sverige 1787—Miranda en Suecia 1787* (Stockholm: Latinoamerika Institutet, 1990).

83. *XVIIIth Century Diary*, p. 129.

84. Ibid., p. 130. Miranda's emphasis.

85. Thorning, *World Citizen*, p. 87.

86. Bernsdorff to Monsieur de St. Saphorin, quoted in *XVIIIth Century Diary*, p. 134.

87. *Miranda i Danmark: Fransisco de Miranda's danske rejsedagnog 1787–88* (Copenhagen: Rhodos, 1987).

88. *XVIIIth Century Diary*, p. 142.

89. Wim Klooster, "De Reis van Francisco Miranda door de Republiek in 1788," *De Achttiende Eeuw* 25 (#1, 1993): 73–88.

90. *XVIIIth Century Diary*, p. 163.

91. Ibid., p. 168.

92. Aranda to del Campo (París, 1 de enero de 1787), and (París, 9 de enero de 1787), *Simancas, Estado 8.175.*

93. Miranda to Her Imperial Majesty Catherine II, Empress and Sovereign of All the Russias (London, July 20, 1789), in *XVIIIth Century Diary*, pp. 195–96.

94. Guthrie to [his father] ([St. Petersburg, September 1787]), and Guthrie to Black (St. Petersburg, September 3, 1787), both in *AGM*, 5:326–28.

Chapter 4, Pages 105–140

1. Yosse Shain, *The Frontier of Loyalty: Political Exiles in the Age of the Nation-State* (Middletown CT: Wesleyan University Press, 1989), pp. 173–74.

2. Jack Hood to Lord Hawkesbury (212 Whitechapel Road, December 11, 1787), *British Museum Add. MSS 38222, ff.176-77.*

3. Miranda to Knox (London, February 2, 1791), in *Massachusetts Historical Society, Knox Papers, reel 27, # 134.*

4. Hester Lucy Stanhope, *Memoirs of the Lady Hester Stanhope*, original edition 1845, reprinted (Austria: Institut für Anglistik und Amerikanistik, 1985),

1:190. The never-married Pitt referred to Hollwood as "his favourite child." Stanhope, *Memoirs*, 2:68. Miranda's notes in *AGM*, 15:109–10.

5. See the "Propuesta de la conferencia tenida en Hollwood el 14 de febrero de 1790," in Miranda, *Diario de viajes y escritos políticos* (Madrid: Editora Nacional, 1977), pp. 336–41.

6. Miranda to Pitt ([47 Jermyn Street], March 9 and 27, 1790), *AGM*, 15:118–19.

7. Grinberg and Grinberg, *Psychoanalytic Perspectives on Migration and Exile*, p. 95

8. César García Rosell, *Miranda y los ex-jesuítas desterrados* ([Caracas]: Ediciones de Estudios Históricos Mirandinos, 1970), p. 31.

9. Miranda to Egerton (Tuesday, May 11, 1790), *British Library, Egerton MSS 3043, ff.70*. On August 12, Miranda agreed to meet with Egerton to give him valuable information for the latter's upcoming trip to Spain. *British Library, Egerton MSS 3043, ff.72*.

10. Miranda to Pitt (47 Jermyn Street, May 4, 1790), *AGM*, 15:120.

11. Miranda to Knox (London, March 13, 1790) and (March 29, 1790), in *Massachusetts Historical Society, Knox Papers, reel 25, #178*, and *MHS, Knox Papers, reel 26, #10* respectively.

12. Miranda to Hamilton (Londres, 5 avril 1791), in *The Papers of Alexander Hamilton*, 8:245.

13. Knox to Miranda (New York, September 5, 1790), *MHS, Knox Papers, reel 26, #177*.

14. Miranda to Charles IV, draft letter (23 de abril de 1790), quoted in Robertson, *The Life of Miranda*, 1:94.

15. Gouverneur Morris, *A Diary of the French Revolution* (Boston: Houghton Mifflin, 1939), 1:554, 557. Entries dated (Friday, July 2, 1790) and (Tuesday, July 6, 1790).

16. Miranda to Knox (Londres, 5 avril 1791), *MHS, Knox Papers, reel 28, #8*.

17. Thomas Paine (New Rochelle, March 20, 1806), in *The Complete Writings of Thomas Paine*, pp. 1480–82.

18. Miranda to Count Novoselov, Russian ambassador to London (late 1790), quoted in García, *Miranda y los ex-jesuítas desterrados*, p. 46.

19. Miranda to Pitt (47 Jermyn Street, June 17, 1791), *AGM*, 15:129.

20. Miranda to Pitt (47 Jermyn Street, June 23, 1791); Miranda to Joseph Smith [Pitt's secretary] (two dated July 6, 1791); Miranda to Smith (July 19, 1791); Miranda to Pitt (47 Jermyn Street, August 19 and 26, 1791), all in *AGM*, 15:130–32.

21. Miranda to Pitt (47 Jermyn Street, August 26, 1791), *AGM*, 15:132.

22. Miranda to Pitt (Londres, 17 de marzo de 1792), in *América espera*, pp. 114–15.

23. *XVIIIth Century Diary*, p. 166.

24. The best narrative account remains Caracciolo Parra-Pérez, *Miranda et la Révolution Française* (Paris: J. Dumoulin, 1925). See also Juan Uslar Pietri, *Miranda y la sonrisa de la guillotina* (Caracas: Editorial Ateneo de Caracas, 1979); Alphonse O'Kelly de Galway, *Francisco de Miranda, Général de Division des Armées de la République (1791–1794), Héro de l'Indépendance Américaine (1756–1816)* (Paris: Campion, 1913); C. F. Pardo de Leygonnier, *Quand Miranda Cherchait l'Independance en France* (Paris: Académie de Marine, 1963); *Francisco de Miranda y la Revolución Francesa: Exposición conmemorativa del bicentenario de la Revolución Francesa* (Caracas: Instituto Autónoma Biblioteca Nacional, 1989).

25. "Notas de Miranda (París, agosto de 1792)," *Francisco de Miranda en Francia*, André-Jean Libourel y Edgardo Mondolfi, eds. (Caracas: Embajada de Francia en Venezuela, Monte Ávila Editores, 1997), pp. 29–30. The dates for the meetings were August 11, 29, 22, 23, 24, and 25, 1792.

26. "Condiciones de Miranda para entrar al servicio de Francia" (París, 25 de agosto de 1792), in *Miranda en Francia*, p. 33.

27. "Brevet de Maréchal de Camp" (Paris, 1 septembre 1792), in *Miranda en Francia*, p. 42.

28. Paul Charles François Adrien Henri Dieudonné, Baron Thiébault, *The Memoirs of Baron Thiébault, late Lieutenant General in the French Army* (New York: The MacMillan Company, 1986), 1:135.

29. Brissot to Dumouriez (Paris, 28 novembre 1792), *AGM*, 15:140–50.

30. Vergniaud to Miranda (September 7, 1792), quoted in Claude Bowers, *Pierre Vergniaud: The Voice of the French Revolution* (New York: Macmillan, 1950), p. 267.

31. Miranda to Brissot (Liège, 19 décembre 1792), *AGM*, 15:160–62.

32. Miranda to Mr. H[enry] Knox (Paris, November 4, 1792), *MHS, Knox Papers, reel 32, #176*; Miranda to Hamilton, Secretary of the U.S. Treasury (Paris, November 4, 1792), in *The Papers of Alexander Hamilton*, 13:16; Miranda's copies are reprinted in *AGM*, 15:145–47.

33. *Lettre-circulaire du général Miranda à tous les commandants temporaires en Belgique, leur ordonnant de procurer au Citoyen Chépy, agent de la République française, sûreté et protection* (Brugge: Weduwe van J. Van Praet, [s.d]); *Lettre du général Miranda, au quartier général d'Anvers, le 4 décembre 1792, l'an premier de la République Française* [1793].

34. "Orden del General Miranda a los representantes de la ciudad de Amberes" (Cuartel General de Amberes, 31 de diciembre de 1792), in *Miranda en Francia*, p. 137.

35. Thiébault, *Memoirs*, 1:136.

36. "Le Général Miranda, Commandante en Chef des armées de la Belgique en absence du Général Dumouriez" (13 février 1793), in *AGM*, 8:179.

37. Thiébault, *Memoirs*, 1:156.

38. Charles-François Dumouriez, *Suite des Mémoires du Général Dumouriez*, M. F. Barrière, ed. (Paris: Firmin-Didot, 1886), 2:136–37.

39. Dumouriez to Pache (Tirlemont, March 19, 1793), translated and reprinted in the *Pennsylvania Gazette* (May 15, 1793).

40. Thiébault, *Memoirs*, 1:158.

41. P. F. J. N. Barras, *Memoirs of Barras: The Directorate up to the 18th Fructidor*, C. E. Roche, transl. (New York: Harper and Brothers, 1895), 2:39.

42. *Mémoires de Jean-Baptiste Louvet de Couvray, Député de la Convention National* (Paris: Badouin Frères, 1823), p. 64n.

43. Francisco de Miranda, *Á ses concitoyens. Discours que je me proposais de prononcer à la Convention Nationale, le 29 mars dernier, le lendemain de mon arrivée à Paris* (Paris: [1793]).

44. *Extrait du procès-verbal des délibérations du Comité de la Guerre, Séance du lundi 8 Avril, huit heures du soir. Interrogatoire du général Miranda* (Paris: Barrois l'Aîné, [1793]).

45. *Original Correspondence between Generals Dumourier* [sic], *Miranda, Pache, and Beurnonville . . . Including the Orders of General Dumourier* [sic] *to General Miranda, from the Invasion of Holland to the Overthrow of the French, after the Battle of Neerwinden* (London: J. Owen, 1794), preface.

46. *Pennsylvania Gazette* (May 15, 1793).

47. Miranda to Pétion (Louvain, March 21, 1793), *Original Correspondence*, pp. 121–24. Another eyewitness account is in *Le Général de Division Leveneur, á ses concitoyens. Notes relatives aux trahisons de Dumouriez, et à mon évasion de l'Armée* (Rouen: Dumesnil, 1793).

48. Bowers, *Vergniaud*, p. 479.

49. Helena Maria Williams, *An Eyewitness Account of the French Revolution by Helena Maria Williams: Letters Continuing a Sketch of the Politics of France*, ed. Jack Fruchtman (New York: Peter Lang reprints, 1997), p. 132.

50. Paine, quoted in David Freeman Hawke, *Paine* (New York: Harper & Row, 1974), p. 284.

51. Paine (New Rochelle, March 20, 1806), in *The Complete Writings of Thomas Paine*, pp. 1480–82.

52. Hawke, *Paine*, p. 285.

53. Paine to Citoyen-President de la Convention Nationale (Maison de l'Arrêt du Luxembourg, le 19 Thermidor, l'An 2 de la République Une et Indivisible), *France, Bibliothèque Nationale, FR 12760, f.227.*

54. Claude-François Chaveau-Lagarde, *Plaidoyer pour le général Miranda, accusé de haute trahison et de complicité avec le général en chef Dumouriez* (Paris: Barrois l'Aîné, [1793]). See also the official published version of the trial, "Interrogatoire du Général Miranda," *Bulletin du Tribunal Criminel Révolutionnaire* #30–37 [1793].

55. Chaveau-Lagarde, *Plaidoyer*, p. 4

56. Ibid., p. 27.

57. Ibid., p. 32. Chaveau-Lagarde's emphasis.

58. Ibid., p. 47.

59. Ibid., p. 49. Chaveau-Lagarde's emphasis.

60. Williams, *Eye-Witness Account*, p. 131.

61. Monseñor Corneille-François de Nelis, quoted in Thorning, *World Citizen*, p. 109.

62. Williams, *Eye-Witness Account*, p. 132.

63. Miranda, in *Le Patriote Française*, #1376 (20 mai 1793), quoted in Thorning, *World Citizen*, p. 117. Italics added.

64. Williams, *Eye-Witness Account*, p. 133.

65. Champagneux, quoted in Rafael María Baralt y Ramón Díaz, *Resumen de la historia de Venezuela desde el año de 1797 hasta el de 1830* (Paris: Desclée de Brouwer, 1939), 1:30–31.

66. Williams, *Eye-Witness Account*, p. 133.

67. Thorning, *World Citizen*, p. 119.

68. *América espera*, p. 572.

69. *Miranda aux réprésentants du peuple français* [1795]. He sent another version, *Miranda á la réprésentation nationale* (Paris: Barrois l'Aîné, l'An III [1795]) to the members of the National Convention; that version had a few minor textual changes and additions.

70. His letters to her have been lost, but hers have been published as *Delphine de Custine, belle amie de Miranda*, Caracciolo Parrá-Pérez, ed. (Paris: Editions Excelsior, 1927).

71. Miranda to Pétion (Valenciennes, 26 de octubre de 1792), in *América espera*, pp. 122–24.

72. *Opinion du général Miranda sur la situation actuelle de la France, et sur les remèdes convenables á ses maux* (Paris: Impr. de la Rue de Vaurigard, l'An III [1795]).

73. Paul Tabori, *Anatomy of Exile* (London: Harrap, 1972), p. 27.

74. *Opinion du général Miranda*, pp. 3–4.

75. Miranda to Knox (Paris, 22 Ventôse, l'année III de la République Française [March 22, 1795]), in *MHS, Knox Papers, reel 37, #52*.

76. *Opinion du général Miranda*, p. 11.

77. Laure Junot, la Duchess d'Abrantés, *Mémoires de la Duchesse d'Abrantés ou souvenirs historiques sur Napoléon, la Révolution, le Directoire, le Consulat, l'Empire et la Restauration*, 18 vols. (Paris: 1831), 1:329; *América espera*, p. 574.

78. The Directory's decree is dated (17th Brumaire, Year IV, [1796]), Barras, *Mémoires*, 2:14, 39–40; a full list of the arrestees, including authors, booksellers, and printers, is found in the *Pennsylvania Gazette* (November 8, 1797).

79. Hélène-Marie Williams, *Souvenirs de la Révolution Française* (Paris: Doncley-Dupré, 1827), pp. 97–99.

80. Antoine C. Quatremère de Quincy, *Lettres à Miranda sur le déplacement des monuments de l'art de l'Italie (1796)*, Édouard Pommier, ed. (Paris: Macula, 1989).

81. The figures remain shadowy. Godoy del Pozo y Sucre may have been an exiled Jesuit; see Miguel Batllori SJ, "Maquinaciones del Abate Godoy en Londres en favor de la independencia hispanoamericana," *Archivum Historicum Societatis Iesu* 21(1952): 84–107.

82. Pitt's copy, the signed original, is held at the *Public Record Office PRO (FO) Pitt Manuscripts 30/8/345*. A printed version, "Acta de París—22 de diciembre de 1797," appears in *América espera*, pp. 194–99.

83. "Acta de Paris," in *América espera*, pp. 194–99. There is one brief study of the Paris Convention: Angel Grisanti, *Miranda, Precursor del Congreso de Panamá y del pan-Americanismo. El convenio de París de 1797* (Caracas: J. E. Grisanti, 1954).

84. The later, more truly representative Venezuelan mission is discussed in chapter 6.

85. "Acta de Paris," in *América espera*, pp. 199.

86. Champagneux, quoted in Baralt and Díaz, *Resumen*, 1:30–31.

87. Adams to James Lloyd (Quincy, 6 March 1815), in *Works of John Adams*, 10:136. The text appears printed in ibid., 1:679–84.

88. Miranda to Hamilton (Londres, 17 août 1798), *The Papers of Alexander Hamilton*, 22:78–79, and (Londres, 4 octubre 1799), 23:496–97.

89. Duque de la Alcudia to Excelentísimo Señor Ministro de Estado (San Lorenzo, 25 de setiembre de 1793), in *Colección de documentos para la historia de Colombia* (Bogotá: Editorial Kelly, 1965), 105:28.

90. See Nariño's description of his travels and activities in Europe in response to Oidor Hernández de Alba's interrogation, in *Archivo Nariño* (Bogotá: Biblioteca de la Presidencia de la República, 1990), 1:133–42.

91. Álvarez to the colonial authorities (San Ildefonso, 21 de agosto de 1798), in *Archivo Nariño*, 1:233–34.

92. "Diario—Mr. Pitt vino a mi sin dilación" (enero de 1798), in *América espera*, p. 203.

93. Miranda to John T.[urnbull] Esq. (Dover, January 12, 1798), in *América espera*, pp. 201–2.

Chapter 5, Pages 141–172

1. Miranda to Pitt (London, January 16 ,1798), in *América espera*, pp. 202–3.
2. "Diario," in *América espera*, p. 205.
3. John Pownall to Miranda (Rodney Place, Clifton, Bristol, Sunday, February 11, 1798), in *AGM*, 15:215.
4. Miranda to William Pitt (1 Great Pulteney Street, May 21, 1798), *Cambridge University Library, Pitt MSS 6958/12/2349*. Miranda to President John Adams (London, March 24, 1798), in *América espera*, pp. 219–21.
5. Hamilton to Rufus King (New York, August 22, 1798), and Hamilton to Miranda (New York, August 22, 1798), both in *Life and Correspondence of Rufus King* (New York: Putnam's, 1895), 2:658–59.
6. King to Hamilton (London, July 31, 1798), in *The Papers of Alexander Hamilton*, 22:44.

7. King to Secretary of State Thomas Pickering (London, February 26, 1798), in *Life and Correspondence of Rufus King,* 2:283–84.

8. Juan Pablo Viscardo to John Udny (Massacarrera, September 23, 1781), in *Colección documental de la independencia del Perú,* César Pacheco Vélez, ed. (Lima: Comisión Nacional del Sesquicentenario de la Independencia del Perú, 1975), 1:123–27.

9. Miguel Batllori, *El Abate Viscardo* (Caracas: Instituto Panamericano de Geografía e Historia, 1953), p. 131n. Although searches in the Public Record Office at London have not unearthed the names of Viscardo or any Jesuits on the government lists, there are contemporary references: Pedro José Caro to Mariano Luis de Urquijo (Hamburgo, 31 de mayo de 1800) reported, "This Jesuit resided in London for several years, recruited and well-paid," in *Colección documental,* pp. 210–11.

10. Carlos Pereyra, quoted in Ernest J. Burrus, "Jesuit Exiles: Precursors of Mexican Independence?" *Mid-America* 36 (#3, July 1954): p. 168; William Spence Robertson, *The Rise of the Spanish American Republics (As Told in the Lives of Their Liberators)* (New York: The Free Press, 1946), p. 39; Jerónimo Alvarado S., *Diálectica democrática de Juan Pablo Viscardo y Guzmán* (Lima: Ediciones "Fanal," 1955), pp. 128–29.

11. "Letter to the Spanish Americans by D. Juan Pablo Viscardo y Guzmán, a Native of Arequipa, in Peru, and Ex-Jesuit." Appendix to Burke, *Additional Reasons for Our Immediately Emancipating Spanish America,* pp. 95–124.

12. Viscardo, "Letter," pp. 97–98.

13. Ibid., p. 99.

14. Ibid., p. 118.

15. Ibid., p. 106. At roughly the same time that Viscardo was working on this argument in London, iconoclastic Mexican priest Fray Servando Teresa de Mier Noriega y Guerra preached his Guadalupe sermon, in which he expressed the controversial opinion that the pre-Columbian evangelization of America abnegated Spain's religious justification for the conquest and colonization. As Viscardo also claimed, the Christianizing mission of the Spaniards in America was both unnecessary and illegal, and could not be used as a valid claim to rule the region.

16. Ibid., p. 109.

17. Ibid., p. 110. Viscardo also copied passages from Montesquieu, William Robertson, and Antonio de Ulloa in his preparatory notes. Contained in *New-York Historical Society, Rufus King Papers, Box 81, Vol. 58.*

18. Viscardo, "Letter," p. 105.

19. Ibid., pp. 123–24.

20. Angel Grisanti, "La personalidad de Juan Pablo Viscardo y Guzmán," *Revista de la Universidad de Arequipa,* 27 (abril–junio 1948): 143–44.

21. Caro to [Excmo Don José Mariano de Urquijo] (Hamburgo, 31 de mayo de 1800), in *Colección de documentos para la historia de Colombia* (Bogotá: Editorial Kelly, 1965), 105:25–32.

22. Miranda to Caro (Londres, 5 de julio de 1799) and (Londres, 2 de setiembre de 1799), in *AGM*, 15:414–17; "I send here a copy of the Carta of Viscardo in case the other 4 I sent you have not arrived."

23. Miranda to Alexander Hamilton (London, 14 November 1799), in *AGM*, 15:384–85.

24. *Carta a los Españoles Americanos* (Londres: P. Boyle, Vine Street Piccadilly, 1801).

25. Cevallos to Josef de Anduaga (Madrid, 14 de mayo de 1804), *Spain, Archivo General de Simancas, Estado 8.253; Nos, los Inquisidores Apostólicos contra la Herética Pravedad y Apostasía . . .* (México: 28 de setiembre de 1810).

26. María Teresa Berruezo León, *La lucha de Hispanoamérica por su independencia en Inglaterra* (Madrid: Ediciones de Cultura Hispánica, 1989), p. 38; Manuel Balborín Moreno and Gustavo Opazo Maturano, *Cinco mujeres en la vida de O'Higgins* (Santiago: Arancibia Hermanos, [1974]), pp. 102–5; Bernardo Riquelme [O'Higgins] to Nicolás de la Cruz (Londres, 1 de octubre de 1799), in *Archivo de Don Bernardo O'Higgins* (Santiago de Chile: Editorial Nascimento, 1946), 1:7–8.

27. Robertson, *The Life of Miranda*, 1:197n. Robertson is following Chilean historiography from Benjamín Vicuña Mackenna, *La corona del héroe: Recopilación de documentos para perpetuar la memoria del Jeneral Don Bernardo O'Higgins* (Santiago de Chile, 1872), pp. 283–89.

28. Riquelme to Ambrosio O'Higgins (Cádiz, 4 de marzo de 1801) in *Archivo O'Higgins*, 1:18.

29. Both versions are reprinted in *Archivo O'Higgins*, 1:19–25.

30. [James Biggs], *History of Don Francisco de Miranda's Attempt to Effect a Revolution in South America* (Boston: Oliver and Munroe, 1808), pp. 290–91.

31. Thomas Blossom, *Antonio Nariño: Hero of Colombian Independence* (Tucson: University of Arizona Press, 1967), p. 36. See also the collection of documents reprinted as "Miranda and the British Admiralty, 1804–1806," *American Historical Review* 6 (#3, April 1901): 508–30.

32. Philip Henry, fifth earl of Stanhope, *Notes of Conversations with the Duke of Wellington, 1831–1851* (London: Oxford University Press, 1938), pp. 68–69.

33. Robertson, *The Life of Miranda*, 1:257.

34. Captain Sir Home Riggs Popham to William Huskisson (HMS *Romney*, February 19, 1801), *British Library, Department of Manuscripts, Add. MSS 38,736, ff.283-84*.

35. Popham to Hardwicke [undated, early January 1804], *British Library, Add. MSS 45,041, ff.1-2*.

36. Popham to Melville (October 11, 1804), *British Library, Add. MSS 41,081 ff.70-73*.

37. Popham to Miranda [Wednesday evening, c. 20 Sept. 1804], *AGM*, 17:79.

38. Mario Rodríguez, *William Burke and Francisco de Miranda: The Word and the Deed in Spanish America's Emancipation* (Lanham, MD: University Press of

America, 1994), p. 39; Popham to Melville [Dundas] (HMS *Antelope*, November 24 and 26, 1804), *British Library, Add. MSS 41,081, ff.90-92*.
   39. Shain, *Frontier of Loyalty*, pp. 173–74.
   40. Miranda to Pitt (Grafton Street, October 22, 1804), *Cambridge University, Pitt MSS, Add. 6958/16/3200*.
   41. Miranda to Popham (Grafton Street, November 12, 1804), *British Library, Add. MSS 41,081, ff. 80-81*.
   42. Miranda to Pitt (Grafton Street, June 13, 1805), *British Library, Add. MSS 31,230, ff.43-46*. Another copy exists in *Cambridge University, Pitt MSS Add 6958/2524*.
   43. See the extensive folder of Caro's reports dated 1799–1803, in *Archivo General de Indias, Estado 61, N.24*. Several have been reprinted in *Colección de documentos para la historia de Colombia* (Bogotá: Editorial Kelly, 1965), vol. 105.
   44. O'Higgins recalled that Miranda referred to him as "my son," in *Epistolario*, 1:29n–30n.
   45. Miranda and his wife, Sarah Andrews, were the third occupants of the house, which was built in 1792. In 1978, the Venezuelan government bought the house and converted it into the seat of their cultural mission. For the physical structure's history, see Guido Acuña, *La Casa de Miranda en Londres* (México DF: Imprenta Madero SA, 1979); José Salcedo-Bastardo, *Crucible of Americanism: Miranda's London House* ([Caracas]: Cuadernos Langoven, 1981); and Miriam Hood, *Cómo adquirió la casa de Miranda en Londres* (Caracas: Instituto de Investigaciones Históricas, Universidad Católica Andrés Bello, 1993).
   46. Miriam Blanco Fombona de Hood, *El Enigma de Sarah Andrews, Esposa de Francisco de Miranda* (Caracas: Instituto de Investigaciones de la Universidad Católica Andrés Bello, 1981); Carlos Pi Sunyer, *Los patriotas americanos en Londres* (Caracas: Monte Avila Editores, 1978), pp. 69, 81.
   47. Francisco Belda, *La lengua de Francisco de Miranda en su diario* (Caracas: Academia Nacional de Historia, 1985), p. 13.
   48. Miranda to Evan Nepean (Grafton Street, July 9, 1805), *Cambridge University, Pitt MSS Add. 6958/17/3538*.
   49. Shain, *Frontier*, pp. 124.
   50. William Jacob to Z. Blacke Esq. (Canonbury, November 26, 1804), in *Cambridge University, Pitt MSS Add. 6958/16/3236*.
   51. Nepean to Pitt (Admiralty, July 16, 1805), and Miranda to Pitt (Grafton Street, 18 juillet 1805), both in *Cambridge University, Pitt MSS Add. 6958/3542*.
   52. [Tomás Molini], "Journal and Remarks on Board the Ship *Polly*, Captain William Coit, from London to New York," *National Maritime Museum (Greenwich), JOD/141*. Although the diarist is unidentified, these notebooks appear to be the daily records of Miranda's faithful secretary.
   53. Richard Rush, "Notes of a Conversation with General Miranda," (Philadelphia, December 4, 1805), *Library of Congress, Department of Manuscripts, Rush Family Papers*.

54. Aaron Burr to Jeremy Bentham (London, October 16, 1811), in *The Private Journal of Aaron Burr*, Matthew Davis, ed. (New York: Harper & Brothers, 1838), 7:254–55. A copy exists at *Library of Congress, Burr Manuscripts, Reel 6, #911.*

55. Casa Yrujo to Cevallos (Filadelfia, 5 de agosto de 1805), *Spain, Archivo Histórico Nacional, Estado 5631, 4. ff.22-23.*

56. Miranda to Smith (Washington, 14 de diciembre de 1805), in *Testigos norteamericanos de la expedición de Miranda*, Edgardo Mondolfi, ed. (Caracas: Monte Ávila Editores, 1992), p. 163.

57. Miranda, "Diario" (martes, 11 de diciembre de 1805), and (jueves, 13 de diciembre de 1805), in *Testigos*, p. 168.

58. Madison to James Monroe (Washington, March 10, 1806), in *Letters and Other Writings of James Madison* (New York: R. Worthington, 1884), 2:220.

59. Jefferson to [Spanish Ambassador] Valentín Foronda (Monticello, October 4, 1809), in *The Writings of Thomas Jefferson* (Washington, DC: The Thomas Jefferson Memorial Association, 1904), 12:319.

60. Casa Yrujo to Cevallos (Philadelphia, 12 de febrero de 1806), *Spain, Archivo Histórico Nacional, Estado 5632, 1. f.15.*

61. Miranda to Jefferson (Nueva York, 22 de enero de 1806), in *Testigos*, p. 181.

62. Miguel A. Villaroel, *El "Leander," un barco con destino de gloria* (Caracas: Instituto de Estudios Históricos Mirandinos, 1969).

63. Adams to James Lloyd (Quincy, April 5, 1815), in *Works of John Adams*, 10:157.

64. John Edsall, *Incidents in the Life of John Edsall* (Catskill, NY, 1831; printed for the author), pp. 9–10; Ingersoll to Barnabas Bidwell (Vaults of St. Clara, Carthagena, October 1, 1808), in "Diary and Letters of Henry Ingersoll, Prisoner at Carthagena 1806–1809," *American Historical Review* 3 (#4, July 1898): pp. 690–91. Ingersoll's original manuscripts are held at the Boston Athenaeum Library.

65. *History of the Adventures and Suffering of Moses Smith, during Five Years of his Life, from the Beginning of the Year 1806 when he was betrayed into the Miranda Expedition, until June 1811 when he was non-suited into an Action at Law, which lasted three years and a half* (Brooklyn, NY: Thomas Kirk, 1812; reprinted for the author), pp. 14–15, 17.

66. Sherman, *A General Account of Miranda's Expedition*, p. 18.

67. [Biggs], *History of Don Francisco de Miranda's Attempt*, pp. 3–4.

68. *Richmond Enquirer* (April 6, 1806).

69. François Dalencour, *Francisco de Miranda et Alexandre Pétion: L'expédition de Miranda, le premier effort de libération hispano-américaine* (Port-au-Prince, 1955).

70. [Tomás Molini] "Journal and Remarks on Board the Ship *Leander*, Captain Thomas Lewis," *National Maritime Museum, JOD/141.*

71. Translated and reprinted in [Sherman], *A General Account of Miranda's Expedition*, pp. 35n–39n. See also Henry Ingersoll to Jonathan Ingersoll (Jacquemel, March 22, 1806), in "Diary and Letters," p. 680.

72. "Form of the Oath" (On board the *Leander*, Jacquemel Harbor, March 24, 1806), in *AGM*, 18:207–8. Biggs reprints an expanded version of the text in *History of Don Francisco de Miranda's Attempt*, pp. 42–43.

73. *History . . . of Moses Smith*, p. 22.

74. José María Peláez to el Gobernador de la Provincia de Cumaná (Carúpano, 8 de abril de 1806), *Venezuela, Archivo General de la Nación, Gobierno y Capitanía General, vol. 165, f.118.*

75. [Biggs], *History of Don Francisco de Miranda's Attempt*, pp. 76, 79–80. Ingersoll gives the date as April 28, "Diary and Letters," p. 681.

76. [Biggs], *History of Don Francisco de Miranda's Attempt*, p. 84; [Molini] "Journal and Remarks on Board the Ship *Leander*," *Great Britain, National Maritime Museum, JOD/141.*

77. José Vázquez y Téllez to Commandante de Nueva Barcelona (Caracas, 25 de junio de 1806) *AGN—Ven, Gob. y Cap.Gen, vol. 167, f.169.*

78. Blossom, *Nariño*, p. xxv.

79. [Biggs], *History of Don Francisco de Miranda's Attempt*, pp. 137–38.

80. Ibid., pp. 157, 190.

81. Miranda to Turnbull (Nueva York, 4 de enero de 1806), in *Testigos*, p. 177.

82. Sarah [Andrews] Martin to Miranda (London, February 9, 1807), in *AGM*, 19:76–78.

83. [Sarah Andrews] to Miranda (London, June 20, 1807), in *AGM*, 19:130–34.

84. Sarah Andrews to Miranda (London, July 4, 1807), in *AGM*, 19:134–38.

85. See, as examples: Miranda to Nicholas Vansittart (Aruba, September 19, 1806), in *AGM*, 18:171–72; Miranda to John Turnbull (Trinidad, June 10, 1807), and Miranda to Vansittart (Trinidad, June 10, 1807), both in *AGM*, 19:50–51, 53.

86. See the transcript of Popham's trial for treason in *Huntington Library, STG Box 150 (58)* and *Minutes of a Court Martial for the Trial of Sir Home Popham* (London: 1807). Naval Records Society, John D. Grainger, ed., *The Royal Navy in the River Plate, 1806–1807: Documents* (Aldershot, UK: Scholar Press, 1996).

87. Extract from the *Morning Post* (June 6, 1806), in *National Archives of Scotland, Cochrane Papers, GD51/1/566/1.*

88. *Times* (London) (June 1806) and (July 1, 1806).

89. "Rolla," in the *Barbados Mercury* (September 6, 1806).

90. Joaquín de Mosquera y Figueroa to Señor Presidente Gobernador y Capitán General (Caracas, 8 de mayo de 1806), *AGN—Ven, Gob y Cap.-Gen, Vol. 166, f.158.*

91. "Mechanics of New York, read the heart-rending Truth!" Broadside [New York: 1806].

92. *History . . . of Moses Smith*, p. 99; Edsall, *Incidents*, p. 25.

93. "The Miranda Expedition," *The Aurora General Advertiser* (October 15, 1807); U.S. Congress, *Report of the Committee to whom was referred the Petition of Sundry Citizens of the United States confined at Carthagena in South America*, 11th Cong. (Washington: A. & G. Way, 1809).

94. Ingersoll to Jonathan and Eunice Ingersoll (July 4, 1808), in "Diary and Letters," p. 689.

95. King to Gore (New York, March 9, 1806), in *Life and Correspondence of Rufus King*, 4:529–30.

96. W. S. Smith to Marqués de Cara Yrujo (New York, June 30, 1806), printed in the *Times* (London) (August 28, 1806).

97. "Acusación contra William S. Smith," *Testigos*, pp. 193–98.

98. *United States v Smith*; *United States v Ogden*, 27 F.Cas. 1189 CC.D.NY (No.16,341a), p. 1191. Washington Morton and Richard Harrison subsequently joined the defense team for the actual trial.

99. *United States v Smith*, 27 F.Cas. 1233 CC.D.NY (No. 16,342a), p. 1244.

100. *United States v Smith*; *United States v Ogden*, 27 F.Cas. 1246 CC.D.NY (No.16,342b), p. 1246.

101. Magdalena to Pedro de Cevallos (Philadelphia, 7 de abril de 1806), *AHN, Estado, Leg. 5632, 8. f.17.*

102. [Regent of the Audiencia Real de Caracas] to El Señor Gobernador y Capitán-General (Caracas, 2 de septiembre de 1806), in *AGN—Ven, Gob. Y Cap.-Gen., vol. 169, f.139*; [unidentified] to Gobernadores de las Provincias de Cumaná, Guayaná, Barinas y Maracaibo, (Caracas, 14 de julio de 1806), *AGN—Ven, Gob. y Cap.-Gen., vol. 168, f.11.*

103. Silvestre Collar, por El Rey Carlos IV to Audiencia of Caracas (El Pardo, 17 de febrero de 1807), *AGN—Ven, Reales Cédulas, vol. 9, ff.34-36.*

104. "Expediente: La sentencia dictada por la Real Audiencia contra las personas que auxiliaron al traidor Miranda en Coro y La Vela" (Coro, 5 de agosto de 1808), *AGN—Ven , Gob. y Cap.-Gen., vol. 198, ff.279-88.*

105. J. Hislop to Castlereagh (Trinidad, October 20, 1807), in *AGM*, 20:344; [Molini], "Journal and Remarks on Board the Ship *Leander*," *National Maritime Museum, JOD/141.*

106. Robertson, *The Life of Miranda*, 2:4; His passport was dated (Portsmouth, December 31, 1807), and signed W[illia]m Goldson, in *AGM*, 20:362. The anonymous diarist claimed that they landed at Falmouth; [Molini], "Journal and Remarks on Board the Ship *Leander*," *National Maritime Museum, JOD/141.*

Chapter 6, Pages 173–208

1. Miranda to Castlereagh (27 Grafton Street, January 3, 1808), *Public Record Office of Northern Ireland, Castlereagh Papers, D3030/2587.*

2. Hislop to Castlereagh (Trinidad, October 20, 1807), *PRONI, Castlereagh Papers, D3030/2589,* and Cochrane Johnstone to Castlereagh (Tortola, November 15, 1807), *PRONI, Castlereagh Papers, D3030/2588.*

3. Alexander Davison to Right Honorable Viscount Melville, (St. James's Square, February 5, 1808), *National Archives of Scotland, Cochrane Papers, GD51/1/135/1;* Canning to Castlereagh (January 4, 1808), *PRONI, Castlereagh Papers, D3030/2590/1.*

4. Miranda to Castlereagh (London, January 10, 1808), *PRONI, Castlereagh Papers, D3030/2594/1-9.* "Memoria Militar para Castlereagh," in *América espera,* pp. 371–76.

5. Robertson, *The Rise of the Spanish American Republics,* p. 60.

6. Vansittart to Miranda (Eden Farm, January 1808), in *AGM,* 20:395–97. Humboldt traveled throughout America between 1799 and 1804 and published thirty volumes of memoirs on the experience, the last of which appeared in 1834.

7. Pelletier to Miranda (7 Duke Street, Portland Place, 19 janvier 1808), in *AGM,* 21:39.

8. Miranda to Rodríguez Peña (Londres, 18 de abril de 1808), *Archivo General de Indias (Sevilla), Estado 81, n.70.* See Roberto Etcheparaborda, *La correspondencia del precursor Miranda con Saturnino Rodríguez Peña, sus conexiones con el grupo patriótico de Belgrano, Castelli, Vieytes, Beruti y Nicolás Rodríguez Peña* (Buenos Aires, 1960).

9. Smith to Castlereagh (October 30, 1808), *Great Britain, Public Record Office, War Office, 1/163.*

10. Philip Henry, fifth earl of Stanhope, *Notes of Conversations with the Duke of Wellington, 1831–1851* (London: Oxford, 1938), pp. 68–69. The Battle of Vimeiro took place on August 21, 1808, when French forces under Junot moved northward from Lisbon and attacked the forces under Wellesley and Sir John Moore, inflicting serious damage on the British position.

11. *The Creevey Papers: A Selection from the Correspondence and Diaries of the Late Thomas Creevey M.P.,* Rt. Hon. Sir Herbert Maxwell, ed. (London: John Murray, 1904), 1:86–87.

12. Undated memorandum, *PRONI, Castlereagh Papers, D3030/2704.* The note indicates that Miranda had previously received £500 per year from the "Emigrant Fund" and a further £200 from private sources, and requested that these sums be renewed since he had reestablished residency in England. He also asked that some provision be made for his secretary, Thomas Molini.

13. John Bergamini, *The Spanish Bourbons: The History of a Tenacious Dynasty* (New York: G. P. Putnam's Sons, 1974), p. 160.

14. Miranda to [Castlereagh] (Grafton Street, May 16, 1808), *PRONI, Castlereagh Papers, D3030/2653/142-144.*

15. [James Mill], review of "Lettre aux Espagnols-Americains, par un de leurs Compatriotes," *Edinburgh Review* 13 (January 1809), p. 311.

16. Kibblethwaite to Miranda (Gray's Inn Place, January 16. 1808), in *AGM*, 21:35–36.

17. McCulloch to John Downie (1 Robert Street, February 10, 1808), in *AGM*, 21:56–57.

18. Miranda to Castlereagh (January 10, 1808), *PRONI, Castlereagh Papers, D3030/2594/1-9.*

19. "A Concise Account of the Present State of the Spanish American Colonies," [1808] in *University of London, Senate House Library, MSS 149*, pp. 1–2.

20. [James Mill], "Lettre," *Edinburgh Review* (January 1809): 230.

21. Ibid., pp. 231, 299–300, 308. In a footnote Mill wrote, "[I]t is worth mentioning, that Inca, as a name dear to South America, is what General Miranda has proposed."

22. The term is coined by Rodríguez, who gives the dates for the "paper assault" as July 20–October 6, 1808; *William Burke and Francisco de Miranda*, p. 18

23. Rodríguez has argued in *William Burke and Francisco de Miranda* that William Burke was in fact a pseudonym used by James Mill. As proof, Rodríguez notes that the language and concepts employed in Burke's books are similar to those espoused by Mill, in particular "the hand of Providence in the natural economic order of the world," p. 64. Rodríguez argues that after 1810 the pseudonym passed to Juan Germán Roscio in Venezuela, who hijacked Burke's name and reputation for columns in *La Gaceta de Caracas*. I remain unconvinced of both attributions; providential appeals were common vehicles of the day and letters from Mill himself to Miranda describe Burke's departure for South America.

24. [J. M. Antepara], *South American Emancipation. Documents Historical and Explanatory, shewing the Designs which have been in Progress and the Exertions made by General Miranda for the South American Emancipation during the last Twenty-Five Years, by J.M. Antepara, a Native of Guayaquil* (London: R. Juigné, 1810).

25. Burke, *Additional Reasons for Our Immediately Emancipating Spanish America*, p. xiv.

26. Ibid., p. xvi.

27. Ibid., p. xxviii.

28. Ibid., pp. 76–77.

29. For an excellent discussion of this symbiotic relationship, see Antonello Gerbi, *The Dispute of the New World: The History of a Polemic, 1750-1900* (Pittsburgh: University of Pittsburgh Press, 1973).

30. Burke, *Additional Reasons for Our Immediately Emancipating Spanish America*, p. 16.

31. Miranda to Castlereagh (Grafton Street, August 19, 1808), *PRONI, Castlereagh Papers, D3030/2703-2706*; Lino Duarte de Level, *Cuadro de la Historia Militar y Civil de Venezuela* (Madrid: Editorial América, 1917), p. 241; Miranda to Capitán General de la Habana y el Virrey de México (27 Grafton Street, Fitzroy Square, Londres, 10 de septiembre de 1808), in *América espera*, pp. 381–82.

32. Rodríguez, *William Burke and Francisco Miranda*, p. 191.

33. Pedro Carbonell (10 de junio de 1797), *Archivo Gual y España* (Caracas: Academia Nacional de la Historia, 1963), 1:70. Quoted in Pedro Grases, *"El Colombiano" de Francisco de Miranda y dos documentos americanistas* (Caracas: 1966), p. 17.

34. Guadalupe Jiménez Codinach, *La Gran Bretaña y la independencia de México 1808–1821* (México: Fondo de Cultura Económica, 1991), p. 26.

35. Canning to Apodaca (May 27, 1809) and Canning to Apodaca (June 3, 1809), *AGI, Estado, 63, N. 31, (2a) and (2b)*.

36. Bentham to Mr. [J.] Mulford (November 1, 1810), in *Memoirs of Jeremy Bentham, Including Autobiographical Conversations and Portions of His Correspondence*, John Bowring, ed. (Edinburgh, 1843) 10:457–58.

37. Bentham to Henry Vassall Fox, Lord Holland (Queen Square Place, October 31, 1808), in Bentham, *Memoirs*, 10:439–44.

38. Bentham to J. Mulford (Queen Square Place, November 8, 1808), in Bentham, *Memoirs*, 10:444–46. "The city of Mexico, in Spanish America, all accounts private, as well as public, concur in representing as being, in this respect, the sort of earthy paradise that I stand in need of."

39. *University College London, Bentham MSS Box 60, ff. 6-11* contains Bentham's 1808 memoranda and notes on Mexico and Veracruz redacted from the *Guía de Comerciantes* and the *Times* (London).

40. Lord Holland to Bentham (Seville, February 18, 1809), in Bentham, *Memoirs*, 10:447–48.

41. Bentham to J. Mulford (Queen Square Place, April 24, 1810), Bentham, *Memoirs,* 10:454-55.

42. See Virginia Childs, *Lady Hester Stanhope: Queen of the Desert* (London: Weidenfeld and Nicolson, 1990), and Alberto Miramón, *La llama que no muere* (Caracas: Instituto Panamericano de Geografía e Historia, 1983).

43. Thorning claims that the two met in October; *World Citizen*, p. 202. Miramón cites Miranda's diary entries and gives the date as April 1809; *La llama*, pp. 20–21.

44. Childs, *Lady Hester Stanhope*, p. 15. She herself frequently referred to a "general want of sympathy toward her own sex," whom she generally viewed as silly, vain, or stupid, and very often all three; Stanhope, *Memoirs*, 1:84.

45. Miramón, *La llama*, pp. 39, 45.

46. J. A. Cova, "Intimidades de don Francisco de Miranda," *Boletín de la Academia Nacional de Historia* 33 (#130, abril–junio de 1950): 177. Robertson, *The Rise of the Spanish American Republics*, p. 79, followed historian Ricardo Becerra and agreed that Miranda's children were born of Sarah Andrews. Carlos Villanueva interpreted an 1850 letter by Leandro Miranda alluding to an inheritance from Lady Hester as proof that she was his mother; in fact, Lady Hester died penniless in Lebanon and had no fortune to leave anyone, son or not; Stanhope, *Memoirs*, 3:338–40.

47. J. R. Dinwiddy, "Bentham's Transition to Political Radicalism, 1809–1810," *Journal of the History of Ideas*, 36 (#4, October–December 1975): 686.

48. Miranda, "Diary" (Wednesday, August 9, 1809) and (Friday, August 11, 1809), in *AGM*, 23:22–24.

49. [Anonymous high-level official] to Virrey de Buenos Ayres (Sevilla, 8 de noviembre de 1809), *AGI, Estado, 71, N.9, (6)*.

50. Apodaca, undated memorandum [late 1809], *AGI, Estado, 71, N. 9.*

51. Saavedra's note (Londres, 15 de febrero de 1810), *Archivo General de Simancas, Estado 8.173.*

52. David Stevenson, *The Origins of Freemasonry: Scotland's Century, 1500–1710* (Cambridge: Cambridge University Press, 1988), p. 124.

53. See the excellent discussion in Mary Ann Clawson, *Constructing Brotherhood: Class, Gender, and Fraternalism* (Princeton, NJ: Princeton University Press, 1989).

54. Mitre, *Historia de San Martín* (Buenos Aires: Editorial 'Suelo Argentino,' 1950), p. 17.

55. María Teresa Berruezo León, "La propaganda independentista de la logia mirandina en Londres," in *Masonería española y americana* (Zaragoza: Centro de Estudios Históricos de la Masonería Española, 1993), 1:112–13; Enrique de Gandía, *La independencia de América y las sociedades secretas* (Santa Fe: Ediciones Sudamérica Santa Fe, 1994).

56. Cortés Campomanes to Miranda (7 de agosto de 1809), in *AGM*, 22:395–96.

57. Cortés Campomanes to Miranda (23 de agosto de 1809), in *AGM*, 23:49–50.

58. Cortés Campomanes to Miranda (30 de diciembre de 1809), in *AGM*, 23:137–38.

59. Miranda to Stanhope (Grafton Street, January 21, 1810), reprinted in Miramón, *La llama*, pp. 45-46.

60. Vansittart to Miranda (Torquay, April 20, 1810), in *AGM*, 23:405–6.

61. *El Colombiano*, #1 (15 de marzo de 1810), p. 1.

62. *El Colombiano*, #4 (1 de mayo de 1810), pp. 57–58.

63. [Unidentified] to Marqués de las Hormazas (28 de marzo de 1810), and Manuel Abella to Juan Ruiz de Apodaca (Londres, 27 de marzo de 1810), both in *Simancas, Estado 8.173.*

64. Eusebio Bardaxi y Azara (Cádiz, 19 de agosto de 1810), *Archivo General de la Nación—México, Reales Cédulas Originales, vol. 23, exp. 95*; González to [Bardaxi] (Guatemala, 24 de noviembre de 1810), *AGI, Estante 100, cajón 3, legajo 15 (2)*; Venegas to Bardaxi (México, 27 de noviembre de 1810), *AGI, Estante 89, cajón 1, legajo 19 (68)*; Abascal to Governador Intendente de Huancavelica (Lima, 17 de enero de 1811), *Indiana University, Lilly Library, Latin American Manuscripts, Peru, box 8.*

65. Salvador Méndez Reyes, "La misteriosa estancia de los Fagoaga en Londres," *Relaciones* 63/64 (verano-ontoño 1995), 128.

66. Allen to Blanco White (Holland House, June 23, 1810), *University of Liverpool, Sydney Jones Library, Blanco White Manuscripts II 3/231 (3).*

67. Albuquerque, "Notas de una conferencia" (4 de julio de 1810), *Simancas, Estado, 8.173.*

68. Wellesley to Apodaca and Albuquerque (Foreign Office, 14 de julio de 1810); translated; *AGI, Estado 63, N.31.*

69. "Minutas de las Conferencias celebradas en Londres en julio de 1810 entre el Marqués de Wellesley y los Comisionados de la Junta de Caracas Coronel Simón Bolívar, don Luis López Méndez y don Andrés Bello, Secretario este último de la Misión," in *Revista de la Sociedad Bolivariana de Venezuela* 27 (#93, 1967): 682–93. These are transcripts of Bello's notes; the originals are held in the Colección Guillermo Hernández de Alba, Bogotá.

70. [Apodaca] to [Bardaxi] (Londres, 17 de julio de 1810), *Simancas, Estado 8.173.*

71. *The Diaries of Sylvester Douglas, Lord Glenbervie*, Francis Bickley, ed. (London: Constable and Co., 1928), 2:129.

72. Wilberforce to Miranda (Kensington Gore, July 28, 1810) and (Friday, August 17, 1810), in *AGM*, 23:484, 530.

73. *Times* (London) (July 26, 1810) and (July 27, 1810).

74. Copy of the note passed by Yrigoyen to the Minister of Foreign Relations [i.e., Foreign Secretary Wellesley] (Londres, 12 de agosto de 1810), in *Archivo General de la Nación, Argentina, Sala X, 1-1-2, ff.3-5.*

75. Joseph Lancaster, *Epitome of Some of the Chief Events and Transactions in the Life of Joseph Lancaster* (New Haven: Baldwin and Peck, 1833), p. 35.

76. Richard Wellesley, "Memorandum of the 9 August 1810 Meeting between Wellesley and the Commissioners" (London, August 10, 1810), in *Las primeras misiones diplomáticas de Venezuela: Documentos*, Cristobal de Mendoza, ed. (Caracas: Academia Nacional de la Historia, Sesquicentenario de Independencia, 1962), pp. 282–87.

77. Cortés Campomanes to Miranda (4 de julio de 1810), in *AGM*, 23:449.

78. Miranda to Junta Suprema de Gobierno de la Provincia de Venezuela Conservadora de los derechos de Fernando VII (Londres, 3 de agosto de 1810), reprinted in *Gazeta de Caracas*, Tomo 1, #7 (martes, 20 de noviembre de 1810).

79. Vansittart to Miranda (Blackheath, August 30, 1810), in *AGM*, 23:531–32.

80. *Times* (London) (August 12, 1810).

81. Apodaca to Richard Wellesley (4 Duke Street, St. James, November 9, 1810), *AGI, Estado 87, N.9 (1)*; Henry Wellesley to His Excellency Eusebio Bardaxi y Azara (Isla de León, November 11, 1810), *AGI, Estado, 87, N.1, ff. 71-73.*

82. [Apodaca] to Bardaxi (Londres, 26 de noviembre de 1810), *Simancas, Estado 8.173.*

83. Rafael María Baralt y Ramón Díaz, *Resumen de la historia de Venezuela desde el año de 1797 hasta él de 1830* (Paris: Desclée de Brouwer, 1939), 1:63.

84. Edmund Burke championed this line in political theory, William Paley in religion. Martin Murphy, *Blanco White: Self-Banished Spaniard* (New Haven: Yale University Press, 1989), p. 78.

Chapter 7, Pages 211–241

1. General accounts of the Venezuelan First Republic can be found in: Pedro Grases, *El regreso de Miranda a Caracas en 1810* (Caracas: [s.p], 1957); *Pensamiento político de la emancipación venezolana*, Pedro Grases, ed. (Caracas: Biblioteca Ayacucho, 1988); and Caracciolo Parra-Pérez, *Historia de la primera república de Venezuela* (Caracas: Biblioteca Ayacucho, 1992).

2. Simon Bolívar, *Memoirs of Simón Bolívar, President Liberator of the Republic of Colombia*, H. L. V. Ducoudray-Holstein, ed. (London: Henry Colburn and Richard Bentley, 1830), 1:115.

3. Robert Semple, *A Sketch of the Present State of Caracas* (London: Robert Baldwin, 1812), pp. 48–49.

4. Mario Rodríguez, "The First Venezuelan Republic and the North American Model," *Revista Interamericana de Bibliografía* 37 (#1, January 1987): 5.

5. Semple, *Sketch*, p. 57.

6. Thorning, *World Citizen*, pp. 211–13.

7. "Proclama de la Junta Suprema de Caracas a los Pueblos de América" (Caracas, 27 de abril de 1810), in *Documentos importantes de Nueva Granada, Venezuela y Colombia* (Bogotá: Imprenta Nacional, 1970), 1:271–22.

8. Semple, *Sketch*, p. 123.

9. *Morning Chronicle* (Monday, February 18, 1811).

10. Roscio to Miranda (Caracas, 12 dec 1810) *AGM* XXIV, pp. 369–70.

11. Bentham, "Constitutional Legislation. On the Evils of Change. Intended for Caraccas on the Occasion of General Miranda's Expedition," *University College, London, Bentham Manuscripts, Box 22, ff.57-76*; and "Proposed Law for Securing the Liberty of the Press Against Persons Having the Exclusive Command of the Printing Presses of a New Country When Small in Number," *UCL, Bentham MSS, Box 21, ff.7-56*. Both dated August–September 1810. Bentham offered the latter proposal to Greece in 1824.

12. "Aviso," *Gaceta de Caracas* #9 (jueves, 4 de diciembre de 1810). See Julio Febres Cordero, *Historia de la imprenta y del periodismo en Venezuela, 1800–1830* (Caracas: Banco Central de Venezuela, 1974).

13. Jeremy Bentham, "Legislación-Libertad de la Imprenta," *La Gaceta de Caracas* (30 de abril de 1811). A general discussion of Bentham's interest in the region can be found in Miriam Williford, *Jeremy Bentham on Spanish America: An*

Account of His Letters and Proposals to the New World (Baton Rouge: Louisiana State University Press, 1980).

14. [Manuel Palacio Fajardo], *Outline of the Revolution in Spanish America* (New York: James Eastburn and Co., 1817), p. 73. Francisco Espejo seconded Miranda's proposal for the club.

15. Semple, *Sketch*, pp. 127–28.

16. Miranda to Wilberforce, (Caracas, January 11, 1811), *Oxford University, Bodleian Library, Wilberforce Manuscripts, d.14, ff.34-35.*

17. Miranda to Junta Suprema del Nuevo Reino de Granada (Caracas, 22 de enero de 1811), in *América espera*, pp. 447–48.

18. Vansittart to Miranda (March 7, 1811), *British Library, Additional MSS 31,230, ff.206-9.*

19. Vansittart to Miranda (March 19, 1811), *British Library, Add MSS 31,230, ff.212-15.*

20. Vansittart to Miranda (July 3, [1811]), *British Library Add MSS, 31,232, f.73*; Vansittart to Miranda (Blackheath, August 11, 1811), *British Library, Add MSS 31,230, ff. 216-19.*

21. Lino Duarte de Level, *Cuadros de la historia militar y civil de Venezuela* (Madrid: Editorial América, 1917), p. 261; Juan Vicente González, *El primer congreso de Venezuela y la Sociedad Patriótica* (Caracas: Ministerio de Educación, 1958), pp .4–5.

22. *Morning Chronicle* (Wednesday, October 2, 1811).

23. Juan Luis Camón to Domingo García de Sena (Caracas, 8 de mayo de 1811), in *Epistolario*, 1:121–22.

24. Roscio to Bello (Caracas, 9 de junio de 1811), reprinted in Miguel Luis Amunátegui, *Vida de Don Andrés Bello* (Santiago de Chile: Pedro G. Ramírez, 1882), pp. 98–111. See also Sergio Fernández Larraín, *Cartas a Bello en Londres, 1810–1829* (Santiago: Editorial Andrés Bello, 1968), p. 66.

25. "Dr. Juan Germán Roscio, calidad mestiza," *Archivo General de la Nación— Venezuela, Limpieza de Sangre, T. 33, f.273.*

26. Benjamin Roberts to John Barber (Trinidad, January 31, 1811), *University of Virginia, Alderman Library, Roberts Manuscripts, Box 2, 1789–1855.*

27. *El Patriota de Venezuela*, #2 (1811).

28. Thorning, *World Citizen*, p. 221.

29. "Discurso redirigido por un miembro de la Sociedad Patriótica, y leído en el Supremo Congreso el día 4 de julio de 1811," *El Patriota de Venezuela* #2 (1811).

30. Lombardi, *Venezuela: The Search for Order, the Dream of Progress*, p. 21.

31. Semple, *Sketch*, pp. 124–25.

32. Ibid., p. 126.

33. Lombardi, *Venezuela*, p. 127; John Lynch, *The Spanish American Revolutions, 1808–1825* (New York: W. W. Norton and Company, 1973), p. 195.

34. *Morning Chronicle* (May 4, 1812).

35. [Palacio Fajardo], *Outline of the Revolution in Spanish America*, p. 72.

36. José Guerra [Fray Servando Teresa de Mier Noriega y Guerra], *Historia de la Revolución de Nueva España, antiguamente Anáhuac, o Verdadera orígen y causas de ella con la relación de sus progresos en el presente año de 1813* (Paris: La Sorbonne, 1990), p. 475n.

37. Cortabarria, *A los pueblos de las provincias de Caracas, Barinas, Cumaná y Nueva Barcelona* . . . (Puerto Rico: 20 de setiembre de 1811), pp. 3–4.

38. *Interesting Official Documents Relating to the United Provinces of Venezuela* (London: Longman and Co., 1812), p. 97. "In the natural order of things, it is the duty of the father to emancipate his son, as soon as getting out of his minority he is able to use his strength and reason to provide for his own subsistence, and also it is the duty of the son to emancipate himself whenever the cruelty or extravagance of the father or tutor endangers his well-being."

39. Cortabarria, *A los pueblos*, p. 12.

40. *Interesting Official Documents*, pp. 85–89.

41. *Discurso que puede servir de preliminar á las noticias de la última conspiración de Caracas.* Escrito por un español americano, que tuvo ocasión de manejar y admirar estos paises (Londres, R. Juigné, 1811).

42. *Interesting Official Documents*, p. 97. In a letter to Juan Martín de Pueyrredón, William Walton claimed that he wrote the preface to this volume and López Méndez paid for it (Londres, 26 de febrero de 1817), in *Archivo General de la Nación—Argentina, Sala 10, 1-3-5*. Others, including Carlos Pi Sunyer and Iván Jaksić, have pointed to Bello as the true author; Jaksić, *Andrés Bello* (Cambridge, UK: Cambridge University Press, 2001), pp. 42–43.

43. *Interesting Official Documents*, p. 33.

44. Semple, *Sketch*, p. 94.

45. Ibid., p. 132.

46. Rodríguez, "First Venezuelan Republic," p. 10.

47. Cortés Madariaga to Miranda (Caracas, 15 de mayo de 1812), and Juan Luis Camón to Domingo García de Sena (Caracas, 8 de mayo de 1811), both in *Epistolario*, 1:121–22, 140-41; "Memoria presentada por la Sociedad Patriótica al Supremo Poder Ejecutivo," *El Patriota de Venezuela* #3 (1811).

48. Miranda to Soublette (Valencia, August 13, 1811), reprinted in Semple, *Sketch*, pp. 159–61; see Miranda's dispatches in *La Gaceta de Caracas* (13 de agosto de 1811) and (16 de agosto de 1811).

49. Carlos Soublette, "Bando" (Quartel General de Valencia, 13 de agosto de 1811), in *La Gaceta de Caracas* (23 de agosto de 1811); [Miranda] "Bando" (Maracay, 9 de setiembre de 1811), in *AGN—Venezuela, Archivo de Aragua, Vol. 71, f.248.*

50. *Morning Chronicle* (Friday, November 22, 1811); *El Español*, vol. 4 (octubre de 1811): 50.

51. Semple, *Sketch*, pp. 137–38.

52. "Acta" (Valencia, 29 de agosto de 1811), in *El Patriota de Venezuela* #3 (1811); "Proclama a los pueblos que componen la Provincia de Caracas," *El Patriota de Venezuela* #2 (1811).

53. "Reflexiones sobre los obstáculos que se oponen al establecimiento sólido del gobierno democrático en las provincias de Venezuela y medios de removerlo," *El Patriota de Venezuela* #3 (1811).

54. "Entrada del General Miranda en Caracas," *El Patriota de Venezuela*, #3 (1811).

55. Letter from La Guaira dated December 23, 1811, quoted in *Morning Chronicle* (Monday, August 16, 1812).

56. Joseph Blanco White, *El Español*, vol. 4 (Oct. 1811), p. 50, quoted in Martin Murphy, *Blanco White: Self-Banished Spaniard* (New Haven: Yale University Press, 1989), p. 79.

57. Burr to Bentham (London, October 16, 1811), *The Private Journal of Aaron Burr*, 7:254–55.

58. Mill to Miranda (Newington Green, January 20, 1812), in *Library of Congress, Burr Papers, Reel 6, #939.*

59. Rodríguez de Ribas, *Caraqueños: Llegó la época feliz del engaño. El fatal error, orígen de vuestras desgracias* . . . (Cádiz: Imprenta Real, 1812). Broadside.

60. Infantado, *Proclama a los habitantes de Ultramar* (Cádiz: Imprenta Real, 30 de agosto de 1812). Broadside.

61. [Augustus Oliver Whipple], *Nine Letters, Particularly Addressed to the People of the Revolting Spanish Provinces of the Caraccas, and to other Spanish Provinces in North and South America, and to the Whole Spanish Nation and the Civilized World* (Baltimore: Printed by Joseph Robinson, 1811).

62. Semple, *Sketch*, p. 72; *Morning Chronicle* (Monday, August 31, 1812).

63. Donald Worcester, *Bolívar* (Boston: Little, Brown & Company, 1977), pp. 28–29. In Caracas today, these words are inscribed on the wall of the Museo Bolivariano.

64. Vansittart to Lord Auckland (Great George Street, June 20, 1812), *British Library, Add MSS, 34,458, ff.264-65.*

65. Miranda to Bentham (Maracay, June 2, 1812), in Bentham, *Memoirs*, 10:468.

66. Miranda to Perceval (Headquarters, Maracay, June 2, 1812), *British Museum, Add. MSS 38,249, f.72*; Miranda to Castlereagh (Maracay, 2 de junio de 1812), in *Epistolario*, 1:243.

67. Soublette to Casas (4 de junio de 1812), and Francisco Iznardy to Miranda (Victoria, 8 de mayo de 1812), in *AGM*, 24:240–41, 446–47.

68. *Defensa documentada de la conducta del comandante de La Guaira Señor Manuel María de las Casas en la prisión del General Miranda y entrega de aquella plaza á los españoles en 1812* (Caracas: George Corser, 1843), p. 21.

69. Semple, *Sketch*, p. 59.

70. *Defensa documentada*, p. 21.

71. José de Anzoátegui, "Representación" (Barcelona, 6 de julio de 1812, 2 de la República de Venezuela), and Miranda et al. to Capitán General de Barcelona Americana (Caracas, 16 de julio de 1811), in *Epistolario de la Primera República* (Caracas: Academia Nacional de la Historia, 1960), 1:54–55, 239–40; "Reflexiones sobre la independencia de Venezuela," *El Patriota de Venezuela* #3 (1811).

72. Cortés Madariaga to Miranda (Caracas, 17 de mayo de 1812), and (Caracas, 15 de mayo de 1812), both in *Epistolario*, 1:140–45.

73. "Juan Contierra, "Carta #1" *El Patriota de Venezuela* #3 (1811). The name, "John With a [Home]land," is a pun on the Spanish exile Joseph Blanco White's favorite pseudonym while writing in *El Español* in London, "Juan Sintierra" or "John Without a [Home]land."

74. Miranda to Francisco Espejo (Cuartel General de Maracay, 16 de mayo de 1812), in *Epistolario*, 1:241–42.

75. Muñoz Tebar to Arzobispo de Caracas (Valencia, 5 de abril de 1812), in *Epistolario*, 1:256–57.

76. *Defensa documentada*, p. 7.

77. *Morning Chronicle* (Friday, August 21, 1812).

78. Cortés Madariaga to Miranda (Caracas, 15 de mayo de 1812), in *Epistolario*, 1:140–42.

79. "Manifiesto, que en nombre de Domingo Monteverde dirige . . . con el obgeto de seducirlos y engañarlos," *La Gaceta de Caracas* (5 de junio de 1812).

80. Miranda, quoted in Worcester, *Bolívar*, p. 31.

81. Bolívar to Miranda (4 de julio de 1812), quoted in Thorning, *World Citizen*, pp. 248–49.

82. Luis Delpech to Tomás Molini, "Relación sucinta de los últimos acontecimientos de Caracas" (Londres, 27 de febrero de 1813), in *Epistolario*, 1:149.

83. "Counter-Revolution in Venezuela," *Morning Chronicle* (Tuesday, October 6, 1812), based on an extract from the *New York Gazette* (August 25, 1812).

84. Monteverde to Miyares (Cuartel General de San Mateo, 27 de julio de 1812), extract reprinted in *El Español* #30 (1812), p. 464. Copy in *Great Britain, Public Record Office, Foreign Office 72/157/160-161.*

85. "Proclama del Comandante Domingo Monteverde á su entrada en la capital de Caracas" (Caracas, 3 de agosto de 1812), included in Miranda to Vansittart (La Carraca, Cádiz, 21 de mayo de 1814), *British Library, Add MSS 31231, f.75.*

86. Worcester, *Bolívar*, p. 41.

87. Gómez quoted in Paul Johnson, *The Birth of the Modern World Society, 1815–1830* (New York: HarperCollins Publishers, 1991), pp. 636–37.

88. Semple, *Sketch*, p. 146.

89. Delpech, "Relación sucinta," *Epistolario*, 1:148.

90. Montilla to López Méndez (St. Bartolomé, 4 de octubre de 1812), and López Méndez to Nicholas Vansittart, "Violación de la capitulación" (Londres, 28

de noviembre de 1812), *Great Britain, PRO, FO 72/157.* Vansittart passed the letter and supporting documents on to Castlereagh.

91. Francisco de Rivera to Señor General [Monteverde] (6 de agosto de 1812), in *AGN—Venezuela, Gobierno y Capitanía-General V.220, f.109.*

92. Bolívar, quoted in Worcester, *Bolívar,* p. 34.

93. Bolívar, *Memoirs,* 1:124.

94. Allen to Bentham (November 3, 1812), *British Library, Add MSS 33,544, f.646.*

95. Delpech, "Relación sucinta," *Epistolario,* 1:149.

Conclusion, 243–258

1. "Memorial de las Bóvedas del Castillo del Puerto Cabello, 8 de marzo de 1813," in *América espera,* pp. 474–80.

2. Miranda to the Royal Audiencia, "Representation of Don Francisco de Miranda, a Native of the City of Caracas . . ." (Dungeons of Puerto Cabello, March 8, 1813), translation included in a letter to Nicholas Vansittart, *British Museum, Add. MSS 31, 231 ff.76-81.*

3. Alberto Miramón, *La llama que no muere* (Caracas: Instituto Panamericano de Geografía e Historia, 1983), pp. 50–51.

4. Thorning, *World Citizen,* p. 206.

5. Spain, Fernando VII, *El torrente de males que afligen á muchas Provincias de mis dominios de América . . .* (Madrid: 2 de julio de 1814); John Bergamini, *The Spanish Bourbons* (New York: Putnam's, 1974), p. 155.

6. Vansittart to Major General Hodgson (January 27, 1814), *British Library, Add. MSS, 31,231, ff.9-10.*

7. Miranda to Ferdinand VII (Carraca, 30 de junio de 1814), in *América espera,* pp. 487–89.

8. Miranda to Ferdinand VII (Carraca, 25 de setiembre de 1814), in *América espera,* pp. 490–92.

9. Miranda to Vansittart (La Carraca, 13 avril 1815), *British Library, Add.MSS 31,231, ff.257-59.*

10. Miranda to Vansittart (La Carraca, August 15, 1815), *British Library 31, 231, Add.MSS, ff.334-35.*

11. A lengthy series of short, increasingly angry and desperate appeals for money is reprinted in *AGM,* 24:547–51.

12. Turnbull to Vansittart (Brighton, December 8, 1814), *British Library, Add. MSS, 31,231, f.208.*

13. Turnbull to [Vansittart] (Gibraltar, April 8, 1816), *British Library, Add. MSS 31,232, f.43.*

14. Peter Livingston to Nicholas Vansittart (Gibraltar, April 7, 1816), *British Library, Add. MSS 31,232, f.39.*

15. Morán to [D. Shaw and Co.] ([14 de] abril [de 1816]), *British Library, Add. MSS 31232, f.41.*

16. Fleeming to [Turnbull] (San Roque, 18 de abril de 1816), *British Library, Add. MSS 31,232, ff.41-42.*

17. José Amindra to [Peter Turnbull] (hoi, lunes, [mayo de 1816]), *British Library, Add.MSS 31,232, f.40.*

18. Sánchez, quoted in Thorning, *World Citizen,* p. 283.

19. Entry in "Libro Quinto de Defunciones del Arsenal de la Carraca, folio 159v.," copy, *Indiana University, Lilly Library, Latin American Manuscripts, Venezuela, 1786–1820.*

20. Morán to Duncan, Shaw and Company (2 de abril de 1816) and (16 de julio de 1816), both in *AGM,* 24:552–53.

21. Sylvester Douglas, Baron Glenbervie (Calais, August 12, 1816), *The Diaries of Sylvester Douglas (Lord Glenbervie),* Francis Bickley, ed. (London: Constable and Co., 1928), 2:194–95.

22. *Morning Chronicle* (Monday, September 9, 1816).

23. *Morning Chronicle* (Friday, November 7, 1817).

24. Bentham, *Memoirs,* 10:468, 487–88.

25. Richard Wellesley to Tomás Molini (Cumberland Place, September 9, 1816), in *AGM,* 24:553–54.

26. Rush to Madison (Washington, September 6, 1815), *Rush Microfilms #1866.*

27. President James Madison to Richard Rush (Montpelier, September 9, 1815), *Rush Microfilms #1292.*

28. John Quincy Adams (August 28, 1815), *Memoirs,* 3:265.

29. *Colombia, Being a Geographical, Statistical, Agricultural, Commercial and Political Account of That Country, Adapted for the General Reader, the Merchant and the Colonist* (London: Baldwin, Cradock and Joy, 1822), 1:302.

30. Mier, *Historia de la revolución de la Nueva España, antiguamente Anáhuac* (Paris: La Sorbonne, 1990), p. 475n.

31. Bolívar, *Memoirs,* 2:211.

32. Daniel Florencio O'Leary, *Memorias del General Daniel Florencio O'Leary* (Caracas: Imprenta Nacional, 1952), 1:33.

33. Daniel F. O'Leary, *Bolívar and the War of Independence,* Robert F. McNerney, transl. (Austin: University of Texas Press, 1970), p. 38.

34. Miranda, quoted in Robertson, *The Life of Miranda,* 1:6.

35. Charles Abbot, Lord Colchester (June 2, 1806), *The Diaries and Correspondence of Charles Abbot, Lord Colchester, Speaker of the House of Commons, 1802–17,* Charles Abbot, Lord Colchester, his son, ed. (London: John Murray, 1861), 2:64–65.

36. Antonio José de Irisarri to Señor Ministro de Estado del Departamento de Relaciones Exteriores (Londres, 9 de enero de 1820), in Chile, Congreso Nacional, *Sesiones de los cuerpos lejislativos de la República de Chile, 1811–1845* (Santiago: Imprenta de Cervantes, 1887–1908), 4:200–201. The Senate discussed this letter during Extraordinary Session #242 on May 31, 1820.

37. O'Higgins to the Senate (Sesión Extraordinaria #242, 31 de mayo de 1820), and Senate Act #203 (Sesión Ordinaria #243, 2 de junio de 1820), both in *Sesiones lejislativas*, 4:199–204. The Senate stated, "[I]t is necessary first to attend to the defense of the country."

38. Evans' auction catalogue remains, giving posterity an idea of the collection's contents. *Catalogue of the Valuable and Extensive Library of the Late General Miranda*; *Catalogue of the Second and Remaining Portion of the Valuable Library of the Late General Miranda* (London: William Nichol, 1833).

39. Bentham to Bolívar (January 6, 1823), copy in *University College London, Bentham Manuscripts, Box 12, ff.86-90.*

40. *Mémoirs de J. B. Boussingault* (Paris: Chamerot et Renouard, 1900), 3:188.

41. *El Conductor* [Bogotá] (7 de noviembre de 1827), quoted in Eloy González, "Los hijos del General Miranda," *Boletín de la Academia Nacional de Historia* 10 (#39, julio–setiembre de 1927): 191.

BIBLIOGRAPHY

Manuscript Sources

Academia Nacional de la Historia—Venezuela
    Archivo Miranda
    Venezuela—Folletos
Alderman Library, University of Virginia
    John Roberts Papers
Archivo General de Indias, Seville
    Estado
    Santo Domingo
    Caracas
Archivo General de la Nación—Argentina
Archivo General de la Nación—México
Archivo General de la Nación—Venezuela
    Archivo de Aragua
    Gobierno y Capitanía General
    Limpieza de Sangre
        Negocios Eclesiásticos
    Real Audiencia—Provisiones
    Real Consulado
Archivo General de Simancas, Valladolid
    Estado
Archivo Histórico Nacional, Madrid
    Estado
Archivo Histórico Nacional, Santiago de Chile

Bibliothèque Nationale—France
     François-Mitterrand-Tolbiac Site
     Richelieu Site, Department of Western Manuscripts
Bodleian Library, Oxford University
     William Wilberforce Papers
Boston Athenaeum Library
British Library, Department of Rare Books and Manuscripts
Cambridge University Library, England
     British and Foreign Bible Society Papers
     William Pitt Papers
Columbia University Library
     Daniel del Río Latin American Collection
Huntington Library
     Thomas Clarkson Papers
     William Wilberforce Papers
John Carter Brown Library, Brown University
     Simón Bolívar Manuscripts
Library of Congress, Washington, DC
     Alexander Hamilton Papers
     Iturbide Papers
     Thomas Jefferson Papers
     Rush Family Papers
     George Washington Papers
Lilly Library, Indiana University
     Latin American Manuscripts
Massachusetts Historical Society
     Adams Family Papers
     Henry Knox Papers
     Miscellaneous Bound Manuscripts
     Timothy Pickering Papers
     Matthew Ridley Papers
National Archives of Scotland
     Melville Papers
     Evan Nepean Papers
National Maritime Museum, Greenwich
Nettie Lee Benson Latin American Collection, University of Texas,
     Austin

Lucas Alamán Papers
Juan Hernández y Dávalos Collection
Servando Teresa de Mier Noriega y Guerra Papers
New-York Historical Society
    Rufus King Papers
Oxford University, Bodleian Library
    Wilberforce Manuscripts
Public Record Office of Great Britain
Public Record Office of Northern Ireland, Belfast
    Castlereagh Papers
Senate House Library, University of London
Stirling Library, Yale University
    Latin American Collection
Sydney Jones Library, University of Liverpool
    Joseph Blanco White Papers
University College—London, Department of Manuscripts
    Jeremy Bentham Collection
    Henry Brougham Papers
Valparaiso University
    Law School Library
    Moellering Library

Contemporary Periodicals

La Aurora de Chile [Santiago]
Aurora General Advertiser [Philadelphia]
Barbados Mercury [Georgetown]
Biblioteca Americana, o Miscelánea de literatura, artes y ciencias
    [London]
El Colombiano [London]
Correo del Orinoco [Angostura]
El Español [London]
Gazeta de Caracas [Caracas]
Morning Chronicle [London]
El Patriota de Venezuela [Caracas]
Pennsylvania Gazette [Philadelphia]

El Repertorio Americano [London]
Semanario Patriótico [Seville]
The Times [London]

Court Cases

United States v Smith; *United States v Ogden*, 27 F.Cas.1189
    CC.D.NY (No.16,341a)
United States v Smith, 27 F.Cas. 1192 CC.D.NY (No. 16,342)
United States v Smith, 27 F.Cas. 1233 CC.D.NY (No. 16,342a)
United States v Smith; *United States v Ogden*, 27 F.Cas. 1246
    CC.D.NY (No.16,342b)

Contemporary Printed Sources

Adams, John. *Works of John Adams, Second President of the United States,*
    with a Life of the Author. Ed. Charles Francis Adams. Vols. 1, 10.
    Boston: Little, Brown, & Co., 1856.
Adams, John Quincy. *Memoirs of John Quincy Adams, Comprising*
    Portions of His Diary from 1795 to 1848. Ed. Charles Francis Adams.
    Philadelphia: J. B. Lippincott & Co., 1874.
Alcalá Galiano, Antonio. *Recuerdos de un anciano.* Madrid: Librería y
    Casa Editorial Hernando S.A., 1927.
Antepara, José María. *South American Emancipation: Documents His-*
    torical and Explanatory, shewing the Designs which have been in
    Progress and the Exertions made by General Miranda for the South
    American Emancipation, during the last Twenty-Five Years. By J. M.
    Antepara, a Native of Guayaquil. London: R. Juigné, 1810.
Archivo Bonpland IV: Londres, Cuartel General de los Patriotas de la
    Emancipación Americana. Buenos Aires: Imprenta y Casa Editora
    "Coni," 1940.
Archivo de San Martín. Buenos Aires: Comisión Nacional del Centen-
    ario, 1910.
Aulard, F. A., ed. *La Société des Jacobins.* Vol. 5, *Janvier 1793–Mars*
    1794. Paris: Maison Quantin, 1895.

Azpurúa, Francisco. *Observaciones á los recuerdos sobre 'La rebelión de Caracas' de José Domingo Díaz.* Madrid: Imprenta de Eusebio Aguado, 1829.

Barras, P. F. J. N. *Memoirs of Barras.* Vol. 2, *The Directorate up to the 18th Fructidor.* New York: Harper and Brothers, 1895.

————. *Mémoires de Barras.* Vol. 2, *Le Directoire jusqu'au 18 Fructidor.* Paris: Librairie Hachette, 1895.

Bentham, Jeremy. *The Correspondence of Jeremy Bentham.* Vol. 7, *January 1802 to December 1808.* Ed. John Dinwiddy. Oxford: Clarendon Press, 1988.

————. *The Correspondence of Jeremy Bentham.* Vol. 8, *January 1809 to December 1816.* Ed. Stephen Conway. Oxford: Clarendon Press, 1988.

————. *Memoirs of Jeremy Bentham, Including Autobiographical Conversations and Correspondence.* Ed. John Bowring. Edinburgh, 1843.

Blanco White, Joseph. *The Life of the Rev. Joseph Blanco White, written by Himself, with portions of his Correspondence.* Ed. John Hamilton Thom. London: John Chapman, 1845.

Bolívar, Simon. *Memoirs of Simón Bolívar, President-Liberator of the Republic of Colombia.* 2 vols. Ed. H. L. V. Ducoudray-Holstein. London: Henry Colburn and Richard Bentley, 1830.

Bolívar, Simón, and Luis López Méndez. "La misión a Londres de Bolívar y López Méndez: Documentos." *Boletín de la Academia Nacional de la Historia* 21, no. 8 (1938): 47–66.

Boussingault, J-B. *Mémoires de J-B Boussingault.* Vol. 3, *1823–1824.* Paris: Chamerot et Renouard, 1900.

Brissot de Warville, Jean Pierre. *Mémoires.* Vol 6. Paris: Picard and Fils, n.d.

Bulletin du tribunal révolutionnaire #30–37. Paris, 1793.

Burke, William. *Additional Reasons for Our Immediately Emancipating Spanish America.* 2d ed. London: J. Ridgway, 1808.

Burr, Aaron. *Political Correspondence and Public Papers of Aaron Burr.* Vol. 2. Ed. Mary Jo Kline. Princeton, NJ: Princeton University Press, 1983.

————. *Private Journal of Aaron Burr.* Vol. 7. Ed. Matthew Davies. New York: Harper & Brothers, 1838.

Castlereagh, Robert Stewart, Viscount. *Memoirs and Correspondence of Viscount Castlereagh.* Vols. 6, 7, 8. London: William Shorberl, 1851.

Catherine II, Empress of Russia. *Memoirs of Catherine the Great.* Trans. Katherine Anthony. New York: Alfred A. Knopf, 1927.

Chateaubriand, François-René de. *Atala and René.* New York: Signet Classics, 1962.

_____. *Mémoires d'outre-tombe.* 2 vols. Paris: Gallimard, 1997.

Chaveau-Lagarde, Claude-François. *Plaidoyer pour le général Miranda, accusé de haute trahison et de complicité avec le général en chef Dumouriez.* Paris: Barrois l'Aîné, [1793].

Chépy, Pierre. *P. Chépy à ses concitoyens.* Paris: Siret, l'an 2 de la République Française.

Chile. Congreso Nacional. *Sesiones de los cuerpos legislativos de la República de Chile, 1811–1845.* Santiago de Chile: Cervantes, 1887–1908.

Colchester, Charles Abbot, Lord. *The Diaries and Correspondence of Charles Abbot, Lord Colchester, Speaker of the House of Commons, 1802–1817.* Ed. Charles Abbot, Lord Colchester, his son. Vol. 2. London: John Murray, 1861.

"Correo insurgente de Londres capturado por un corsario puertorriqueño, 1811." *Boletín de la Academia Chilena de la Historia* 63 (1960): 125–55.

Cortabarria, Antonio Ignacio. *A los pueblos de la provincias de Caracas, Barinas, Cumaná y Nueva Barcelona.* [Puerto Rico], 20 de setiembre de 1811.

Costa Pereira Furtado de Mendonça, Hippolyto Joseph da. *A Narrative of the Persecution of Hippolyto Joseph da Costa Pereira Furtado de Mendonça, a Native of Colonia-do-Sacramento, on the River La Plata, imprisoned and tried in Lisbon, by the Inquisition for the Pretended Crime of Free-Masonry.* London: W. Lewis, 1811.

Creevey, Thomas. *The Creevey Papers: A Selection from the Correspondence and Diaries of the Late Thomas Creevey MP.* Ed. Rt. Hon. Sir Herbert Maxwell. London: John Murray, 1903.

Custine, Delphine. *Delphine de Custine, belle amie de Miranda.* Ed. Caracciolo Parra-Pérez. Paris: Editions Excelsior, 1927.

Discurso que puede servir de preliminar á las noticias de la última conspiración de Caracas. Escrito por un español americano que tuvo ocasión de manejar y admirar estos papeles. Londres: R. Juigné, 1811.

Dumouriez, Charles François. *Mémoires du Général Dumouriez, pour servir a l'Histoire de la Convention Nationale.* 2 vols. Paris: Fermin-Didot et Cie., 1884–1886.

Edsall, John. *Incidents in the Life of John Edsall.* Catskill, NY, 1831.

"English Policy toward America in 1790–91: Documents." Ed. Frederick Jackson Turner. *American Historical Review* 7, no. 4 (July 1902): 706–35.

Epistolario de la Primera República. Vol. 1. Caracas: Academia Nacional de la Historia, 1960.

Eustace, John Skey. *Le citoyen des Etats-Unis d'Amérique Jean-Skey Eustace, Général de brigade des armées de la république française, à ses frères d'armes.* Paris: Imprimerie du Cercle Social, 1793, l'an deux de la République Française.

Flinter, George. *A History of the Revolution of Caracas, Comprising an Impartial Narrative of the Atrocities Committed by the Contending Parties.* London: T. and J. Allman, 1819.

France. National Convention. *Lettres des généraux Miranda, D'Arçon et Valence au Ministre de la Guerre.* [Paris]: Imprimerie Nationale, [s.d].

Francisco de Miranda en Francia: documentos. Caracas: Embajada de Francia en Venezuela, Monte Avila Editores, 1997.

Franklin, Benjamin. *The Autobiography and Other Writings.* New York: Penguin, 1986.

García del Río, Juan. "Vindicación de J. García del Río." *El Mercurio* (Valparaíso) 12 de marzo de 1843.

George, Prince of Wales. *The Correspondence of George, Prince of Wales, 1770–1812.* Vol. 7. Ed. A. Aspinall. London: Oxford University Press, 1970.

Glenbervie, Sylvester Douglas, Baron. *The Diaries of Sylvester Douglas, Lord Glenbervie.* Vol. 2. Ed. Francis Bickley. London: Constable and Co., 1928.

Grases, Pedro, ed. *Pensamiento político de la emancipación venezolana.* Caracas: Biblioteca Ayacucho, 1988.

Hackett, James. *Narrative of the Expedition which sailed from England in 1817, to join the South American Patriots.* London: John Murray, 1818.

Hall, Col. Francis. *Colombia: Its Present State.* London: Baldwin, Cradock, and Joy, 1827.

———. *Letters written from Colombia, being a Journey from Caracas to Bogotá, and thence to Santa Martha in 1823.* London: G. Cowie and Co., 1824.

Hamilton, Alexander. *The Papers of Alexander Hamilton.* Ed. Harold Syrett. Vols. 22, 23. New York: Columbia University Press, 1963–1967.

Hippisley, Gustavus. *A Narrative of the Expedition to the Rivers Orinoco and Apuré in South America.* London: John Murray, 1819.

Infantado, Duque del. *Proclama a los Habitantes de Ultramar.* Cádiz: Imprenta Real, 30 de agosto de 1812.

Ingersoll, Henry. "The Diary and Letters of Henry Ingersoll, Prisoner at Carthagena, 1806–1809." *American Historical Review* 3, no. 4 (July 1898): 674–702.

Interesting Official Documents Relating to the United Provinces of Venezuela... In Spanish and English. London: Longman and Co., 1812.

Jefferson, Thomas. *The Papers of Thomas Jefferson.* Ed. John Catzanti. Vols. 9, 13, 17, 18, 25, 26. Princeton, NJ: Princeton University Press, 1997.

———. *The Writings of Thomas Jefferson.* Washington, DC: The Jefferson Memorial Association, 1904.

Junius [pseud.]. *A Jean Skei Eustace. Soi-disant Citoyen des Etats Unis d'Amérique and Général de Brigade des Armées Françaises.* [Paris]: Barrois l'Aîné [1793].

[Keith, Lieut. Sir George Mouat]. *A Voyage to South America and the Cape of Good Hope in His Majesty's Gun Brig, the Protector.* London: Richard Phillips, 1810.

King, Rufus. *Life and Correspondence of Rufus King.* Vols. 3, 4, 5. New York: Putnam's, 1895–1897.

Knutsford, Viscountess. *The Life and Letters of Zachary Macaulay.* London: Edward Arnold, 1900.

Lafayette. *Mémoires, correspondance et manuscrits.* 6 Vols. Paris: H. Fournier Ainé, 1838.

Lancaster, Joseph. *Epitome of Some of the Chief Events and Transactions in the Life of Joseph Lancaster.* New Haven: Baldwin and Peck, 1833.

[Las Casas, Manuel María de]. *Defensa documentada de la conducta del comandante de La Guaira en la prisión del General Miranda.* Caracas: George Corser, 1843.

López, Casto Fulgencio, ed. *Juan Picornell y la conspiración de Gual y España (documentos).* Caracas: Ediciones Nueva Cádiz, 1954.

López Méndez, Luis. "Correspondencia de Luis López Méndez para el Libertador." *Revista de la Sociedad Bolivariana de Venezuela* 17, no. 54 (abril 1958): 67–75.

Louvet de Couvray, J. B. *Mémoires du Louvet de Couvray, Député à la Convention Nationale.* Paris: Badouin Frères, 1823.

Madison, James. *Letters and Other Writings of James Madison.* Vol. 2. New York: R. Worthington, 1884.

Mallet du Pan. *Correspondance inédite de Mallet du Pan avec la Cour de Vienne (1794–1798).* Vol. 1. Paris: F. Plon, Nourrit and Cie., 1884.

"Mechanics of New York, read the heart-rending Truth!" [New York, 1806]. Broadside.

Mendoza, Cristobal, ed. *Primeras misiones diplomáticas de Venezuela: documentos.* Caracas: Academia Nacional de la Historia Sesquicentenario de Independencia, 1962.

Mier Noriega y Guerra, José Servando Teresa de. *Memorias.* Ed. y prólogo de Antonio Castro Leal. México: Editorial Porrúa, 1946.

————. "Masonería establecida en Cádiz: Rito Americano Logia 'Caballeros Racionales'—Declaraciones de Fray Servando Teresa de Mier sobre dicha Masonería." *Boletín del Archivo General de la Nación* 3 (1932): 381–89.

Mill, John Stuart. *Autobiography of John Stuart Mill.* Toronto: New American Library, 1965.

Minutes of a Court Martial for the Trial of Captain Sir Home Popham. London, 1807.

Miranda, Francisco de. *Archivo del General Miranda.* 25 vols. Caracas: Tipografía "La Nación," 1929–1933.

————. *El Colombiano de Francisco de Miranda y dos documentos americanistas.* Ed. Pedro Grases. Caracas, 1966.

————. *América espera.* Caracas: Biblioteca Ayacucho, 1982.

_____. *Diario y viajes y escritos políticos*. Madrid: Editora Nacional, 1977.

_____. *Extrait du procès-verbal des déliberations du Comité de la Guerre, séance du lundi 8 avril huit heures du soir. Interrogatoire du général Miranda*. [Paris]: Barrois l'Aîné, [1793].

_____. *Miranda á ses concitoyens. Discours que je me proposais de prononcer à la Convention nationale, le 29 mars dernier, le lendemain de mon arrivée à Paris*. Paris, [1793].

_____. *Miranda aux répresentants du peuple français*. [N.p., 1795].

_____. *Lettre-circulaire du général Miranda à tous les commandants temporaires en Belgique, leur ordonnant de procurer au Citoyen Chépy, agent de la République française, sûreté et protection*. Brugge: Weduwe van J. Van Praet, [s.d].

_____. *Lettre du général Miranda, au quartier général d'Anvers, le 4 décembre 1792, l'an premier de la République Française*. [N.p., n.d.].

_____. *A la Représentation nationale*. Paris: Barrois l'Aîné, an 3 [1795].

_____. *Opinion du général Miranda sur la situation actuelle de la France et sur les remèdes convenables à ses maux*. Paris: Imprimerie de la rue de Vaurigard, an 3 [1795].

_____. *Original Correspondence between Generals Dumourier, Miranda, Pache and Beurnonville, Ministers at War, since 1793*. London: J. Owen, 1794.

_____. *Fragments from an XVIIIth Century Diary: 1771–1789*. Ed. Jordan Herbert Stabler. Caracas: Tipografía "La Nación," 1931.

_____. *The New Democracy in America: Travels of Francisco de Miranda in the United States, 1783–84*. Ed. Judson P. Wood. Norman: University of Oklahoma Press, 1963.

_____, [attrib.] "Emancipation of South America." *Edinburgh Review* 13 (January 1809): 227–311.

"Miranda and the British Admiralty, 1804–1806: Documents." *American Historical Review* 6, no. 3 (April 1901): 508–30.

Molina, Ignacio. *The Geographical, Natural and Civil History of Chili, by Abbé Don J. Ignacius Molina*. 2 vols. Middletown, CT: I. Riley, 1808.

Moreno, Manuel. *Vida y memorias de Mariano Moreno*. Buenos Aires: Editorial Universitaria de Buenos Aires, 1968.

Morris, Gouverneur. *A Diary of the French Revolution*. Ed. Beatrix Cary Davenport. Vol. 1. Boston: Houghton Mifflin, 1939.

Nariño, Antonio. *Archivo Nariño*. 6 vols. Bogotá: Fundación Francisco de Paula Santander, 1990.

Naval Records Society. *The Royal Navy in the River Plate, 1806–1807*. Ed. John D. Grainger. Aldershot, UK: Scholar Press, 1996.

O'Higgins, Bernardo. *Archivo de don Bernardo O'Higgins*. Santiago de Chile: Editorial Nascimento, 1946.

————. *Epistolario de Bernardo O'Higgins: 1798–1819*. Madrid: Editorial América, 1920.

O'Leary, Daniel Florencio. *The "Detached Recollections" of General D. F. O'Leary*. Ed. R. A. Humphreys. London: Athlone, 1969.

————. *Memorias del General Daniel Florencio O'Leary*. Caracas: Imprenta Nacional, 1952.

————. *Bolívar and the War of Independence*. Trans. Robert J. McNerney. Austin: University of Texas Press, 1970.

Páez, José Antonio. *Autobiografía del General José Antonio Páez*. 2 vols. Caracas: Ministerio de Educación Nacional, Dirección de Cultura, 1946.

Paine, Thomas. *Life and Works of Thomas Paine*. Vols. 5, 7. New York: Thomas Paine National Historical Association, 1925.

————. *Life and Writings of Thomas Paine*. Vol. 10. Ed. Daniel Wheeler. New York: Vincent Parke and Co., 1908.

————. *The Complete Writings of Thomas Paine*. Ed. Philip S. Foner. New York: The Citadel Press, 1945.

[Palacio Fajardo, Manuel]. *Outline of the Revolution in Spanish America, or an Account of the Origin, Progress, and Actual State of the War Carried on between Spain and America*. By a South American. New York: James Eastburn and Co., 1817.

Perú de Lacroix, Luis. *Diario de Bucaramanga*. Paris: Librería P. Ollendorf, [n.d.].

Pike, Zebulon M. "The Papers of Zebulon M. Pike, 1806–1807." Ed. Herbert E. Bolton. *American Historical Review* 13, no. 4 (June 1908): 798–827.

Porter, Sir Robert Ker. *Sir Robert Ker Porter's Caracas Diary, 1825–42: A British Diplomat in a New Nation*. Ed. Walter Dupuoy. Caracas, 1966.

Pownall, Thomas. *Memorial, Most Humbly Addressed to the Sovereigns of Europe on the Present State of Affairs between the Old and New World.* 2d ed. London: J. Almon, 1780.

_____. *Memorial Addressed to the Sovereigns of Europe and the Atlantic.* London: J. Debrett, 1803.

Quatremère de Quincy, Antoine C. *Lettres à Miranda sur le déplacement des monuments de l'art de l'Italie (1796).* Introduction et notes par Edouard Pommier. Paris: Macula, 1989.

Retrato y vida del traidor Miranda, incertada en la Gazeta de Lima, del sabado 7 de Febrero del presente año. Buenos Aires: En la Real Imprenta de Niños Expositos, 1807.

Rodríguez de Ribas, Ignacio. *"Caraqueños: llegó la época feliz del desengaño. El fatal error, orígen de vuestras desgracias . . ."* [Cádiz]: Imprenta Real, 1812.

Roscio, Juan Germán. *Pensamiento sobre una biblioteca pública en Caracas.* [Caracas, 1811]. Broadside.

Rush, Benjamin. *The Autobiography of Benjamin Rush.* Ed. George W. Corner. Philadelphia: American Philosophical Society, 1948.

Rush, Richard. *A Residence at the Court of London.* London: Century, 1987.

_____. *The Letters and Papers of Richard Rush.* Ed. Anthony M. Brescia. Wilmington, DE: Scholarly Resources, 1980. Microfilm.

Ségur, Louis-Philippe. *Mémoires, ou Souvenirs et Anecdotes par M. Le Comte de Ségur.* Paris: Henri Colburn, 1825.

Semple, Robert. *Sketch of the Present State of Caracas.* London: Robert Baldwin, 1812.

Sevilla, Capt. Rafael. *Memorias de un oficial del ejército español: Campañas contra Bolívar y los separatistas de América.* Madrid: Editorial América, [n.d.].

[Sherman, John H.] *A General Account of Miranda's Expedition, including the Trial and Execution of Ten of His Officers.* New York: McFarlane and Long, 1808.

Smith, Moses. *History of the Adventures and Suffering of Moses Smith, during Five Years of his Life; From the Beginning of the Year 1806, when he was Betrayed into the Miranda Expedition, until June 1811, when he was Non-suited into an Action at Law, which lasted Three Years and a Half.* Brooklyn: Thomas Kirk, 1812.

Smyth, Captain W. H. *The Life and Services of Captain Philip Beaver*. London: John Murray, 1829.

Stanhope, Lady Hester. *Memoirs of Lady Hester Stanhope*. 3 vols. Salzburg: Institut für Anglistik und Amerikanistik, 1985.

Stanhope, Philip Henry, the fifth earl. *Notes of Conversations with the Duke of Wellington, 1831–1851*. London: Oxford University Press, 1938.

Stephens, H. Morse, ed. *Orators of the French Revolution*. 2 vols. Oxford: Clarendon Press, 1892.

Stiles, Ezra. *The Literary Diary of Ezra Stiles*. Ed. Franklin Bowditch Dexter. New York: Scribner's 1901.

Testigos norteamericanos de la expedición norteamericana de Miranda (Sherman, Smith, Ingersoll). Ed. Edgardo Mondolfi. Caracas: Monte Avila Editores, 1992.

Testimonios de la época emancipadora. Caracas: Academia Nacional de la Historia, 1961.

Thiébault, Paul Charles François Adrien Henri Dieudonné, Baron. *Mémoires du Général Baron Thiébault*. Vol. 1. Paris: Librairie Plon, 1908.

_____. *The Memoirs of Baron Thiébault, Late Lieutenant-General in the French Army*. Ed. Arthur John Butler. Vol. 1. New York: MacMillan, 1896.

U.S. Congress. *Report of the Committee to whom was Referred the Petition of Sundry Citizens of the United States, confined at Carthagena in South America*. 11th Cong. Washington, DC: A. and G. Way, 1809.

[Viscardo y Guzmán, Juan Pablo]. *Colección documental de la independencia del Perú: Tomo 1*. Lima: Comisión Nacional del Sesquicentenario de la Independencia del Perú, 1975.

Walton, William. *Present State of the Spanish Colonies*. London: Longman, Hurst, Rees, Orme, and Brown, 1810.

_____. *An Exposé of the Dissentions of Spanish America*. London: Printed for the Author and sold by John Booth, 1814.

Webster, C. K., ed. *Britain and the Independence of Latin America, 1812–1830: Selected Documents from the Foreign Service Archives*. 2 vols. London: Oxford University Press, 1938.

Wellington, Arthur Wellesley, Duke of. *Supplementary Despatches, Correspondence and Memoranda of Field Marshal Arthur, Duke of Wellington K.G.* Vol. 6, *1807–1810*. London: John Murray, 1860.

[Whipple, Augustus Oliver]. *Nine Letters, Particularly Addressed to the People of the Revolting Spanish Provinces of the Caraccas.* Baltimore: Printed by Joseph Robinson, 1811.

Wilberforce, William. *Correspondence.* Ed. Robert Isaac Wilberforce and Samuel Wilberforce. Philadelphia: Henry Perkins, 1841.

Williams, Helena Maria. *Souvenirs de la Révolution Française.* Paris: Dupré, 1827.

_____. *An Eyewitness Account of the French Revolution by Helen Maria Williams; Letters Continuing a Sketch of the Politics of France.* Ed. Jack Fruchtman. New York. Peter Lang Reprints, 1997.

Secondary Works

Acuña, Guido. *La casa de Miranda en Londres.* México DF: Imprenta Madero, S.A., 1979.

Adams, Jerome. *Liberators and Patriots of Latin America: Biographies of 23 Leaders.* Jefferson, NC: McFarland and Co., 1991.

Alexander, James T. *Catherine the Great: Life and Legend.* New York: Oxford University Press, 1989.

Alvarado S., Jerónimo. *Dialéctica democrática de Juan Pablo Viscardo Guzmán.* Lima: Ediciones "Fanal," 1955.

Amúnategui, Miguel Luis. *Vida de Don Andrés Bello.* Santiago de Chile: Pedro G. Ramírez, 1882.

Anderson, Benedict. *Imagined Communities: Reflections on the Origin and Spread of Nationalism.* London: Verso, 1983.

Andrien, Kenneth, and Lyman Johnson, eds. *The Political Economy of Spanish America in the Age of Revolution, 1750–1850.* Albuquerque: University of New Mexico Press, 1994.

Arciniegas, Germán. *America in Europe: A History of the New World in Reverse.* San Diego: Harcourt, Brace, Jovanovich, 1985.

Balborín Moreno, Manuel, and Gustavo Opazo Maturano. *Cinco mujeres en la vida de O'Higgins.* Santiago: Arancibia Hermanos, [1974].

Baralt, Rafael, and Ramón Díaz. *Resumen de la historia de Venezuela desde el año de 1797 hasta el de 1830.* Paris: Descléee de Brouwer, 1939.

Batllori, Miguel, SJ. *La cultura hispano-italiana de los jesuítas expulsos: Españoles, hispanoamericanos, filipinos, 1767–1814.* Madrid: Editorial Gredos, 1966.

————. *El Abate Viscardo.* Caracas: Instituto Panamericano de Geografía e Historia, 1953.

————. "Maquinaciones del Abate Godoy en Londres en favor de la independencia hispanoamericana." *Archivum Historicum Societatis Iesu* 21 (1952): 84–107.

————. "América en el pensamiento de los jesuítas expulsos." *Boletín de la Academia Nacional de Historia* [Buenos Aires] 23 (1950): 221–23.

————. "El mito de la intervención de los jesuítas en la independencia hispanoamericana." *Razón y Fé* 145 (1952): 505–19.

————. "William Pitt y los proyectos constitucionales de Miranda y Viscardo." *Atlante* 2, no. 1 (enero 1954): 18–21.

Baur, John Edward. "Mulatto Machiavelli: Jean-Pierre Boyer and the Haiti of His Day." *Journal of Negro History* 32, no. 3 (July 1947): 307–53.

Baylen, Joseph, and Dorothy Woodward. "Francisco de Miranda and Russian Diplomacy, 1787–1788." *The Historian* 13 (1950): 52–65.

Belda, Francisco de. *La lengua de Francisco de Miranda en su diario.* Caracas: Academia Nacional de la Historia, 1985.

Bello y Londres. 2 vols. Caracas: La Casa de Bello, 1980.

Berruezo León, María Teresa. *La lucha de Hispanoamérica por su independencia en Inglaterra, 1800–1830.* Madrid: Ediciones de Cultura Hispánica, 1989.

————. "La propaganda independentista de la logia mirandina en Londres." In *Masonería Española y Americana.* Ed. J.A. Ferrer Benimeli. Zaragoza: Centro de Estudios Históricos de la Masonería Española, 1993. Vol. 1: 95–113.

Blanco-Fombona de Hood, Miriam. *El enigma de Sarah Andrews, esposa de Francisco de Miranda.* Caracas: Instituto de Investigaciones Históricas de la Universidad Católica Andrés Bello, 1981.

Blossom, Thomas. *Nariño: Hero of Colombian Independence.* Tucson: University of Arizona Press, 1967.

Botero Saladarriaga, Roberto. *Francisco Antonio Zea.* Bogotá: Ediciones del Consejo, 1945.

Boulton, Alfredo. "Bolívar en Londres." *Boletín de la Academia Nacional de la Historia* 26, no. 143 (1953): 290–95.

Bowers, Claude. *Pierre Vergniaud: The Voice of the French Revolution.* New York: MacMillan, 1950.

Bowman, Charles Harwood. *Vicente Pazos Kanki: Un boliviano en la libertad de América.* Traducción de Raúl Mariaca G. y Samuel Mendoza. La Paz: Editorial Los Amigos del Libro, 1975.

Caldera, Rafael. *Caracas, London, Santiago de Chile: Three Periods in the Life of Andrés Bello.* Caracas: Republic of Venezuela, Ministry of Foreign Affairs, 1981.

Carnicelli, Américo. *La masonería en la independencia de América.* 2 vols. Bogotá: [n.p.], 1970.

Castillo Didier, Miguel. *Miranda de la Senda de Bello.* Caracas: Ediciones de la Presidencia de la República, 1991.

Childs, Virginia. *Lady Hester Stanhope: Queen of the Desert.* London: Weidenfeld and Nicolson, 1990.

Colley, Linda. *Britons: Forging the Nation, 1707–1837.* New Haven: Yale University Press, 1992.

Corbin, Alain. *The Foul and the Fragrant: Odour and the Social Imagination.* London: Picador, 1994.

Cova, Jesús Antonio. "Intimidades de don Francisco de Miranda." *Boletín de la Academia Nacional de la Historia* 33 (1950): 173–81.

———. "Miranda y las mujeres." *Vida y Letras* 43–44 (nov–dic 1956): 43–79.

Crompton, Louis. *Byron and Greek Love: Homophobia in Nineteenth-Century England.* Berkeley and Los Angeles: University of California Press, 1985.

Cussen, Antonio. *Bello and Bolívar: Poetry and Politics in the Spanish American Revolution.* Cambridge: Cambridge University Press, 1992.

Dinwiddy, J. R. "Bentham's Transition to Political Radicalism, 1809–10." *Journal of the History of Ideas* 36, no. 4 (October–December 1795): 683–700.

Dupouy, Walter. *Catalina de Miranda (novela)*. Caracas: Tipografiía Garrida, 1945.

Ernst, Robert. *Rufus King: American Federalist*. Chapel Hill: University of North Carolina Press, 1968.

Eyzaguirre, Jaime. *La logia lauterina y otros estudios sobre la independencia*. Buenos Aires: Editorial Francisco de Aguirre, S.A., 1973.

Febres Cordero, Julio. *Historia de la imprenta y del periodismo en Venezuela, 1800–1830*. Caracas: Banco Central de Venezuela, 1974.

Fernández, David W. *La familia de Miranda*. Caracas: Instituto de Estudios Históricos Mirandinos, 1972.

Ford, John. *Ackermann, 1783–1983: The Business of Art*. London: Ackermann, 1983.

Gálvez, Manuel. *Don Francisco de Miranda: El más universal de los americanos*. Buenos Aires: Emece Editores, S.A., 1946.

Gandía, Enrique. "La Carta a los Españoles Americanos." *Revista del Centro de Estudios Históricos-militares del Perú* 12 (1956–57): 77–93.

García, Lautico, SJ. *Francisco de Miranda y el antiguo regimen español*. Caracas: Academia Nacional de la Historia, 1961.

García Rosell, César. *Miranda y los ex-jesuítas desterrados*. [Caracas]: Ediciones del Instituto de Estudios Históricos Mirandinos, 1970.

Gleijeses, Piero. "Haiti's Contribution to the Independence of Spanish America: A Forgotten Chapter." *Revista Interamerica* 9, no. 4 (Winter 1979–80): 511–28.

Gómez, Carlos Alarico. *Miranda, periodista*. Caracas: Comercial Neliu [1979].

González, Eloy. "Los hijos del General Miranda." *Boletín de la Academia Nacional de la Historia* 10, no. 39 (1927): 191–98.

González Echeverría, Roberto. *Myth and Archive: A Theory of Latin American Narrative*. Cambridge: Cambridge University Press, 1990.

Grases, Pedro. *Tiempo de Bello en Londres y otros ensayos*. Caracas: Biblioteca Venezolana de Cultura, 1962.

Grinberg, León, and Rebeca Grinberg. *Psychoanalytic Perspectives on Migration and Exile*. Transl. Nancy Festinger. New Haven: Yale University Press, 1989.

Grisanti, Angel. "Los jesuítas a quienes conoció el General Miranda (Esteban de Arteaga y Tomás Belón)." *Cultura Universitaria* 50 (1955): 135–45.

_____. "La personalidad de Juan Pablo Viscardo y Guzmán." *Revista de la Universidad de Arequipa* 27 (abril–junio 1948): 115–51.

_____. *El proceso contra Don Sebastián de Miranda, padre del precursor de la independencia continental.* Caracas: Editorial Avila Gráfica, 1950.

_____. *Miranda y la Emperatriz Catalina la Grande.* Caracas: Empresa Gutenberg, 1928.

_____. *El Precursor Miranda y su familia: primera biografía de la familia Miranda.* Madrid: Talleres Artegráficas, 1950.

_____. *Miranda juzgado por los funcionarios españoles de su tiempo.* Caracas: SPI, 1954.

_____. *La reconstrucción de La Guaira despues del terromoto de 1812.* Caracas: SPI, 1964.

Guzmán, José R. "Una sociedad secreta en Londres al servicio de la independencia hispanoamericana." *Boletín del Archivo General de la Nación*, Segunda Série, 8 (1967): 111–28.

Harris, Jonathan. "Bernardino Rivadavia and Benthamite Discipleship." *Latin American Research Review* 33, no. 1 (1998): 129–49.

Harvey, Robert. *Liberators: Latin America's Struggle for Independence.* New York: Overlook Press, 2000.

Hasbrouck, Alfred. *Foreign Legionaries in the Liberation of Spanish America.* New York: Octagon Books, 1969.

Helg, Aline. *Civiliser les peuples et former les élites.* Paris: Editions L'Harmattan, 1984.

Henríquez, Gloria. *Historia de un archivo Francisco de Miranda Reconstitución de la Memoria.* Caracas: Fundación para la Cultura Urbana, 2001.

Hernández y Sánchez-Barba, Mario. "La Paz de 1783 y la misión de Bernardo del Campo en Londres." *Estudios de Historia Moderna* 2 (1952): 179–229.

Herrick, Jane. "The Reluctant Revolutionist: A Study of the Political Ideas of Hipólito da Costa, 1774–1823." *The Americas* 7, no. 2 (1950): 171–81.

Hibbert, Christopher. *Wellington: A Personal History*. Reading, MA: Perseus Books, 1997.

Holzinger, Walter. "Stephen Sayre and Frederick the Great: A Proposal for a Prussian Protectorate for Dominica (1777)." *William and Mary Quarterly* 37, no. 2 (April 1980): 302–11.

Jaksić, Iván. *Andrés Bello: Scholarship and Nation-Building in Nineteenth-Century Latin America*. Cambridge: Cambridge University Press, 2001.

Jarrett, Derek. *Pitt the Younger*. New York: Charles Scribner's Sons, 1974.

Jiménez Codinach, Guadalupe. *La Gran Bretaña y la independencia de México, 1808–1821*. México: Fondo de Cultura Económico, 1991.

Jones, Calvin P. "The Images of Simón Bolívar as Reflected in Ten Leading British Periodicals, 1816–1830." *The Americas* 40, no. 3 (1984): 377–97.

Jones, Robert F. *"King of the Alley": William Duer, Politician, Entrepreneur and Speculator, 1769–1799*. Philadelphia: American Philosophical Society, 1992.

Langley, Lester. *The Americas in the Age of Revolution, 1750–1850*. New Haven, CT: Yale University Press, 1996.

Le Roy, Marcel. "Pedro Antonio Leleux." *Boletín de la Academia Nacional de la Historia* 12 (1929): 176–78.

Level, Lino Duarte. *Cuadros de la historia militar y civil de Venezuela*. Madrid: Editorial América, [n.d.].

Llorens, Vicente. *Liberales y románticos: Una emigración española en Inglaterra, 1823–1834*. Madrid: Editorial Castilla, 1979.

Lombardi, John V. *Venezuela: The Search for Order, the Dream of Progress*. New York: Oxford University Press, 1982.

Lynch, John. *The Spanish American Revolutions, 1808–1826*. New York: W. W. Norton and Company, 1973.

———, ed. *Andrés Bello: The London Years*. Surrey: The Richmond Publishing Co., 1982.

Madariaga, Isabel de. *Russia in the Age of Catherine the Great*. New Haven: Yale University Press, 1981.

———. *The Travels of General Francisco de Miranda in Russia*. London: [n.p.], 1950.

Madariaga, Salvador. *The Fall of the Spanish American Empire*. New York: Collier Books, 1967.

Martínez Zaldua, Ramón. *Historia de la Masonería en Hispanoamérica*. México: B. Costa Amic, 1877.

Mathiez, Albert. *The French Revolution*. Trans. Catherine Alison Phillips. New York: Alfred A. Knopf, 1929.

Méndez Reyes, Salvador. "La misteriosa estancia de los Fagoaga en Londres." *Relaciones* 63/64 (verano–otoño 1995): 123–38.

Mendoza, Cristobal. "La misión de Bolívar y López Méndez a Londres." *Boletín de la Academia Nacional de la Historia* 18, no. 72 (1935): 648–710.

———. "Las relaciones entre Bolívar y Miranda." *Revista de la Sociedad Bolivariana de Venezuela* 35, no. 18 (1978): 12–20.

———. "Bolívar y Miranda." In *Temas de Historia Americana*, Vol. 2. Caracas: [Sociedad Bolivariana de Venezuala], 1965.

Miramón, Alberto. *La llama que no muere*. Caracas: Instituto Panamericano de Geografía e Historia, 1983.

———. *Dos vidas no ejemplares (Pedro Fermín de Vargas y Manuel Mallo)*. Bogotá: Biblioteca Eduardo Santos, 1962.

Mitre, Bartolomé. *Historia de San Martín*. Buenos Aires: Editorial "Suelo Argentino," 1950.

Moreno Alonso, Manuel. "La Independencia de las colonias americanas y la política de Cádiz (1810–1814) en 'El Español' de Blanco White." In *Andalucía y América en el siglo XIX*. Sevilla: Escuela de Estudios Hispano-americanos de Sevilla, 1986. Vol. 1: 85–128.

Morgan, Edmund. *Inventing the People: The Rise of Popular Sovereignty in England and America*. New York: W. W. Norton and Company, 1988.

Murphy, Martin. *Blanco White: Self-Banished Spaniard*. New Haven: Yale University Press, 1989.

———. "Blanco White: An Anglicized Spaniard." *History Today* 28 (1978): 40–46.

Navarro, Bernabé. "Los jesuítas y la independencia." *Abside* 16, no. 1 (1952): 43–62.

Nucete-Sardi, José. *Aventura y tragedia de Don Francisco de Miranda*. Barcelona: Plaza y Janes, 1971.

Onís, José de. *The United States as Seen by Spanish American Writers, 1776–1890.* New York: Hispanic Institute, 1952.

Onsari, Fabián. *San Martín, La Logia Lautaro y la Francmasonería.* Buenos Aires: Supremo Consejo del Grado 33 y Gran Logia de la Masonería Argentina, 1964.

Parra Pérez, Caracciolo. "Bolívar y sus amigos del estrangero." *Revista de la Sociedad Bolivariano de Venezuela* 36, no. 122 (1979): 61–71.

_____. *Historia de la primera república de Venezuela.* Caracas: Biblioteca Ayacucho, 1992.

Peers, E. Allison. "The Literary Activities of the Spanish Emigrados in England, 1814–1834." *Modern Language Review* 2 (1924): 315–24, 445–58.

Perazzo, Nicolás. *José Cortes Madariaga.* [Caracas]: Ediciones del Cuatricentenario de Caracas, [1965].

Pérez Cabrera, José Manuel. *Miranda en Cuba (1780–1783).* La Habana: Academia de la Historia de Cuba, 1950.

Pérez Díaz, Lucila. "Miranda según sus contemporáneos." *Boletín de la Academia Nacional de la Historia* 33 (1950): 162–72.

Pérez Vila, Manuel. "José Lancaster: Un educador británico en Caracas." *Revista de la Sociedad Bolivariana de Venezuela* 24, no. 85 (1965): 773–76.

Pi Sunyer, Carlos. *Patriotas americanos en Londres (Miranda, Bello y otros figuras).* Caracas: Monte Avila Editores, 1978.

Pineda, Rafael. *Iconografía de Francisco de Miranda (retratos, estatuas, y medallas, hechos y cosas relacionados con su memoria).* Caracas: Ministerio del Interior y Justicia, Banco Industrial de Venezuela, 2001.

Plá y Beltrán, Pascual. "Un fiel amigo de Miranda: John Turnbull." *Boletín de la Academia Nacional de la Historia* 45, no. 179 (1962): 425–29.

Polanco Alcántara, Tomás. *Francisco de Miranda, ¿Don Juan o Don Quijote?* Caracas: Ediciones Ge, 1997.

Pons, André. "Blanco White et la crise du monde hispanique, 1808–1814." Université de Paris III - Sorbonne Nouvelle, Thèse pour le Doctorat d'Etat, 1990.

Portell Vilá, Herminio. *Juan de Miralles, un habanero amigo de Jorge Washington*. La Habana, 1947.

Robertson, William Spence. *Rise of the Spanish American Republics (As Told in the Lives of Their Liberators)*. Rev. ed. New York: The Free Press, 1946.

————. *The Life of Miranda*. 2 vols. Chapel Hill: University of North Carolina Press, 1929.

————. "The Recognition of the Spanish Colonies by the Motherland." *Hispanic American Historical Review* 1 (1918): 70–91.

Rodríguez, Mario. *"William Burke" and Francisco de Miranda: The Word and the Deed in Spanish America's Emancipation*. Lanham, MD: University Press of America, 1994.

————. "The First Venezuelan Republic and the North American Model." *Revista Interamericana de Bibliografía* 37, no. 1 (Enero 1897): 3–17.

Rodríguez O., Jaime. *The Emergence of Spanish America: Vicente Rocafuerte and Spanish Americanism, 1808–1832*. Berkeley and Los Angeles: University of California Press, 1975.

Rumeu de Armas, Antonio. *El científico mejicano José María Lanz: fundador de la cinemática industrial*. Madrid: Instituto de España, 1983.

Salcedo Bastardo, José. *Crucible of Americanism: Miranda's London House*. Caracas: Cuadernos Langoven, 1981.

Schneider, Louis, ed. *The Scottish Moralists on Human Nature and Society*. Chicago: University of Chicago Press, 1967.

Sepinwall, Alyssa. "Regenerating France, Regenerating the World: The Abbé Grégoire and the French Revolution, 1750–1831." Ph.D. diss., Stanford University, 1998.

Severn, John Kenneth. *A Wellesley Affair: Richard Marquess Wellesley and the Conduct of Anglo-Spanish Diplomacy, 1809–1812*. Tallahassee: University Presses of Florida, 1981.

Shain, Yossi. *The Frontier of Loyalty: Political Exiles in the Age of the Nation State*. Middletown, CT: Wesleyan University Press, 1989.

Simmons, Merle E. "Una polémica sobre la independencia de Hispanoamérica." *Boletín de la Academia Nacional de la Historia* 30 (1947): 82–126.

————. "Tom Paine and Spanish American Independence." *The American Hispanist* 1 (1975): 4–6.

_____. "Spanish and Spanish American Writers—Politicians in Philadelphia, 1790–1830." *Dieciocho* 3, no. 1 (1980): 27–39.

_____. *Los escritos de Juan Pablo Viscardo y Guzmán: Precursor de la independencia hispanoamericano.* Caracas: Universidad Católica Andrés Bello, 1983.

Smith, Robert Sidney. " 'The Wealth of Nations' in Spain and Hispanic America, 1780–1830." *Journal of Political Economy* 65 (April 1957): 104–25.

Stephen, Leslie. *The English Utilitarians.* 3 vols. Bristol: Thoemmes, 1991.

Stevenson, David. *The Origins of Freemasonry: Scotland's Century, 1590–1710.* Cambridge: Cambridge University Press, 1988.

Stoetzer, Carlos. *The Scholastic Roots of the Spanish American Revolution.* New York: Fordham University Press, 1979.

Thorning, Joseph. *Miranda: World Citizen.* Gainesville: University of Florida Press, 1952.

El Times de Londres y la expedición de Miranda a Venezuela (1806). Caracas: Universidad Central de Venezuela, 1964.

Tisnés, Roberto María. *Un Precursor: Don Pedro Fermín de Vargas.* Bogotá: Editorial Kelly, 1969.

Turley, David. *The Culture of English Anti-Slavery, 1780–1860.* London: Routledge, 1991.

Ullrick, Laura. "Morillo's Attempt to Pacify Venezuela." *Hispanic American Historical Review* 111 (120): 535–65.

Uslar Pietri, Arturo. *Los libros de Miranda.* Caracas: Fundación de Caracas, 1966.

Valéry S, Rafael. *Miranda en Pensacola.* Los Teques: Biblioteca de Autores y Temas Mirandinos, 1991.

Vargas Ugarte, Rubén, SJ. *La Carta a los españoles americanos de Don Juan Pablo Viscardo y Guzmán.* Lima: Gil, S.A., 1964.

_____. *Jesuítas peruanos desterrados en Italia.* Lima: 1930.

Vejarano, Jorge Ricardo. "La vida fabulosa de Miranda en la corte de Catalina de Rusia." *Revista de América* 1 (1945): 181–98.

Warren, Harris Gaylord. "The Southern Career of Don Juan Mariano Picornell." *Journal of Southern History* 8, no. 3 (August 1942): 311–33.

Weiner, Margery. *The French Exiles, 1789–1815.* London: John Murray, 1960.

Williford, Miriam. *Jeremy Bentham on Spanish America.* Baton Rouge: Louisiana State University Press, 1980.

Wright, Winthrop. *Café con Leche: Race, Class and National Image in Venezuela.* Austin: University of Texas Press, 1990.

INDEX

Mestizos, 146
Mexico-Guatemala, proposed
viceroyalty of, 175
Mier Noriega y Guerra, Servando
Teresa de, 195; *Historia* by, 223;
on Miranda's death, 254
Milan, Miranda's visit to, 101
Military career of Miranda: as aide-
de-camp to Cagigal, 22, 24, 25,
26; appointed as *generalíssimo,*
233; Battle of Pensacola, role in,
21, 22–24; complaints against, 19;
decision to leave military service,
28; desertion charges against, 51–
52; duties in Spain, 12–13;
English skills in negotiations
during, 23; in expedition of Army
of American Operations, 21;
French military, service in, 113,
114–28; French War Committee
charges against, 121–30; inscrip-
tion of name on Arc de Triomphe,
135; Jamaica, role in prisoner
exchange of, 24–26; personal
library on military subjects, 22,
23; purchase of three slaves during
service, 23; in Regiment of
Aragón, 20; at siege of Melilla,
12–16, 17; tour of duty in North
Africa, 12–16; traitor and spy
charges against, 26; transfer to
Madrid, 18; trial for actions in
battle at Maastricht, 119–20,
122–27; Venezuela, service in,
226–30
Military sites, Miranda's visits to, 50,
74, 76–77, 83
Mill, James: on abolition of slavery,
234; Miranda's communications
with, 81, 155, 192; on Miranda's
plans for Spanish American
independence, 174, 181–83, 214,
230

Milton, John, 23
Miralles, Señor, 58
Miranda, Ana Antonia, 2
Miranda, Avelina, 257
Miranda, Francisco Antonio Gabriel, 2
Miranda, Francisco de, 2; *Additional
Reasons* by, 183, 184; "Advice from
an Old South American" by, 148,
149; alias of Count Mirandov,
139; alias of George Martin, 155,
211; alias of José de Amindra,
249; alias of Martín de Mariland,
81; alias of Monsieur de Méran,
101; arrest for Vendémiaire Plot,
133; arrest in Venezuela, 238–39;
arrival in Caracas (1811), 213;
attentions of Lady Hester
Stanhope, 187, 189–92, 196–97;
book collection of, 255; claims of
American lineage, 3; collection of
introductions and recommendations, 47, 68–69; death of mother,
20; departure for Venezuela
(1810), 207; education and
studies of, 3; European style of
rule and battle, 254; exile, impacts
of, 96, 108, 109–10, 152;
language studies of, 10; marriage
to Sarah Andrews, 153–55, 165–
66, 173, 178, 206, 222, 257;
Masonic membership of, 193–95;
*Opinion . . . sur la situation actuelle
de la France* by, 130–31, 132,
219–20; plans for emancipating
Spanish America, 59–60, 106–7,
167, 174, 181–83, 206, 214, 219,
230; as Principal Agent of Spanish
American Colonies, 140, 141,
142, 143; *Proclamation* by, 160; as
representative of Pao province,
218; second arrest by French
Jacobins, 127–29; secular world
view of, 9; *South American*

Latin American Silhouettes
Studies in History and Culture

William H. Beezley and
Judith Ewell
Editors

Volumes Published

Brian Loveman and Thomas M. Davies, Jr., eds., *The Politics of Antipolitics: The Military in Latin America*, 3d ed., revised and updated (1996).
Cloth ISBN 0-8420-2609-6
Paper ISBN 0-8420-2611-8

Dianne Walta Hart, *Undocumented in L.A.: An Immigrant's Story* (1997).
Cloth ISBN 0-8420-2648-7
Paper ISBN 0-8420-2649-5

William H. Beezley and Judith Ewell, eds., *The Human Tradition in Modern Latin America* (1997). Cloth ISBN 0-8420-2612-6   Paper ISBN 0-8420-2613-4

Donald F. Stevens, ed., *Based on a True Story: Latin American History at the Movies* (1997).
Cloth ISBN 0-8420-2582-0
Paper ISBN 0-8420-2781-5

Jaime E. Rodríguez O., ed., *The Origins of Mexican National Politics, 1808–1847* (1997). Paper ISBN 0-8420-2723-8

Che Guevara, *Guerrilla Warfare*, with revised and updated introduction and case studies by Brian Loveman and Thomas M. Davies, Jr., 3d ed. (1997). Cloth ISBN 0-8420-2677-0   Paper ISBN 0-8420-2678-9

Adrian A. Bantjes, *As If Jesus Walked on Earth: Cardenismo, Sonora, and the Mexican Revolution* (1998; rev. ed., 2000). Cloth ISBN 0-8420-2653-3
Paper ISBN 0-8420-2751-3

A. Kim Clark, *The Redemptive Work: Railway and Nation in Ecuador, 1895–1930* (1998). Cloth ISBN 0-8420-2674-6
Paper ISBN 0-8420-5013-2

Louis A. Pérez, Jr., ed., *Impressions of Cuba in the Nineteenth Century: The Travel Diary of Joseph J. Dimock* (1998).
Cloth ISBN 0-8420-2657-6
Paper ISBN 0-8420-2658-4

June E. Hahner, ed., *Women through Women's Eyes: Latin American Women in*

Nineteenth-Century Travel Accounts (1998). Cloth ISBN 0-8420-2633-9
Paper ISBN 0-8420-2634-7

James P. Brennan, ed., *Peronism and Argentina* (1998). ISBN 0-8420-2706-8

John Mason Hart, ed., *Border Crossings: Mexican and Mexican-American Workers* (1998). Cloth ISBN 0-8420-2716-5
Paper ISBN 0-8420-2717-3

Brian Loveman, *For* la Patria: *Politics and the Armed Forces in Latin America* (1999). Cloth ISBN 0-8420-2772-6 Paper ISBN 0-8420-2773-4

Guy P. C. Thomson, with David G. LaFrance, *Patriotism, Politics, and Popular Liberalism in Nineteenth-Century Mexico: Juan Francisco Lucas and the Puebla Sierra* (1999).
ISBN 0-8420-2683-5

Robert Woodmansee Herr, in collaboration with Richard Herr, *An American Family in the Mexican Revolution* (1999).
ISBN 0-8420-2724-6

Juan Pedro Viqueira Albán, trans. Sonya Lipsett-Rivera and Sergio Rivera Ayala, *Propriety and Permissiveness in Bourbon Mexico* (1999).
Cloth ISBN 0-8420-2466-2
Paper ISBN 0-8420-2467-0

Stephen R. Niblo, *Mexico in the 1940s: Modernity, Politics, and Corruption* (1999).
Cloth ISBN 0-8420-2794-7
Paper (2001) ISBN 0-8420-2795-5

David E. Lorey, *The U.S.-Mexican Border in the Twentieth Century* (1999).
Cloth ISBN 0-8420-2755-6
Paper ISBN 0-8420-2756-4

Joanne Hershfield and David R. Maciel, eds., *Mexico's Cinema: A Century of Films and Filmmakers* (2000). Cloth ISBN 0-8420-2681-9 Paper ISBN 0-8420-2682-7

Peter V. N. Henderson, *In the Absence of Don Porfirio: Francisco León de la Barra*

and the Mexican Revolution (2000).
ISBN 0-8420-2774-2
Mark T. Gilderhus, The Second Century: U.S.-
Latin American Relations since 1889
(2000). Cloth ISBN 0-8420-2413-1
Paper ISBN 0-8420-2414-X
Catherine Moses, Real Life in Castro's Cuba
(2000). Cloth ISBN 0-8420-2836-6
Paper ISBN 0-8420-2837-4
K. Lynn Stoner, ed./comp., with Luis
Hipólito Serrano Pérez, Cuban and
Cuban-American Women: An
Annotated Bibliography (2000).
ISBN 0-8420-2643-6
Thomas D. Schoonover, The French in
Central America: Culture and
Commerce, 1820–1930 (2000).
ISBN 0-8420-2792-0
Enrique C. Ochoa, Feeding Mexico: The
Political Uses of Food since 1910
(2000). Cloth ISBN 0-8420-2812-9
(2002) Paper ISBN 0-8420-2813-7
Thomas W. Walker and Ariel C. Armony,
eds., Repression, Resistance, and
Democratic Transition in Central
America (2000). Cloth ISBN 0-8420-
2766-1   Paper ISBN 0-8420-2768-8
William H. Beezley and David E. Lorey,
eds., ¡Viva México! ¡Viva la
Independencia! Celebrations of
September 16 (2001).
Cloth ISBN 0-8420-2914-1
Paper ISBN 0-8420-2915-X
Jeffrey M. Pilcher, Cantinflas and the Chaos
of Mexican Modernity (2001).
Cloth ISBN 0-8420-2769-6
Paper ISBN 0-8420-2771-8
Victor M. Uribe-Uran, ed., State and Society
in Spanish America during the Age of
Revolution (2001). Cloth ISBN 0-8420-
2873-0   Paper ISBN 0-8420-2874-9
Andrew Grant Wood, Revolution in the
Street: Women, Workers, and Urban
Protest in Veracruz, 1870–1927 (2001).
Cloth ISBN 0-8420-2879-X
(2002) Paper ISBN 0-8420-2880-3
Charles Bergquist, Ricardo Peñaranda, and
Gonzalo Sánchez G., eds., Violence in
Colombia, 1990–2000: Waging War and
Negotiating Peace (2001).
Cloth ISBN 0-8420-2869-2
Paper ISBN 0-8420-2870-6

William Schell, Jr., Integral Outsiders: The
American Colony in Mexico City, 1876–
1911 (2001). ISBN 0-8420-2838-2
John Lynch, Argentine Caudillo: Juan
Manuel de Rosas (2001).
Cloth ISBN 0-8420-2897-8
Paper ISBN 0-8420-2898-6
Samuel Basch, M.D., ed. and trans. Fred D.
Ullman, Recollections of Mexico: The
Last Ten Months of Maximilian's Empire
(2001). ISBN 0-8420-2962-1
David Sowell, The Tale of Healer
Miguel Perdomo Neira: Medicine,
Ideologies, and Power in the
Nineteenth-Century Andes (2001).
Cloth ISBN 0-8420-2826-9
Paper ISBN 0-8420-2827-7
June E. Hahner, ed., A Parisian in Brazil:
The Travel Account of a Frenchwoman
in Nineteenth-Century Rio de Janeiro
(2001). Cloth ISBN 0-8420-2854-4
Paper ISBN 0-8420-2855-2
Richard A. Warren, Vagrants and Citizens:
Politics and the Masses in Mexico City
from Colony to Republic (2001).
ISBN 0-8420-2964-8
Roderick J. Barman, Princess Isabel of
Brazil: Gender and Power in the
Nineteenth Century (2002).
Cloth ISBN 0-8420-2845-5
Paper ISBN 0-8420-2846-3
Stuart F. Voss, Latin America in the
Middle Period, 1750–1929 (2002).
Cloth ISBN 0-8420-5024-8
Paper ISBN 0-8420-5025-6
Lester D. Langley, The Banana Wars:
United States Intervention in the
Caribbean, 1898–1934, with new
introduction (2002). Cloth ISBN 0-8420-
5046-9   Paper ISBN 0-8420-5047-7
Mariano Ben Plotkin, Mañana es San Perón:
A Cultural History of Perón's Argentina
(2003). Cloth ISBN 0-8420-5028-0
Paper ISBN 0-8420-5029-9
Allen Gerlach, Indians, Oil, and Politics:
A Recent History of Ecuador (2003).
Cloth ISBN 0-8420-5107-4
Paper ISBN 0-8420-5108-2
Karen Racine, Francisco de Miranda: A
Transatlantic Life in the Age of
Revolution (2003). Cloth ISBN 0-8420-
2909-5   Paper ISBN 0-8420-2910-9